D1292385

# HAZLITT ON
# ENGLISH LITERATURE

## AN INTRODUCTION TO THE
## APPRECIATION OF LITERATURE

BY

## JACOB ZEITLIN

## AMS PRESS
### NEW YORK

Reprinted from the edition of 1913, New York
First AMS EDITION published 1970
Manufactured in the United States of America


International Standard Book Number: 0-404-03193-5


Library of Congress Catalog Card Number: 71-127904


AMS PRESS, INC.
NEW YORK, N.Y. 10003

# PREFACE

THE present selection of Hazlitt's critical essays has been planned to serve two important purposes. In the first place it provides the materials for an estimate of the character and scope of Hazlitt's contributions to criticism and so acquaints students with one of the greatest of English critics. And in the second place, what is perhaps more important, such a selection, embodying a series of appreciations of the great English writers, should prove helpful in the college teaching of literature. There is no great critic who by his readableness and comprehensiveness is as well qualified as Hazlitt to aid in bringing home to students the power and the beauty of the essential things in literature. There is in him a splendid stimulating energy which has not yet been sufficiently utilized.

The contents have been selected and arranged to present a chronological and almost continuous account of English literature from its beginning in the age of Elizabeth down to Hazlitt's own day, the period of the romantic revival. To the more strictly critical essays there have been added a few which reveal Hazlitt's intimate intercourse with books and also with their writers, whether he knew them in the flesh or only through the printed page. Such vivid revelations of personal contact contribute much to further the chief aim of this volume, which is to introduce the reader to a direct and spontaneous view of literature.

The editor's introduction, in trying to fix formally Hazlitt's position as a critic, of necessity takes account of his personality, which cannot be dissociated from his critical

practice. The notes, in addition to identifying quotations and explaining allusions, indicate the nature of Hazlitt's obligations to earlier and contemporary critics. They contain a body of detailed information, which may be used, if so desired, for disciplinary purposes. The text here employed is that of the last form published in Hazlitt's own lifetime, namely, that of the second edition in the case of the Characters of Shakespeare's Plays, the lectures on the poets and on the age of Elizabeth, and the Spirit of the Age, and the first edition of the Comic Writers, the Plain Speaker, and the Political Essays. A slight departure from this procedure in the case of the essay on "Elia" is explained in the notes. "My First Acquaintance with Poets," and "Of Persons One Would Wish to Have Seen" are taken from the periodicals in which they first appeared, as they were not republished in book-form till after Hazlitt's death. Hazlitt's own spellings and punctuation are retained.

To all who have contributed to the study and appreciation of Hazlitt, the present editor desires to make general acknowledgement—to Alexander Ireland, Mr. W. C. Hazlitt, Mr. Birrell, and Mr. Saintsbury. Mention should also be made of Mr. Nichol Smith's little volume of Hazlitt's Essays on Poetry (Blackwood's), and of the excellent treatment of Hazlitt in Professor Oliver Elton's Survey of English Literature from 1780 to 1830, which came to hand after this edition had been completed. A debt of special gratitude is owing to Mr. Glover and Mr. Waller for their splendid edition of Hazlitt's Collected Works (in twelve volumes with an index, Dent 1902-1906). All of Hazlitt's quotations have been identified with the help of this edition. References to Hazlitt's own writings, when cited by volume and page, apply to the edition of Glover and Waller.

Finally I wish to express my sincere thanks to Professor G. P. Krapp for his friendly cooperation in the planning

and carrying out of this volume, and to him and to my colleague, Professor S. P. Sherman, for helpful criticism of the introduction.

JACOB ZEITLIN.

February 20, 1913.

# CONTENTS

vii

# CHRONOLOGY OF HAZLITT'S LIFE AND WRITINGS

1778   William Hazlitt born at Maidstone in Kent, April 10.
1783-1786  Residence in America.
1787 ff.  Residence at Wem in Shropshire.
1793-1794  Student in the Hackney Theological College.
1798   Meeting with Coleridge and Wordsworth.
1798?-1805  Study and practice of painting.
1802   Visit to Paris.
1805   *Essay on the Principles of Human Action.*
1806   *Free Thoughts on Public Affairs.*
1807   *An Abridgment of the Light of Nature Revealed, by Abraham Tucker.*
       *Reply to the Essay on Population by the Rev. T. R. Malthus.*
       *Eloquence of the British Senate.*
1808   Marriage with Sarah Stoddart and settlement at Winterslow.
1810   *A New and Improved Grammar of the English Tongue.*
1812   Removal to London.—Lectures on philosophy at the Russell Institution.
1812-1814  On the staff of the *Morning Chronicle.*
1814   Begins contributing to the *Champion, Examiner,* and the *Edinburgh Review.*
1816   *Memoirs of the Late Thomas Holcroft.*
1817   *The Round Table.*
       *The Characters of Shakespeare's Plays.*
1818   *A View of the English Stage.*
       *Lectures on the English Poets.* (Delivered at the Surrey Institution.)
1819   *Lectures on the_ English Comic Writers.* (Delivered at the Surrey Institution at the close of 1818.)
       *A Letter to William Gifford Esq., from William Hazlitt Esq.*
       *Political Essays.*
1820   *Lectures on the Dramatic Literature of the Age of Elizabeth.* (Delivered at the Surrey Institution at the close of 1819.)
       Joins the staff of the *London Magazine.*
1821-22  *Table Talk, or Original Essays* (2 volumes).
1822   Episode of Sarah Walker.—Journey to Scotland to obtain a divorce from his wife.
1823   *Liber Amoris, or the New Pygmalion.*
       *Characteristics in the Manner of Rochefoucauld's Maxims.*
1824   *Sketches of the Principal Picture-Galleries in England.*

ix

*Select British Poets.*
Marriage with Mrs. Bridgewater.—Tour of the Continent.
1825  *The Spirit of the Age.*
1826  *Notes of a Journey through France and Italy.*
     *The Plain Speaker, Opinions on Books, Men, and Thing* (2 volumes).
1828-1830  *Life of Napoleon Buonaparte* (4 volumes).
1830  *Conversations of James Northcote.*
     Death of William Hazlitt, September 18.

# INTRODUCTION

## WILLIAM HAZLITT

### I

HAZLITT characterized the age he lived in as "critical, didactic, paradoxical, romantic." [1] It was the age of the Edinburgh Review, of the Utilitarians, of Godwin and Shelley, of Wordsworth and Byron—in a word of the French Revolution and all that it brought in its train. Poetry in this age was impregnated with politics; ideas for social reform sprang from the ground of personal sentiment. Hazlitt was born early enough to partake of the ardent hopes which the last decade of the eighteenth century held out, but his spirit came to ripeness in years of reaction in which the battle for reform seemed a lost hope. While the changing events were bringing about corresponding changes in the ideals of such early votaries to liberty as Coleridge and Wordsworth, Hazlitt continued to cling to his enthusiastic faith, but at the same time the spectacle of a world which turned away from its brightest dreams made of him a sharp critic of human nature, and his sense of personal disappointment turned into a bitterness hardly to be distinguished from cynicism. In a passionate longing for a better order of things, in the merciless denunciation of the cant and bigotry which was enlisted in the cause of the existing order, he resembled Byron. The rare union in his nature of the analytic and the emo-

[1] *Dramatic Essays*, VIII, 415.

tional gave to his writings the very qualities which he enumerated as characteristic of the age, and his consistent sincerity made his voice distinct above many others of his generation.

Hazlitt's earlier years reveal a restless conflict of the sensitive and the intellectual. His father, a friend of Priestley's, was a Unitarian preacher, who, in his vain search for liberty of conscience, had spent three years in America with his family. Under him the boy was accustomed to the reading of sermons and political tracts, and on this dry nourishment he seemed to thrive till he was sent to the Hackney Theological College to begin his preparation for the ministry. His dissatisfaction there was not such as could be put into words—perhaps a hunger for keener sensations and an appetite for freer inquiry than was open to a theological student even of a dissenting church. After a year at Hackney he withdrew to his father's home, where he found nothing more definite to do than to "solve some knotty point, or dip in some abstruse author, or look at the sky, or wander by the pebbled sea-side." [2] This was probably the period of his most extensive reading. He absorbed the English novelists and essayists; he saturated himself with the sentiment of Rousseau; he studied Bacon and Hobbes and Berkeley and Hume; he became fascinated, in Burke, by the union of a wide intellect with a brilliant fancy and consummate rhetorical skill. [3] Though he called himself at this time dumb and inarticulate, and the idea of ever making literature his profession had not suggested itself to him, he was eager to talk about the things he read, and in Joseph Fawcett, a retired minister, he found an agreeable companion. " A heartier friend or honester critic I never coped

[2] "On Living to One's Self," in *Table Talk*.
[3] "On Reading Old Books," pp. 344-45.

withal." [4]   " The writings of Sterne, Fielding, Cervantes, Richardson, Rousseau, Godwin, Goethe, etc. were the usual subjects of our discourse, and the pleasure I had had, in reading these authors, was more than doubled." [5]   How acutely sensitive he was to all impressions at this time is indicated by the effect upon him of the meeting with Coleridge and Wordsworth of which he has left a record in one of his most eloquent essays, " My First Acquaintance with Poets." But his active energies were concentrated on the solution of a metaphysical problem which was destined to possess his brain for many years: in his youthful enthusiasm he was grappling with a theory concerning the natural disinterestedness of the human mind, apparently adhering to the bias which he had received from his early training.

But being come of age and finding it necessary to turn his mind to something more marketable than abstract speculation, he determined, though apparently without any natural inclination toward the art, to become a painter. He apprenticed himself to his brother John Hazlitt, who had gained some reputation in London for his miniatures. During the peace of Amiens in 1802, he travelled to the Louvre to study and copy the masterpieces which Napoleon had brought over from Italy as trophies of war. Here, as he " marched delighted through a quarter of a mile of the proudest efforts of the mind of man, a whole creation of genius, a universe of art," [6] he imbibed a love of perfection which may have been fatal to his hopes of a career. At any rate it was soon after, while he was following the profession of itinerant painter through England, that he wrote to his father of " much dissatisfaction and much sorrow,"

[4] " On Criticism," in *Table Talk*.
[5] *Life of Holcroft,* Works, II, 171, n.
[6] " On the Pleasure of Painting," in *Table Talk*.

of "that repeated disappointment and that long dejection which have served to overcast and to throw into deep obscurity some of the best years of my life." [7]

When Hazlitt abandoned painting, he fell back upon his analytic gift as a means of earning a living. Not counting his first published work, the Essay on the Principles of Human Action, which was purely a labor of love and fell still-born from the press, the tasks to which he now devoted his time were chiefly of the kind ordinarily rated as job work. He prepared an abridgement of Abraham Tucker's Light of Nature, compiled the Eloquence of the British Senate, wrote a reply to Malthus's Essay on Population, and even composed an elementary English Grammar. It would be a mistake to suppose that these labors were performed according to a system of mechanical routine. Hazlitt impressed something of his personality on whatever he touched. His violent attack on the inhuman tendencies of Malthus's doctrines is pervaded by a glow of humanitarian indignation. For the Eloquence of the British Senate he wrote a sketch of Burke, which for fervor of appreciation and judicious analysis ranks with his best things of this class. Even the Grammar bears evidence of his enthusiasm for an idea. Whenever he has occasion to express his feelings on a subject of popular interest, his manner begins to grow animated and his language to gain in force and suppleness.

But Hazlitt continued firmly in the faith that it was his destiny to be a metaphysician. In 1812 he undertook to deliver a course of lectures on philosophy at the Russell Institution with the ambitious purpose of founding a system

---

[7] W. C. Hazlitt: *Lamb and Hazlitt* (1900), p. 44. The letter in which these phrases are to be found is dated 1793 by Mr. W. C. Hazlitt, but the present writer has given a detailed statement of his reasons for believing that it was written in 1803. See *Nation,* October 19, 1911.

of philosophy "more conformable to reason and experience" than that of the modern material school which
resolved "all thought into sensation, all morality into the
love of pleasure, and all action into mechanical impulse." [8]
Though he did not succeed in founding a system, he probably interested his audience by a stimulating review of the
main tendencies of English thought from Bacon and Hobbes
to Priestley and Godwin.

At the conclusion of his last lecture, Hazlitt told the
story of a Brahmin who, on being transformed into a
monkey, " had no other delight than that of eating cocoanuts
and studying metaphysics." "I too," he added, "should
be very well contented to pass my life like this monkey,
did I but know how to provide myself with a substitute
for cocoanuts." But it must have become apparent to Hazlitt and his friends that he possessed a talent more profitable
than that of abstract speculation. The vigor and vitality
of the prose in these lectures, compared with the heavy,
inert style of his first metaphysical writing, the freedom
of illustration and poetic allusion, suggested the possibility of success in more popular forms of literature. He
tried to work for the newspapers as theatrical and parliamentary reporter, but his temper and his habits were not
adaptable to the requirements of daily journalism, and
editors did not long remain complacent toward him. He
did however, in the course of a few years, succeed in
gaining admission to the pages of the Edinburgh Review
and in establishing an enviable reputation as a writer of
critical and miscellaneous essays. Even in that anonymous
generation he could not long contribute to any periodical
without attracting attention. Readers were aroused by his
bold paradox and by the tonic quality of his style. Editors
appealed to him for " dashing articles," for something

[8] XI, 26.

"brilliant or striking" on any subject. Authors looked forward to a favorable notice from Hazlitt, and Keats even declared that it would be a compensation for being damned-if Hazlitt were to do the damning.

In his essays the features of Hazlitt's personality may be plainly recognized, and these reveal a triple ancestry. He claims descent from Montaigne by virtue of his original observation of humanity with its entire accumulation of custom and prejudice; he is akin to Rousseau in a highstrung susceptibility to emotions, sentiments, and ideas; and he is tinged with a cynicism to which there is no closer parallel than in the maxims of La Rochefoucauld. The union of the philosopher, the enthusiast, and the man of the world is fairly unusual in literature, but in Hazlitt's case the union was not productive of any sharp contradictions. His common sense served as a ballast to his buoyant emotions; the natural strength of his feelings loosened the bonds which attached him to his favorite theories; his cynicism, by sharpening his perception of the frailty of human nature, prevented his philanthropic dreams from imposing themselves on him for reality.

The analytical gift manifested itself in Hazlitt precociously in the study of human nature. He characterized some of his schoolmates disdainfully as " fit only for fighting like stupid dogs and cats," and at the age of twelve, while on a visit, he communicated to his father a caustic sketch of some English ladies who "require an Horace or a Shakespeare to describe them," and whose " ceremonial unsociality " made him wish he were back in America. His metaphysical studies determined the direction which his observation of life should take. He became a remarkable anatomist of the constitution of human nature in the abstract, viewing the motives of men's actions from a speculative plane. He excels in sharp etchings which bring the outline of a character into bold prominence. He is happy in defining isolated traits and in throwing a new light on much used words. "Cleverness," he writes, "is a certain *knack* or aptitude at doing certain things, which depend more on a particular adroitness and off-hand readiness than on force or perseverance, such as making puns, making epigrams, making extempore verses, mimicking the company, mimicking a style, etc. . . . Accomplishments are certain external graces, which are to be learnt from others, and which are easily displayed to the admiration of the beholder, *viz.* dancing, riding, fencing, music, and so on. . . . Talent is the capacity of doing anything that depends on application and industry, such as writing a criticism, making a speech, studying the law."[9] These innocent looking definitions are probably not without an ironic sting. It requires no great stretch of the imagination, for example, to catch in Hazlitt's eye a sly wink at Lamb or a disdainful glance toward Leigh Hunt as he gives the reader his idea cr cleverness or accomplishment.

Hazlitt's definitions often startle and give a vigorous buffet to our preconceptions. He is likely to open an essay on "Good-Nature" by declaring that a good-natured man is "one who does not like to be put out of his way. . . . Good-nature is humanity that costs nothing;"[10] and he may describe a respectable man as "a person whom there is no reason for respecting, or none that we choose to name."[11] Against the imputation of paradox, which such expressions expose him to, he has written his own defence, applying his usual analytical acuteness to distinguish between originality and singularity.[12] The contradiction of

[9] *Table Talk,* "On the Indian Jugglers."
[10] *Round Table.*
[11] "On Respectable People," in *Plain Speaker.*
[12] "On Paradox and Commonplace," in *Table Talk.*

a common prejudice, which always passes for paradox, is often such only in appearance. It is true that an ingenious person may take advantage of the elusive nature of language to play tricks with the ordinary understanding, but it is equally true that words of themselves have a way of imposing on the uninquiring mind and passing themselves off at an inflated value. No process is more familiar than that by which words in the course of a long life lose all their original power, and yet they will sometimes continue to exercise a disproportionate authority. Then comes the original mind, which, looking straight at the thing instead of accepting the specious title, discovers the incongruity between the pretence and the reality, and in the first shock of the disclosure annoyingly overturns our settled ideas. This is the spirit in which Carlyle seeks to strip off the clothes in which humanity has irrecognizably disguised itself, and it is the spirit in which Robert Louis Stevenson tries to free his old-world conscience from the old-world forms. To take a more recent parallel, it is the manner, somewhat exaggerated, in which Mr. G. K. Chesterton examines the upstart heresies of our own agitated day. There would be nothing fanciful in suggesting that all these men owed a direct debt to Hazlitt—Stevenson on many occasions acknowledged it.[13]   Hazlitt was as honest and

---

[13] Hazlitt's *Table Talk* was included by Stevenson in a youthful *Catalogus Librorum Carissimorum*. It is interesting that at the same time that Carlyle was composing *Sartor Resartus*, Hazlitt should have penned this bit of savage satire. "It has been often made a subject of dispute, What is the distinguishing characteristic of man? And the answer may, perhaps, be given that *he is the only animal that dresses. . . .* Swift has taken a good bird's-eye view of man's nature, by abstracting the habitual notions of size, and looking at it in *great* or in *little:* would that some one had the boldness and the art to do a similar service, by stripping off the coat from his back, the vizor from his thoughts, or by dressing up some other creature in similar mummery! It is not his body alone

sincere as any of them. Though the opening of an essay
may appear perverse, he is sure to enforce his point before
proceeding very far. He accumulates familiar instances
in such abundance as to render obvious what at first seemed
paradoxical. He writes "On the Ignorance of the
Learned" and makes it perfectly clear that no person knows
less of the actual life of the world than he whose experience
is confined to books. On the other hand he has a whole-
hearted appreciation of pedantry: "The power of attaching
an interest to the most trifling or painful pursuits, in
which our whole attention and faculties are engaged, is
one of the greatest happinesses of our nature. . . . He
who is not in some measure a pedant, though he may be
a wise, cannot be a very happy man." [14] These two examples illustrate Hazlitt's manner of presenting both views of
a subject by concentrating his attention on each separately
and examining it without regard to the other. On one
occasion he anatomizes the faults of the dissenters, and on
another he extols their virtues. "I have inveighed all my

that he tampers with, and metamorphoses so successfully; he tricks
out his mind and soul in borrowed finery, and in the admired costume
of gravity and imposture. If he has a desire to commit a base
or a cruel action without remorse and with the applause of the
spectators, he has only to throw the cloak of religion over it, and
invoke Heaven to set its seal on a massacre or a robbery. At one
time dirt, at another indecency, at another rapine, at a fourth rancorous malignity, is decked out and accredited in the garb of
sanctity. The instant there is a flaw, a 'damned spot' to be concealed, it is glossed over with a doubtful name. Again, we dress
up our enemies in nicknames, and they march to the stake as
assuredly as in *san Benitos*. . . . Strange, that a reptile should wish
to be thought an angel; or that he should not be content to writhe
and grovel in his native earth, without aspiring to the skies! It
is from the love of dress and finery. He is the Chimney-sweeper on
May-day all the year round: the soot peeps through the rags
and tinsel, and all the flowers of sentiment!" *Aphorisms on
Man*, LXIV, Works, XII, 227.
[14] *Round Table*, "On Pedantry."

life against the insolence of the Tories, and for this I have
the authority both of Whigs and Reformers; but then I
have occasionally spoken against the imbecility of the
Whigs, and the extravagance of the Reformers, and thus
have brought all three on my back, though two out of the
three regularly agree with all I say of the third party." [15]
The strange thing is not that he should have incurred the
wrath of all parties, but that he should show surprise at the
result.

Very often Hazlitt's reflections are the generalization of
his personal experience. The essay " On the Disadvantages
of Intellectual Superiority " is but a record of the trials
to which he was exposed by his morbid sensitiveness and
want of social tact, and amid much excellent advice " On
the Conduct of Life," there are passages which merely
reflect his own marital misfortunes. It is not so much that
he is a dupe of his emotions, but in his view of life he
attaches a higher importance to feeling than to reason, and
so provides a philosophic basis for his strongest prejudices.
" Custom, passion, imagination," he declares, " insinuate
themselves into and influence almost every judgment we
pass or sentiment we indulge, and are a necessary help (as
well as hindrance) to the human understanding; to attempt
to refer every question to abstract truth and precise definition, without allowing for the frailty of prejudice, which
is the unavoidable consequence of the frailty and imper-
fection of reason, would be to unravel the whole web and
texture of human understanding and society." [16]

It is this infusion of passion and sentiment, the addition
of the warm breath of his personal experience, that gives
the motion of life to his analytic essays, and a deep and
solemn humanity to his abstract speculations. Hazlitt felt

[15] " Knowledge of the World," XII, 307.
[16] " On Prejudice," XII, 396.

life with an intensity which reminds us of a more spacious age. " What a huge heap, a ' huge, dumb heap,' of wishes, thoughts, feelings, anxious cares, soothing hopes, loves, joys, friendships, it is composed of! How many ideas and trains of sentiment, long and deep and intense, often pass through the mind in only one day's thinking or reading, for instance! How many such days are there in a year, how many years in a long life, still occupied with something interesting, still recalling some old impression, still recurring to some difficult question and making progress in it, every step accompanied with a sense of power, and every moment conscious of the ' high endeavour and the glad success! ' " [17] What an exultant sense of power over the resources of life! What an earnest delight in the tasting of every pleasure which the senses and the intelligence afford! His enjoyments comprehended the widest range of sensations and activities. He loved nature, he loved books, he loved pictures, he loved the theatre, he loved music and dancing. He loved good talk and good fellowship; he loved an idea and anyone who was susceptible to an idea. He also loved a spirited game of rackets, and though he hated brutality, he has left us a very vivid and sympathetic account of a prize-fight. Above all he loved the words truth and justice and humanity. With such sensibilities, it is no wonder that his last words should have been " I have had a happy life."

As the phrase is ordinarily understood, Hazlitt's dying expression might seem unaccountable. Outwardly few authors have been more miserable. Like the great French sentimentalist with whom we have compared him, a suspicious distrust of all who came near him converted his social existence into a restless fever. He had the gift of interpreting every contradiction to one of his favorite prin-

[17] *Table Talk,* " On the Past and Future."

ciples as a personal injury to himself, and in the tense state of party feeling then prevailing, the opportunities for taking offence were not limited. Hazlitt was one of the chief marks singled out for abuse by the critics of Government. To constant self-tormentings from within and persecution from without, there was added the misfortune of an unhappy marriage and of a still more unhappy love affair which lowered him in his own eyes as well as in the eyes of the world. From the point of view of the practical man, Hazlitt's life would be declared a failure.

The result of Hazlitt's hard experiences with the realities of life was to confirm him in a devoted attachment to the past. All his high enthusiasms, his sanguine dreams, his purest feelings continued to live for him in the past, and it was only by recurring to their memory in the dim distance that he could find assurance to sustain his faith. In the past all his experiences were refined, subtilized, transfigured. A sunny afternoon on Salisbury Plain, a walk with Charles and Mary Lamb under a Claude Lorraine sky, a visit to the Montpelier Gardens where in his childhood he drank tea with his father—occurrences as common as these were enveloped in a haze of glory. And rarer events, such as a visit to the pictures at Burleigh House, or to the galleries in the Louvre, tender visions of feminine grace and sweetness, were touched in the recollection with a depth and pathos which subdued even the most joyous impressions to a refined melancholy. In no other English writer is this rich sentiment of the past so eloquent, and no one was better qualified to describe its sources. " Time takes out the sting of pain; our sorrows after a certain period have been so often steeped in a medium of thought and passion, that they ' unmould their essence '; and all that remains of our original impressions is what we would wish them to have been. . . . Seen in the distance, in the long

perspective of waning years, the meanest incidents, en-
larged and enriched by countless recollections, become interesting; the most painful, broken and softened by time,
soothe." [18] The "Farewell to Essay Writing" is perfumed with the odor of grateful memories from which the
writer draws his "best consolation for the future." He
almost erects his feeling for the past into a religion.
"Happy are they," he exclaims, "who live in the dream of
their own existence, and see all things in the light of their
own minds; who walk by faith and hope; to whom the
guiding star of their youth still shines from afar, and into
whom the spirit of the world has not entered! . . . The
world has no hold on them. They are in it, not of it; and
a dream and a glory is ever around them!" [19]

But this impassioned sentiment for the past was only a
refuge such as Byron might seek among the glories of
by-gone ages or amid the solitary Alpine peaks, where
it was possible to regain the strength spent in grappling
with the forces of the actual world and return newly nerved
to the battle. For fighting was Hazlitt's more proper element. He could hate with the same intensity that he loved,
and his hatred was aroused most by those whom he regarded
as responsible for the overturning of his political hopes.
Politics had played the most important part in his early
education. In his father's house he had absorbed the spirit
of protest, accustomed himself to arguing for the repeal
of the Test Act, and to declaiming against religious and
political persecution. At the age of twelve he had written
an indignant letter to the Shrewsbury Chronicle against the
mob of incendiaries which had destroyed the house of
Priestley, and as a student at Hackney he showed sufficient
self-reliance to develop an original "Essay on Laws." The

[18] *Table Talk*, "Why Distant Objects Please."
[19] "Love of Power," XI, 268.

defence of the popular cause was with him not an academic exercise, but a religious principle. " Since a little child, I knelt and lifted up my hands in prayer for it." [20] The emotional warmth of his creed was heightened by the reading of Rousseau, and in Napoleon it found a living hero on whom it could expend itself.

An uncompromising attachment to certain fundamental principles of democracy and an unceasing devotion to Napoleon constitute the chief elements of Hazlitt's political character. He sets forth his idea of representative government exactly in the manner of Rousseau when he proclaims that " in matters of feeling and common sense, of which each individual is the best judge, the majority are in the right. . . . It is an absurdity to suppose that there can be any better criterion of national grievances, or the proper remedies for them, than the aggregate amount of the actual, dear-bought experience, the honest feelings, and heart-felt wishes of a whole people, informed and directed by the greatest power of understanding in the community, unbiassed by any sinister motive." [21] Hazlitt was not a republican, and he disapproved of the Utopian rhapsodies of Shelley, woven as they seemed of mere moonshine, without applicability to the evils that demanded immediate reform. But he did insist that there was a power in the people to change its government and its governors, and hence grew his idolatry of Napoleon, who, through all vicissitudes, remained the " Child and Champion of the Revolution," the hero who had shown Europe how its established despots could be overthrown.

The news of Waterloo plunged Hazlitt into deep distress, as if it had been the shock of a personal calamity. According to Haydon, " he walked about unwashed, unshaven,

---

[20] *Life of Napoleon,* chap. 34.
[21] " What is the People? " in *Political Essays,* III, 292.

hardly sober by day, always intoxicated by night, literally for weeks." But his disappointment only strengthened his attachment to his principles. These remained enshrined with the brightest dreams of his youth, and in proportion as the vision faded and men were beginning to scoff at it as a shadow, Hazlitt bent his energies to fix its outline and prove its reality. " I am attached to my conclusions," he says, " in consequence of the pain, the anxiety, and the waste of time they have cost me." [22]  His doctrines contained nothing that was subversive of social order, and their ultimate triumph lends the color of heroism to a consistency which people have often interpreted as proof of a limited horizon. It is at least certain that he did not put his conscience out to market, and that his reward came in the form of the vilest calumny ever visited upon a man of letters.

These were the most infamous years of the Quarterly Review and Blackwood's Magazine, both of which had been founded as avowed champions of reaction. Their purpose was to discredit all writers whose politics or the politics of whose friends differed from the Government. Everybody knows of the fate which Keats and Shelley suf-

[22] He tells of an experience in crossing the Alps which he intends should be symbolic of his whole life. From a great distance he thought he perceived Mont Blanc, but as the driver insisted that it was only a cloud, " I supposed that I had taken a sudden fancy for a reality. I began in secret to take myself to task, and to lecture myself for my proneness to build theories on the foundation of my conjectures and wishes. On turning round occasionally, however, I observed that this cloud remained in the same place, and I noticed the circumstance to our guide, as favoring my first suggestion; for clouds do not usually remain long in the same place. We disputed the point for half a day, and it was not till the afternoon when we had reached the other side of the lake of Neufchatel, that this same cloud rising like a canopy over the point where it had hovered, ' in shape and station proudly eminent,' he acknowledged it to be Mont Blanc." *Notes of a Journey Through France and Italy.* Works, IX, 296.

fered at their hands, chiefly because they were friends of
Leigh Hunt, who was the editor of a Liberal newspaper
which had displeased George IV. Even the unoffending
Lamb did not escape their brutality, perhaps because he
was guilty of admitting Hazlitt to his house. The weapons
were misrepresentation and unconfined abuse, wielded with
an utter disregard of where the blows might fall, in the
spirit of a gang of young ruffians who knew that they were
protected in their wantonness by a higher authority. In
the chastened sadness of his later years Lockhart, who
was one of the offenders, confessed that he had no personal
grudge against any of Blackwood's victims, in fact that he
knew nothing about any of them, but that at the request
of John Wilson, his fellow-editor, he had composed " some
squibberies . . . with as little malice as if the assigned
subject had been the court of Pekin." The sincere regret
he expressed for the pain which his " jokes " had inflicted
ought perhaps to be counted in extenuation of his errors.
It may be true, as his generous biographer suggests, that
" his politics and his feud with many of these men was an
affair of ignorance and accidental associations in Edinburgh," that under different circumstances " he might have
been found inditing sonnets to Leigh Hunt, and supping with
Lamb, Haydon, and Hazlitt." [23] But meanwhile irreparable
mischief had been done to many reputations, and the life
of one man had been sacrificed to his sportiveness.[24]

The signal for the attack on Hazlitt was given by the
Quarterly in connection with a review of The Round Table,
Hazlitt's first book. The contents of this volume were

---

[23] Andrew Lang's *Life of Lockhart,* I, 63, 128-130.

[24] John Scott, the editor of the *London Magazine,* was killed in
a duel arising from his retaliatory attacks on Lockhart and the
Blackwood School of Criticism. See *London Magazine,* II, 509,
666; III, 76, and " Statement " prefatory to number for February,
1821.

characterized as "vulgar descriptions, silly paradox, flat
truisms, misty sophistry, broken English, ill humour and
rancorous abuse." [25] A little later, when the Characters of
Shakespeare's Plays seemed to be finding such favor with
the public that one edition was quickly exhausted, the Quarterly extinguished its sale by "proving that Mr. Hazlitt's
knowledge of Shakespeare and the English language is on
a par with the purity of his morals and the depth of his
understanding." [26] The cry was soon taken up by the
Blackwood's people in a series on the Cockney School of
Prose. Lockhart invented the expression "pimpled Hazlitt." It so happened that Hazlitt's complexion was unusu-
ally clear, but the epithet clung to him with a cruel tenacity.
When an ill-natured reviewer could find nothing else to say,
he had recourse to "pimpled essays" or "pimpled criticism." [27] The climax of abuse was reached in an article
entitled "Hazlitt Cross-Questioned," which a sense of decency makes it impossible to reproduce, and which resulted
in the payment of damages to the victim. Even the publisher Blackwood speaks of it, with what sincerity it is not
safe to say, as disgusting in tone, and Murray, who was
the London agent for the Magazine, refused to have any
further dealings with it. But the harm was done. Hazlitt
could not walk out without feeling that every passer-by had
read the atrocious article and saw the brand of the social
outcast on his features.

In an atmosphere like this, it is scarcely to be wondered
at if Hazlitt's temper, never of the amiable sort, should

[25] April, 1817.
[26] January, 1818
[27] "I have been reading Frederick Schlegel. . . . He is like
Hazlitt, in English, who *talks pimples*—a red and white corruption
rising up (in little imitations of mountains upon maps), but containing nothing, and discharging nothing, except their own humours." Byron's *Letters*, Jan. 28, 1821 (ed. Prothero, V, 191).

have become embittered, nor is it strange that he should sometimes, through ignorance, have committed the fault of which his enemies had been guilty in wantonness. Not content with retaliating the full measure of malice upon the heads of his immediate assailants, he turned the stream of his abuse upon Sir Walter Scott, whom he singled out deliberately as the towering head of a supposed literary conspiracy. He is credited with remarking: "To pay these fellows in their own coin, the way would be to begin with Walter Scott, and have at his clump foot."[28] Very meanspirited this sounds to us, who are acquainted with the nobility of Scott's character and who know with what magnanimous wisdom he kept himself above the petty altercations of the day. But for Hazlitt, Sir Walter was the father-in-law and friendly patron of John Lockhart, he was the person who had thrown the weight of his powerful influence to make John Wilson Professor of Moral Philosophy at the University of Edinburgh! He did not carry his prejudice against the Author of Waverley.

In some instances Hazlitt was consciously the aggressor, but his attacks were never wanton. He denounced Wordsworth and Coleridge and Southey because they were renegades from the cause which lay nearest to his heart. Their apostasy was an unforgivable offence in his eyes, and his wrath was proportioned to the admiration which he otherwise entertained for them. It is true that he treated their motives hastily and unjustly, but none of his opponents set him the example of charity. In the earlier years of their acquaintance Coleridge had spoken of Hazlitt as a "thinking, observant, original man," one who "says things that are his own in a way of his own,"[29] whereas after their

[28] Charles and Mary Cowden Clarke's *Recollections of Writers*, 147.
[29] Joseph Cottle: *Reminiscences of Samuel Taylor Coleridge*, 465.

estrangement he discovered that Hazlitt was completely
lacking in originality. Wordsworth, being offended at Hazlitt's review of the "Excursion," peevishly raked up an old
scandal and wrote to Haydon that he was "not a proper
person to be admitted into respectable society." [30] Perhaps
Hazlitt was not as "respectable" as his poet-friends, but
he had a better sense of fair play. At any rate, in a complete balancing of the accounts, Hazlitt's frequent displays
of ill-temper are offset by the insidious, often unscrupulous
baitings which he suffered from his opponents.

Naturally his bitterness was extended to his reflections
on mankind in general. He felt as if the human race had
wilfully deceived his sanguine expectations, and he poured
out his grievances against its refractoriness, taking revenge
for his public and his private wrongs, in a passage in
which high idealism is joined with personal spite,' in which
he has revealed himself in all his strength and weakness, and involved his enemies in a common ruin with
himself. It concludes the essay "On the Pleasure of
Hating":

"Instead of patriots and friends of freedom, I see nothing
but the tyrant and the slave, the people linked with kings
to rivet on the chains of despotism and superstition. I see
folly join with knavery, and together make up public spirit
and public opinions. I see the insolent Tory, the blind
Reformer, the coward Whig! If mankind had wished for
what is right, they might have had it long ago. The theory
is plain enough; but they are prone to mischief, 'to every
good work reprobate.' I have seen all that had been done
by the mighty yearnings of the spirit and intellect of men,
'of whom the world was not worthy,' and that promised
a proud opening to truth and good through the vista of
future years, undone by one man, with just glimmering of

[30] Haydon's *Correspondence and Table Talk*, II, 32.

understanding enough to feel that he was a king, but not
to comprehend how he could be king of a free people! I
have seen this triumph celebrated by poets, the friends of
my youth and the friends of man, but who were carried
away by the infuriate tide that, setting in from a throne,
bore down every distinction of right reason before it; and
I have seen all those who did not join in applauding this
insult and outrage on humanity proscribed, hunted down
(they and their friends made a bye-word of), so that it
has become an understood thing that no one can live by his
talents or knowledge who is not ready to prostitute those
talents and that knowledge to betray his species, and prey
upon his fellow-man. . . . In private life do we not see
hypocrisy, servility, selfishness, folly, and impudence succeed, while modesty shrinks from the encounter, and merit is
trodden under foot? How often is ' the rose plucked from
the forehead of a virtuous love to plant a blister there!'
What chance is there of the success of real passion? What
certainty of its continuance? Seeing all this as I do, and
unravelling the web of human life into its various threads of
meanness, spite, cowardice, want of feeling, and want of
understanding, of indifference towards others and ignorance
of ourselves—seeing custom prevail over all excellence,
itself giving way to infamy—mistaken as I have been in
my public and private hopes, calculating others from
myself, and calculating wrong; always disappointed where
I placed most reliance; the dupe of friendship, and the
fool of love; have I not reason to hate and to despise
myself? Indeed I do; and chiefly for not having hated and
despised the world enough." [31]—This is not exactly downright cynicism; it is more like disappointment, beating its
head frantically against the wall of circumstance. Yet
through his bitterest utterances there is felt the warm senti-

[31] *Plain Speaker.*

ment that, " let people rail at virtue, at genius and friendship as long as they will—the very *names* of these disputed
qualities are better than anything else that could be sub-
stituted for them, and embalm even the most angry abuse
of them." [32]

It is no wonder that Hazlitt has never been a popular
favorite. With a stronger attachment to principles than
to persons, lavishing upon ideas or the fanciful creations of
art a passionate affection which he grudgingly withheld
from human beings, stubbornly tenacious of a set of political dogmas to which he was ready to sacrifice his dearest
friends, morbidly sensitive to the faintest suggestion of a
personal slight, and prompter than the serpent to vent
against the aggressor the bitterness of his poison, he plays
the role of Ishmael among the men of letters in his day.
The violence of his retorts when he felt himself injured
and his capacity for giving offence even when he was not
directly provoked, begot a resentment in his adversaries
which blinded them to an appreciation of his genuine worth.
At best they might have assented, after his death, to the
sublime pity with which Carlyle, from his spiritual altitudes,
moralized upon his struggles. " How many a poor Hazlitt
must wander on God's verdant earth, like the Unblest on
burning deserts; passionately dig wells, and draw up only
the dry quicksand; believe that he is seeking Truth, yet
only wrestle among endless Sophisms, doing desperate
battle as with spectre-hosts; and die and make no sign!" [33]
We must appeal to the issue to determine whether Hazlitt's battle was altogether against spectre-hosts, and whether
in his quest for truth and beauty he has drawn up nothing
but quicksand. But at least Carlyle's expression recognizes

---

[32] *Characteristics*, CCCVII.
[33] "Characteristics," in Carlyle's *Critical and Miscellaneous Essays* (Chapman and Hall, 1898), III, 32.

the earnestness of his purpose and the bravery with which he maintained the conflict.

Hazlitt gave himself freely and without reserve to his reader. By his side Leigh Hunt appears affected, De Quincey theatrical, Lamb—let us say discreet. Affectation and discretion were equally alien to Hazlitt's nature, as they concerned either his personal conduct or his literary exercises. In regard to every impression, every prejudice, every stray thought that struggled into consciousness, his practice was, to use his own favorite quotation,

> " To pour out all as plain
> As downright Shippen or as old Montaigne."

He has drifted far from the tradition of Addison and Steele with which his contemporaries sought to associate him. There was nothing in him of the courtier-like grace employed in the good-humored reproof of unimportant vices, of the indulgent, condescending admonition to the " gentle reader," particularly of the fair sex. In Hazlitt's hands the essay was an instrument for the expression of serious thought and virile passion. He lacked indeed the temperamental balance of Lamb. His insight into human nature was intellectual rather than sympathetic. Though as a philosopher he understood that the web of life is of a mingled yarn, he has given us none of those rare glimpses of laughter ending in tears or of tears subsiding in a tender smile which are the sources of Lamb's depth and his charm. The same thing is true of his humor. He relished heartily its appearance in others and had a most wholesome laugh; but in himself there is no real merriment, only an ironic realization of the contrasts of life. When he writes, the smile which sometimes seeks to overpower the grim fixity of his features, is frozen before it can emerge to the sur- face. He lacks all the ingratiating arts which make a

writer beloved. But if one enjoys a keen student of the
intricacies of character, a bold and candid critic of human
imperfections, a stimulating companion full of original ideas
and deep feelings, he will find in Hazlitt an inexhaustible
source of instruction and delight. Hazlitt has long appealed to men of vigorous character and acute intellect,
men like Landor, Froude, Walter Bagehot, Robert Louis
Stevenson, and Ernest Henley, who have either proclaimed
his praise or flattered him with imitation. By the friend
who knew him longest and was better qualified than any
other to speak of him, he has been pronounced as "in his
natural and healthy state, one of the wisest and finest spirits
breathing." [34]

## II

THE discovery in the seventeenth century of the Greek
treatise "On the Sublime," attributed to Longinus, with its
inspired appreciation of the great passages in Greek literature so different from the analytic manner of Aristotle,
gave a decided impulse to English criticism. It was at the
same time that English prose, under the influence of French
models, was developing a more familiar tone than it had
hitherto been acquainted with. The union of the enthusiasm
of Longinus with this moderated French prose resulted in
the graceful prefaces of Dryden, which remained unmatched for more than a century. The Longinian fire,
breathed upon too by the genius of Shakespeare, preserved
the eighteenth century from congealing into the utter
formalism of pseudo-Aristotelian authority. Though they
did not produce an even warmth over the whole surface,
the flames are observed darting through the crust even
where the crust seems thickest. It is significant that Dr.

[34] "Letter of Elia to Robert Southey," Lamb's Works, ed. Lucas,
I, 233.

Johnson should exclaim with admiration at the criticism of
Dryden, not because Dryden judged according to rules but
because his was the criticism of a poet. And he singles
out as the best example of such criticism the well-known
appreciation of Shakespeare, the very passage which Hazlitt later quoted as "the best character of Shakespeare
that has ever been written." [35]  The high-priest of classi-
cism wavered frequently in his allegiance to some of the
sacred fetishes of his cult, and had enough grace, once
at least, to speak with scorn of the "cant of those who
judged by principles rather than by perception." [36]

But to judge by perception is a comparatively rare accomplishment, and so most critics continued to employ the
foot-rule as if they were measuring flat surfaces, while
occasionally going so far as to recognize the existence of
certain mountain-peaks as "irregular beauties." In a more
or less conscious distinction from the criticism of external
rules there developed also during the eighteenth century
what its representatives were pleased to call metaphysical
criticism, to which we should now probably apply the term
psychological. This consisted in explaining poetic effects
by reference to strictly mental processes in a tone of calm
analysis eminently suited to the rationalistic temper of the
age. It methodically traced the sources of grandeur or
of pathos or of humor, and then illustrated its generalization by the practice of the poets. It could thereby pride
itself on going back of the rules to the fundamental laws
of human nature. Kames's Elements of Criticism, written
in 1761, became a work of standard reference, though it
did not impose on the great critics. In commending it
Dr. Johnson was careful to remark, "I do not mean that
he has taught us anything; but he has told us old things

---

[35] "On Criticism," in *Table Talk.*
[36] Life of Pope, Johnson's Lives, ed. Birkbeck Hill, IV, 248.

in a new way." [37]  But in general Kames was considered
a safer guide than the enthusiastic Longinus, who throughout the century was looked upon with distrust. "Instead
of shewing for what reason a sentiment or image is sublime, and discovering the secret power by which they affect
a reader with pleasure, he is ever intent on producing
something sublime *himself,* and strokes of his *own* eloquence." So runs the complaint of Joseph Warton. [38] The
distrust was not without ground. The danger that the
method of Longinus in the hands of ungifted writers would
become a cloak for critical ignorance and degenerate into
empty bluster was already apparent. [39]  Only rarely was
there a reader who could distinguish between the false and
the true application of the method. Gibbon did it in a
passage which impressed itself upon the younger critics
of Hazlitt's generation. "I was acquainted only with two
ways of criticising a beautiful passage: the one, to shew,
by an exact anatomy of it, the distinct beauties of it, and
whence they sprung; the other, an idle exclamation, or
a general encomium, which leaves nothing behind it.
Longinus has shewn me that there is a third. He tells me
his own feelings upon reading it; and tells them with such
energy, that he communicates them." [40] That vital element, the commentator's power of communicating his own
feelings, constituting as it does the difference between
phrase-making and valuable criticism, did not become prominent in English literature before the nineteenth century.

The official criticism of the early nineteenth century as
represented by the Edinburgh and Quarterly Reviews, de-

[37] Boswell's Johnson, ed. Birkbeck Hill, II, 89.
[38] *Essay on the Genius and Writings of Pope,* I, 170.
[39] See an essay by John Foster on "Poetical Criticism," in
*Critical Essays,* ed. Bohn, I, 144.
[40] Gibbon's Journal, October 3, 1762. Miscellaneous Works, ed.
1814, V, 263.

rives its descent directly from the eighteenth. Whatever
the Government might have thought of the politics of the
Edinburgh, its literary outlook remained unexceptionably
orthodox. Jeffrey's "Essay on Beauty" is a direct copy
of Alison's "Essay on Taste." Much as Dr. Johnson in
the preceding age, Jeffrey prided himself on the moral
tendency of his criticism—a morality which consisted in
censuring the life of Burns and in exalting the virtuous
insipidities of Maria Edgeworth's tales as it might have
been done by any faithful minister of the gospel. To be
sure he cannot be said to have held tenaciously to the
old ·set of canons. Though he stanchly withstood the
new-fangled poetic practices of Wordsworth and of Southey,
he bowed before the great popularity of Scott and Byron,
even at the cost of some of his favorite maxims. In his
writings the solvents of the older criticism are best seen
at work. Jeffrey both by instinct and training was a
lawyer, and his position at the head of the most respected
periodical formed a natural temptation to a dictatorial
manner. He was a judge who tried to uphold the literary
constitution but wavered in the face of a strong popular
opposition. When the support of precedent failed him,
he remained without any firm conviction of his own. While
his poetic taste was quite adequate to the appreciation of
a Samuel Rogers or a Barry Cornwall, it was incomparably
futile in the perception of a Wordsworth or a Shelley. In
a passage composed at the end of his long editorial career
in 1829, he unconsciously announced his own extinction
as a critic:

"Since the beginning of our critical career, we have
seen a vast deal of beautiful poetry pass into oblivion, in
spite of our feeble efforts to recall or retain it in remembrance. The tuneful quartos of Southey are already little
better than lumber:—and the rich melodies of Keats and

Shelley,—and the fantastical emphasis of Wordsworth,—and the plebeian pathos of Crabbe, are melting fast from the field of our vision. The novels of Scott have put out his poetry. Even the splendid strains of Moore are fading into distance and dimness, except where they have been married to immortal music; and the blazing star of Byron himself is receding from its place of pride. We need say nothing of Milman, and Croly, and Atherstone, and Hood, and a legion of others, who, with no ordinary gifts of taste and fancy, have not so properly survived their fame, as been excluded by some hard fatality, from what seemed their just inheritance. The two who have the longest withstood this rapid withering of the laurel, and with the least marks of decay on their branches, are Rogers and Campbell; neither of them, it may be remarked, voluminous writers, and both distinguished rather for the fine taste and consummate elegance of their writings, than for that fiery passion, and disdainful vehemence, which seemed for a time to be so much more in favour with the public." [41]

But the authority of Jeffrey did not long remain unchallenged. His unfortunate " This will never do " became a by-word among the younger writers who were gradually awaking to the realization of a new spirit in criticism. The protest against the methods of the dictatorial quarterlies found expression in the two brilliant monthly periodicals, Blackwood's and the London Magazine, founded respectively in 1817 and 1820. In these no opportunity was neglected to thrust at the inflated pretensions of the established reviews, and, though the animus of rivalry might be suspected of playing its part, the blows usually struck home. There is an air of absolute finality about Lockhart's " Remarks on the Periodical Criticism of

[41] Review of Mrs. Hemans's Poems, *Edinburgh Review,* October, 1829. Jeffrey's Works, III, 296.

England," and his characterization of Jeffrey in this article is a bold anticipation of the judgment of posterity.[42] The editor of the London Magazine [43] writes with equal assurance, "We must protest against considering the present taste as the standard of excellence, or the criticisms on poetry in the Edinburgh Review as the voice even of the present taste." The test of critical eligibility in this age is an appreciation of Wordsworth and a proper understanding of Coleridge his prophet, and it is by virtue of what inspiration they drew from these oracles that John Lockhart and John Scott became better qualified than Jeffrey or Gifford to form the literary opinions of the public.

Coleridge more than any other person was responsible for bringing about a change in the attitude of literature toward criticism. As Hazlitt puts it with his inimitable vividness, he "threw a great stone into the standing pool of criticism, which splashed some persons with the mud, but which gave a motion to the surface and a reverberation to the neighbouring echoes, which has not since subsided." [44] Whether his ideas were borrowed from the Germans or evolved in his own brain, their importance for English literature remains the same. Coleridge's service lay in asserting and reasserting such fundamental principles as that a critical standard is something quite distinct from a set of external rules; that the traditional opposition between genius and laws was based on a misconception as to the function of the critic; that all great genius necessarily worked in accordance with certain laws which it was the function of the critic to determine by a study of each particular work of art; that art, being vital and organic, assumed different shapes at different epochs of human cul-

[42] *Blackwood's Magazine,* II, 670-79.
[43] I, 281 (March, 1820).
[44] *Spirit of the Age,* "William Godwin."

ture; that only the spirit of poetry remained constant, while
its form was molded anew by each age in accordance with
the demands of its own life; that it was no more reasonable to judge Shakespeare's plays by the practice of Sophocles than to judge sculpture by the rules of painting. "O!
few have there been among critics, who have followed with
the eye of their imagination the imperishable yet ever
wandering spirit of poetry through its various metempsy-
choses; or who have rejoiced with the light of clear perception at beholding with each new birth, with each rare
*avatar,* the human race frame to itself a new body, by
assimilating materials of nourishment out of its new circumstances, and work for itself new organs of power appropriate to the new sphere of its motion and activity." [45]
This rare grasp of general principles was combined in
Coleridge with poetic vision and a declamatory eloquence
which enabled him to seize on the more ardent and open-
minded men of letters and to determine their critical view-
point.

William Hazlitt was among the earliest to fall under
Coleridge's spell. Just how much he owed to Coleridge
beyond the initial impulse it is impossible to prove, because
so much of the latter's criticism was expressed during
improvised monologues at the informal meetings of friends,
or in lectures of which only fragmentary notes remain. At
any rate, while Coleridge's chief distinction lay in the
enunciation of general principles, Hazlitt's practice, in so
far as it took account of these general principles at all,
assumed their existence, and displayed its strength in concrete judgments of individual literary works. His criticism
may be said to imply at every step the existence of Coleridge's, or to rise like an elegant superstructure on the solid
foundation which the other had laid. Hazlitt communi-

[45] Works, ed. Shedd, IV, 35.

cated to the general public that love and appreciation of great literature which Coleridge inspired only in the few elect. The latter, even more distinctly than a poet for poets, was a *critic for critics,*[46] and three generations have not succeeded in absorbing all his doctrines. But Hazlitt, with a delicate sensitiveness to the impressions of genius, with a boundless zest of poetic enjoyment, with a firm common sense to control his taste, and with a gift of original expression unequalled in his day, arrested the attention of the ordinary reader and made effective the principles which Coleridge with some vagueness had projected. To analyze in cold blood such living criticism as Hazlitt's may expose one to unflattering imputations, but the attempt may serve to bring to light what is so often overlooked, that Hazlitt's criticism is no random, irresponsible discharge of his sensibilities, but has an implicit basis of sound theory.

In his History of Criticism, Mr. Saintsbury takes as his motto for the section on the early nineteenth century a sentence from Sainte-Beuve to the effect that nearly the whole art of the critic consists in knowing how to read a book with judgment and without ceasing to relish it.[47] We are almost ready to believe that the French critic, in the significant choice of the words judgment and relish, is consciously summarizing the method of Hazlitt, the more so as he elsewhere explicitly confesses a sympathy with the English critic.[48] Hazlitt has indeed himself characterized his art in some such terms. In one of his lectures he modestly describes his undertaking " merely to read over a set of authors with the audience, as I would do with

---

[46] Mr. Saintsbury has applied this phrase to Hazlitt himself, but we prefer to transfer the honor.

[47] " Savoir bien lire un livre en le jugeant chemin faisant, et sans cesser de le goûter, c'est presque tout l'art du critique." *Chateaubriand et son Groupe Littéraire*, I, 234.

[48] *Portraits Contemporains,* " Sonnet d'Hazlitt," II, 515.

a friend, to point out a favorite passage, to explain an
objection; or if a remark or a theory occurs, to state it in
illustration of the subject, but neither to tire him nor
puzzle myself with pedantical rules and pragmatical *formulas* of criticism that can do no good to anybody." [49] This
sounds dangerously like dilettantism. It suggests the
method of what in our day is called impressionism, one of
the most delightful forms of literary entertainment when
practiced by a master of literature. The impressionist's
aim is to record whatever impinges on his brain, and
though with a writer of fine discernment it is sure to be
productive of exquisite results, as criticism it is under-
mined by the impressionist's assumption that every appreciation is made valid by the very fact of its existence. But
this was scarcely Hazlitt's idea of criticism. Against universal suffrage in matters literary he would have been
among the first to protest. We might almost imagine we
were listening to some orthodox theorist of the eighteenth
century when we hear him declaring that the object of
taste "must be that, not which *does,* but which *would*
please universally, supposing all men to have paid an equal
attention to any subject and to have an equal relish for it,
which can only be guessed at by the imperfect and yet more
than casual agreement among those who have done so from
choice and feeling." [50] Though not the surest kind of clue,
this indicates at least that Hazlitt's rejection of " pedantical
rules and pragmatical formulas " was not equivalent to
a declaration of anarchy.

For Hazlitt the assertion of individual taste meant eman-
cipation from arbitrary codes and an opportunity to embrace a compass as wide as the range of literary excellence.
Realizing that every reader, even the professed critic, is

[49] *Age of Elizabeth,* "On Miscellaneous Poems," V, 301.
[50] "Thoughts on Taste," XI, 460.

hemmed in by certain prejudices arising from his temperament, his education, his environment, he was unwilling to
pledge his trust to any school or fashion of criticism. The
favorite oppositions of his generation—Shakespeare and
Pope, Fielding and Richardson, English poetry and French
—had no meaning for him. He was glad to enjoy each
in its kind. "The language of taste and moderation is,
*I prefer this, because it is best to me;* the language of
dogmatism and intolerance is, *Because I prefer it, it is best
in itself, and I will allow no one else to be of a different
opinion.*" [51] This passage, in connection with the one last
quoted, may be considered as fixing the limits within which
Hazlitt gave scope to personal preference. The sum of
his literary judgments reveals a taste for a greater variety
of the works of genius than is displayed by any contemporary, and the absence of "a catholic and many-sided
sympathy" [52] is one of the last imputations that should
have been brought against him. His criticism has limitations, but not such as are due to a narrowness of literary
perception.

Even Hazlitt's shortcomings may frequently be turned to
his glory as a critic. The most remarkable thing about his
violent political prejudices is the success with which he
dissociated his literary estimates from them. Such a serious
limitation in a critic as deficiency of reading in his case
only raises our astonishment at the sureness of instinct
which enabled him to pronounce unerringly on the scantest
information. Never was there a critic of nearly equal pretensions who had as little of the scholar's equipment. If,
as he tells us, he applied himself too closely to his studies
at a certain period in his youth,[53] he atoned for it by his

[51] *Conversations of Northcote,* VI, 457.
[52] Cf. Herford: *Age of Wordsworth,* p. 51.
[53] "On the Conduct of Life," XII, 427.

neglect of books in later life.[54]  A desultory education had
left him without that intimacy with the classics which belonged of right to every cultivated Englishman.  His allusions to the Greek and Latin writers are in the most
general terms, but with a note of reverence which did not
enter into his speech concerning even Shakespeare.  "I
would have you learn Latin (he is writing to his son)
because there is an atmosphere round this sort of classical
ground, to which that of actual life is gross and vulgar." [55]
His knowledge of Italian was no more thorough, though
here he was more nearly on a level with his contemporaries.
For Boccaccio indeed he showed an intense affection, and
he could write intelligently, if not deeply, concerning Dante
and Ariosto and Tasso.[56]  With French he naturally had
a wider acquaintance, but still nothing beyond the reach
of the very general reader.  The notable point is that he
refrains from passing judgment on the entire body of
French poetry because it is unlike English poetry.  He is
not infected with the wilful provincialism of Lamb nor
with the spirit of John Bullishness which seriously proclaims in its rivals " equally a want of books and men." [57]
"We may be sure of this," says Hazlitt, "that when we
see nothing but grossness and barbarism, or insipidity and
verbiage in a writer that is the God of a nation's idolatry,
it is we and not they who want true taste and feeling." [58]
Having this wholesome counsel ever before him, he can
be more generously appreciative of the genius of Molière,
more justly discerning in his analysis of the spirit of

---

[54] Patmore: *My Friends and Acquaintances,* III, 122.
[55] "On the Conduct of Life," XII, 428.  See also the paper "On
the Study of the Classics," in the *Round Table.*
[56] See a note to p. 329.
[57] See Wordsworth's sonnet, "Great men have been among us."
[58] "On Criticism," in *Table Talk.*

Rousseau,[59] and more free of the puritanical clatter against Voltaire than any of his fellow-critics. With German literature his familiarity was bounded on the one hand by Schiller's "Robbers," on the other by the first part of "Faust," the entire gap between these being filled by the popular versions of Kotzebue's plays and Mme. de Staël's book on Germany. Yet he dared to write a character of the German people which is almost worth quoting.[60]

In English his range of reading was correspondingly narrow. Such a piece of waywardness as his enthusiasm for John Buncle,[61] derived no doubt from Lamb, is unique. Broadly speaking, he prefers to accept the established canon and approaches new discoveries with a deep distrust. He is very little concerned with writers of the second order, and in his Lecture on the Living Poets he shocked his audience unspeakably, when he came to the name of Hannah More, by merely remarking, "She has written a great deal which I have never read." He looked upon most living writers through the eyes of the somewhat jaded reviewer, who, though susceptible to a romantic thrill from one or the other, is usually on his guard against spurious blandishments and reluctant to admit the claims of new pretenders. Even in poets of the first rank he slurred over a great deal; but what he loved he dwelt on with a kind of rapt inspiration until it became his second nature, its spirit and its language fused intimately with his own.

[59] "He is the most illuminating and the most thoughtful of all Rousseau's early English critics. . . . His essay 'On the Character of Rousseau' was not surpassed, or approached, as a study of the great writer until the appearance of Lord Morley's monograph nearly sixty years afterwards." E. Gosse: *Fortnightly Review,* July, 1912, p. 30.

[60] In the review of Schlegel's *Lectures on the Drama,* Works, X, 78.

[61] See the paper on "John Buncle," in the *Round Table.*

This revolutionist in politics was a jealous aristocrat in
the domains of art, and this admission does not impair
our earlier assertion of his openness to a greater variety
of impressions than any of his contemporaries in criticism.
Hazlitt's professed indifference to system is probably due
as much to lack of deep reading as to romantic impatience
of restraint. When he declared that it was beyond his
powers "to condense and combine all the facts relating to
a subject " [62] or that " he had no head for arrangement," [63]
it was only because he did not happen to be a master of
the facts which required combination or arrangement. For
he did have an unusual gift for penetrating to the core of
a subject and tearing out the heart of its mystery; in fact,
his power of concrete literary generalization was in his age
unmatched. To reveal the distinctive virtue of a literary
form, to characterize the sources of weakness or of strength
in a new or a by-gone fashion of poetry, to analyze accurately the forces impelling a whole mighty age—these
things, requiring a deep and steady concentration of mind,
are among his most solid achievements. In a paragraph he
distils for us the essence of what is picturesque and worth
dwelling on in the comedy of the Restoration. In a page
he triumphantly establishes the boundary-line between the
poetry of art and nature—Pope and Shakespeare—which to
the present day remains as a clear guide, while at the same
time Campbell and Byron and Bowles are filling the periodicals with protracted and often irrelevant arguments on
one side or the other which only the critically curious now
venture to look into. In the space of a single lecture he
takes a sweeping view of all the great movements which
gave vitality and grandeur to the Elizabethan spirit and
found a voice in its literature, so that in spite of his little

[62] *Correspondence of Macvey Napier,* p. 21.
[63] " On the Pleasure of Painting," in *Table Talk.*

learning he seems to have left nothing for his followers but
to fill in his outline. The same keenness of discernment
he applied casually in dissecting the genius of his own
time. He associated the absence of drama with the French
Revolution, its tendency to deal in abstractions and to regard everything in relation to *man* and not men—a tendency
irreconcilable with dramatic literature, which is essentially
individual and concrete.[64] To be sure the eighteenth century before the Revolution was as void of drama as Hazlitt's generation, but what is true of the period which produced Political Justice and the Edinburgh Review would
hold equally of the time which produced the "Essay on
Man" and the deistic controversy. He sometimes harshly
exposes the weaker side of contemporary lyricism as a
"mere effusion of natural sensibility," and he regrets the
absence of "imaginary splendor and human passion" as of
a glory departed.[65] But with all this he had the true historical sense. It breaks out most unmistakably when he
says, "If literature in our day has taken this decided turn
into a critical channel, is it not a presumptive proof that
it ought to do so?"[66] Of the actual application of
historical principles, which were just beginning to be
realized in the study of literature, we find only a few faint
traces in Hazlitt. Some remarks on the influence of climate
and of religious and political institutions occur in his contributions to the Edinburgh, but occasionally their per-
functory manner suggests the editorial pen of Jeffrey.
Doubtless Hazlitt's discriminating judgment would have
enabled him to excel in this field, had he been equipped
with the necessary learning.

It may also be a serious limitation of Hazlitt's that he

[64] *Dramatic Essays,* VIII, 415.
[65] "On Shakespeare and Milton," p. 44.
[66] "The Periodical Press," X, 203.

neglects questions of structure and design. Doubtless he
was reacting against the jargon of the older criticism with
its lifeless and monotonous repetitions about invention and
fable and unity, giving nothing but the "superficial plan
and elevation, as if a poem were a piece of formal architecture." [67] In avoiding the study of the design of "Paradise Lost" or of the "Faerie Queene" he may have
brought his criticism nearer to the popular taste; but he
deliberately shut himself off from a vision of some of the
higher reaches of poetic art, perhaps betraying thereby that
lack of "imagination" with which he has sometimes been
charged.[68] His interpretation of an author is therefore
occasionally in danger of becoming an appreciation of isolated characters, or scenes, or passages, as if he were actually reading him over with his audience. But this is a
limitation which Hazlitt shares with all the finer critics of
his day.

After all these shortcomings have been acknowledged,
the permanence of Hazlitt's achievement appears only the
more remarkable. It is clear that the gods made him
critical. The two essential qualities of judgment and taste
he seems to have possessed from the very beginning. It is
impossible to trace in him any development of taste; his
growth is but the succession of his literary experiences.
One looks in vain for any of those errors of youth such
as are met even in a Coleridge enamored of Bowles. What
extravagance of tone Hazlitt displayed in his early criticism
he carried with him to his last day. If any change is to
be noted, it is in the growing keenness of his appreciation.
The early maturity of his judicial powers is attested by
the political and metaphysical tendency of his youthful

---

[67] "On Criticism," in *Table Talk*.
[68] Cf. "On Reading Old Books," pp. 338-9, where this charge is
curiously echoed by Hazlitt himself.

studies. His birth as a full-fledged critic awaited only the
stirring of the springs of his eloquence, as is evident from
the excellence of what is practically his first literary essay,
the " Character of Burke."

No critic has approached books with so intense a passion
as Hazlitt. That sentimental fondness for the volumes
themselves, especially when enriched by the fragrance of
antiquity, which gives so delicious a savor to the bookish-
ness of Lamb, was in him conspicuously absent. For him
books were only a more vivid aspect of life itself. " Tom
Jones," he tells us, was the novel that first broke the spell
of his daily tasks and made of the world " a dance through
life, a perpetual gala-day." [69] Keats could not have romped
through the " Faerie Queene " with more spirit than did
Hazlitt through the length and breadth of eighteenth century romance, and the young poet's awe before the majesty
of Homer was hardly greater than that of the future critic
when a Milton or a Wordsworth swam into his ken. This
hot and eager interest, deprived of its outlet in the form
of direct emulation, sought a vent in communicating itself
to others and in making converts to its faith. So intimately
did Hazlitt feel the spell of a work of genius, that its
life-blood was transfused into his own almost against his
will. " I wish," he exclaims, " I had never read the Emilius
. . . I had better have formed myself on the model of
Sir Fopling Flutter." [70] He entered into the poet's creation
with a sympathy amounting almost to poetic vision, and
the ever-present sense of the reality of the artist's world
led him to interpret literature primarily in relation to life.
The poetry of character and passion is what he regards of
most essential interest.[71] This point of view unintention-
ally converts his familiar essays on life into a literary dis-

[69] Ibid., p. 337.    [70] Ibid., p. 340.
[71] " On Shakespeare and Milton," p. 109.

course, and gives to his formal criticism the tone of a
study of life at its sources, raising it at once to the same
level with creative literature. Though he nowhere em-
ploys the now familiar formula of " literature and life," the
lecture "On Poetry in General" is largely an exposition
of this outlook.

Life in its entire compass is regarded as the rough material of literature, but it does not become literature until
the artist's imagination, as with a divine ray, has pene-
trated the mass and inspired it with an ideal existence.
Among the numerous attempts of his contemporaries to
define the creative faculty of the poet, this comparatively
simple one of Hazlitt's is worth noting. "This intuitive
perception of the hidden analogies of things, or, as it may
be called, this *instinct of imagination,* is perhaps what stamps
the character of genius on the productions of art more than
any other circumstance: for it works unconsciously, like
nature, and receives its impressions from a kind of inspiration." [72] It is this power that he has in mind when he says
" Poetry is infusing the same spirit in a number of things,
or bathing them all as it were, in the same overflowing
sense of delight." [73] It shows Hazlitt to have fully appre-
hended the guiding principle of the new ideal of criticism
which, looking upon the work of art as an act of original
creation and not of mechanical composition, based its judgment on a direct sympathy with the artist's mind instead
of resorting to a general rule. In the light of this principle he is enabled to avoid the pitfalls of a moralistic
interpretation of literature and to decide the question as to
the relative importance of substance and treatment with
a certainty which seems to preclude the possibility of any
other answer.

[72] " The English Novelists," VIII, 109.
[73] " Thoughts on Taste," XI, 463.

It is not the dignity of the theme which constitutes the great work of art, for in that case a prose summary of the " Divine Comedy " would be as exalted as the original, and it would be necessary merely to know the subject of a poem in order to pass judgment upon it. A low or a trivial subject may be raised by the imagination of the artist who recognizes in it the elements of beauty or power. No definition of poetry can be worth anything which would exclude " The Rape of the Lock "; and Murillo's painting of " The Two Beggar Boys " is as much worth having " as almost any picture in the world." [74] " Yet it is not true that execution is everything, and the class or subject nothing. The highest subjects, equally well-executed (which, however, rarely happens), are the best." [75] Though each is perfect in its kind, there can be no difficulty in deciding the question of greatness between " King Lear " and " The Comedy of Errors." " The greatest strength of genius is shewn in describing the strongest passions: for the power of imagination, in works of invention, must be in proportion to the force of the natural impressions, which are the subject of them." [76] One also finds a test of relative values in the measure of fulness with which the work of art reflects the complex elements of life. If we estimate a tragedy of Shakespeare above one of Lillo or Moore, it is because " impassioned poetry is an emanation of the moral and intellectual part of our nature, as well as of the sensitive—of the desire to know, the will to act, and the power to feel; and ought to appeal to these different parts of the constitution, in order to be perfect." [77]

In treating of the specific distinction of poetry Hazlitt

[74] " On Criticism," in *Table Talk.*
[75] Ibid.
[76] *Characters of Shakespeare,* " Lear."
[77] " On Poetry in General," p. 258.

does not escape the usual difficulties. Taking his point of departure from Milton's "thoughts that voluntary move harmonious numbers," he defines poetry in a passage that satisfactorily anticipates the familiar one of Carlyle, as "the music of language answering to the music of the mind. . . . Wherever any object takes such a hold of the mind as to make us dwell upon it, and brood over it, melting the heart in tenderness, or kindling it' to a sentiment of enthusiasm;—wherever a movement of imagination or passion is impressed on the mind, by which it seeks to prolong or repeat the emotion, to bring all other objects into accord with it, and to give the same movement of harmony, sustained and continuous, or gradually varied according to the occasion, to the sounds that express it—this is poetry. The musical in sound is the sustained and continuous; the musical in thought is the sustained and continuous also. There is a near connection between music and deep-rooted passion." [78] In this mystical direction a definition could go no further, but like nearly all writers and speakers Hazlitt is inclined to use the word poetry in a variety of more or less connected meanings,[79] ordinarily legitimate enough, but somewhat embarrassing when it is a question of definition. "That which lifts the spirit above the earth, which draws the soul out of itself with indescribable longings, is," he says, "poetry in kind, and generally fit to become so in name, by 'being married to immortal verse.'" [80] If it is true that Pilgrim's Progress and Robinson Crusoe possess the "essence and the power of poetry"

[78] "On Poetry in General," p. 266.
[79] Hazlitt defends himself on the ground that "the word has these three *distinct* meanings in the English language, that is, it signifies the composition produced, the state of mind or faculty producing it, and, in certain cases, the subject-matter proper to call forth that state of mind." *Letter to Gifford*, I, 396.
[80] "On Poetry in General," pp. 268-9.

and require only the addition of verse to become absolutely so,[81] then the musical expression is only a factitious ornament, to be added or removed at the caprice of the writer. But Hazlitt is careful to declare that verse does not make the whole difference between poetry and prose, leaving the whole question as vaguely suspended as ever.[82] Bare theorizing, according to his own confession, was no favorite pursuit with Hazlitt. He enjoyed himself much more in the analysis of an individual author or his work. His aversion to literary cant, his love of " saying things that are his own in a way of his own," were here most in evidence. What he says of Milton might appropriately be applied to himself, that he formed the most intense conception of things and then embodied them by a single stroke of his pen. In a phrase or in a sentence he stamped the character of an author indelibly, and, enemy to commonplace though he was, became a cause of commonplace in others. No matter how much might already have been written on a subject (and Hazlitt did not make a practice of celebrating neglected obscurity) his own view stood out fresh and clear, and yet his judgments were never eccentric. He wrestled with a writer's thoughts, absorbed his most passionate feelings, and mirrored back his most exquisite perceptions with " all the color, the light and the shade." His fertility is more amazing than his intensity, for no critic of nearly equal rank has enriched English literature with so many valuable and enduring judgments on so great a variety of subjects. Dr. Johnson is by common consent the spokesman of the eighteenth century, or of its dominant class; Coleridge and

[81] Ibid., p. 268.

[82] Those interested in the perennial discussion of the relation of poetry to verse or metre would do well to read the recent interesting contribution to the subject by Professor Mackail in his *Lectures on Poetry* (Longmans, 1912).

Lamb are entitled to the glory of revealing the literature between Spenser and Milton to English readers, and the former rendered the additional service of acting as the interpreter of Wordsworth. But to give an idea of Hazlitt's scope would require a summary of opinions embracing poetry from Chaucer and Spenser to Wordsworth and Byron, prose sacred and profane from Bacon and Jeremy Taylor to Burke and Edward Irving, the drama in its two flourishing periods, the familiar essay from Steele and Addison to Lamb and Leigh Hunt, the novel from Defoe to Sir Walter Scott. This does not begin to suggest Hazlitt's versatility. His own modest though somewhat over-alliterative words are that he has "at least glanced over a number of subjects—painting, poetry, prose, plays, politics, parliamentary speakers, metaphysical lore, books, men, and things." [83]

The importance of Hazlitt's Shakespearian criticism is no longer open to question. Though Coleridge alluded to them slightingly as out-and-out imitations of Lamb, [84] Hazlitt's dicta on the greatest English genius are equal in depth to Lamb's and far more numerous; and while in profoundness and subtlety they fall short of the remarks of Coleridge himself, they surpass them in intensity and carrying power. To both of these men Hazlitt owed a great deal in his appreciation of Shakespeare, and perhaps even more to August Wilhelm Schlegel, whose Lectures on Dramatic Literature he reviewed in 1815. [85] His allusions to Schlegel border on enthusiasm and he makes it a proud claim that he has done "more than any one except Schlegel to vindicate the Characters of Shakespeare's Plays

[83] "On the Causes of Popular Opinion," XII, 320.
[84] Coleridge: *Table Talk*, Aug. 6, 1832.
[85] *Edinburgh Review*, Feb., 1816. The nature of Hazlitt's debt to Coleridge, Lamb and Schlegel is to some extent illustrated in the notes to the present text.

from the stigma of French criticism."[86] But however
great his obligation, there was some point in the compliment of the German critic when he declared that Hazlitt
had gone beyond him (l'avoit dépassé) in his Shakespearian opinions.[87] A few years later Heine maintained
that the only significant commentator of Shakespeare produced by England was William Hazlitt.[88] Coleridge's
notes, it is to be remembered, were not at that time generally accessible.

Hazlitt's attitude toward Shakespeare was wholesomely
on this side of idolatry. He did not make it an article
of faith to admire everything that Shakespeare had written,
and refused his praise to the poems and most of the sonnets. Even Schlegel and Coleridge could not persuade him
to see beauties in what appeared to be blemishes, but in
a general estimate of Shakespeare's all-embracing genius
he conceived his faults to be " of just as much consequence
as his bad spelling."[89] He saw in him a genius who comprehended all humanity, who represented it poetically in all
its shades and varieties. He examined all the fine distinctions of character, he studied Shakespeare's manner of
combining and contrasting them so as to produce a unity
of tone above even the art of the classic unities. From
the irresponsible comedy of Falstaff to the deepest tragic
notes of Lear, the whole gamut of human emotions en-
counters responsive chords in the critic's mind—the young
love of Romeo and Juliet or the voluptuous abandonment
of Antony and Cleopatra, the intellect of Iago irresistibly
impelled to malignant activity or Hamlet entangled in the
coils of a fatal introspection. To the sheer poetry of

---

[86] " Whether Genius is Conscious of its Powers," in *Plain Speaker*.
[87] Moore's *Letters and Journals*, May 21, 1821, III, 235.
[88] *Shakespeare's Mädchen und Frauen*.
[89] Review of Schlegel's Lectures, Works, X, 111.

Shakespeare he is also acutely sensitive, to the soft moonlit
atmosphere of the " Midsummernight's Dream," to the
tender gloom of " Cymbeline," to the " philosophic poetry "
of " As You Like It." Some of his interpretations of isolated passages are hardly to be surpassed. He comments
minutely and exquisitely on what he considers to be a touchstone of poetic feeling,

> " Daffodils
> That come before the swallow dares, and take
> The winds of March with beauty." °°

And with what complete insight he translates a speech of
Antony's :

" This precarious state and the approaching dissolution
of his greatness are strikingly displayed in the dialogue of
Antony with Eros :

> ' *Antony.*  Eros, thou yet behold'st me?
> *Eros.*  Ay, noble lord.
> *Antony.*  Sometime we see a cloud that's dragonish ;
> A vapour sometime, like a bear or lion,
> A towered citadel, a pendant rock,
> A forked mountain, or blue promontory
> With trees upon't, that nod unto the world
> And 'mock our eyes with air.  Thou hast seen these signs,
> They are black vesper's pageants.
> *Eros.*  Ay, my lord.
> *Antony.*  That which is now a horse, even with a thought
> The rack dislimns, and makes it indistinct
> As water is in water.
> *Eros.*  It does, my lord.
> *Antony.*  My good knave, Eros, now thy captain is
> Even such a body,' etc.

" This is, without doubt, one of the finest pieces of poetry
in Shakspeare.  The splendour of the imagery, the semblance of reality, the lofty range of picturesque objects

°° " Poetry," XII, 339.

hanging over the world, their evanescent nature, the total
uncertainty of what is left behind, are just like the mouldering schemes of human greatness. It is finer than Cleopatra's passionate lamentation over his fallen grandeur, because it is more dim, unstable, unsubstantial." [91]
If an understanding of Shakespeare in Hazlitt's day may
be taken as a measure of a critic's depth of insight, his
attitude toward Shakespeare's fellow-dramatists will just
as surely reveal his powers of discrimination. Lamb was
often carried away by a pioneer's fervor and misled persons
like Lowell, who, returning to Ford late in life, found
"that the greater part of what [he] once took on trust
as precious was really paste and pinchbeck," and that as
far as the celebrated closing scene in "The Broken Heart"
was concerned, Charles Lamb's comment on it was "worth
more than all Ford ever wrote." [92]  Hazlitt's dispassionate
sanity in this instance forms an instructive contrast: "Except the last scene of the Broken Heart (which I think
extravagant—others may think it sublime, and be right)
they [Ford's plays] are merely exercises of style and effusion of wire-drawn sentiment." [93]  The same strength of
judgment rendered Hazlitt proof against the excessive
sentimentality in Beaumont and Fletcher and gave a distinct value to his opinions even when they seemed to be
wrong, which was not often. But in writing of Marlowe,
of Dekker and of Webster, he spreads out all his sail to
make a joyous run among the beauties in his course.

And it is so with the rest of his criticism—throughout
the same susceptibility to all that is true, or lofty, or refined, vigilantly controlled by a firm common sense, the

[91] *Characters of Shakespeare's Plays,* "Antony and Cleopatra."
[92] Lowell: *Old English Dramatists.*
[93] *Lecture on the Age of Elizabeth,* "On Beaumont and Fletcher"
V, 269.

same stamp of originality unmistakably impressed on all. " I like old opinions with new reasons," he once said to Northcote, " not new opinions without any." [94] But he did not hesitate to express a new opinion where the old one appeared to be unjust. His heretical preference of Steele over Addison has found more than one convert in later days. On Spenser or Pope, on Fielding or Richardson, he is equally happy and unimprovable. In the opinion of Mr. Saintsbury, Hazlitt's general lecture on Elizabethan literature, his treatment of the dramatists of the Restoration, of Pope, of the English Novelists, and of Cobbett have never been excelled; and who is better qualified than Mr. Saintsbury by width of reading to express such an opinion? [95]

Of Hazlitt's treatment of his own contemporaries an additional word needs to be said. No charge has been repeated more often than that of the inconsistency, perversity, and utter unreliableness of his judgments on the writers of his day. To distinguish between the claims of living poets, particularly in an age of new ideas and changing forms, is a task which might test the powers of the most discerning critics, and in which perfection is hardly to be attained. Yet one may ask whether in the entire extent of Hazlitt's writing a great living genius has been turned into a mockery or a figurehead been set up for the admiration of posterity. Of his personal and political antipathies enough has been said, but against literary orthodoxy his only great sin is a harsh review of " Christabel." [96] If in general we look at the age through Hazlitt's eyes, we shall see its literature dominated by the figures

---

[94] *Conversation of Northcote,* VI, 393.

[95] *Essays in English Literature,* Second Series, 159-161.

[96] There seems to be no reason for doubting Hazlitt's authorship of the article in the *Examiner.* See Works, XI, 580.

of Wordsworth and Scott, the one regarded as the restorer
of life to poetry, the other as the creator or transcriber
of a whole world of romance and humanity. Coleridge
stands out prominently as the widest intellect of his age.
Byron's poetry bulks very large, though it is not estimated
as superlatively as in the criticism of our own day. It is
a pity that Hazlitt never wrote formally of Keats, for his
casual allusions indicate a deep enjoyment of the "rich
beauties and the dim obscurities" of the "Eve of St.
Agnes"[97] and an appreciation of the perfection of the
great odes.[98] If he failed to give Shelley his full dues, he
did not overlook his exquisite lyrical inspiration. He spoke
of Shelley as a man of genius, but "'all air,' disdaining
the bars and ties of mortal mould;" he praised him for
"single thoughts of great depth and force, single images
of rare beauty, detached passages of extreme tenderness,"
and he rose to enthusiasm in commending his translations,
especially the scenes from Faust.[99] He has been accused
of writing a Spirit of the Age which omitted to give
an account of Shelley and Keats, but in the title of the
book consists his excuse. As it was not his idea to anticipate
the decision of posterity but only to sketch the personalities
who were in control of the public attention, he passed over
the finer poets who were still neglected, and wrote instead
about Campbell and Moore and Crabbe. It is sufficient
praise for the critic that those of whom he has undertaken
to treat stand irreversibly judged in his pages. He is generous toward Campbell and Moore, who were both personally hostile to him; he is scrupulously honest toward
Bentham, with whose system he had no sympathy. The
concluding pages of his sketch of Southey, in view of that

[97] "William Gifford," in *Spirit of the Age.*
[98] *Select British Poets.* See Works, V, 378.
[99] "Shelley's Posthumous Poems," Works, X, 256 ff.

poet's rancor against him, are almost defiant in their magnanimity.  His adverse judgments, moreover, are as permanent as his favorable ones.  He pronounced the verdict
against the naked realism of Crabbe's poetry, which persons like Jeffrey thought superior to Wordsworth's, and
he pricked the bubble of Edward Irving's popularity while
it was at its pitch of highest glory.  If he was often bitter
toward men whom he at other times eulogized, it was
in the heat and hurry of journalistic publication in a period
when blows were freely dealt and freely taken.  If he
sometimes censured even Wordsworth and Scott and grew
impatient with Byron and Coleridge, it must be remembered that these men of genius had imperfections, and that
the imperfections of men of genius are of far greater
concern to their contemporaries than to posterity.  Time
dispels the mists and allows the gross matter to settle to
the bottom.  We now have Wordsworth in the selections
of Matthew Arnold, we read the Waverley Novels with
Lockhart's Life of Scott before us, and we render praise
to Coleridge for what he has accomplished since his death.
With none of these advantages, Hazlitt's performance
seems remarkable enough.  No contemporary with the exception of Leigh Hunt displayed as wide a sympathy with
the writers of that time, and Hazlitt so far surpasses Hunt
in discrimination and strength, that he deserves to be called,
strange as it may sound, the best contemporary judge of
the literature of his age.

It has already been suggested that much of Hazlitt's
appeal as a critic rests on the force of his popular eloquence,
so that a brief consideration of his prose is not in this connection out of place.  "We may all be fine fellows," said
Stevenson, "but none of us can write like Hazlitt."  To
write a style that is easy yet incisive, lively and at the
same time substantial, buoyant without being frothy, glit-

tering but with no tinsel frippery, a style combining the
virtues of homeliness and picturesqueness, has been given
to few mortals. Writing in a generation in which the
standards of prose were conspicuously unsettled, when the
most ambitious writers were seeking an escape from the
frozen patterns of the eighteenth century in a restoration
of the elaborate artifices of the seventeenth, when quaintness
and ornateness were the evidence of a distinguished style,
Hazlitt succeeded in preserving the note of familiarity without fading into colorlessness or in any degree effacing his
individuality. He cannot be counted among the masters
of finished prose, he is as a matter of fact often very negli-
gent,[100] but he developed the best model of an undiluted,
sturdy, popular style that is to be found in the English
language.

Perhaps an adherence to the eighteenth century tradition
of plainness is the most prominent characteristic of Hazlitt's
prose. But his plainness is not precisely of the blunt type
associated with Swift and Arbuthnot. It is modified by the
Gallic tone of easy familiarity, by the ideal deemed appropriate for dignified converse among educated people of the
world. His periods are of the simplest construction and
they are not methodically combined in the artificial patterns
beloved of the eighteenth century followers of the plain
style. Not that he altogether neglects the devices of
parallelism and antithesis when he wishes to give epigrammatic point to his remarks, but he more generally develops
his ideas in a series of easily flowing sentences which are
as near as writing can be to " the tone of lively and sensible

---

[100] Hazlitt's syntax is often abbreviated, elliptical, and unregardful
of book rules. Constructions like the following are not uncommon
in his prose: " As a novelist, his Vicar of Wakefield has charmed
all Europe. . . . As a comic writer, his Tony Lumpkin draws forth
new powers from Mr. Liston's face." *Lectures on the English
Poets*, " On Swift, Young," etc., V, 119, 120.

conversation." It is impossible to match in the English essay such talk as Hazlitt reproduces in his accounts of the evenings at Lamb's room or of his meeting with Coleridge, in which high themes and spirited eloquence find spontaneous and unaffected expression through the same medium as might be employed in a deliberate definition of the nature of poetry. The various sets of lectures are pitched in the same conversational key and are found adequate to conveying a notion of the grandeur of Milton as well as of the familiarity of Lamb.

Those who have praised Hazlitt's simplicity have often given the impression that his prose is a single-stringed instrument, and have failed to suggest the range comprised between the simple hammer-strokes of the essay on Cobbett and the magnificent diapason in which he unrolls the panorama of Coleridge's mind. In both passages there is the same sentence-norm. In the first, the periods, not bound by any connecting words, strike distinctly, sharply, with staccato abruptness. The movement is that of a clean-limbed wrestler struggling with confident energy to pin down a difficult opponent:

" His principle is repulsion, his nature contradiction: he is made up of mere antipathies; an Ishmaelite indeed, without a fellow. He is always playing at *hunt-the-slipper* in politics. He turns round upon whoever is next to him. The way to wean him from any opinion, and make him conceive an intolerable hatred against it, would be to place somebody near him who was perpetually dinning it in his ears. When he is in England, he does nothing but abuse the Boroughmongers, and laugh at the whole system: when he is in America, he grows impatient of freedom and a republic. If he had staid there a little longer, he would have become a loyal and a loving subject of his Majesty King George IV. He lampooned the French Revolution when it was hailed as the dawn of liberty by millions: by the time it was brought into almost universal ill-odour by some means or other (partly no doubt by himself) he had turned, with one or two or three others, staunch Bonapartist. He is always of the militant, not of the triumphant party: so far he bears a gallant show of magnanimity; but his gallantry is hardly of the right stamp: it wants principle. For though he is not servile or mercenary, he is the victim of self-will. He must pull down and pull in pieces: it is not in his disposition to do otherwise. It is a pity; for with his great talents he might do great things, if he would go right forward to any useful object, make thorough-stitch work of any question, or join hand and heart with any principle. He changes his opinions as he does his friends, and much on the same account. He has no comfort in fixed principles: as soon as anything is settled in his own mind, he quarrels with it. He has no satisfaction but in the chase after truth, runs a question down, worries and kills it, then quits it like vermin, and starts some new game, to lead him a new dance, and give him a fresh breathing through bog and brake, with the rabble yelping at his heels and the leaders perpetually at fault." [101]

In the other passage the clauses and phrases follow in their natural order, but they are united by the simplest kind of connective device in an undistinguishable stream over which the reader is driven with a steady swell and fall, sometimes made breathlessly rapid by the succession of its uniformly measured word-groups, but delicately modulated here and there to provide restful pauses in the long onward career:

"Next, he was engaged with Hartley's tribes of mind, 'etherial braid, thought-woven,'—and he busied himself for a year or two with vibrations and vibratiuncles and the

---

[101] *Spirit of the Age*, "William Cobbett."

great law of association that binds all things in its mystic
chain, and the doctrine of Necessity (the mild teacher of
Charity) and the Millennium, anticipative of a life to come
—and he plunged deep into the controversy on Matter and
Spirit, and, as an escape from Dr. Priestley's Materialism,
where he felt himself imprisoned by the logician's spell, like
Ariel in the cloven pine-tree, he became suddenly enamoured of Bishop Berkeley's fairy-world, and used in all
companies to build the universe, like a brave poetical fiction,
of fine words—and he was deep-read in Malebranche, and
in Cudworth's Intellectual System (a huge pile of learning,
unwieldly, enormous) and in Lord Brook's hieroglyphic theories, and in Bishop Butler's Sermons, and in the Duchess
of Newcastle's fantastic folios, and in Clarke and South
and Tillotson, and all the fine thinkers and masculine reasoners of that age—and Leibnitz's *Pre-established Harmony* reared its arch above his head, like the rainbow in
the cloud, covenanting with the hopes of man—and then he
fell plump, ten thousand fathoms down (but his wings saved
him harmless) into the *hortus siccus* of Dissent " etc.[102]

The same style which glistens and sparkles in describing
the fancy of Pope rises to an inspired chant with a clearly
defined cadence at the recollection of the past glory of
Coleridge :

" He was the first poet I ever knew. His genius at that
time had angelic wings, and fed on manna. He talked
on for ever; and you wished him to talk on for ever. His
thoughts did not seem to come with labour and effort; but
as if borne on the gusts of genius, and as if the wings of
his imagination lifted him from off his feet. His voice
rolled on the ear like the pealing organ, and its sound
alone was the music of thought. His mind was clothed
with wings; and raised on them, he lifted philosophy to

[102] See pp. 210-213.

heaven. In his descriptions, you then saw the progress of human happiness and liberty in bright and never-ending succession, like the steps of Jacob's ladder, with airy shapes ascending and descending, and with the voice of God at the top of the ladder. And shall I, who heard him then, listen to him now? Not I! That spell is broke; that time is gone for ever; that voice is heard no more: but still the recollection comes rushing by with thoughts of long-past years, and rings in my ears with never-dying sound." [103]

It would take much space to illustrate all the notes to which Hazlitt's voice responds—the pithy epigram of the Characteristics, the Chesterfieldian grace in his advice "On the Conduct of Life," the palpitating movement with which he gives expression to his keen enjoyment of his sensual or intellectual existence, and the subdued solemnity of his reveries which sometimes remind us that he was writing in an age which had rediscovered Sir Thomas Browne. The following sentence proves how accurately he could catch the rhythm of the seventeenth century. " That we should wear out by slow stages, and dwindle at last into nothing, is not wonderful, when even in our prime our strongest impressions leave little trace but for the moment, and we are the creatures of petty circumstance." [104] Other passages in the same essay echo this manner only less strikingly:

[103] "On the Living Poets," in *Lectures on the English Poets*, V, 167.

[104] This is the form of the passage as published in the *Literary Remains* (1836). That Hazlitt did not attain effects like this offhand, is evident from the comparative feebleness of the original sound of the passage in the *Monthly Magazine:* "That we should thus in a manner outlive ourselves, and dwindle imperceptibly into nothing, is not surprising, when even in our prime the strongest impressions leave so little traces of themselves behind, and the last object is driven out by the succeeding one." " On the Feeling of Immortality in Youth," Works, XII, 160.

"Life is indeed a strange gift, and its privileges are most mysterious. No wonder when it is first granted to us, that our gratitude, our admiration, and our delight, should prevent us from reflecting on our own nothingness, or from thinking it will ever be recalled. Our first and strongest impressions are borrowed from the mighty scene that is opened to us, and we unconsciously transfer its durability as well as its splendour to ourselves. So newly found we cannot think of parting with it yet, or at least put off that consideration *sine die*. Like a rustic at a fair, we are full of amazement and rapture, and have no thought of going home, or that it will soon be night. We know our existence only by ourselves, and confound our knowledge with the objects of it. We and nature are therefore one. Otherwise the illusion, the 'feast of reason and the flow of soul,' to which we are invited, is a mockery and a cruel insult. We do not go from a play till the last act is ended, and the lights are about to be extinguished. But the fairy face of nature still shines on: shall we be called away before the curtain falls, or ere we have scarce had a glimpse of what is going on? Like children, our stepmother nature holds us up to see the raree-show of the universe, and then, as if we were a burden to her to support, lets us fall down agan. Yet what brave sublunary things does not this pageant present, like a ball or *fête* of the universe!" [105]

In Hazlitt's vocabulary there is nothing striking unless it be the scrupulousness with which he avoids the danger of commonplaceness and of pedantry. It is easy to forget that the transparent obviousness of his style was attained only after many years of groping. We may well believe

---

[105] This passage also shows alterations from the first form. Cf. XII, 152.

that "there is a research in the choice of a plain, as well as of an ornamental or learned style; and, in fact, a great deal more." [106] Though he did not go in pursuit of the word to the extent of some later refiners of style, he had a clear realization that the appropriate word was what chiefly gave vitality to writing.[107] For this reason he constantly denounced Johnsonese with its polysyllabic Latin words which reduced language to abstract generalization. His own vocabulary is concrete and vivid, and of a purity which makes one wonder how even the Quarterly Review could have ventured to apply to him the epithet "slangwhanger."

In spite of all that may be said in honor of the unadorned style of composition, writers have ever found that even in prose ideas are most forcibly conveyed by means of imagery. Hazlitt, it should be remembered, was an ardent admirer of the picturesque qualities in the prose of Burke, the most brilliant of the eighteenth century. In recalling his first reading of Burke, he tells how he despaired of emulating his felicities. But whether by dint of meditating over Burke or by the native vigor of his fancy, Hazlitt learned to write as boldly and as brilliantly as the great orator. As a rule his rhetorical passages are not deliberately contrived, in the manner for example of

---

[106] *Lectures on the English Poets.* "On Swift, Young, etc.," V, 104. See also the paper in *Table Talk* on "Familiar Style."

[107] "I grant thus much, that it is in vain to seek for the word we want, or endeavour to get at it second-hand, or as a paraphrase on some other word—it must come of itself, or arise out of an immediate impression or lively intuition of the subject; that is, the proper word must be suggested immediately by the thoughts, but it need not be presented as soon as called for. . . . Proper expressions rise to the surface from the heat and fermentation of the mind, like bubbles on an agitated stream. It is this which produces a clear and sparkling style." "On Application to Study," in *Plain Speaker.*

his esteemed contemporary De Quincey. His tropes and images rise directly out of his subject or his feelings. Instead of dissecting the qualities of a character or a work of art, he translates its tone and its spirit as closely as language will permit. That is why his criticism, like Lamb's or that of the master of this form, Longinus, is itself first-rate literature, recreating the impression of a masterpiece and sometimes even going beyond it.

Of his picturesque quality examples enough may be found in the present volume, yet one cannot forbear to add a few illustrations at this point. There is his irresistible comparison of Cobbett in his political inconsistency to "a young and lusty bridegroom, that divorces a favorite speculation every morning, and marries a new one every night. He is not wedded to his notions, not he. He has not one Mrs. Cobbett among all his opinions." [108] There is a good deal more than mere wit in the analogy between Godwin's mechanical laboriousness and "an eight-day clock that must be wound up long before it can strike." [109] And there is real grandeur in his description of Fame: "Fame is the sound which the stream of high thoughts, carried down to future ages, makes as it flows—deep, distant, murmuring evermore like the waters of the mighty ocean. He who has ears truly touched to this music, is in a manner deaf to the voice of popularity." [110] In representing the brilliant hues of Restoration comedy, he allows an even freer play to his fancy:

"In turning over the pages of the best comedies, we are almost transported to another world, and escape from this dull age to one that was all life, and whim, and mirth, and humour. The curtain rises, and a gayer scene presents

---

[108] *Spirit of the Age*, "Mr. Cobbett."
[109] Ibid., "William Godwin."
[110] "On the Living Poets," *Lectures on English Poets*, V, 144.

itself, as on the canvas of Watteau. We are admitted
behind the scenes like spectators at court, on a levee or
birthday; but it is the court, the gala-day of wit and
pleasure, of gallantry and Charles II.! What an air
breathes from the name! what a rustling of silks and wav-
ing of plumes! what a sparkling of diamond ear-rings and
shoe-buckles! What bright eyes, (Ah, those were Waller's
Sacharissa's as she passed!) what killing looks and graceful motions! How the faces of the whole ring are dressed
in smiles! how the repartee goes round! how wit and folly,
elegance and awkward imitation of it, set one another off!
Happy, thoughtless age, when kings and nobles led purely
ornamental lives; when the utmost stretch of a morning's
study went no farther than the choice of a sword-knot, or
the adjustment of a side-curl; when the soul spoke out in
all the pleasing eloquence of dress; and beaux and belles,
enamoured of themselves in one another's follies, fluttered
like gilded butterflies, in giddy mazes, through the walks of
St. James's Park!" [111]

Sometimes, it is true, he allows his spirits to run away
with his judgment, although in such instances the manner is
so obviously exaggerated as to suggest deliberate mimicry.
His account of the tawdry sentimentality of Moore's poetry
sounds like pure travesty:

" His verse is like a shower of beauty; a dance of images;
a stream of music; or like the spray of the water-fall,
tinged by the morning-beam with rosy light. The characteristic distinction of our author's style is this continuous
and incessant flow of voluptuous thoughts and shining allusions. He ought to write with a crystal pen on silver
paper. His subject is set off by a dazzling veil of poetic
diction, like a wreath of flowers gemmed with innumerous

[111] *Lectures on the Comic Writers,* " On Wycherley, Congreve,
etc.," VIII, 70.

dew-drops, that weep, tremble, and glitter in liquid softness
and pearly light, while the song of birds ravishes the ear,
and languid odours breathe around, and Aurora opens
Heaven's smiling portals, Peris and nymphs peep through
the golden glades, and an Angel's wing glances over the
glossy scene." [112]

One feature of Hazlitt's style concerning which much
has been said both in praise and in blame is his inveterate
use of quotations. His pages, particularly when he is in
a contemplative mood, are sown with snatches from the
great poets, and the effect generally is of the happiest. A
line of Shakespeare's or of Wordsworth's, blending with
a vein of high feeling or deep reflection, transfigures the
entire passage as if by magic. Sometimes the phrase is
merely woven into the general texture of the prose without
in any way raising its tone, and on occasion some fine poetic
expression is vulgarized by being thrown into very common
company. It is vandalism to muster a sonnet of Shakespeare's into such a service and it in no way enhances the
expressiveness of the passage to say, " A flashy pamphlet
has been run to a five-and-thirtieth edition, and thus ensured
the writer a ' deathless date ' among political charlatans." [113]
The fact is that quotations were a part of Hazlitt's vocabulary, which he used with the same freedom as common
locutions and with less scrupulous regard for the associations which were gathered about them. He negligently
misquoted or wantonly adapted to his purpose, but the
reader is willing to pardon the moments of irritation for
the numerous delightful thrills which he has provoked by
some happy poetic memory " stealing and giving odor "
to a sentiment in itself dignified or elevated.

Hazlitt's influence as a critic may be inferred from a

[112] *Spirit of the Age,* " Mr. T. Moore," IV, 353.
[113] *Table Talk,* " On Patronage and Puffing."

summary of his opinions. It was not so much through the
infusion of a new spirit in literature that he acted on
other minds. Though his criticism owes much of its value
to the freshness and boldness of his approach, this temperamental virtue was not something which could be imitated
by a less gifted writer. Sainte-Beuve indeed seems to
recognize Hazlitt as the exponent of the impetuous and
inspired vein in criticism—"the kind of inspiration which
accompanies and follows those frequent articles dashingly
improvised and launched under full steam. One puts himself completely into it: its value is exaggerated for the
time being, its importance is measured by its fury, and if
this leads to better results, there is no great harm after
all." [114] But though he professed these to be his own
feelings as a critic, they were in him so modified by the
traditional French moderation and suavity of tone, as well
as by a greater precision of method, as to make the resemblance to Hazlitt inconspicuous. It is hard to determine
to what extent Hazlitt's individualism is responsible for the
lawless impressionism of some later critics,[115] but it is not
to be imputed to him as a sin if, in the course of a century,
one of his virtues has become exaggerated into a fault.
He has but suffered human destiny.

[114] "L'espèce d'entrain qui accompagne et suit ces fréquents
articles improvisés de verve et lancés à toute vapeur. On s'y met
tout entier: on s'en exagère la valeur dans le moment même, on en
mesure l'importance au bruit, et si cela mène à mieux faire, il n'y
a pas grand mal après tout." *Portraits Contemporains,* II, 515.
[115] "'Range and keenness of appreciation' do not by themselves
give taste, but merely romantic gusto or perceptiveness. In order
that gusto may be elevated to taste it needs to be disciplined and
selective. To this end it must come under the control of an
entirely different order of intuitions, of what I have called the
'back pull toward the centre.' The romantic one-sidedness that is
already so manifest in Hazlitt's conception of taste has, I maintain,
gone to seed in Professor Saintsbury." Irving Babbitt, in *Nation,*
May 16, 1912.

Hazlitt's influence has been wide in guiding the taste
of readers and in creating or giving currency to a body
of opinions on literature which has found acceptance
among critics. If the tributes of Schlegel and Heine to
Hazlitt's Shakespearian criticism were insufficient, we have
the word of his own countrymen for it that numberless
readers were initiated into a proper understanding of
Shakespeare by means of his writings.[116] In our own days
Mr. Howells has told us that Hazlitt " helped him to clarify
and formulate his opinions of Shakespeare as no one else
has yet done." [117] Critics no less than readers owe him
a large debt. Hazlitt had not been writing many years
before his fellow-laborers in literature began to recognize
and pay homage to his superior insight. His opinions were
quoted as having the weight of authority by those who
were friendly to him, the writers in the London Magazine
or in the Edinburgh Review; they were appropriated without acknowledgement by the hostile contributors to Blackwood's. Many writers deferred to him as respectfully as
he himself deferred to Coleridge and Lamb, even though
Byron's respectable friends adjured the noble poet not to
dignify Hazlitt in open controversy except by mentioning
him as " a certain lecturer." Leigh Hunt was frequently
indebted to him, but generally paid the tribute due.
Macaulay sometimes assimilated a passage of Hazlitt's to
the needs of his own earlier essays. In the essay on Milton
his balancing of Charles's political vices against his domestic
virtues is strikingly reminiscent of a similar treatment of
Southey by the older critic. Personal dislike of Hazlitt,
persisting after his death, for a long time prevented a
proper respect being paid to his memory without much
diminishing the weight of his influence. The attitude to-

---

[116] T. N. Talfourd: *Edinburgh Review*, Nov., 1820.
[117] *My Literary Passions*, 120.

ward him is summed up by a writer whose treatment in
general does not err on the side of enthusiasm.  Hazlitt,
he tells us, is " a writer with whose reputation fashion has
hitherto had very little to do—who is even now more read
than praised, more imitated than extolled, and whose various
productions still interest many who care and know very
little about the author." [118]  But this very utterance was on
the occasion of the turning of the tide.  It was in a review
of Hazlitt's Literary Remains which had been introduced
by appreciative essays from the pens of Bulwer-Lytton
and Thomas Noon Talfourd, the former not a little patron-
izing, but Talfourd's excellent in its discrimination of the
strength and weakness of Hazlitt.  A few years later came
the implied compliment of Horne's New Spirit of the
Age, which would hardly be worth mentioning were it
not that Thackeray in reviewing it took occasion to pay
an exquisite tribute to Hazlitt.[119]  From this time forth
he was not wanting in stout champions, though most people
still maintained a cautious reserve in their judgments of
him.  So sound and penetrating a critic as Walter Bagehot
became an earnest convert, and in Bagehot's writings Mr.
Birrell has pointed out more than one resemblance to Hazlitt.  James Russell Lowell has not been profuse in his
expressions of admiration, but he has probably followed
Hazlitt's track more closely than any other important critic.
Many of his essays seem to have been composed with a
volume of Hazlitt on the desk before him.  There is the
essay on Pope with its general correspondence of points
and occasional startling parallel of phrase.  Hazlitt at the
end of his lecture on Pope and Dryden remarks that poetry
had " declined by successive gradations from the poetry
of imagination in the age of Elizabeth to the poetry of

[118] *Edinburgh Review,* January, 1837.
[119] Thackeray's Works, ed. Trent and Henneman, XXV, 350-51.

fancy in the time of Charles I," and Lowell repeats this with some amplification. In the same connection he characterizes Shakespeare, Chaucer, Spenser, and Milton in the sharp epigrammatic manner reminding one of Hazlitt. In the concluding pages of the essay on Spenser we are also kept in a reminiscent mood, till Lowell tells us that "to read him is like dreaming awake," and at once there flashes upon us Hazlitt's expression that "Spenser is the poet of our waking dreams." It is through missionary work like this, not altogether conscious and therefore all the more genuine, that his opinions have been diffused through the length and breadth of English and been incorporated into the common stock. "Gracious rills from the Hazlitt watershed have flowed in all directions, fertilizing a dry and thirsty land"—is the happily turned phrase of Mr. Birrell. If in our own day there are still persons who, looking upon criticism as a severe science, occasionally sneer at him as a "facile eulogist," [120] those who regard it rather as a gift have seen in him "the greatest critic that England has yet produced." [121] Wherever the golden mean between these two extremes of opinion may lie, there is no doubt that for introducing readers to an appreciation of the great things in English literature, Hazlitt still remains without an equal.

[120] Robertson: *Essays Toward a Critical Method,* 81.
[121] Saintsbury's *History of Criticism* and John Davidson's *Sentences and Paragraphs,* 113.

# I

## THE AGE OF ELIZABETH

The age of Elizabeth was distinguished, beyond, perhaps, any other in our history, by a number of great men, famous in different ways, and whose names have come down to us with unblemished honours; statesmen, warriors, divines, scholars, poets, and philosophers, Raleigh, Drake, Coke, Hooker, and higher and more sounding still, and still more frequent in our mouths, Shakspeare, Spenser, Sidney, Bacon, Jonson, Beaumont and Fletcher, men whom fame has eternised in her long and lasting scroll, and who, by their words and acts, were benefactors of their country, and ornaments of human nature. Their attainments of different kinds bore the same general stamp, and it was sterling: what they did, had the mark of their age and country upon it. Perhaps the genius of Great Britain (if I may so speak without offence or flattery), never shone out fuller or brighter, or looked more like itself, than at this period. Our writers and great men had something in them that savoured of the soil from which they grew: they were not French, they were not Dutch, or German, or Greek, or Latin; they were truly English. They did not look out of themselves to see what they should be; they sought for truth and nature, and found it in themselves. There was no tinsel, and but little art; they were not the spoiled children of affectation and refinement, but a bold, vigorous, independent race of thinkers, with prodigious strength and energy, with none but natural grace, and heartfelt unob-

trusive delicacy. They were not at all sophisticated. The
mind of their country was great in them, and it prevailed.
With their learning and unexampled acquirement, they did
not forget that they were men: with all their endeavours
after excellence, they did not lay aside the strong original
bent and character of their minds. What they performed
was chiefly nature's handy-work; and time has claimed it
for his own.—To these, however, might be added others
not less learned, nor with a scarce less happy vein, but less
fortunate in the event, who, though as renowned in their
day, have sunk into "mere oblivion," and of whom the
only record (but that the noblest) is to be found in their
works. Their works and their names, "poor, poor dumb
names," are all that remains of such men as Webster,
Deckar, Marston, Marlow, Chapman, Heywood, Middleton,
and Rowley! "How lov'd, how honour'd once, avails them
not:" though they were the friends and fellow-labourers
of Shakspeare, sharing his fame and fortunes with him, the
rivals of Jonson, and the masters of Beaumont and
Fletcher's well-sung woes! They went out one by one
unnoticed, like evening lights; or were swallowed up in the
headlong torrent of puritanic zeal which succeeded, and
swept away everything in its unsparing course, throwing
up the wrecks of taste and genius at random, and at long
fitful intervals, amidst the painted gew-gaws and foreign
frippery of the reign of Charles II. and from which we
are only now recovering the scattered fragments and broken
images to erect a temple to true Fame! How long, before
it will be completed?

If I can do anything to rescue some of these writers
from hopeless obscurity, and to do them right, without
prejudice to well-deserved reputation, I shall have succeeded
in what I chiefly propose. I shall not attempt, indeed,
to adjust the spelling, or restore the pointing, as if the

genius of poetry lay hid in errors of the press, but leaving these weightier matters of criticism to those who are more able and willing to bear the burden, try to bring out their real beauties to the eager sight, " draw the curtain of Time, and shew the picture of Genius," restraining my own admiration within reasonable bounds! . . .

We affect to wonder at Shakspeare, and one or two more of that period, as solitary instances upon record; whereas it is our own dearth of information that makes the waste; for there is no time more populous of intellect, or more prolific of intellectual wealth, than the one we are speaking of. Shakspeare did not look upon himself in this light, as a sort of monster of poetical genius, or on his contemporaries as " less than smallest dwarfs," when he speaks with true, not false modesty, of himself and them, and of his wayward thoughts, " desiring this man's art, and that man's scope." We fancy that there were no such men, that could either add to or take anything away from him, but such there were. He indeed overlooks and commands the admiration of posterity, but he does it from the *tableland* of the age in which he lived. He towered above his fellows, " in shape and gesture proudly eminent; " but he was one of a race of giants, the tallest, the strongest, the most graceful, and beautiful of them; but it was a common and a noble brood. He was not something sacred and aloof from the vulgar herd of men, but shook hands with nature and the circumstances of the time, and is distinguished from his immediate contemporaries, not in kind, but in degree and greater variety of excellence. He did not form a class or species by himself, but belonged to a class or species. His age was necessary to him; nor could he have been wrenched from his place in the edifice of which he was so conspicuous a part, without equal injury to himself and it. Mr. Wordsworth says of Milton, that " his soul

was like a star, and dwelt apart." This cannot be said
with any propriety of Shakspeare, who certainly moved in
a constellation of bright luminaries, and " drew after him
a third part of the heavens." If we allow, for argument's
sake (or for truth's, which is better), that he was in himself
equal to all his competitors put together; yet there was
more dramatic excellence in that age than in the whole
of the period that has elapsed since. If his contemporaries,
with their united strength, would hardly make one Shakspeare, certain it is that all his successors would not make
half a one. With the exception of a single writer, Otway,
and of a single play of his (Venice Preserved), there is
nobody in tragedy and dramatic poetry (I do not here
speak of comedy) to be compared to the great men of the
age of Shakspeare, and immediately after. They are a
mighty phalanx of kindred spirits closing him round, moving in the same orbit, and impelled by the same causes in
their whirling and eccentric career. They had the same
faults and the same excellences; the same strength and
depth and richness, the same truth of character, passion,
imagination, thought and language, thrown, heaped, massed
together without careful polishing or exact method, but
poured out in unconcerned profusion from the lap of nature
and genius in boundless and unrivalled magnificence. The
sweetness of Deckar, the thought of Marston, the gravity
of Chapman, the grace of Fletcher and his young-eyed wit,
Jonson's learned sock, the flowing vein of Middleton, Heywood's ease, the pathos of Webster, and Marlow's deep
designs, add a double lustre to the sweetness, thought,
gravity, grace, wit, artless nature, copiousness, ease, pathos,
and sublime conceptions of Shakspeare's Muse. They are
indeed the scale by which we can best ascend to the true
knowledge and love of him. Our admiration of them does
not lessen our relish for him: but, on the contrary, increases

and confirms it.—For such an extraordinary combination and development of fancy and genius many causes may be assigned; and we may seek for the chief of them in religion, in politics, in the circumstances of the time, the recent diffusion of letters, in local situation, and in the character of the men who adorned that period, and availed themselves so nobly of the advantages placed within their reach.

I shall here attempt to give a general sketch of these causes, and of the manner in which they operated to mould and stamp the poetry of the country at the period of which I have to treat; independently of incidental and fortuitous causes, for which there is no accounting, but which, after all, have often the greatest share in determining the most important results.

The first cause I shall mention, as contributing to this general effect, was the Reformation, which had just then taken place. This event gave a mighty impulse and increased activity to thought and inquiry, and agitated the inert mass of accumulated prejudices throughout Europe. The effect of the concussion was general; but the shock was greatest in this country. It toppled down the full-grown, intolerable abuses of centuries at a blow; heaved the ground from under the feet of bigotted faith and slavish obedience; and the roar and dashing of opinions, loosened from their accustomed hold, might be heard like the noise of an angry sea, and has never yet subsided. Germany first broke the spell of misbegotten fear, and gave the watch-word; but England joined the shout, and echoed it back with her island voice, from her thousand cliffs and craggy shores, in a longer and a louder strain. With that cry, the genius of Great Britain rose, and threw down the gauntlet to the nations. There was a mighty fermentation: the waters were out; public opinion was in a state of projection. Lib-

erty was held out to all to think and speak the truth. Men's
brains were busy; their spirits stirring; their hearts full;
and their hands not idle. Their eyes were opened to expect
the greatest things, and their ears burned with curiosity
and zeal to know the truth, that the truth might make them
free. The death-blow which had been struck at scarlet
vice and bloated hypocrisy, loosened their tongues, and
made the talismans and love-tokens of Popish superstition,
with which she had beguiled her followers and committed
abominations with the people, fall harmless from their
necks.

The translation of the Bible was the chief engine in the
great work. It threw open, by a secret spring, the rich
treasures of religion and morality, which had been there
locked up as in a shrine. It revealed the visions of the
prophets, and conveyed the lessons of inspired teachers
(such they were thought) to the meanest of the people.
It gave them a common interest in the common cause.
Their hearts burnt within them as they read. It gave a
*mind* to the people, by giving them common subjects of
thought and feeling. It cemented their union of character
and sentiment: it created endless diversity and collision
of opinion. They found objects to employ their faculties,
and a motive in the magnitude of the consequences attached
to them, to exert the utmost eagerness in the pursuit of
truth, and the most daring intrepidity in maintaining it.
Religious controversy sharpens the understanding by the
subtlety and remoteness of the topics it discusses, and braces
the will by their infinite importance. We perceive in the
history of this period a nervous masculine intellect. No
levity, no feebleness, no indifference; or if there were, it
is a relaxation from the intense activity which gives a tone
to its general character. But there is a gravity approaching to piety; a seriousness of impression, a conscientious

severity of argument, an habitual fervour and enthusiasm in their mode of handling almost every subject. The debates of the schoolmen were sharp and subtle enough; but they wanted interest and grandeur, and were besides confined to a few: they did not affect the general mass of the community. But the Bible was thrown open to all ranks and conditions "to run and read," with its wonderful table of contents from Genesis to the Revelations. Every village in England would present the scene so well described in Burns's Cotter's Saturday Night. I cannot think that all this variety and weight of knowledge could be thrown in all at once upon the mind of a people, and not make some impression upon it, the traces of which might be discerned in the manners and literature of the age. For to leave more disputable points, and take only the historical parts of the Old Testament, or the moral sentiments of the New, there is nothing like them in the power of exciting awe and admiration, or of rivetting sympathy. We see what Milton has made of the account of the Creation, from the manner in which he has treated it, imbued and impregnated with the spirit of the time of which we speak. Or what is there equal (in that romantic interest and patriarchal simplicity which goes to the heart of a country, and rouses it, as it were, from its lair in wastes and wildernesses) equal to the story of Joseph and his Brethren, of Rachael and Laban, of Jacob's Dream, of Ruth and Boaz, the descriptions in the Book of Job, the deliverance of the Jews out of Egypt, or the account of their captivity and return from Babylon? There is in all these parts of the Scripture, and numberless more of the same kind, to pass over the Orphic hymns of David, the prophetic denunciations of Isaiah, or the gorgeous visions of Ezekiel, an originality, a vastness of conception, a depth and tenderness of feeling, and a touching simplicity in the mode of narration, which he who does

not feel, need be made of no " penetrable stuff." There
is something in the character of Christ too (leaving religious
faith quite out of the question) of more sweetness and
majesty, and more likely to work a change in the mind of
man, by the contemplation of its idea alone, than any to
be found in history, whether actual or feigned. This character is that of a sublime humanity, such as was never
seen on earth before, nor since. This shone manifestly
both in his words and actions. We see it in his washing
the Disciples' feet the night before his death, that unspeakable instance of humility and love, above all art, all meanness, and all pride, and in the leave he took of them on
that occasion, " My peace I give unto you, that peace
which the world cannot give, give I unto you;" and in
his last commandment, that " they should love one another."
Who can read the account of his behaviour on the cross,
when turning to his mother he said, " Woman, behold thy
son," and to the Disciple John, " Behold thy mother," and
" from that hour that Disciple took her to his own home,"
without having his heart smote within him! We see it in
his treatment of the woman taken in adultery, and in his
excuse for the woman who poured precious ointment on
his garment as an offering of devotion and love, which is
here all in all. His religion was the religion of the heart.
We see it in his discourse with the Disciples as they walked
together towards Emmaus, when their hearts burned within
them; in his sermon from the Mount, in his parable of
the good Samaritan, and in that of the Prodigal Son—in
every act and word of his life, a grace, a mildness, a dignity
and love, a patience and wisdom worthy of the Son of
God. His whole life and being were imbued, steeped in
this word, *charity;* it was the spring, the well-head from
which every thought and feeling gushed into act; and it
was this that breathed a mild glory from his face in that

last agony upon the cross, "when the meek Saviour bowed his head and died," praying for his enemies. He was the first true teacher of morality; for he alone conceived the idea of a pure humanity. He redeemed man from the worship of that idol, self, and instructed him by precept and example to love his neighbour as himself, to forgive our enemies, to do good to those that curse us and despitefully use us. He taught the love of good for the sake of good, without regard to personal or sinister views, and made the affections of the heart the sole seat of morality, instead of the pride of the understanding or the sternness of the will. In answering the question, "who is our neighbour?" as one who stands in need of our assistance, and whose wounds we can bind up, he has done more to humanize the thoughts and tame the unruly passions, than all who have tried to reform and benefit mankind. The very idea of abstract benevolence, of the desire to do good because another wants our services, and of regarding the human race as one family, the offspring of one common parent, is hardly to be found in any other code or system. It was "to the Jews a stumbling block, and to the Greeks foolishness." The Greeks and Romans never thought of considering others, but as they were Greeks or Romans, as they were bound to them by certain positive ties, or, on the other hand, as separated from them by fiercer antipathies. Their virtues were the virtues of political machines, their vices were the vices of demons, ready to inflict or to endure pain with obdurate and remorseless inflexibility of purpose. But in the Christian religion, "we perceive a softness coming over the heart of a nation, and the iron scales that fence and harden it, melt and drop off." It becomes malleable, capable of pity, of forgiveness, of relaxing in its claims, and remitting its power. We strike it, and it does not hurt us: it is not steel or marble, but flesh and blood, clay tempered with tears, and " soft as sinews of the new-born babe." The gospel was first preached to the poor, for it consulted their wants and interests, not its own pride and arrogance. It first promulgated the equality of mankind in the community of duties and benefits. It denounced the iniquities of the chief Priests and Pharisees, and declared itself at variance with principalities and powers, for it sympathizes not with the oppressor, but the oppressed. It first abolished slavery, for it did not consider the power of the will to inflict injury, as clothing it with a right to do so. Its law is good, not power. It at the same time tended to wean the mind from the grossness of sense, and a particle of its divine flame was lent to brighten and purify the lamp of love!

There have been persons who, being sceptics as to the divine mission of Christ, have taken an unaccountable prejudice to his doctrines, and have been disposed to deny the merit of his character; but this was not the feeling of the great men in the age of Elizabeth (whatever might be their belief) one of whom says of him, with a boldness equal to its piety:

> " The best of men
> That e'er wore earth about him was a sufferer;
> A soft, meek, patient, humble, tranquil spirit;
> The first true gentleman that ever breathed."

This was old honest Deckar, and the lines ought to embalm his memory to every one who has a sense either of religion, or philosophy, or humanity, or true genius. Nor can I help thinking, that we may discern the traces of the influence exerted by religious faith in the spirit of the poetry of the age of Elizabeth, in the means of exciting terror and pity, in the delineation of the passions of grief, remorse, love, sympathy, the sense of shame, in the fond desires, the longings after immortality, in the heaven of hope, and the abyss of despair it lays open to us.*

The literature of this age then, I would say, was strongly influenced (among other causes), first by the spirit of Christianity, and secondly by the spirit of Protestantism.

The effects of the Reformation on politics and philosophy may be seen in the writings and history of the next and of the following ages. They are still at work, and will continue to be so. The effects on the poetry of the time were chiefly confined to the moulding of the character, and giving a powerful impulse to the intellect of the country. The immediate use or application that was made of religion to subjects of imagination and fiction was not (from an obvious ground of separation) so direct or frequent, as that which was made of the classical and romantic literature.

For much about the same time, the rich and fascinating stores of the Greek and Roman mythology, and those of the romantic poetry of Spain and Italy, were eagerly explored by the curious, and thrown open in translations to the admiring gaze of the vulgar. This last circumstance could hardly have afforded so much advantage to the poets of that day, who were themselves, in fact, the translators, as it shews the general curiosity and increasing interest in such subjects, as a prevailing feature of the times. There were translations of Tasso by Fairfax, and of Ariosto by Harrington, of Homer and Hesiod by Chapman, and of Virgil long before, and Ovid soon after; there was Sir Thomas North's translation of Plutarch, of which Shakspeare has made such admirable use in his Coriolanus and Julius Cæsar; and Ben Jonson's tragedies of Catiline and Sejanus may themselves be considered as almost literal

---

* In some Roman Catholic countries, pictures in part supplied the place of the translations of the Bible: and this dumb art arose in the silence of the written oracles.

translations into verse, of Tacitus, Sallust, and Cicero's Orations in his consulship. Boccacio, the divine Boccacio, Petrarch, Dante, the satirist Aretine, Machiavel, Castiglione, and others, were familiar to our writers, and they make occasional mention of some few French authors, as Ronsard and Du Bartas; for the French literature had not at this stage arrived at its Augustan period, and it was the imitation of their literature a century afterwards, when it had arrived at its greatest height (itself copied from the Greek and Latin), that enfeebled and impoverished our own. But of the time that we are considering, it might be said, without much extravagance, that every breath that blew, that every wave that rolled to our shores, brought with it some accession to our knowledge, which was engrafted on the national genius. In fact, all the disposeable materials that had been accumulating for a long period of time, either in our own, or in foreign countries, were now brought together, and required nothing more than to be wrought up, polished, or arranged in striking forms, for ornament and use. To this every inducement prompted, the novelty of the acquisition of knowledge in many cases, the emulation of foreign wits, and of immortal works, the want and the expectation of such works among ourselves, the opportunity and encouragement afforded for their production by leisure and affluence; and, above all, the insatiable desire of the mind to beget its own image, and to construct out of itself, and for the delight and admiration of the world and posterity, that excellence of which the idea exists hitherto only in its own breast, and the impression of which it would make as universal as the eye of heaven, the benefit as common as the air we breathe. The first impulse of genius is to create what never existed before: the contemplation of that, which is so created, is sufficient to satisfy the demands of taste; and it is the habitual study and imita-

tion of the original models that takes away the power, and
even wish to do the like. Taste limps after genius, and
from copying the artificial models, we lose sight of the
living principle of nature. It is the effort we make, and
the impulse we acquire, in overcoming the first obstacles,
that projects us forward; it is the necessity for exertion
that makes us conscious of our strength; but this necessity
and this impulse once removed, the tide of fancy and enthusiasm, which is at first a running stream, soon settles
and crusts into the standing pool of dulness, criticism, and
*virtù.*

What also gave an unusual *impetus* to the mind of man
at this period, was the discovery of the New World, and
the reading of voyages and travels. Green islands and
golden sands seemed to arise, as by enchantment, out of
the bosom of the watery waste, and invite the cupidity, or
wing the imagination of the dreaming speculator. Fairy
land was realized in new and unknown worlds. " Fortunate
fields and groves and flowery vales, thrice happy isles,"
were found floating " like those Hesperian gardens famed
of old," beyond Atlantic seas, as dropt from the zenith.
The people, the soil, the clime, every thing gave unlimited
scope to the curiosity of the traveller and reader. Other
manners might be said to enlarge the bounds of knowledge,
and new mines of wealth were tumbled at our feet. It is
from a voyage to the Straits of Magellan that Shakspeare
has taken the hint of Prospero's Enchanted Island, and of
the savage Caliban with his god Setebos.* Spenser seems
to have had the same feeling in his mind in the production
of his Faery Queen, and vindicates his poetic fiction on
this very ground of analogy.

> " Right well I wote, most mighty sovereign,
>     That all this famous antique history

*See *A Voyage to the Straits of Magellan,* 1594.

Of some the abundance of an idle brain
Will judged be, and painted forgery,
Rather than matter of just memory:
Since none that breatheth living air, doth know
Where is that happy land of faery
Which I so much do vaunt, but no where show,
But vouch antiquities, which nobody can know.

But let that man with better sense avise,
That of the world least part to us is read:
And daily how through hardy enterprize
Many great regions are discovered,
Which to late age were never mentioned.
Who ever heard of th' Indian Peru?
Or who in venturous vessel measured
The Amazons' huge river, now found true?
Or fruitfullest Virginia who did ever view?

Yet all these were when no man did them know,
Yet have from wisest ages hidden been:
And later times things more unknown shall show.
Why then should witless man so much misween
That nothing is but that which he hath seen?
What if within the moon's fair shining sphere,
What if in every other star unseen,
Of other worlds he happily should hear,
He wonder would much more; yet such to some appear."

Fancy's air-drawn pictures after history's waking dream shewed like clouds over mountains; and from the romance of real life to the idlest fiction, the transition seemed easy.— Shakspeare, as well as others of his time, availed himself of the old Chronicles, and of the traditions or fabulous inventions contained in them in such ample measure, and which had not yet been appropriated to the purposes of poetry or the drama. The stage was a new thing; and those who had to supply its demands laid their hands upon whatever came within their reach: they were not particular as to the means, so that they gained the end. Lear is founded upon an old ballad; Othello on an Italian novel; Hamlet on a Danish, and Macbeth on a Scotch tradition:

one of which is to be found in Saxo-Grammaticus, and the last in Hollingshed. The Ghost-scenes and the Witches in each, are authenticated in the old Gothic history. There was also this connecting link between the poetry of this age and the supernatural traditions of a former one, that the belief in them was still extant, and in full force and visible operation among the vulgar (to say no more) in the time of our authors. The appalling and wild chimeras of superstition and ignorance, "those bodiless creations that ecstacy is very cunning in," were inwoven with existing manners and opinions, and all their effects on the passions of terror or pity might be gathered from common and actual observation—might be discerned in the workings of the face, the expressions of the tongue, the writhings of a troubled conscience. "Your face, my Thane, is as a book where men may read strange matters." Midnight and secret murders too, from the imperfect state of the police, were more common; and the ferocious and brutal manners that would stamp the brow of the hardened ruffian or hired assassin, more incorrigible and undisguised. The portraits of Tyrrel and Forrest were, no doubt, done from the life. We find that the ravages of the plague, the destructive rage of fire, the poisoned chalice, lean famine, the serpent's mortal sting, and the fury of wild beasts, were the common topics of their poetry, as they were common occurrences in more remote periods of history. They were the strong ingredients thrown into the cauldron of tragedy, to make it "thick and slab." Man's life was (as it appears to me) more full of traps and pit-falls; of hair-breadth accidents by flood and field; more way-laid by sudden and startling evils; it trod on the brink of hope and fear; stumbled upon fate unawares; while the imagination, close behind it, caught at and clung to the shape of danger, or "snatched a wild and fearful joy" from its escape. The accidents of nature were less provided against; the excesses of the passions and of lawless power were less regulated, and produced more strange and desperate catastrophes. The tales of Boccacio are founded on the great pestilence of Florence, Fletcher the poet died of the plague, and Marlow was stabbed in a tavern quarrel. The strict authority of parents, the inequality of ranks, or the hereditary feuds between different families, made more unhappy loves or matches.

> "The course of true love never did run even."

Again, the heroic and martial spirit which breathes in our elder writers, was yet in considerable activity in the reign of Elizabeth. "The age of chivalry was not then quite gone, nor the glory of Europe extinguished for ever." Jousts and tournaments were still common with the nobility in England and in foreign countries: Sir Philip Sidney was particularly distinguished for his proficiency in these exercises (and indeed fell a martyr to his ambition as a soldier) —and the gentle Surrey was still more famous, on the same account, just before him. It is true, the general use of fire-arms gradually superseded the necessity of skill in the sword, or bravery in the person: and as a symptom of the rapid degeneracy in this respect, we find Sir John Suckling soon after boasting of himself as one—

> "Who prized black eyes, and a lucky hit
> At bowls, above all the trophies of wit."

It was comparatively an age of peace,

> "Like strength reposing on his own right arm;"

but the sound of civil combat might still be heard in the distance, the spear glittered to the eye of memory, or the clashing of armour struck on the imagination of the ardent and the young. They were borderers on the savage state, on the times of war and bigotry, though in the lap of arts, of luxury, and knowledge. They stood on the shore and saw the billows rolling after the storm: " they heard the tumult, and were still." The manners and out-of-door amusements were more tinctured with a spirit of adventure and romance. The war with wild beasts, &c. was more strenuously kept up in country sports. I do not think we could get from sedentary poets, who had never mingled in the vicissitudes, the dangers, or excitements of the chase, such descriptions of hunting and other athletic games, as are to be found in Shakspeare's Midsummer Night's Dream or Fletcher's Noble Kinsmen.

With respect to the good cheer and hospitable living of those times, I cannot agree with an ingenious and agreeable writer of the present day, that it was general or frequent. The very stress laid upon certain holidays and festivals, shews that they did not keep up the same Saturnalian licence and open house all the year round. They reserved themselves for great occasions, and made the best amends they could, for a year of abstinence and toil by a week of merriment and convivial indulgence. Persons in middle life at this day, who can afford a good dinner every day, do not look forward to it as any particular subject of exultation: the poor peasant, who can only contrive to treat himself to a joint of meat on a Sunday, considers it as an event in the week. So, in the old Cambridge comedy of the Return from Parnassus, we find this indignant description of the progress of luxury in those days, put into the mouth of one of the speakers.

> " Why is't not strange to see a ragged clerke,
> Some stammell weaver, or some butcher's sonne,
> That scrubb'd a late within a sleeveless gowne,
> When the commencement, like a morrice dance,
> Hath put a bell or two about his legges,
> Created him a sweet cleane gentleman:

How then he 'gins to follow fashions.
He whose thin sire dwelt in a smokye roofe,
Must make tobacco, and must wear a locke.
His thirsty dad drinkes in a wooden bowle,
But his sweet self is served in silver plate.
His hungry sire will scrape you twenty legges
For one good Christmas meal on new year's day,
But his mawe must be capon cramm'd each day."

*Act III.  Scene 2.*

This does not look as if in those days " it snowed of meat
and drink," as a matter of course throughout the year!—
The distinctions of dress, the badges of different professions, the very signs of the shops, which we have set aside
for written inscriptions over the doors, were, as Mr. Lamb
observes, a sort of visible language to the imagination, and
hints for thought.  Like the costume of different foreign
nations, they had an immediate striking and picturesque
effect, giving scope to the fancy.  The surface of society
was embossed with hieroglyphics, and poetry existed " in
art and compliment extern."  The poetry of former times
might be directly taken from real life, as our poetry is
taken from the poetry of former times.  Finally, the face
of nature, which was the same glorious object then that it
is now, was open to them; and coming first, they gathered
her fairest flowers to live for ever in their verse:—the
movements of the human heart were not hid from them,
for they had the same passions as we, only less disguised,
and less subject to controul.  Deckar has given an admirable description of a mad-house in one of his plays.  But it
might be perhaps objected, that it was only a literal account
taken from Bedlam at that time; and it might be answered,
that the old poets took the same method of describing the
passions and fancies of men whom they met at large, which
forms the point of communion between us: for the title of
the old play, " A Mad World, my Masters," is hardly yet

obsolete; and we are pretty much the same Bedlam still, perhaps a little better managed, like the real one, and with more care and humanity shewn to the patients!

Lastly, to conclude this account; what gave a unity and common direction to all these causes, was the natural genius of the country, which was strong in these writers in proportion to their strength. We are a nation of islanders, and we cannot help it; nor mend ourselves if we would. We are something in ourselves, nothing when we try to ape others. Music and painting are not our *forte:* for what we have done in that way has been little, and that borrowed from others with great difficulty. But we may boast of our poets and philosophers. That's something. We have had strong heads and sound hearts among us. Thrown on one side of the world, and left to bustle for ourselves, we have fought out many a battle for truth and freedom. That is our natural style; and it were to be wished we had in no instance departed from it. Our situation has given us a certain cast of thought and character; and our liberty has enabled us to make the most of it. We are of a stiff clay, not moulded into every fashion, with stubborn joints not easily bent. We are slow to think, and therefore impressions do not work upon us till they act in masses. We are not forward to express our feelings, and therefore they do not come from us till they force their way in the most impetuous eloquence. Our language is, as it were, to begin anew, and we make use of the most singular and boldest combinations to explain ourselves. Our wit comes from us, " like birdlime, brains and all." We pay too little attention to form and method, leave our works in an unfinished state, but still the materials we work in are solid and of nature's mint; we do not deal in counterfeits. We both under and over-do, but we keep an eye to the prominent features, the main chance. We are more for weight than show; care only about what interests ourselves, instead of trying to impose upon others by plausible appearances, and are obstinate and intractable in not conforming to common rules, by which many arrive at their ends with half the real waste of thought and trouble. We neglect all but the principal object, gather our force to make a great blow, bring it down, and relapse into sluggishness and indifference again. *Materiam superabat opus,* cannot be said of us. We may be accused of grossness, but not of flimsiness; of extravagance, but not of affectation; of want of art and refinement, but not of a want of truth and nature. Our literature, in a word, is Gothic and grotesque; unequal and irregular; not cast in a previous mould, nor of one uniform texture, but of great weight in the whole, and of incomparable value in the best parts. It aims at an excess of beauty or power, hits or misses, and is either very good indeed, or absolutely good for nothing. This character applies in particular to our literature in the age of Elizabeth, which is its best period, before the introduction of a rage for French rules and French models; for whatever may be the value of our own original style of composition, there can be neither offence nor presumption in saying, that it is at least better than our second-hand imitations of others. Our understanding (such as it is, and must remain to be good for anything) is not a thoroughfare for common places, smooth as the palm of one's hand, but full of knotty points and jutting excrescences, rough, uneven, overgrown with brambles; and I like this aspect of the mind (as some one said of the country), where nature keeps a good deal of the soil in her own hands. Perhaps the genius of our poetry has more of Pan than of Apollo; "but Pan is a God, Apollo is no more!"

## II

## SPENSER

SPENSER flourished in the reign of Queen Elizabeth, and was sent with Sir John Davies into Ireland, of which he has left behind him some tender recollections in his description of the bog of Allan, and a record in an ably written paper, containing observations on the state of that country and the means of improving it, which remain in full force to the present day. Spenser died at an obscure inn in London, it is supposed in distressed circumstances. The treatment he received from Burleigh is well known. Spenser, as well as Chaucer, was engaged in active life; but the genius of his poetry was not active: it is inspired by the love of ease, and relaxation from all the cares and business of life. Of all the poets, he is the most poetical. Though much later than Chaucer, his obligations to preceding writers were less. He has in some measure borrowed the plan of his poem (as a number of distinct narratives) from Ariosto; but he has engrafted upon it an exuberance of fancy, and an endless voluptuousness of sentiment, which are not to be found in the Italian writer. Farther, Spenser is even more of an inventor in the subject-matter. There is an originality, richness, and variety in his allegorical personages and fictions, which almost vies with the splendor of the ancient mythology. If Ariosto transports us into the regions of romance, Spenser's poetry is all fairy-land. In Ariosto, we walk upon the ground, in a company, gay, fantastic, and adventurous enough. In

Spenser, we wander in another world, among ideal beings.
The poet takes and lays us in the lap of a lovelier nature,
by the sound of softer streams, among greener hills and
fairer valleys. He paints nature, not as we find it, but
as we expected to find it; and fulfils the delightful promise
of our youth. He waves his wand of enchantment—and at
once embodies airy beings, and throws a delicious veil
over all actual objects. The two worlds of reality and of
fiction are poised on the wings of his imagination. His
ideas, indeed, seem more distinct than his perceptions. He
is the painter of abstractions, and describes them with dazzling minuteness. In the Mask of Cupid he makes the God
of Love " clap on high his coloured winges *twain;* " and
it is said of Gluttony in the Procession of the Passions,

> " In green vine leaves he was right fitly clad."

At times he becomes picturesque from his intense love of
beauty; as where he compares Prince Arthur's crest to the
appearance of the almond tree:

> "Upon the top of all his lofty crest,
> A bunch of hairs discolour'd diversely
> With sprinkled pearl and gold full richly drest
> Did shake and seem'd to daunce for jollity;
> Like to an almond tree ymounted high
> On top of green Selenis all alone,
> With blossoms brave bedecked daintily;
> Her tender locks do tremble every one
> At every little breath that under heav'n is blown."

The love of beauty, however, and not of truth, is the moving
principle of his mind; and he is guided in his fantastic
delineations by no rule but the impulse of an inexhaustible
imagination. He luxuriates equally in scenes of Eastern
magnificence; or the still solitude of a hermit's cell—in the
extremes of sensuality or refinement.

In reading the Faery Queen, you see a little withered old man by a wood-side opening a wicket, a giant, and a dwarf lagging far behind, a damsel in a boat upon an enchanted lake, wood-nymphs, and satyrs; and all of a sudden you are transported into a lofty palace, with tapers burning, amidst knights and ladies, with dance and revelry, and song, "and mask, and antique pageantry." What can be more solitary, more shut up in itself, than his description of the house of Sleep, to which Archimago sends for a dream:

> "And more to lull him in his slumber soft
>   A trickling stream from high rock tumbling down,
> And ever-drizzling rain upon the loft,
>   Mix'd with a murmuring wind, much like the sound
> Of swarming Bees, did cast him in a swound.
>   No other noise, nor people's troublous cries
> That still are wont t' annoy the walled town
>   Might there be heard; but careless Quiet lies
> Wrapt in eternal silence, far from enemies."

It is as if "the honey-heavy dew of slumber" had settled on his pen in writing these lines. How different in the subject (and yet how like in beauty) is the following description of the Bower of Bliss:

> "Eftsoones they heard a most melodious sound
>   Of all that mote delight a dainty ear;
> Such as at once might not on living ground,
>   Save in this Paradise, be heard elsewhere:
> Right hard it was for wight which did it hear,
>   To tell what manner musicke that mote be;
> For all that pleasing is to living eare
>   Was there consorted in one harmonee:
> Birds, voices, instruments, windes, waters, all agree.
>
> The joyous birdes shrouded in chearefull shade
>   Their notes unto the voice attempred sweet:
> The angelical soft trembling voices made
>   To th' instruments divine respondence meet.

> The silver sounding instruments did meet
>     With the base murmur of the water's fall;
> The water's fall with difference discreet,
>     Now soft, now loud, unto the wind did call;
> The gentle warbling wind low answered to all."

The remainder of the passage has all that voluptuous pathos, and languid brilliancy of fancy, in which this writer excelled:

> "The whiles some one did chaunt this lovely lay;
>     Ah! see, whoso fayre thing dost fain to see,
> In springing flower the image of thy day!
>     Ah! see the virgin rose, how sweetly she
> Doth first peep forth with bashful modesty,
>     That fairer seems the less ye see her may!
> Lo! see soon after, how more bold and free
>     Her bared bosom she doth broad display;
> Lo! see soon after, how she fades and falls away!

> So passeth in the passing of a day
>     Of mortal life the leaf, the bud, the flower;
> Ne more doth flourish after first decay,
>     That erst was sought to deck both bed and bower
> Of many a lady and many a paramour!
>     Gather therefore the rose whilst yet is prime,
> For soon comes age that will her pride deflower;
>     Gather the rose of love whilst yet is time,
> Whilst loving thou mayst loved be with equal crime." *

> He ceased; and then gan all the quire of birds
>     Their divers notes to attune unto his lay,
> As in approvance of his pleasing wordes.
>     The constant pair heard all that he did say,
> Yet swerved not, but kept their forward way
>     Through many covert groves and thickets close,
> In which they creeping did at last display †
>     That wanton lady with her lover loose,
> Whose sleepy head she in her lap did soft dispose.

---

* Taken from Tasso.

† This word is an instance of those unwarrantable freedoms which Spenser sometimes took with language.

Upon a bed of roses she was laid
  As faint through heat, or dight to pleasant sin;
And was arrayed or rather disarrayed,
  All in a veil of silk and silver thin,
That hid no whit her alabaster skin,
  But rather shewed more white, if more might be:
More subtle web Arachne cannot spin;
  Nor the fine nets, which oft we woven see
Of scorched dew, do not in the air more lightly flee.

Her snowy breast was bare to greedy spoil
  Of hungry eyes which n'ote therewith be fill'd.
And yet through languor of her late sweet toil
  Few drops more clear than nectar forth distill'd,
That like pure Orient perles adown it trill'd;
  And her fair eyes sweet smiling in delight
Moisten'd their fiery beams, with which she thrill'd
  Frail hearts, yet quenched not; like starry light,
Which sparkling on the silent waves does seem more bright."

The finest things in Spenser are, the character of Una, in the first book; the House of Pride; the Cave of Mammon, and the Cave of Despair; the account of Memory, of whom it is said, among other things,

"The wars he well remember'd of King Nine,
  Of old Assaracus and Inachus divine;"

the description of Belphœbe; the story of Florimel and the Witch's son; the Gardens of Adonis, and the Bower of Bliss; the Mask of Cupid; and Colin Clout's vision, in the last book. But some people will say that all this may be very fine, but that they cannot understand it on account of the allegory. They are afraid of the allegory, as if they thought it would bite them: they look at it as a child looks at a painted dragon, and think it will strangle them in its shining folds. This is very idle. If they do not meddle with the allegory, the allegory will not meddle with them. Without minding it at all, the whole is as plain as a pikestaff. It might as well be pretended that we cannot see Poussin's pictures for the allegory, as that the allegory prevents us from understanding Spenser. For instance, when Britomart, seated amidst the young warriors, lets fall her hair and discovers her sex, is it necessary to know the part she plays in the allegory, to understand the beauty of the following stanza?

> " And eke that stranger knight amongst the rest
>     Was for like need enforc'd to disarray.
> Tho when as vailed was her lofty crest,
>     Her golden locks that were in trammels gay
> Upbounden, did themselves adown display,
>     And raught unto her heels like sunny beams
> That in a cloud their light did long time stay;
>     Their vapour faded, shew their golden gleams,
> And through the persant air shoot forth their azure streams."

Or is there any mystery in what is said of Belphœbe, that her hair was sprinkled with flowers and blossoms which had been entangled in it as she fled through the woods? Or is it necessary to have a more distinct idea of Proteus, than that which is given of him in his boat, with the frighted Florimel at his feet, while

> "—the cold icicles from his rough beard
> Dropped adown upon her snowy breast ! "

Or is it not a sufficient account of one of the sea-gods that pass by them, to say—

> " That was Arion crowned :—
> So went he playing on the watery plain."

Or to take the Procession of the Passions that draw the coach of Pride, in which the figures of Idleness, of Gluttony, of Lechery, of Avarice, of Envy, and of Wrath speak, one should think, plain enough for themselves; such as this of Guttony:

"And by his side rode loathsome Gluttony,
  Deformed creature, on a filthy swine;
His belly was up blown with luxury;
  And eke with fatness swollen were his eyne;
And like a crane his neck was long and fine,
  With which he swallowed up excessive feast,
For want whereof poor people oft did pine.

In green vine leaves he was right fitly clad;
  For other clothes he could not wear for heat;
And on his head an ivy garland had,
  From under which fast trickled down the sweat:
Still as he rode, he somewhat still did eat,
  And in his hand did bear a bouzing can,
Of which he supt so oft, that on his seat
  His drunken corse he scarce upholden can;
In shape and life more like a monster than a man."

Or this of Lechery:

"And next to him rode lustfull Lechery
  Upon a bearded goat, whose rugged hair
And whaly eyes (the sign of jealousy)
  Was like the person's self whom he did bear:
Who rough and black, and filthy did appear.
  Unseemly man to please fair lady's eye:
Yet he of ladies oft was loved dear,
  When fairer faces were bid standen by:
O! who does know the bent of woman's fantsay?

In a green gown he clothed was full fair,
  Which underneath did hide his filthiness;
And in his hand a burning heart he bare,
  Full of vain follies and new fangleness;
For he was false and fraught with fickleness;
  And learned had to love with secret looks;
And well could dance; and sing with ruefulness;
  And fortunes tell; and read in loving books;
And thousand other ways to bait his fleshly hooks.

Inconstant man that loved all he saw,
  And lusted after all that he did love;
Ne would his looser life be tied to law;
  But joyed weak women's hearts to tempt and prove,
If from their loyal loves he might them move."

This is pretty plain-spoken.  Mr. Southey says of Spenser:

> "Yet not more sweet
> Than pure was he, and not more pure than wise;
> High priest of all the Muses' mysteries!"

On the contrary, no one was more apt to pry into mysteries which do not strictly belong to the Muses.

Of the same kind with the Procession of the Passions, as little obscure, and still more beautiful, is the Mask of Cupid, with his train of votaries:

> "The first was Fancy, like a lovely boy
> Of rare aspect, and beauty without peer;
>
> His garment neither was of silk nor say,
> But painted plumes in goodly order dight,
> Like as the sun-burnt Indians do array
> Their tawny bodies in their proudest plight;
> As those same plumes so seem'd he vain and light,
> That by his gait might easily appear;
> For still he far'd as dancing in delight,
> And in his hand a windy fan did bear
> That in the idle air he mov'd still here and there.
>
> And him beside march'd amorous Desire,
> Who seem'd of riper years than the other swain,
> Yet was that other swain this elder's sire,
> And gave him being, common to them twain:
> His garment was disguised very vain,
> And his embroidered bonnet sat awry;
> 'Twixt both his hands few sparks he close did strain,
> Which still he blew, and kindled busily,
> That soon they life conceiv'd and forth in flames did fly.
>
> Next after him went Doubt, who was yclad
> In a discolour'd coat of strange disguise,
> That at his back a broad capuccio had,
> And sleeves dependant *Albanese-wise;*
> He lookt askew with his mistrustful eyes,
> And nicely trod, as thorns lay in his way,
> Or that the floor to shrink he did avise;
> And on a broken reed he still did stay
> His feeble steps, which shrunk when hard thereon he lay.

With him went Daunger, cloth'd in ragged weed,
  Made of bear's skin, that him more dreadful made;
Yet his own face was dreadfull, ne did need
  Strange horror to deform his grisly shade;
A net in th' one hand, and a rusty blade
  In th' other was; this Mischiefe, that Mishap;
With th' one his foes he threat'ned to invade,
  With th' other he his friends meant to enwrap;
For whom he could not kill he practiz'd to entrap.

Next him was Fear, all arm'd from top to toe,
  Yet thought himself not safe enough thereby,
But fear'd each shadow moving to and fro;
  And his own arms when glittering he did spy
Or clashing heard, he fast away did fly,
  As ashes pale of hue, and winged-heel'd;
And evermore on Daunger fixt his eye,
  'Gainst whom he always bent a brazen shield,
Which his right hand unarmed fearfully did wield.

With him went Hope in rank, a handsome maid,
  Of chearfull look and lovely to behold;
In silken samite she was light array'd,
  And her fair locks were woven up in gold;
She always smil'd, and in her hand did hold
  An holy-water sprinkle dipt in dew,
With which she sprinkled favours manifold
  On whom she list, and did great liking shew,
Great liking unto many, but true love to few.

Next after them, the winged God himself
  Came riding on a lion ravenous,
Taught to obey the menage of that elfe
  That man and beast with power imperious
Subdueth to his kingdom tyrannous:
  His blindfold eyes he bade awhile unbind,
That his proud spoil of that same dolorous
  Fair dame he might behold in perfect kind;
Which seen, he much rejoiced in his cruel mind.

Of which full proud, himself uprearing high,
  He looked round about with stern disdain,
And did survey his goodly company;
  And marshalling the evil-ordered train,
With that the darts which his right hand did strain,

Full dreadfully he shook, that all did quake,
And clapt on high his colour'd winges twain,
   That all his many it afraid did make:
Tho, blinding him again, his way he forth did take."

The description of Hope, in this series of historical portraits, is one of the most beautiful in Spenser: and the triumph of Cupid at the mischief he has made, is worthy of the malicious urchin deity. In reading these descriptions, one can hardly avoid being reminded of Rubens's allegorical pictures; but the account of Satyrane taming the lion's whelps and lugging the bear's cubs along in his arms while yet an infant, whom his mother so naturally advises to "go seek some other play-fellows," has even more of this high picturesque character. Nobody but Rubens could have painted the fancy of Spenser; and he could not have given the sentiment, the airy dream that hovers over it!

With all this, Spenser neither makes us laugh nor weep. The only jest in his poem is an allegorical play upon words, where he describes Malbecco as escaping in the herd of goats, "by the help of his fayre horns on hight." But he has been unjustly charged with a want of passion and of strength. He has both in an immense degree. He has not indeed the pathos of immediate action or suffering, which is more properly the dramatic; but he has all the pathos of sentiment and romance—all that belongs to distant objects of terror, and uncertain, imaginary distress. His strength, in like manner, is not strength of will or action, of bone and muscle, nor is it coarse and palpable—but it assumes a character of vastness and sublimity seen through the same visionary medium, and blended with the appalling associations of preternatural agency. We need only turn, in proof of this, to the Cave of Despair, or the Cave of Mammon, or to the account of the change of Malbecco into

Jealousy. The following stanzas, in the description of the
Cave of Mammon, the grisly house of Plutus, are unrivalled
for the portentous massiness of the forms, the splendid
chiaro-scuro, and shadowy horror.

" That house's form within was rude and strong,
 Like an huge cave hewn out of rocky clift,
From whose rough vault the ragged breaches hung,
 Embossed with massy gold of glorious gift,
And with rich metal loaded every rift,
 That heavy ruin they did seem to threat:
And over them Arachne high did lift
 Her cunning web, and spread her subtle net,
Enwrapped in foul smoke, and clouds more black than jet.

Both roof and floor, and walls were all of gold,
 But overgrown with dust and old decay,*
And hid in darkness that none could behold
 The hue thereof: for view of cheerful day
Did never in that house itself display,
 But a faint shadow of uncertain light;
Such as a lamp whose light doth fade away;
 Or as the moon clothed with cloudy night
Does shew to him that walks in fear and sad affright,

　　.　　.　　.　　.　　.　　.

And over all sad Horror with grim hue
 Did always soar, beating his iron wings;
And after him owls and night-ravens flew,
 The hateful messengers of heavy things,
Of death and dolour telling sad tidings;
 While sad Celleno, sitting on a clift,
A song of bale and bitter sorrow sings,
 That heart of flint asunder could have rift;
Which having ended, after him she flieth swift."

The Cave of Despair is described with equal gloominess and
power of fancy; and the fine moral declamation of the

* " That all with one consent praise new-born gauds,
 Tho' they are made and moulded of things past,
 And give to Dust, that is a little gilt,
 More laud than gold o'er-dusted."
　　　　　　　　　　*Troilus and Cressida.*

owner of it, on the evils of life, almost makes one in love
with death.  In the story of Malbecco, who is haunted by
jealousy, and in vain strives to run away from his
own thoughts—

"High over hill and over dale he flies"—

the truth of human passion and the preternatural ending are
equally striking.—It is not fair to compare Spenser with
Shakspeare, in point of interest.  A fairer comparison
would be with Comus; and the result would not be unfavourable to Spenser.  There is only one work of the same
allegorical kind, which has more interest than Spenser
(with scarcely less imagination): and that is the Pilgrim's
Progress.  The three first books of the Faery Queen are
very superior to the three last.  One would think that Pope,
who used to ask if any one had ever read the Faery Queen
through, had only dipped into these last.  The only things
in them equal to the former, are the account of Talus, the
Iron Man, and the delightful episode of Pastorella.

The language of Spenser is full, and copious, to overflowing: it is less pure and idiomatic than Chaucer's, and
is enriched and adorned with phrases borrowed from the
different languages of Europe, both ancient and modern.
He was, probably, seduced into a certain license of expression by the difficulty of filling up the moulds of his
complicated rhymed stanza from the limited resources of
his native language.  This stanza, with alternate and repeatedly recurring rhymes, is borrowed from the Italians.
It is peculiarly fitted to their language, which abounds in
similar vowel terminations, and is as little adapted to ours,
from the stubborn, unaccommodating resistance which the
consonant endings of the northern languages make to this
sort of endless sing-song.—Not that I would, on that account, part with the stanza of Spenser.  We are, perhaps,

indebted to this very necessity of finding out new forms of expression, and to the occasional faults to which it led, for a poetical language rich and varied and magnificent beyond all former, and almost all later example. His versification is, at once, the most smooth and the most sounding in the language. It is a labyrinth of sweet sounds, "in many a winding bout of linked sweetness long drawn out" —that would cloy by their very sweetness, but that the ear is constantly relieved and enchanted by their continued variety of modulation—dwelling on the pauses of the action, or flowing on in a fuller tide of harmony with the movement of the sentiment. It has not the bold dramatic transitions of Shakspeare's blank verse, nor the high-raised tone of Milton's; but it is the perfection of melting harmony, dissolving the soul in pleasure, or holding it captive in the chains of suspense. Spenser was the poet of our waking dreams; and he has invented not only a language, but a music of his own for them. The undulations are infinite, like those of the waves of the sea: but the effect is still the same, lulling the senses into a deep oblivion of the jarring noises of the world, from which we have no wish to be ever recalled.

# III

## SHAKSPEARE

THE four greatest names in English poetry, are almost the four first we come to—Chaucer, Spenser, Shakspeare, and Milton. There are no others that can really be put in competition with these. The two last have had justice done them by the voice of common fame. Their names are blazoned in the very firmament of reputation; while the two first, (though "the fault has been more in their stars than in themselves that they are underlings") either never emerged far above the horizon, or were too soon involved in the obscurity of time. The three first of these are excluded from Dr. Johnson's Lives of the Poets (Shakspeare indeed is so from the dramatic form of his compositions): and the fourth, Milton, is admitted with a reluctant and churlish welcome.

In comparing these four writers together, it might be said that Chaucer excels as the poet of manners, or of real life; Spenser, as the poet of romance; Shakspeare, as the poet of nature (in the largest use of the term): and Milton, as the poet of morality. Chaucer most frequently describes things as they are; Spenser, as we wish them to be; Shakspeare, as they would be; and Milton as they ought to be. As poets, and as great poets, imagination, that is, the power of feigning things according to nature, was common to them all: but the principle or moving power, to which this faculty was most subservient in Chaucer, was habit, or inveterate prejudice; in Spenser, novelty, and the

34

love of the marvellous; in Shakspeare, it was the force of
passion, combined with every variety of possible circumstances; and in Milton, only with the highest. The characteristic of Chaucer is intensity; of Spenser, remoteness;
of Milton, elevation; of Shakspeare, everything.—It has
been said by some critic, that Shakspeare was distinguished
from the other dramatic writers of his day only by
his wit; that they had all his other qualities but
that; that one writer had as much sense, another as
much fancy, another as much knowledge of character,
another the same depth of passion, and another as great
a power of language. This statement is not true; nor is
the inference from it well-founded, even if it were. This
person does not seem to have been aware that, upon his
own shewing, the great distinction of Shakspeare's genius
was its virtually including the genius of all the great men
of his age, and not his differing from them in one accidental particular. But to have done with such minute and
literal trifling.

The striking peculiarity of Shakspeare's mind was its
generic quality, its power of communication with all other
minds—so that it contained a universe of thought and
feeling within itself, and had no one peculiar bias, or
exclusive excellence more than another. He was just like
any other man, but that he was like all other men. He
was the least of an egotist that it was possible to be. He
was nothing in himself; but he was all that others were,
or that they could become. He not only had in himself
the germs of every faculty and feeling, but he could follow
them by anticipation, intuitively, into all their conceivable
ramifications, through every change of fortune or conflict
of passion, or turn of thought. He had " a mind reflecting
ages past," and present:—all the people that ever lived are
there. There was no respect of persons with him. His

genius shone equally on the evil and on the good, on the wise and the foolish, the monarch and the beggar: " All corners of the earth, kings, queens, and states, maids, matrons, nay, the secrets of the grave," are hardly hid from his searching glance. He was like the genius of humanity, changing places with all of us at pleasure, and playing with our purposes as with his own. He turned the globe round for his amusement, and surveyed the generations of men, and the individuals as they passed, with their different concerns, passions, follies, vices, virtues, actions, and mo-tives—as well those that they knew, as those which they did not know, or acknowledge to themselves. The dreams of childhood, the ravings of despair, were the toys of his fancy. Airy beings waited at his call, and came at his bid-ding. Harmless fairies " nodded to him, and did him curtesies : " and the night-hag bestrode the blast at the com-mand of " his so potent art." The world of spirits lay open to him, like the world of real men and women: and there is the same truth in his delineations of the one as of the other ; for if the preternatural characters he describes could be supposed to exist, they would speak, and feel, and act, as he makes them. He had only to think of any thing in order to become that thing, with all the circumstances belonging to it. When he conceived of a character whether real or imaginary, he not only entered into all its thoughts and feelings, but seemed instantly, and as if by touching a secret spring, to be surrounded with all the same objects, " subject to the same skyey influences," the same local, outward, and unforeseen accidents which would occur in reality. Thus the character of Caliban not only stands before us with a language and manners of its own, but the scenery and situation of the enchanted island he inhabits, the traditions of the place, its strange noises, its hidden recesses, " his frequent haunts and ancient neighbourhood,"

are given with a miraculous truth of nature, and with all
the familiarity of an old recollection. The whole " coheres
semblably together " in time, place, and circumstance. In
reading this author, you do not merely learn what his characters say,—you see their persons. By something expressed
or understood, you are at no loss to decypher their peculiar
physiognomy, the meaning of a look, the grouping, the bye-
play, as we might see it on the stage. A word, an epithet
paints a whole scene, or throws us back whole years in
the history of the person represented. So (as it has been
ingeniously remarked) when Prospero describes himself as
left alone in the boat with his daughter, the epithet which
he applies to her, " Me and thy *crying* self," flings the imagination instantly back from the grown woman to the helpless condition of infancy, and places the first and most
trying scene of his misfortunes before us, with all that
he must have suffered in the interval. How well the silent
anguish of Macduff is conveyed to the reader, by the friendly
expostulation of Malcolm—" What! man, ne'er pull your
hat upon your brows! " Again, Hamlet, in the scene with
Rosencrans and Guildenstern, somewhat abruptly concludes
his fine soliloquy on life by saying, " Man delights not me,
nor woman neither, though by your smiling you seem to
say so." Which is explained by their answer—" My lord,
we had no such stuff in our thoughts. But we smiled to
think, if you delight not in man, what lenten entertainment
the players shall receive from you, whom we met on the
way: "—as if while Hamlet was making this speech, his two
old schoolfellows from Wittenberg had been really standing
by, and he had seen them smiling by stealth, at the idea of
the players crossing their minds. It is not " a combination
and a form " of words, a set speech or two, a preconcerted
theory of a character, that will do this : but all the persons
concerned must have been present in the poet's imagination,

as at a kind of rehearsal; and whatever would have passed through their minds on the occasion, and have been observed by others, passed through his, and is made known to the reader.—I may add in passing, that Shakspeare always gives the best directions for the costume and carriage of his heroes. Thus, to take one example, Ophelia gives the following account of Hamlet; and as Ophelia had seen Hamlet, I should think her word ought to be taken against that of any modern authority.

> "*Ophelia.* My lord, as I was reading in my closet,
> Prince Hamlet, with his doublet all unbrac'd,
> No hat upon his head, his stockings loose,
> Ungartred, and down-gyved to his ancle,
> Pale as his shirt, his knees knocking each other,
> And with a look so piteous,
> As if he had been sent from hell
> To speak of horrors, thus he comes before me.
>    *Polonius.* Mad for thy love!
>    *Oph.* My lord, I do not know,
> But truly I do fear it.
>    *Pol.*         What said he?
>    *Oph.* He took me by the wrist and held me hard.
> Then goes he to the length of all his arm;
> And with his other hand thus o'er his brow,
> He falls to such perusal of my face,
> As he would draw it: long staid he so;
> At last, a little shaking of my arm,
> And thrice his head thus waving up and down,
> He rais'd a sigh so piteous and profound,
> As it did seem to shatter all his bulk,
> And end his being. That done, he lets me go,
> And with his head over his shoulder turn'd,
> He seem'd to find his way without his eyes;
> For out of doors he went without their help,
> And to the last bended their light on me."
>                             *Act II. Scene 1.*

How after this airy, fantastic idea of irregular grace and bewildered melancholy any one can play Hamlet, as we have seen it played, with strut, and stare, and antic right-

angled sharp-pointed gestures, it is difficult to say, unless
it be that Hamlet is not bound, by the prompter's cue, to
study the part of Ophelia.  The account of Ophelia's death
begins thus:

> "There is a willow hanging o'er a brook,
> That shows its hoary leaves in the glassy stream."——

Now this is an instance of the same unconscious power
of mind which is as true to nature as itself.  The leaves of
the willow are, in fact, white underneath, and it is this part
of them which would appear " hoary " in the reflection in
the brook.  The same sort of intuitive power, the same
faculty of bringing every object in nature, whether present
or absent, before the mind's eye, is observable in the speech
of Cleopatra, when conjecturing what were the employments of Antony in his absence:—" He's speaking now, or
murmuring, where's my serpent of old Nile? "   How fine to
make Cleopatra have this consciousness of her own character, and to make her feel that it is this for which Antony
is in love with her!  She says, after the battle of Actium,
when Antony has resolved to risk another fight, " It is my
birth-day; I had thought to have held it poor: but since my
lord is Antony again, I will be Cleopatra."   What other
poet would have thought of such a casual resource of the
imagination, or would have dared to avail himself of it?
The thing happens in the play as it might have happened
in fact.—That which, perhaps, more than any thing else
distinguishes the dramatic productions of Shakspeare from
all others, is this wonderful truth and individuality of conception.  Each of his characters is as much itself, and as
absolutely independent of the rest, as well as of the author,
as if they were living persons, not fictions of the mind.  The
poet may be said, for the time, to identify himself with the

character he wishes to represent, and to pass from one to another, like the same soul successively animating different bodies. By an art like that of the ventriloquist, he throws his imagination out of himself, and makes every word appear to proceed from the mouth of the person in whose name it is given. His plays alone are properly expressions of the passions, not descriptions of them. His characters are real beings of flesh and blood; they speak like men, not like authors. One might suppose that he had stood by at the time, and overheard what passed. As in our dreams we hold conversations with ourselves, make remarks, or communicate intelligence, and have no idea of the answer which we shall receive, and which we ourselves make, till we hear it: so the dialogues in Shakspeare are carried on without any consciousness of what is to follow, without any appearance of preparation or premeditation. The gusts of passion come and go like sounds of music borne on the wind. Nothing is made out by formal inference and analogy, by climax and antithesis: all comes, or seems to come, immediately from nature. Each object and circumstance exists in his mind, as it would have existed in reality: each several train of thought and feeling goes on of itself, without confusion or effort. In the world of his imagination, every thing has a life, a place, and being of its own!

Chaucer's characters are sufficiently distinct from one another, but they are too little varied in themselves, too much like identical propositions. They are consistent, but uniform; we get no new idea of them from first to last; they are not placed in different lights, nor are their subordinate *traits* brought out in new situations; they are like portraits or physiognomical studies, with the distinguishing features marked with inconceivable truth and precision, but that preserve the same unaltered air and attitude. Shak-

speare's are historical figures, equally true and correct, but
put into action, where every nerve and muscle is displayed
in the struggle with others, with all the effect of collision
and contrast, with every variety of light and shade.
Chaucer's characters are narrative, Shakspeare's dramatic,
Milton's epic. That is, Chaucer told only as much of his
story as he pleased, as was required for a particular purpose. He answered for his characters himself. In Shakspeare they are introduced upon the stage, are liable to be
asked all sorts of questions, and are forced to answer for
themselves. In Chaucer we perceive a fixed essence of
character. In Shakspeare there is a continual composition
and decomposition of its elements, a fermentation of every
particle in the whole mass, by its alternate affinity or
antipathy to other principles which are brought in contact
with it. Till the experiment is tried, we do not know the
result, the turn which the character will take in its new
circumstances. Milton took only a few simple principles of
character, and raised them to the utmost conceivable
grandeur, and refined them from every base alloy. His
imagination, "nigh sphered in Heaven," claimed kindred
only with what he saw from that height, and could raise
to the same elevation with itself. He sat retired, and
kept his state alone, "playing with wisdom;" while Shakspeare mingled with the crowd, and played the host, "to
make society the sweeter welcome."

The passion in Shakspeare is of the same nature as his
delineation of character. It is not some one habitual feeling or sentiment preying upon itself, growing out of itself,
and moulding every thing to itself; it is passion modified
by passion, by all the other feelings to which the individual
is liable, and to which others are liable with him; subject to
all the fluctuations of caprice and accident; calling into
play all the resources of the understanding and all the

energies of the will; irritated by obstacles or yielding to
them; rising from small beginnings to its utmost height;
now drunk with hope, now stung to madness, now sunk in
despair, now blown to air with a breath, now raging like
a torrent. The human soul is made the sport of fortune, the
prey of adversity: it is stretched on the wheel of destiny,
in restless ecstacy. The passions are in a state of projection. Years are melted down to moments, and every instant
teems with fate. We know the results, we see the process.
Thus after Iago has been boasting to himself of the effect
of his poisonous suggestions on the mind of Othello,
" which, with a little act upon the blood, will work like
mines of sulphur," he adds—

> " Look where he comes! not poppy, nor mandragora,
>   Nor all the drowsy syrups of the East,
>   Shall ever medicine thee to that sweet sleep
>   Which thou ow'dst yesterday."——

And he enters at this moment, like the crested serpent,
crowned with his wrongs and raging for revenge! The
whole depends upon the turn of a thought. A word, a
look, blows the spark of jealousy into a flame; and the
explosion is immediate and terrible as a volcano. The
dialogues in Lear, in Macbeth, that between Brutus and
Cassius, and nearly all those in Shakspeare, where the
interest is wrought up to its highest pitch, afford examples
of this dramatic fluctuation of passion. The interest in
Chaucer is quite different; it is like the course of a river,
strong, and full, and increasing. In Shakspeare, on the
contrary, it is like the sea, agitated this way and that, and
loud-lashed by furious storms; while in the still pauses of
the blast, we distinguish only the cries of despair or the
silence of death! Milton, on the other hand, takes the
imaginative part of passion—that which remains after the

event, which the mind reposes on when all is over, which
looks upon circumstances from the remotest elevation of
thought and fancy, and abstracts them from the world of
action to that of contemplation. The objects of dramatic
poetry affect us by sympathy, by their nearness to ourselves, as they take us by surprise, or force us upon action,
" while rage with rage doth sympathise : " the objects of
epic poetry affect us through the medium of the imagination, by magnitude and distance, by their permanence and
universality. The one fill us with terror and pity, the
other with admiration and delight. There are certain
objects that strike the imagination, and inspire awe in the
very idea of them, independently of any dramatic interest,
that is, of any connection with the vicissitudes of human
life. For instance, we cannot think of the pyramids of
Egypt, of a Gothic ruin, or an old Roman encampment,
without a certain emotion, a sense of power and sublimity
coming over the mind. The heavenly bodies that hang over
our heads wherever we go, and " in their untroubled element
shall shine when we are laid in dust, and all our cares forgotten," affect us in the same way. Thus Satan's address
to the Sun has an epic, not a dramatic interest; for though
the second person in the dialogue makes no answer and feels
no concern, yet the eye of that vast luminary is upon him,
like the eye of heaven, and seems conscious of what he
says, like an universal presence. Dramatic poetry and epic,
in their perfection, indeed, approximate to and strengthen
one another. Dramatic poetry borrows aid from the dignity
of persons and things, as the heroic does from human passion, but in theory they are distinct.—When Richard II.
calls for the looking-glass to contemplate his faded majesty
in it, and bursts into that affecting exclamation : " Oh, that
I were a mockery-king of snow, to melt away before the
sun of Bolingbroke," we have here the utmost force of

human passion, combined with the ideas of regal splendour and fallen power. When Milton says of Satan:

> "—His form had not yet lost
> All her original brightness, nor appear'd
> Less than archangel ruin'd, and th' excess
> Of glory obscur'd; "—

the mixture of beauty, of grandeur, and pathos, from the sense of irreparable loss, of never-ending, unavailing regret, is perfect.

The great fault of a modern school of poetry is, that it is an experiment to reduce poetry to a mere effusion of natural sensibility; or what is worse, to divest it both of imaginary splendour and human passion, to surround the meanest objects with the morbid feelings and devouring egotism of the writers' own minds. Milton and Shakspeare did not so understand poetry. They gave a more liberal interpretation both to nature and art. They did not do all they could to get rid of the one and the other, to fill up the dreary void with the Moods of their own Minds. They owe their power over the human mind to their having had a deeper sense than others of what was grand in the objects of nature, or affecting in the events of human life. But to the men I speak of there is nothing interesting, nothing heroical, but themselves. To them the fall of gods or of great men is the same. They do not enter into the feeling. They cannot understand the terms. They are even debarred from the last poor, paltry consolation of an unmanly triumph over fallen greatness; for their minds reject, with a convulsive effort and intolerable loathing, the very idea that there ever was, or was thought to be, any thing superior to themselves. All that has ever excited the attention or admiration of the world they look upon with the most perfect indifference; and they are

surprised to find that the world repays their indifference
with scorn. "With what measure they mete, it has been
meted to them again."

Shakspeare's imagination is of the same plastic kind as
his conception of character or passion. "It glances from
heaven to earth, from earth to heaven." Its movement is
rapid and devious. It unites the most opposite extremes;
or, as Puck says, in boasting of his own feats, "puts a girdle
round about the earth in forty minutes." He seems always
hurrying from his subject, even while describing it; but the
stroke, like the lightning's, is sure as it is sudden. He
takes the widest possible range, but from that very range
he has his choice of the greatest variety and aptitude of
materials. He brings together images the most alike, but
placed at the greatest distance from each other; that is,
found in circumstances of the greatest dissimilitude. From
the remoteness of his combinations, and the celerity with
which they are effected, they coalesce the more indissolubly
together. The more the thoughts are strangers to each
other, and the longer they have been kept asunder, the more
intimate does their union seem to become. Their felicity
is equal to their force. Their likeness is made more dazzling
by their novelty. They startle, and take the fancy prisoner
in the same instant. I will mention one or two which are
very striking, and not much known, out of Troilus and
Cressida. Æneas says to Agamemnon,

> "I ask that I may waken reverence,
> And on the cheek be ready with a blush
> Modest as morning, when she coldly eyes
> The youthful Phœbus."

Ulysses urging Achilles to shew himself in the field, says—

> "No man is the lord of any thing,
> Till he communicate his parts to others:

> Nor doth he of himself know them for aught,
> Till he behold them formed in the applause,
> Where they're extended! which like an arch reverberates
> The voice again, or like a gate of steel,
> Fronting the sun, receives and renders back
> Its figure and its heat."

Patroclus gives the indolent warrior the same advice.

> " Rouse yourself; and the weak wanton Cupid
> Shall from your neck unloose his amorous fold,
> And like a dew-drop from the lion's mane
> Be shook to air."

Shakspeare's language and versification are like the rest of him. He has a magic power over words: they come winged at his bidding; and seem to know their places. They are struck out at a heat, on .the spur of the occasion, and have all the truth and vividness which arise from an actual impression of the objects. His epithets and single phrases are like sparkles, thrown off from an imagination, fired by the whirling rapidity of its own motion. His language is hieroglyphical. It translates thoughts into visible images. It abounds in sudden transitions and elliptical expressions. This is the source of his mixed metaphors, which are only abbreviated forms of speech. These, however, give no pain from long custom. They have, in fact, become idioms in the language. They are the building, and not the scaffolding to thought. We take the meaning and effect of a well-known passage entire, and no more stop to scan and spell out the particular words and phrases, than the syllables of which they are composed. In trying to recollect any other author, one sometimes stumbles, in case of failure, on a word as good. In Shakspeare, any other word but the true one, is sure to be wrong. If any body, for instance, could not recollect the words of the following description,

> "—Light thickens,
> And the crow makes wing to the rooky wood,"

he would be greatly at a loss to substitute others for them equally expressive of the feeling. These remarks, however, are strictly applicable only to the impassioned parts of Shakspeare's language, which flowed from the warmth and originality of his imagination, and were his own. The language used for prose conversation and ordinary business is sometimes technical, and involved in the affectation of the time. Compare, for example, Othello's apology to the senate, relating " his whole course of love," with some of the preceding parts relating to his appointment, and the official dispatches from Cyprus. In this respect, " the business of the state does him offence."—His versification is no less powerful, sweet, and varied. It has every occasional excellence, of sullen intricacy, crabbed and perplexed, or of the smoothest and loftiest expansion—from the ease and familiarity of measured conversation to the lyrical sounds

> "—Of ditties highly penned,
> Sung by a fair queen in a summer's bower,
> With ravishing division to her lute."

It is the only blank verse in the language, except Milton's, that for itself is readable. It is not stately and uniformly swelling like his, but varied and broken by the inequalities of the ground it has to pass over in its uncertain course,

> " And so by many winding nooks it strays,
> With willing sport to the wild ocean."

It remains to speak of the faults of Shakspeare. They are not so many or so great as they have been represented ; what there are, are chiefly owing to the following causes :—

The universality of his genius was, perhaps, a disadvantage to his single works; the variety of his resources sometimes diverting him from applying them to the most effectual purposes.  He might be said to combine the powers of Æschylus and Aristophanes, of Dante and Rabelais, in his own mind.  If he had been only half what he was, he would perhaps have appeared greater.  The natural ease and indifference of his temper made him sometimes less scrupulous than he might have been.  He is relaxed and careless in critical places; he is in earnest throughout only in Timon, Macbeth, and Lear.  Again, he had no models of acknowledged excellence constantly in view to stimulate his efforts, and by all that appears, no love of fame.  He wrote for the "great vulgar and the small," in his time, not for posterity.  If Queen Elizabeth and the maids of honour laughed heartily at his worst jokes, and the catcalls in the gallery were silent at his best passages, he went home satisfied, and slept the next night well.  He did not trouble himself about Voltaire's criticisms.  He was willing to take advantage of the ignorance of the age in many things; and if his plays pleased others, not to quarrel with them himself.  His very facility of production would make him set less value on his own excellences, and not care to distinguish nicely between what he did well or ill.  His blunders in chronology and geography do not amount to above half a dozen, and they are offences against chronology and geography, not against poetry.  As to the unities, he was right in setting them at defiance.  He was fonder of puns than became so great a man.  His barbarisms were those of his age.  His genius was his own.  He had no objection to float down with the stream of common taste and opinion: he rose above it by his own buoyancy, and an impulse which he could not keep under, in spite of himself or others, and "his delights did shew most dolphin-like."

He had an equal genius for comedy and tragedy; and his tragedies are better than his comedies, because tragedy is better than comedy. His female characters, which have been found fault with as insipid, are the finest in the world. Lastly, Shakspeare was the least of a coxcomb of any one that ever lived, and much of a gentleman.

## IV

# THE CHARACTERS OF SHAKSPEARE'S PLAYS

## CYMBELINE

CYMBELINE is one of the most delightful of Shakspeare's historical plays. It may be considered as a dramatic romance, in which the most striking parts of the story are thrown into the form of a dialogue, and the intermediate circumstances are explained by the different speakers, as occasion renders necessary. The action is less concentrated in consequence; but the interest becomes more aerial and refined from the principle of perspective introduced into the subject by the imaginary changes of scene, as well as by the length of time it occupies. The reading of this play is like going a journey with some uncertain object at the end of it, and in which the suspense is kept up and heightened by the long intervals between each action. Though the events are scattered over such an extent of surface, and relate to such a variety of characters, yet the links which bind the different interests of the story together are never entirely broken. The most straggling and seemingly casual incidents are contrived in such a manner as to lead at last to the most complete developement of the catastrophe. The ease and conscious unconcern with which this is effected only makes the skill more wonderful. The business of the plot evidently thickens in the last act: the story moves forward with increasing rapidity at every step; its various ramifications are drawn from the most distant points to the same centre; the principal characters are brought together, and placed in very critical situations; and the fate of almost every person in the drama is made to depend on the solution of a single circumstance—the answer of Iachimo to the question of Imogen respecting the obtaining of the ring from Posthumus. Dr. Johnson is of opinion that Shakspeare was generally inattentive to the winding-up of his plots. We think the contrary is true; and we might cite in proof of this remark not only the present play, but the conclusion of *Lear,* of *Romeo and Juliet,* of *Macbeth,* of *Othello,* even of *Hamlet,* and of other plays of less moment, in which the last act is crowded with decisive events brought about by natural and striking means.

The pathos in Cymbeline is not violent or tragical, but of the most pleasing and amiable kind. A certain tender gloom overspreads the whole. Posthumus is the ostensible hero of the piece, but its greatest charm is the character of Imogen. Posthumus is only interesting from the interest she takes in him; and she is only interesting herself from her tenderness and constancy to her husband. It is the peculiar excellence of Shakspeare's heroines, that they seem to exist only in their attachment to others. They are pure abstractions of the affections. We think as little of their persons as they do themselves, because we are let into the secrets of their hearts, which are more important. We are too much interested in their affairs to stop to look at their faces, except by stealth and at intervals. No one ever hit the true perfection of the female character, the sense of weakness leaning on the strength of its affections for support, so well as Shakspeare—no one ever so well painted natural tenderness free from affectation and disguise—no one else ever so well shewed how delicacy and timidity, when driven to extremity, grow romantic and extravagant; for the romance of his heroines (in which they abound) is only an excess of the habitual prejudices of their sex, scrupulous of being false to their vows, truant to their affections, and taught by the force of feeling when to forego the forms of propriety for the essence of it. His women were in this respect exquisite logicians; for there is nothing so logical as passion. They knew their own minds exactly; and only followed up a favourite purpose, which they had sworn to with their tongues, and which was engraven on their hearts, into its untoward consequences. They were the prettiest little set of martyrs and confessors on record.—Cibber, in speaking of the early English stage, accounts for the want of prominence and theatrical display in Shakspeare's female characters from the circumstance, that women in those days were not allowed to play the parts of women, which made it necessary to keep them a good deal in the back-ground. Does not this state of manners itself, which prevented their exhibiting themselves in public, and confined them to the relations and charities of domestic life, afford a truer explanation of the matter? His women are certainly very unlike stage-heroines; the reverse of tragedy-queens.

We have almost as great an affection for Imogen as she had for Posthumus; and she deserves it better. Of all Shakspeare's women she is perhaps the most tender and the most artless. Her incredulity in the opening scene with Iachimo, as to her husband's infidelity, is much the same as Desdemona's backwardness to believe Othello's jealousy. Her answer to the most distressing part of the picture is only, " My lord, I fear, has forgot Britain." Her readiness to pardon Iachimo's false imputations and his designs against herself, is a good lesson to prudes; and may shew that where there is a real attachment to virtue, it has no need to bolster itself up with an outrageous or affected antipathy to vice. The scene in which Pisanio

gives Imogen his master's letter, accusing her of incon-
tinency on the treacherous suggestions of Iachimo, is as
touching as it is possible for anything to be:—

> "*Pisanio.* What cheer, Madam?
> *Imogen.* False to his bed! What is it to be false?
> To lie in watch there, and to think on him?
> To weep 'twixt clock and clock? If sleep charge nature,
> To break it with a fearful dream of him,
> And cry myself awake? That's false to 's bed, is it?
> *Pisanio.* Alas, good lady!
> *Imogen.* I false? thy conscience witness, Iachimo,
> Thou didst accuse him of incontinency,
> Thou then look'dst like a villain: now methinks,
> Thy favour's good enough. Some Jay of Italy,
> Whose mother was her painting, hath betray'd him:
> Poor I am stale, a garment out of fashion,
> And for I am richer than to hang by th' walls,
> I must be ript; to pieces with me. Oh,
> Men's vows are women's traitors. All good seeming
> By thy revolt, oh husband, shall be thought
> Put on for villainy: not born where't grows,
> But worn a bait for ladies.
> *Pisanio.* Good Madam, hear me—
> *Imogen.* Talk thy tongue weary, speak:
> I have heard I am a strumpet, and mine ear,
> Therein false struck, can take no greater wound,
> Nor tent to bottom that."——

When Pisanio, who had been charged to kill his mistress, puts her in a way to live, she says,

> "Why, good fellow,
> What shall I do the while? Where bide? How live?
> Or in my life what comfort, when I am
> Dead to my husband?"

Yet when he advises her to disguise herself in boy's
clothes, and suggests "a course pretty and full in view,"
by which she may "happily be near the residence of Posthumus," she exclaims,

> " Oh, for such means,
> Though peril to my modesty, not death on't,
> I would adventure."

And when Pisanio, enlarging on the consequences, tells
her she must change

> ——" Fear and niceness,
> The handmaids of all women, or more truly,
> Woman its pretty self, into a waggish courage,
> Ready in gibes, quick-answer'd, saucy, and
> As quarrellous as the weazel "——

she interrupts him hastily :—

> " Nay, be brief;
> I see into thy end, and am almost
> A man already."

In her journey thus disguised to Milford-Haven, she
loses her guide and her way; and unbosoming her complaints, says beautifully—

> ——" My dear lord,
> Thou art one of the false ones; now I think on thee,
> My hunger's gone; but even before, I was
> At point to sink for food."

She afterwards finds, as she thinks, the dead body of
Posthumus, and engages herself as a foot-boy to serve a
Roman officer, when she has done all due obsequies to him
whom she calls her former master—

> ——" And when
> With wild wood-leaves and weeds I ha' strew'd his grave,
> And on it said a century of pray'rs,
> Such as I can, twice o'er, I'll weep and sigh,
> And leaving so his service, follow you,
> So please you entertain me."

Now this is the very religion of love.  She all along
relies little on her personal charms, which she fears may

have been eclipsed by some painted Jay of Italy; she relies
on her merit, and her merit is in the depth of her love,
her truth and constancy.   Our admiration of her beauty
is excited with as little consciousness as possible on her
part.   There are two delicious descriptions given of her,
one when she is asleep, and one when she is supposed dead.
Arviragus thus addresses her—

> ——" With fairest flowers,
> While summer lasts, and I live here, Fidele,
> I'll sweeten thy sad grave; thou shalt not lack
> The flow'r that's like thy face, pale primrose, nor
> The azur'd hare-bell, like thy veins, no, nor
> The leaf of eglantine, which not to slander,
> Out-sweeten'd not thy breath."

The yellow Iachimo gives another thus, when he steals
into her bedchamber:—

> ——" Cytherea,
> How bravely thou becom'st thy bed!  Fresh lily,
> And whiter than the sheets!  That I might touch—
> But kiss, one kiss—'Tis her breathing that
> Perfumes the chamber thus: the flame o' th' taper
> Bows toward her, and would under-peep her lids
> To see th' enclosed lights now canopied
> Under the windows, white and azure, laced
> With blue of Heav'ns own tinct—on her left breast
> A mole cinque-spotted, like the crimson drops
> I' th' bottom of a cowslip."

There is a moral sense in the proud beauty of this last
image, a rich surfeit of the fancy,—as that well-known
passage beginning, " Me of my lawful pleasure she restrained, and prayed me oft forbearance," sets a keener
edge upon it by the inimitable picture of modesty and self-
denial.

The character of Cloten, the conceited, booby lord, and
rejected lover of Imogen, though not very agreeable in

itself, and at present obsolete, is drawn with much humour and quaint extravagance. The description which Imogen gives of his unwelcome addresses to her—" Whose love-suit hath been to me as fearful as a siege "—is enough to cure the most ridiculous lover of his folly. It is remarkable that though Cloten makes so poor a figure in love, he is described as assuming an air of consequence as the Queen's son in a council of state, and with all the absurdity of his person and manners, is not without shrewdness in his observations. So true is it that folly is as often owing to a want of proper sentiments as to a want of understanding! The exclamation of the ancient critic—Oh Menander and Nature, which of you copied from the other! would not be misapplied to Shakspeare.

The other characters in this play are represented with great truth and accuracy, and as it happens in most of the author's works, there is not only the utmost keeping in each separate character; but in the casting of the different parts, and their relation to one another, there is an affinity and harmony, like what we may observe in the gradations of colour in a picture. The striking and powerful contrasts in which Shakspeare abounds could not escape observation; but the use he makes of the principle of analogy to reconcile the greatest diversities of character and to maintain a continuity of feeling throughout, has not been sufficiently attended to. In CYMBELINE, for instance, the principal interest arises out of the unalterable fidelity of Imogen to her husband under the most trying circumstances. Now the other parts of the picture are filled up with subordinate examples of the same feeling, variously modified by different situations, and applied to the purposes of virtue or vice. The plot is aided by the amorous importunities of Cloten, by the persevering determination of Iachimo to conceal the defeat of his project by a daring imposture: the faithful attachment of Pisanio to his mistress is an affecting accompaniment to the whole; the obstinate adherence to his purpose in Bellarius, who keeps the fate of the young princes so long a secret in resentment for the ungrateful return to his former services, the incorrigible wickedness of the Queen, and even the blind uxorious confidence of Cymbeline, are all so many lines of the same story, tending to the same point. The effect of this coincidence is rather felt than observed; and as the impression exists unconsciously in the mind of the reader, so it probably arose in the same manner in the mind of the author, not from design, but from the force of natural association, a particular train of thought suggesting different inflections of the same predominant feeling, melting into, and strengthening one another, like chords in music.

The characters of Bellarius, Guiderius, and Arviragus, and the romantic scenes in which they appear, are a fine relief to the intrigues and artificial refinements of the court from which they are banished. Nothing can surpass the wildness and simplicity of the descriptions of the mountain life they lead. They follow the business of huntsmen, not of shepherds; and this is in keeping with the spirit of adventure and uncertainty in the rest of the story, and with the scenes in which they are afterwards called on to act. How admirably the youthful fire and impatience to emerge from their obscurity in the young princes is opposed to the cooler calculations and prudent resignation of their more experienced counsellor! How well the disadvantages of knowledge and of ignorance, of solitude and society, are placed against each other!

" *Guiderius.*   Out of your proof you speak: we poor unfledg'd
Have never wing'd from view o' th' nest; nor know not
What air's from home.   Haply this life is best,
If quiet life is best; sweeter to you

That have a sharper known; well corresponding
With your stiff age: but unto us it is
A cell of ignorance; travelling a-bed,
A prison for a debtor, that not dares
To stride a limit.
　　*Arviragus.* What should we speak of
When we are old as you? When we shall hear
The rain and wind beat dark December! How,
In this our pinching cave, shall we discourse
The freezing hours away? We have seen nothing.
We are beastly; subtle as the fox for prey,
Like warlike as the wolf for what we eat:
Our valour is to chase what flies; our cage
We make a quire, as doth the prison'd bird,
And sing our bondage freely."

The answer of Bellarius to this expostulation is hardly
satisfactory; for nothing can be an answer to hope, or the
passion of the mind for unknown good, but experience.—
The forest of Arden in *As you like it* can alone compare
with the mountain scenes in CYMBELINE: yet how different
the contemplative quiet of the one from the enterprising
boldness and precarious mode of subsistence in the other!
Shakspeare not only lets us into the minds of his characters, but gives a tone and colour to the scenes he describes
from the feelings of their supposed inhabitants. He at the
same time preserves the utmost propriety of action and passion, and gives all their local accompaniments. If he was
equal to the greatest things, he was not above an attention
to the smallest. Thus the gallant sportsmen in CYMBELINE
have to encounter the abrupt declivities of hill and valley:
Touchstone and Audrey jog along a level path. The deer
in CYMBELINE are only regarded as objects of prey, " The
game's a-foot," etc.—with Jaques they are fine subjects to
moralise upon at leisure, " under the shade of melancholy
boughs."

We cannot take leave of this play, which is a favourite
with us, without noticing some occasional touches of nat-

ural piety and morality.   We may allude here to the opening of the scene in which Bellarius instructs the young
princes to pay their orisons to heaven:

> ——"See, boys! this gate
> Instructs you how t' adore the Heav'ns; and bows you
> To morning's holy office.
> *Guiderius.*   Hail, Heav'n!
> *Arviragus.*   Hail, Heav'n!
> *Bellarius.*   Now for our mountain-sport, up to yon hill."

What a grace and unaffected spirit of piety breathes in
this passage!   In like manner, one of the brothers says to
the other, when about to perform the funeral rites to
Fidele,

> " Nay, Cadwall, we must lay his head to the east;
> My Father hath a reason for't "—

—as if some allusion to the doctrines of the Christian faith
had been casually dropped in conversation by the old man,
and had been no farther inquired into.

Shakspeare's morality is introduced in the same simple,
unobtrusive manner.   Imogen will not let her companions
stay away from the chase to attend her when sick, and
gives her reason for it—

> " Stick to your journal course; *the breach of custom*
> *Is breach of all!* "

When the Queen attempts to disguise her motives for
procuring the poison from Cornelius, by saying she means
to try its effects on " creatures not worth the hanging,"
his answer conveys at once a tacit reproof of her hypocrisy,
and a useful lesson of humanity—

> ——"Your Highness
> Shall from this practice but make hard your heart."

## MACBETH

> "The poet's eye in a fine frenzy rolling
> Doth glance from heaven to earth, from earth to heaven;
> And as imagination bodies forth
> The forms of things unknown, the poet's pen
> Turns them to shape, and gives to airy nothing
> A local habitation and a name."

MACBETH and *Lear, Othello* and *Hamlet,* are usually reckoned Shakspeare's four principal tragedies. *Lear* stands first for the profound intensity of the passion; *Macbeth* for the wildness of the imagination and the rapidity of the action; *Othello* for the progressive interest and powerful alternations of feeling: *Hamlet* for the refined development of thought and sentiment. If the force of genius shewn in each of these works is astonishing, their variety is not less so. They are like different creations of the same mind, not one of which has the slightest reference to the rest. This distinctness and originality is indeed the necessary consequence of truth and nature. Shakspeare's genius alone appeared to possess the resources of nature. He is " your only *tragedy-maker."* His plays have the force of things upon the mind. What he represents is brought home to the bosom as a part of our experience, implanted in the memory as if we had known the places, persons, and things of which he treats. MACBETH is like a record of a preternatural and tragical event. It has the rugged severity of an old chronicle with all that the imagination of the poet can engraft upon traditional belief. The castle of Macbeth, round which " the air smells wooingly," and where " the temple-haunting martlet builds," has a real subsistence in the mind; the Weird Sisters meet us in person on " the blasted heath;" the " air-drawn dagger " moves slowly before our eyes; the " gracious Dun-

can," the "blood-boultered Banquo" stand before us; all
that passed through the mind of Macbeth passes, without
the loss of a tittle, through our's.   All that could actually
take place, and all that is only possible to be conceived, what
was said and what was done, the workings of passion, the
spells of magic, are brought before us with the same absolute truth and vividness.—Shakspeare excelled in the open-
ings of his plays: that of MACBETH is the most striking of
any.   The wildness of the scenery, the sudden shifting of
the situations and characters, the bustle, the expectations
excited, are equally extraordinary.   From the first entrance
of the Witches and the description of them when they meet
Macbeth,

> ——"What are these
> So wither'd and so wild in their attire,
> That look not like the inhabitants of th' earth
> And yet are on't?"

the mind is prepared for all that follows.

This tragedy is alike distinguished for the lofty imagination it displays, and for the tumultuous vehemence of the
action; and the one is made the moving principle of the
other.   The overwhelming pressure of preternatural agency
urges on the tide of human passion with redoubled force.
Macbeth himself appears driven along by the violence of
his fate like a vessel drifting before a storm: he reels to
and fro like a drunken man; he staggers under the weight
of his own purposes and the suggestions of others; he
stands at bay with his situation; and from the superstitious
awe and breathless suspense into which the communications
of the Weird Sisters throw him, is hurried on with daring
impatience to verify their predictions, and with impious and
bloody hand to tear aside the veil which hides the uncertainty of the future.   He is not equal to the struggle with
fate and conscience.   He now "bends up each corporal

instrument to the terrible feat;" at other times his heart
misgives him, and he is cowed and abashed by his success.
"The deed, no less than the attempt, confounds him." His
mind is assailed by the stings of remorse, and full of
"preternatural solicitings." His speeches and soliloquies
are dark riddles on human life, baffling solution, and en-
tangling him in their labyrinths. In thought he is absent
and perplexed, sudden and desperate in act, from a distrust
of his own resolution. His energy springs from the anxiety and agitation of his mind. His blindly rushing forward on the objects of his ambition and revenge, or his
recoiling from them, equally betrays the harassed state of
his feelings.—This part of his character is admirably set
off by being brought in connection with that of Lady Macbeth, whose obdurate strength of will and masculine firmness give her the ascendancy over her husband's faultering
virtue. She at once seizes on the opportunity that offers
for the accomplishment of all their wished-for greatness,
and never flinches from her object till all is over. The
magnitude of her resolution almost covers the magnitude
of her guilt. She is a great bad woman, whom we hate,
but whom we fear more than we hate. She does not excite
our loathing and abhorrence like Regan and Gonerill. She
is only wicked to gain a great end; and is perhaps more
distinguished by her commanding presence of mind and
inexorable self-will, which do not suffer her to be diverted
from a bad purpose, when once formed, by weak and
womanly regrets, than by the hardness of her heart or want
of natural affections. The impression which her lofty determination of character makes on the mind of Macbeth is well
described where he exclaims,

> ——"Bring forth men children only;
> For thy undaunted mettle should compose
> Nothing but males!"

Nor do the pains she is at to "screw his courage to the sticking-place," the reproach to him, not to be "lost so poorly in himself," the assurance that "a little water clears them of this deed," shew anything but her greater consistency in depravity. Her strong-nerved ambition furnishes ribs of steel to "the sides of his intent;" and she is herself wound up to the execution of her baneful project with the same unshrinking fortitude in crime, that in other circumstances she would probably have shewn patience in suffering. The deliberate sacrifice of all other considerations to the gaining "for their future days and nights sole sovereign sway and masterdom," by the murder of Duncan, is gorgeously expressed in her invocation on hearing of "his fatal entrance under her battlements:" —

> ——"Come all you spirits
> That tend on mortal thoughts, unsex me here:
> And fill me, from the crown to th' toe, top-full
> Of direst cruelty; make thick my blood,
> Stop up the access and passage to remorse,
> That no compunctious visitings of nature
> Shake my fell purpose, nor keep peace between
> The effect and it. Come to my woman's breasts,
> And take my milk for gall, you murthering ministers,
> Wherever in your sightless substances
> You wait on nature's mischief. Come, thick night!
> And pall thee in the dunnest smoke of hell,
> That my keen knife see not the wound it makes,
> Nor heav'n peep through the blanket of the dark,
> To cry, hold, hold!"——

When she first hears that "Duncan comes there to sleep" she is so overcome by the news, which is beyond her utmost expectations, that she answers the messenger, "Thou'rt mad to say it:" and on receiving her husband's account of the predictions of the Witches, conscious of his instability of purpose, and that her presence is necessary to goad him on to the consummation of his promised greatness, she exclaims—

>———" Hie thee hither,
> That I may pour my spirits in thine ear,
> And chastise with the valour of my tongue
> All that impedes thee from the golden round,
> Which fate and metaphysical aid doth seem
> To have thee crowned withal."

This swelling exultation and keen spirit of triumph, this uncontroulable eagerness of anticipation, which seems to dilate her form and take possession of all her faculties, this solid, substantial flesh and blood display of passion, exhibit a striking contrast to the cold, abstracted, gratuitous, servile malignity of the Witches, who are equally instrumental in urging Macbeth to his fate for the mere love of mischief, and from a disinterested delight in deformity and cruelty. They are hags of mischief, obscene panders to iniquity, malicious from their impotence of enjoyment, enamoured of destruction, because they are themselves unreal, abortive, half-existences—who become sublime from their exemption from all human sympathies and contempt for all human affairs, as Lady Macbeth does by the force of passion! Her fault seems to have been an excess of that strong principle of self-interest and family aggrandisement, not amenable to the common feelings of compassion and justice, which is so marked a feature in barbarous nations and times. A passing reflection of this kind, on the resemblance of the sleeping king to her father, alone prevents her from slaying Duncan with her own hand.

In speaking of the character of Lady Macbeth, we ought not to pass over Mrs. Siddons's manner of acting that part. We can conceive of nothing grander. It was something above nature. It seemed almost as if a being of a superior order had dropped from a higher sphere to awe the world

with the majesty of her appearance. Power was seated on
her brow, passion emanated from her breast as from a
shrine; she was tragedy personified. In coming on in the
sleeping-scene, her eyes were open, but their sense was
shut. She was like a person bewildered and unconscious
of what she did. Her lips moved involuntarily—all her
gestures were involuntary and mechanical. She glided on
and off the stage like an apparition. To have seen her in
that character was an event in every one's life, not to be
forgotten.

The dramatic beauty of the character of Duncan, which
excites the respect and pity even of his murderers, has
been often pointed out. It forms a picture of itself. An
instance of the author's power of giving a striking effect
to a common reflection, by the manner of introducing it,
occurs in a speech of Duncan, complaining of his having
been deceived in his opinion of the Thane of Cawdor, at
the very moment that he is expressing the most unbounded
confidence in the loyalty and services of Macbeth.

> " There is no art
> To find the mind's construction in the face :
> He was a gentleman, on whom I built
> An absolute trust.
> O worthiest cousin, (*addressing himself to Macbeth.*)
> The sin of my Ingratitude e'en now
> Was great upon me," etc.

Another passage to shew that Shakspeare lost sight of
nothing that could in any way give relief or heightening
to his subject, is the conversation which takes place between
Banquo and Fleance immediately before the murder-scene
of Duncan.

> " *Banquo.*   How goes the night, boy?
> *Fleance.*   The moon is down: I have not heard the clock.
> *Banquo.*   And she goes down at twelve.
> *Fleance.*   I take't, 'tis later, Sir.

> *Banquo.* Hold, take my sword. There's husbandry in heav'n,
> Their candles are all out.—
> A heavy summons lies like lead upon me,
> And yet I would not sleep: Merciful Powers,
> Restrain in me the cursed thoughts that nature
> Gives way to in repose."

In like manner, a fine idea is given of the gloomy coming on of evening, just as Banquo is going to be assassinated.

> " Light thickens and the crow
> Makes wing to the rooky wood."
> .    .    .    .    .    .
> " Now spurs the lated traveller apace
> To gain the timely inn."

MACBETH (generally speaking) is done upon a stronger and more systematic principle of contrast than any other of Shakspeare's plays.   It moves upon the verge of an abyss, and is a constant struggle between life and death. The action is desperate and the reaction is dreadful.   It is a huddling together of fierce extremes, a war of opposite natures which of them shall destroy the other.   There is nothing but what has a violent end or violent beginnings. The lights and shades are laid on with a determined hand; the transitions from triumph to despair, from the height of terror to the repose of death, are sudden and startling; every passion brings in its fellow-contrary, and the thoughts pitch and jostle against each other as in the dark.   The whole play is an unruly chaos of strange and forbidden things, where the ground rocks under our feet.   Shakspeare's genius here took its full swing, and trod upon the farthest bounds of nature and passion.   This circumstance will account for the abruptness and violent antitheses of the style, the throes and labour which run through the expression, and from defects will turn them into beauties.   " So

fair and foul a day I have not seen," etc.  "Such welcome
and unwelcome news together."  "Men's lives are like the
flowers in their caps, dying or ere they sicken."  "Look
like the innocent flower, but be the serpent under it."  The
scene before the castle-gate follows the appearance of the
Witches on the heath, and is followed by a midnight murder.
Duncan is cut off betimes by treason leagued with witch-
craft, and Macduff is ripped untimely from his mother's
womb to avenge his death.  Macbeth, after the death of
Banquo, wishes for his presence in extravagant terms, " To
him and all we thirst," and when his ghost appears, cries
out, "Avaunt and quit my sight," and being gone, he is
"himself again."  Macbeth resolves to get rid of Macduff,
that "he may sleep in spite of thunder;" and cheers his
wife on the doubtful intelligence of Banquo's taking-off
with the encouragement—"Then be thou jocund: ere the
bat has flown his cloistered flight; ere to black Hecate's
summons the shard-born beetle has rung night's yawning peal, there shall be done—a deed of dreadful note."
In Lady Macbeth's speech "Had he not resembled my
father as he slept, I had done 't," there is murder and filial
piety together; and in urging him to fulfil his vengeance
against the defenceless king, her thoughts spare the blood
neither of infants nor old age.  The description of the
Witches is full of the same contradictory principle; they
"rejoice when good kings bleed," they are neither of the
earth nor the air, but both; they "should be women, but
their beards forbid it;" they take all the pains possible to
lead Macbeth on to the height of his ambition, only to
betray him "in deeper consequence," and after showing
him all the pomp of their art, discover their malignant delight in his disappointed hopes, by that bitter taunt, "Why
stands Macbeth thus amazedly?"  We might multiply such
instances every where.

The leading features in the character of Macbeth are striking enough, and they form what may be thought at first only a bold, rude, Gothic outline.  By comparing it with other characters of the same author we shall perceive the absolute truth and identity which is observed in the midst of the giddy whirl and rapid career of events.  Macbeth in Shakspeare no more loses his identity of character in the fluctuations of fortune or the storm of passion, than Macbeth in himself would have lost the identity of his person. Thus he is as distinct a being from Richard III. as it is possible to imagine, though these two characters in common hands, and indeed in the hands of any other poet, would have been a repetition of the same general idea, more or less exaggerated.  For both are tyrants, usurpers, murderers, both aspiring and ambitious, both courageous, cruel, treacherous.  But Richard is cruel from nature and constitution.  Macbeth becomes so from accidental circumstances. Richard is from his birth deformed in body and mind, and naturally incapable of good.  Macbeth is full of " the milk of human kindness," is frank, sociable, generous.  He is tempted to the commission of guilt by golden opportunities, by the instigations of his wife, and by prophetic warnings. Fate and metaphysical aid conspire against his virtue and his loyalty.  Richard on the contrary needs no prompter, but wades through a series of crimes to the height of his ambition from the ungovernable violence of his temper and a reckless love of mischief.  He is never gay but in the prospect or in the success of his villainies: Macbeth is full of horror at the thoughts of the murder of Duncan, which he is with difficulty prevailed on to commit, and of remorse after its perpetration.  Richard has no mixture of common humanity in his composition, no regard to kindred or posterity, he owns no fellowship with others, he is " himself alone."  Macbeth is not destitute of feelings of sympathy, is accessible to pity, is even made in some measure the dupe of his uxoriousness, ranks the loss of friends, of the cordial love of his followers, and of his good name, among the causes which have made him weary of life, and regrets that he has ever seized the crown by unjust means, since he cannot transmit it to his posterity—

> "For Banquo's issue have I fil'd my mind—
> For them the gracious Duncan have I murther'd,
> To make them kings, the seed of Banquo kings."

In the agitation of his mind, he envies those whom he has sent to peace. "Duncan is in his grave; after life's fitful fever he sleeps well."—It is true, he becomes more callous as he plunges deeper in guilt, "direness is thus rendered familiar to his slaughterous thoughts," and he in the end anticipates his wife in the boldness and bloodiness of his enterprises, while she for want of the same stimulus of action, "is troubled with thick-coming fancies that rob her of her rest," goes mad and dies. Macbeth endeavours to escape from reflection on his crimes by repelling their consequences, and banishes remorse for the past by the meditation of future mischief. This is not the principle of Richard's cruelty, which displays the wanton malice of a fiend as much as the frailty of human passion. Macbeth is goaded on to acts of violence and retaliation by necessity; to Richard, blood is a pastime.—There are other decisive differences inherent in the two characters. Richard may be regarded as a man of the world, a plotting, hardened knave, wholly regardless of everything but his own ends, and the means to secure them.—Not so Macbeth. The superstitions of the age, the rude state of society, the local scenery and customs, all give a wildness and imaginary grandeur to his character. From the strangeness of the events that surround him, he is full of amazement and fear;

and stands in doubt between the world of reality and the world of fancy. He sees sights not shewn to mortal eye, and hears unearthly music. All is tumult and disorder within and without his mind; his purposes recoil upon himself, are broken and disjointed; he is the double thrall of his passions and his evil destiny. Richard is not a character either of imagination or pathos, but of pure self-will. There is no conflict of opposite feelings in his breast. The apparitions which he sees only haunt him in his sleep; nor does he live like Macbeth in a waking dream. Macbeth has considerable energy and manliness of character; but then he is "subject to all the skyey influences." He is sure of nothing but the present moment. Richard in the busy turbulence of his projects never loses his self-possession, and makes use of every circumstance that happens as an instrument of his long-reaching designs. In his last extremity we can only regard him as a wild beast taken in the toils: while we never entirely lose our concern for Macbeth; and he calls back all our sympathy by that fine close of thoughtful melancholy,

> "My way of life is fallen into the sear,
> The yellow leaf; and that which should accompany old age,
> As honour, troops of friends, I must not look to have;
> But in their stead, curses not loud but deep,
> Mouth-honour, breath, which the poor heart
> Would fain deny, and dare not."

We can conceive a common actor to play Richard tolerably well; we can conceive no one to play Macbeth properly, or to look like a man that had encountered the Weird Sisters. All the actors that we have ever seen, appear as if they had encountered them on the boards of Coventgarden or Drury-lane, but not on the heath at Fores, and as if they did not believe what they had seen. The Witches of MACBETH indeed are ridiculous on the modern stage, and we doubt if the Furies of Æschylus would be more respected. The progress of manners and knowledge has an influence on the stage, and will in time perhaps destroy both tragedy and comedy. Filch's picking pockets in the *Beggar's Opera* is not so good a jest as it used to be: by the force of the police and of philosophy, Lillo's murders and the ghosts in Shakspeare will become obsolete. At last, there will be nothing left, good nor bad, to be desired or dreaded, on the theatre or in real life.—A question has been started with respect to the originality of Shakspeare's witches, which has been well answered by Mr. Lamb in his notes to the " Specimens of Early Dramatic Poetry."

" Though some resemblance may be traced between the charms in MACBETH, and the incantations in this play, (The Witch of Middleton) which is supposed to have preceded it, this coincidence will not detract much from the originality of Shakspeare. His Witches are distinguished from the Witches of Middleton by essential differences. These are creatures to whom man or woman plotting some dire mischief might resort for occasional consultation. Those originate deeds of blood, and begin bad impulses to men. From the moment that their eyes first meet with Macbeth's, he is spell-bound. That meeting sways his destiny. He can never break the fascination. These Witches can hurt the body; those have power over the soul.—Hecate in Middleton has a son, a low buffoon: the hags of Shakspeare have neither child of their own, nor seem to be descended from any parent. They are foul anomalies, of whom we know not whence they are sprung, nor whether they have beginning or ending. As they are without human passions, so they seem to be without human relations. They come with thunder and lightning, and vanish to airy music. This is all we know of them.—Except Hecate, they have no names, which heightens their mysteriousness. The names, and some of the properties which Middleton has given to his hags, excite smiles. The Weird Sisters are serious things. Their presence cannot co-exist with mirth. But, in a lesser degree, the Witches of Middleton are fine creations. Their power too is, in some measure, over the mind. They raise jars, jealousies, strifes, *like a thick scurf o'er life.*"

## IAGO

The character of Iago is one of the supererogations of Shakspeare's genius. Some persons, more nice than wise, have thought this whole character unnatural, because his villainy is *without a sufficient motive.* Shakspeare, who was as good a philosopher as he was a poet, thought otherwise. He knew that the love of power, which is another name for the love of mischief, is natural to man. He would know this as well or better than if it had been demonstrated to him by a logical diagram, merely from seeing children paddle in the dirt or kill flies for sport. Iago in fact belongs to a class of character, common to Shakspeare and at the same time peculiar to him; whose heads are as acute and active as their hearts are hard and callous. Iago is to be sure an extreme instance of the kind; that is to say, of diseased intellectual activity, with the most perfect indifference to moral good or evil, or rather with a decided preference of the latter, because it falls more readily in with his favourite propensity, gives greater zest to his thoughts and scope to his actions. He is quite or nearly as indifferent to his own fate as to that of others; he runs all risks for a trifling and doubtful advantage; and is himself the dupe and victim of his ruling passion—an insatiable craving after action of the most difficult and dangerous kind. " Our ancient " is a philosopher, who fancies that a lie that kills has more point in it than an alliteration or an antithesis; who thinks a fatal experiment on the peace of a family a better thing than watching the palpitations in the heart of a flea in a microscope; who plots the ruin of his friends as an exercise for his ingenuity, and stabs men in the dark to prevent *ennui.* His gaiety, such as it is, arises from the success of his treachery; his ease from the torture he has inflicted on others. He is an amateur of tragedy in real life; and instead of employing his invention on imaginary characters, or long-forgotten incidents, he takes the bolder and more desperate course of getting up his plot at home, casts the principal parts among his nearest friends and connections, and rehearses it in downright earnest, with steady nerves and unabated resolution. We will just give an illustration or two.

One of his most characteristic speeches is that immediately after the marriage of Othello.

> "*Roderigo*.   What a full fortune does the thick lips owe,
> If he can carry her thus!
> *Iago*.   Call up her father:
> Rouse him (*Othello*) make after him, poison his delight,
> Proclaim him in the streets, incense her kinsmen,
> And tho' he in a fertile climate dwell,
> Plague him with flies: tho' that his joy be joy,
> Yet throw such changes of vexation on it,
> As it may lose some colour."

In the next passage, his imagination runs riot in the mischief he is plotting, and breaks out into the wildness and impetuosity of real enthusiasm.

> "*Roderigo*.   Here is her father's house: I'll call aloud.
> *Iago*.   Do, with like timourous accent and dire yell
> As when, by night and negligence, the fire
> Is spied in populous cities."

One of his most favourite topics, on which he is rich indeed, and in descanting on which his spleen serves him for a Muse, is the disproportionate match between Desdemona and the Moor. This is a clue to the character of the lady which he is by no means ready to part with. It is brought forward in the first scene, and he recurs to it, when in answer to his insinuations against Desdemona, Roderigo says,

"I cannot believe that in her—she's full of most blest conditions.
*Iago.*  Bless'd fig's end.  The wine she drinks is made of grapes.
If she had been blest, she would never have married the Moor."

And again with still more spirit and fatal effect afterwards, when he turns this very suggestion arising in Othello's own breast to her prejudice.

"*Othello.*  And yet how nature erring from itself—
*Iago.*  Ay, there's the point;—as to be bold with you,
Not to affect many proposed matches
Of her own clime, complexion, and degree," etc.

This is probing to the quick.  Iago here turns the character of poor Desdemona, as it were, inside out.  It is certain that nothing but the genius of Shakspeare could have preserved the entire interest and delicacy of the part, and have even drawn an additional elegance and dignity from the peculiar circumstances in which she is placed.—The habitual licentiousness of Iago's conversation is not to be traced to the pleasure he takes in gross or lascivious images, but to his desire of finding out the worst side of everything, and of proving himself an over-match for appearances.  He has none of "the milk of human kindness" in his composition.  His imagination rejects everything that has not a strong infusion of the most unpalatable ingredients; his mind digests only poisons.  Virtue or goodness or whatever has the least "relish of salvation in it," is, to his depraved appetite, sickly and insipid: and he even resents the good opinion entertained of his own integrity, as if it were an affront cast on the masculine sense and spirit of his character.  Thus at the meeting between Othello and Desdemona, he exclaims—"Oh, you are well tuned now: but I'll set down the pegs that make this music, *as honest as I am*"—his character of *bonhommie* not sitting at all easy upon him.  In the scenes, where he tries to work Othello to his purpose, he is proportionably guarded, insidious, dark, and deliberate. We believe nothing ever came up to the profound dissimulation and dextrous artifice of the well-known dialogue in the third act, where he first enters upon the execution of his design.

> "*Iago.*  My noble lord.
> *Othello.*  What dost thou say, Iago?
> *Iago.*  Did Michael Cassio,
> When you woo'd my lady, know of your love?
> *Othello.*  He did from first to last.
> Why dost thou ask?
> *Iago.*  But for a satisfaction of my thought,
> No further harm.
> *Othello.*  Why of thy thought, Iago?
> *Iago.*  I did not think he had been acquainted with it.
> *Othello.*  O yes, and went between us very oft—
> *Iago.*  Indeed!
> *Othello.*  Indeed? Ay, indeed. Discern'st thou aught of that?
> Is he not honest?
> *Iago.*  Honest, my lord?
> *Othello.*  Honest? Ay, honest.
> *Iago.*  My lord, for aught I know.
> *Othello.*  What do'st thou think?
> *Iago.*  Think, my lord!
> *Othello.*  Think, my lord! Alas, thou echo'st me,
> As if there was some monster in thy thought
> Too hideous to be shewn."—

The stops and breaks, the deep workings of treachery under the mask of love and honesty, the anxious watchfulness, the cool earnestness, and if we may so say, the *passion* of hypocrisy, marked in every line, receive their last finishing in that inconceivable burst of pretended indignation at Othello's doubts of his sincerity.

> "O grace! O Heaven forgive me!
> Are you a man? Have you a soul or sense?
> God be wi' you; take mine office. O wretched fool,
> That lov'st to make thine honesty a vice!
> Oh monstrous world! Take note, take note, O world!
> To be direct and honest, is not safe.

> I thank you for this profit, and from hence
> I'll love no friend, since love breeds such offence."

If Iago is detestable enough when he has business on his hands and all his engines at work, he is still worse when he has nothing to do, and we only see into the hollowness of his heart. His indifference when Othello falls into a swoon, is perfectly diabolical.

> "*Iago.* How is it, General? Have you not hurt your head?
> *Othello.* Do'st thou mock me?
> *Iago.* I mock you not, by Heaven," etc.

The part indeed would hardly be tolerated, even as a foil to the virtue and generosity of the other characters in the play, but for its indefatigable industry and inexhaustible resources, which divert the attention of the spectator (as well as his own) from the end he has in view to the means by which it must be accomplished.—Edmund the Bastard in *Lear* is something of the same character, placed in less prominent circumstances. Zanga is a vulgar caricature of it.

## HAMLET

This is that Hamlet the Dane, whom we read of in our youth, and whom we may be said almost to remember in our after-years; he who made that famous soliloquy on life, who gave the advice to the players, who thought " this goodly frame, the earth, a steril promontory, and this brave o'er-hanging firmament, the air, this majestical roof fretted with golden fire, a foul and pestilent congregation of vapours;" whom " man delighted not, nor woman neither;" he who talked with the grave-diggers, and moralised on Yorick's skull; the school-fellow of Rosencrans and

Guildenstern at Wittenberg; the friend of Horatio; the lover of Ophelia; he that was mad and sent to England; the slow avenger of his father's death; who lived at the court of Horwendillus five hundred years before we were born, but all whose thoughts we seem to know as well as we do our own, because we have read them in Shakspeare.

Hamlet is a name; his speeches and sayings but the idle coinage of the poet's brain. What then, are they not real? They are as real as our own thoughts. Their reality is in the reader's mind. It is *we* who are Hamlet. This play has a prophetic truth, which is above that of history. Whoever has become thoughtful and melancholy through his own mishaps or those of others; whoever has borne about with him the clouded brow of reflection, and thought himself " too much i' th' sun; " whoever has seen the golden lamp of day dimmed by envious mists rising in his own breast, and could find in the world before him only a dull blank with nothing left remarkable in it; whoever has known " the pangs of despised love, the insolence of office, or the spurns which patient merit of the unworthy takes; " he who has felt his mind sink within him, and sadness cling to his heart like a malady, who has had his hopes blighted and his youth staggered by the apparitions of strange things; who cannot be well at ease, while he sees evil hovering near him like a spectre; whose powers of action have been eaten up by thought, he to whom the universe seems infinite, and himself nothing; whose bitterness of soul makes him careless of consequences, and who goes to a play as his best resource to shove off, to a second remove, the evils of life by a mock representation of them—this is the true Hamlet.

We have been so used to this tragedy that we hardly know how to criticise it any more than we should know how to describe our own faces. But we must make such observations as we can. It is the one of Shakspeare's plays that we think of the oftenest, because it abounds most in striking reflections on human life, and because the distresses of Hamlet are transferred, by the turn of his mind, to the general account of humanity. Whatever happens to him we apply to ourselves, because he applies it so himself as a means of general reasoning.. He is a great moraliser; and what makes him worth attending to is, that he moralises on his own feelings and experience. He is not a common-place pedant. If *Lear* is distinguished by the greatest depth of passion, HAMLET is the most remarkable for the ingenuity, originality, and unstudied developement of character. Shakspeare had more magnanimity than any other poet, and he has shewn more of it in this play than in any other. There is no attempt to force an interest: everything is left for time and circumstances to unfold. The attention is excited without effort, the incidents succeed each other as matters of course, the characters think and speak and act just as they might do, if left entirely to themselves. There is no set purpose, no straining at a point. The observations are suggested by the passing scene—the gusts of passion come and go like sounds of music borne on the wind. The whole play is an exact transcript of what might be supposed to have taken place at the court of Denmark, at the remote period of time fixed upon, before the modern refinements in morals and manners were heard of. It would have been interesting enough to have been admitted as a by-stander in such a scene, at such a time, to have heard and witnessed something of what was going on. But here we are more than spectators. We have not only "the outward pageants and the signs of grief;" but "we have that within which passes shew." We read the thoughts of the heart, we catch the passions living as they rise. Other dramatic writers give us very fine versions and paraphrases of nature; but Shakspeare, together with his own comments, gives us the original text, that we may judge for ourselves. This is a very great advantage.

The character of Hamlet stands quite by itself. It is not a character marked by strength of will or even of passion, but by refinement of thought and sentiment. Hamlet is as little of the hero as a man can well be: but he is a young and princely novice, full of high enthusiasm and quick sensibility—the sport of circumstances, questioning with fortune and refining on his own feelings, and forced from the natural bias of his disposition by the strangeness of his situation. He seems incapable of deliberate action, and is only hurried into extremities on the spur of the occasion, when he has no time to reflect, as in the scene where he kills Polonius, and again, where he alters the letters which Rosencrans and Guildenstern are taking with them to England, purporting his death. At other times, when he is most bound to act, he remains puzzled, undecided, and sceptical, dallies with his purposes, till the occasion is lost, and finds out some pretence to relapse into indolence and thoughtfulness again. For this reason he refuses to kill the King when he is at his prayers, and by a refinement in malice, which is in truth only an excuse for his own want of resolution, defers his revenge to a more fatal opportunity, when he shall be engaged in some act "that has no relish of salvation in it."

> "He kneels and prays,
> And now I'll do't, and so he goes to heaven,
> And so am I reveng'd: *that would be scann'd.*
> He kill'd my father, and for that,
> I, his sole son, send him to heaven.
> Why this is reward, not revenge.
> Up sword and know thou a more horrid time,
> When he is drunk, asleep, or in a rage."

He is the prince of philosophical speculators; and because he cannot have his revenge perfect, according to the most refined idea his wish can form, he declines it altogether. So he scruples to trust the suggestions of the ghost, contrives the scene of the play to have surer proof of his uncle's guilt, and then rests satisfied with this confirmation of his suspicions, and the success of his experiment, instead of acting upon it. Yet he is sensible of his own weakness, taxes himself with it, and tries to reason himself out of it.

> "How all occasions do inform against me,
> And spur my dull revenge! What is a man,
> If his chief good and market of his time
> Be but to sleep and feed? A beast; no more.
> Sure he that made us with such large discourse,
> Looking before and after, gave us not
> That capability and·god-like reason
> To rust in us unus'd. Now whether it be
> Bestial oblivion, or some craven scruple
> Of thinking too precisely on th' event,—
> A thought which quarter'd, hath but one part wisdom,
> And ever three parts coward;—I do not know
> Why yet I live to say, this thing's to do;
> Sith I have cause, and will, and strength, and means
> To do it. Examples gross as earth exhort me:
> Witness this army of such mass and charge,
> Led by a delicate and tender prince,
> Whose spirit with divine ambition puff'd,
> Makes mouths at the invisible event,
> Exposing what is mortal and unsure
> To all that fortune, death, and danger dare,
> Even for an egg-shell. 'Tis not to be great
> Never to stir without great argument;
> But greatly to find quarrel in a straw,
> When honour's at the stake. How stand I then,
> That have a father kill'd, a mother stain'd,
> Excitements of my reason and my blood,
> And let all sleep, while to my shame I see
> The imminent death of twenty thousand men,
> That for a fantasy and trick of fame,
> Go to their graves like beds, fight for a plot
> Whereon the numbers cannot try the cause,

Which is not tomb enough and continent
To hide the slain?—O, from this time forth,
My thoughts be bloody or be nothing worth."

Still he does nothing; and this very speculation on his
own infirmity only affords him another occasion for indulging it.  It is not from any want of attachment to his
father or of abhorrence of his murder that Hamlet is thus
dilatory, but it is more to his taste to indulge his imagination in reflecting upon the enormity of the crime and refining
on his schemes of vengeance, than to put them into immediate practice.  His ruling passion is to think, not to act:
and any vague pretext that flatters this propensity instantly
diverts him from his previous purposes.

The moral perfection of this character has been called
in question, we think, by those who did not understand it.
It is more interesting than according to rules; amiable,
though not faultless.  The ethical delineations of " that noble
and liberal casuist " (as Shakspeare has been well called)
do not exhibit the drab-coloured quakerism of morality.
His plays are not copied either from The Whole Duty of
Man, or from The Academy of Compliments!  We confess
we are a little shocked at the want of refinement in those
who are shocked at the want of refinement in Hamlet.
The neglect of punctilious exactness in his behaviour either
partakes of the " licence of the time," or else belongs to
the very excess of intellectual refinement in the character,
which makes the common rules of life, as well as his own
purposes, sit loose upon him.  He may be said to be amenable only to the tribunal of his own thoughts, and is too
much taken up with the airy world of contemplation to lay
as much stress as he ought on the practical consequences
of things.  His habitual principles of action are unhinged
and out of joint with the time.  His conduct to Ophelia
is quite natural in his circumstances.  It is that of assumed

severity only. It is the effect of disappointed hope, of bitter regrets, of affection suspended, not obliterated, by the distractions of the scene around him! Amidst the natural and preternatural horrors of his situation, he might be excused in delicacy from carrying on a regular courtship. When "his father's spirit was in arms," it was not a time for the son to make love in. He could neither marry Ophelia, nor wound her mind by explaining the cause of his alienation, which he durst hardly trust himself to think of. It would have taken him years to have come to a direct explanation on the point. In the harassed state of his mind, he could not have done much otherwise than he did. His conduct does not contradict what he says when he sees her funeral,

> "I loved Ophelia: forty thousand brothers
> Could not with all their quantity of love
> Make up my sum."

Nothing can be more affecting or beautiful than the Queen's apostrophe to Ophelia on throwing the flowers into the grave.

> ——"Sweets to the sweet, farewell.
> I hop'd thou should'st have been my Hamlet's wife:
> I thought thy bride-bed to have deck'd, sweet maid,
> And not have strew'd thy grave."

Shakspeare was thoroughly a master of the mixed motives of human character, and he here shews us the Queen, who was so criminal in some respects, not without sensibility and affection in other relations of life.—Ophelia is a character almost too exquisitely touching to be dwelt upon. Oh rose of May, oh flower too soon faded! Her love, her madness, her death, are described with the truest touches of tenderness and pathos. It is a character which nobody but Shakspeare could have drawn in the way that he has done, and to the conception of which there is not even the smallest approach, except in some of the old romantic ballads.*  Her brother, Laertes, is a character we do not like so well: he is too hot and choleric, and somewhat rhodomontade.  Polonius is a perfect character in its kind; nor is there any foundation for the objections which have been made to the consistency of this part.  It is said that he acts very foolishly and talks very sensibly. There is no inconsistency in that.  Again, that he talks wisely at one time and foolishly at another; that his advice to Laertes is very excellent, and his advice to the King and Queen on the subject of Hamlet's madness very ridiculous.  But he gives the one as a father, and is sincere in it; he gives the other as a mere courtier, a busy-body, and is accordingly officious, garrulous, and impertinent.  In short, Shakspeare has been accused of inconsistency in this and other characters, only because he has kept up the distinction which there is in nature, between the understandings and the moral habits of men, between the absurdity of their ideas and the absurdity of their motives.  Polonius is not a fool, but he makes himself so.  His folly, whether in his actions or speeches, comes under the head of impropriety of intention.

We do not like to see our author's plays acted, and least of all, HAMLET.  There is no play that suffers so much in being transferred to the stage.  Hamlet himself seems hardly

---

* In the account of her death, a friend has pointed out an instance of the poet's exact observation of nature :—
     "There is a willow growing o'er a brook,
     That shews its hoary leaves i' th' glassy stream."
The inside of the leaves of the willow, next the water, is of a whitish colour, and the reflection would therefore be "hoary."

capable of being acted. Mr. Kemble unavoidably fails in
this character from a want of ease and variety. The character of Hamlet is made up of undulating lines; it has
the yielding flexibility of " a wave o' th' sea." Mr. Kemble
plays it like a man in armour, with a determined inveteracy
of purpose, in one undeviating straight line, which is as
remote from the natural grace and refined susceptibility of
the character, as the sharp angles and abrupt starts which
Mr. Kean introduces into the part. Mr. Kean's Hamlet
is as much too splenetic and rash as Mr. Kemble's is too
deliberate and formal. His manner is too strong and
pointed. He throws a severity, approaching to virulence,
into the common observations and answers. There is nothing of this in Hamlet. He is, as it were, wrapped up
in his reflections, and only *thinks aloud*. There should
therefore be no attempt to impress what he says upon others
by a studied exaggeration of emphasis or manner; no *talking at* his hearers. There should be as much of the gentleman and scholar as possible infused into the part, and
as little of the actor. A pensive air of sadness should sit
reluctantly upon his brow, but no appearance of fixed and
sullen gloom. He is full of weakness and melancholy, but
there is no harshness in his nature. He is the most amiable of misanthropes.

## ROMEO AND JULIET

ROMEO AND JULIET is the only tragedy which Shakspeare
has written entirely on a love-story. It is supposed to have
been his first play, and it deserves to stand in that proud
rank. There is the buoyant spirit of youth in every line,
in the rapturous intoxication of hope, and in the bitterness
of despair. It has been said of ROMEO AND JULIET by a
great critic, that " whatever is most intoxicating in the

odour of a southern spring, languishing in the song of the nightingale, or voluptuous in the first opening of the rose, is to be found in this poem." The description is true; and yet it does not answer to our idea of the play. For if it has the sweetness of the rose, it has its freshness too; if it has the languor of the nightingale's song, it has also its giddy transport; if it has the softness of a southern spring, it is as glowing and as bright. There is nothing of a sickly and sentimental cast. Romeo and Juliet are in love, but they are not love-sick. Everything speaks the very soul of pleasure, the high and healthy pulse of the passions: the heart beats, the blood circulates and mantles throughout. Their courtship is not an insipid interchange of sentiments lip-deep, learnt at second-hand from poems and plays,—made up of beauties of the most shadowy kind, of " fancies wan that hang the pensive head," of evanescent smiles, and sighs that breathe not, of delicacy that shrinks from the touch, and feebleness that scarce supports itself, an elaborate vacuity of thought, and an artificial dearth of sense, spirit, truth, and nature! It is the reverse of all this. It is Shakspeare all over, and Shakspeare when he was young.

## MIDSUMMER NIGHT'S DREAM

Puck, or Robin Goodfellow, is the leader of the fairy band. He is the Ariel of the MIDSUMMER NIGHT'S DREAM; and yet as unlike as can be to the Ariel in the *Tempest*. No other poet could have made two such different characters out of the same fanciful materials and situations. Ariel is a minister of retribution, who is touched with the sense of pity at the woes he inflicts. Puck is a mad-cap sprite, full of wantonness and mischief, who laughs at those whom he misleads—" Lord, what fools

these mortals be!'" Ariel cleaves the air, and executes
his mission with the zeal of a winged messenger; Puck is
borne along on his fairy errand like the light and glittering
gossamer before the breeze. He is, indeed, a most Epicurean little gentleman, dealing in quaint devices, and faring
in dainty delights. Prospero and his world of spirits are
a set of moralists: but with Oberon and his fairies we are
launched at once into the empire of the butterflies. How
beautifully is this race of beings contrasted with the men
and women actors in the scene, by a single epithet which
Titania gives to the latter, "the human mortals"! It is
astonishing that Shakspeare should be considered, not only
by foreigners, but by many of our own critics, as a gloomy
and heavy writer, who painted nothing but "gorgons and
hydras, and chimeras dire." His subtlety exceeds that
of all other dramatic writers, insomuch that a celebrated
person of the present day said that he regarded him rather
as a metaphysician than a poet. His delicacy and sportive
gaiety are infinite. In the MIDSUMMER NIGHT'S DREAM
alone, we should imagine, there is more sweetness and
beauty of description than in the whole range of French
poetry put together. What we mean is this, that we will
produce out of that single play ten passages, to which we
do not think any ten passages in the works of the French
poets can be opposed, displaying equal fancy and imagery.
Shall we mention the remonstrance of Helena to Hermia,
or Titania's description of her fairy train, or her disputes
with Oberon about the Indian boy, or Puck's account of
himself and his employments, or the Fairy Queen's exhorta-
tion to the elves to pay due attendance upon her favourite,
Bottom; or Hippolita's description of a chace, or Theseus's
answer? The two last are as heroical and spirited as the
others are full of luscious tenderness. The reading of this
play is like wandering in a grove by moonlight: the de-

scriptions breathe a sweetness like odours thrown from beds of flowers. . . .

The MIDSUMMER NIGHT'S DREAM, when acted, is converted from a delightful fiction into a dull pantomime. All that is finest in the play is lost in the representation. The spectacle was grand; but the spirit was evaporated, the genius was fled.—Poetry and the stage do not agree well together. The attempt to reconcile them in this instance fails not only of effect, but of decorum. The *ideal* can have no place upon the stage, which is a picture without perspective: everything there is in the fore-ground. That which was merely an airy shape, a dream, a passing thought, immediately becomes an unmanageable reality. Where all is left to the imagination (as is the case in reading) every circumstance, near or remote, has an equal chance of being kept in mind, and tells accordingly to the mixed impression of all that has been suggested. But the imagination cannot sufficiently qualify the actual impressions of the senses. Any offence given to the eye is not to be got rid of by explanation. Thus Bottom's head in the play is a fantastic illusion, produced by magic spells: on the stage it is an ass's head, and nothing more; certainly a very strange costume for a gentleman to appear in. Fancy cannot be embodied any more than a simile can be painted; and it is as idle to attempt it as to personate *Wall* or *Moonshine*. Fairies are not incredible, but fairies six feet high are so. Monsters are not shocking, if they are seen at a proper distance. When ghosts appear at mid-day, when apparitions stalk along Cheapside, then may the MIDSUMMER NIGHT'S DREAM be represented without injury at Coventgarden or at Drury-lane. The boards of a theatre and the regions of fancy are not the same thing.

## FALSTAFF

If Shakspeare's fondness for the ludicrous sometimes
led to faults in his tragedies (which was not often the
case) he has made us amends by the character of Falstaff.
This is perhaps the most substantial comic character that
ever was invented. Sir John carries a most portly presence
in the mind's eye; and in him, not to speak it profanely,
" we behold the fulness of the spirit of wit and humour
bodily." We are as well acquainted with his person as
his mind, and his jokes come upon us with double force
and relish from the quantity of flesh through which they
make their way, as he shakes his fat sides with laughter,
or " lards the lean earth as he walks along." Other comic
characters seem, if we approach and handle them, to resolve
themselves into air, " into thin air; " but this is embodied
and palpable to the grossest apprehension: it lies "three
fingers deep upon the ribs," it plays about the lungs and
the diaphragm with all the force of animal enjoyment.
His body is like a good estate to his mind, from which he
receives rents and revenues of profit and pleasure in kind,
according to its extent, and the richness of the soil. Wit
is often a meagre substitute for pleasurable sensation; an
effusion of spleen and petty spite at the comforts of others,
from feeling none in itself. Falstaff's wit is an emanation
of a fine constitution; an exuberance of good-humour and
good-nature; an overflowing of his love of laughter and
good-fellowship; a giving vent to his heart's ease, and over-
contentment with himself and others. He would not be
in character, if he were not so fat as he is; for there is
the greatest keeping in the boundless luxury of his imagination and the pampered self-indulgence of his physical appetites. He manures and nourishes his mind with jests,
as he does his body with sack and sugar. He carves out

his jokes, as he would a capon or a haunch of venison, where there is *cut and come again;* and pours out upon them the oil of gladness. His tongue drops fatness, and in the chambers of his brain " it snows of meat and drink." He keeps up perpetual holiday and open house, and we live with him in a round of invitations to a rump and dozen.—Yet we are not to suppose that he was a mere sensualist. All this is as much in imagination as in reality. His sensuality does not engross and stupify his other faculties, but "ascends me into the brain, clears away all the dull, crude vapours that environ it, and makes it full of nimble, fiery, and delectable shapes." His imagination keeps up the ball after his senses have done with it. He seems to have even a greater enjoyment of the freedom from restraint, of good cheer, of his ease, of his vanity, in the ideal exaggerated description which he gives of them, than in fact. He never fails to enrich his discourse with allusions to eating and drinking, but we never see him at table. He carries his own larder about with him, and he is himself " a tun of man." His pulling out the bottle in the field of battle is a joke to shew his contempt for glory accompanied with danger, his systematic adherence to his Epicurean philosophy in the most trying circumstances. Again, such is his deliberate exaggeration of his own vices, that it does not seem quite certain whether the account of his hostess's bill, found in his pocket, with such an out-of-the-way charge for capons and sack with only one halfpenny-worth of bread, was not put there by himself as a trick to humour the jest upon his favourite propensities, and as a conscious caricature of himself. He is represented as a liar, a braggart, a coward, a glutton, etc. and yet we are not offended but delighted with him; for he is all these as much to amuse others as to gratify himself. He openly assumes all these characters to shew

the humourous part of them. The unrestrained indulgence
of his own ease, appetites, and convenience, has neither
malice nor hypocrisy in it. In a word, he is an actor in
himself almost as much as upon the stage, and we no more
object to the character of Falstaff in a moral point of view
than we should think of bringing an excellent comedian,
who should represent him to the life, before one
of the police offices. We only consider the number of
pleasant lights in which he puts certain foibles (the more
pleasant as they are opposed to the received rules and
necessary restraints of society) and do not trouble ourselves
about the consequences resulting from them, for no mis-
chievous consequences do result. Sir John is old as well
as fat, which gives a melancholy retrospective tinge to the
character; and by the disparity between his inclinations and
his capacity for enjoyment, makes it still more ludicrous
and fantastical.

The secret of Falstaff's wit is for the most part a masterly presence of mind, an absolute self-possession, which
nothing can disturb. His repartees are involuntary suggestions of his self-love; instinctive evasions of everything that
threatens to interrupt the career of his triumphant jollity and
self-complacency. His very size floats him out of all his
difficulties in a sea of rich conceits; and he turns round on
the pivot of his convenience, with every occasion and at
a moment's warning. His natural repugnance to every
unpleasant thought or circumstance, of itself makes light of
objections, and provokes the most extravagant and licentious answers in his own justification. His indifference to
truth puts no check upon his invention, and the more improbable and unexpected his contrivances are, the more
happily does he seem to be delivered of them, the anticipation of their effect acting as a stimulus to the gaiety of
his fancy. The success of one adventurous sally gives him

spirits to undertake another: he deals always in round.
numbers, and his exaggerations and excuses are "open,
palpable, monstrous as the father that begets them." His
dissolute carelessness of what he says discovers itself in
the first dialogue with the Prince.

> "*Falstaff.* By the lord, thou say'st true, lad; and is not mine
> hostess of the tavern a most sweet wench?
> *P. Henry.* As the honey of Hibla, my old lad of the castle;
> and is not a buff-jerkin a most sweet robe of durance?
> *Falstaff.* How now, how now, mad wag, what in thy quips and
> thy quiddities? what a plague have I to do with a buff-jerkin?
> *P. Henry.* Why, what a pox have I to do with mine hostess
> of the tavern?"

In the same scene he afterwards affects melancholy, from
pure satisfaction of heart, and professes reform, because
it is the farthest thing in the world from his thoughts. He
has no qualms of conscience, and therefore would as soon
talk of them as of anything else when the humour takes
him.

> "*Falstaff.* But Hal, I pr'ythee trouble me no more with vanity.
> I would to God thou and I knew where a commodity of good
> names were to be bought: an old lord of council rated me the
> other day in the street about you, sir; but I mark'd him not, and
> yet he talked very wisely, and in the street too.
> *P. Henry.* Thou didst well, for wisdom cries out in the street,
> and no man regards it.
> *Falstaff.* O, thou hast damnable iteration, and art indeed able
> to corrupt a saint. Thou hast done much harm unto me, Hal;
> God forgive thee for it. Before I knew thee, Hal, I knew nothing,
> and now I am, if a man should speak truly, little better than one
> of the wicked. I must give over this life, and I will give it over,
> by the Lord; an I do not, I am a villain. I'll be damned for never
> a king's son in Christendom.
> *P. Henry.* Where shall we take a purse to-morrow, Jack?
> *Falstaff.* Where thou wilt, lad, I'll make one; an I do not, call
> me villain, and baffle me.

*P. Henry.* I see good amendment of life in thee, from praying to purse-taking.
*Falstaff.* Why, Hal, 'tis my vocation, Hal. 'Tis no sin for a man to labour in his vocation."

Of the other prominent passages, his account of his pretended resistance to the robbers, " who grew from four men in buckram into eleven " as the imagination of his own valour increased with his relating it, his getting off when the truth is discovered by pretending he knew the Prince, the scene in which in the person of the old king he lectures the prince and gives himself a good character, the soliloquy on honour, and description of his new-raised recruits, his meeting with the chief justice, his abuse of the Prince and Poins, who overhear him, to Doll Tearsheet, his reconciliation with Mrs. Quickly who has arrested him for an old debt, and whom he persuades to pawn her plate to lend him ten pounds more, and the scenes with Shallow and Silence, are all inimitable. Of all of them, the scene in which Falstaff plays the part, first, of the King, and then of Prince Henry, is the one that has been the most often quoted. We must quote it once more in illustration of our remarks.

" *Falstaff.* Harry, I do not only marvel where thou spendest thy time, but also how thou art accompanied: for though the camomile, the more it is trodden on, the faster it grows, yet youth, the more it is wasted, the sooner it wears. That thou art my son, I have partly thy mother's word, partly my own opinion; but chiefly, a villainous trick of thine eye, and a foolish hanging of thy nether lip, that doth warrant me. If then thou be son to me, here lies the point;——Why, being son to me, art thou so pointed at? Shall the blessed sun of heaven prove a micher, and eat blackberries? A question not to be ask'd. Shall the son of England prove a thief, and take purses? a question to be ask'd. There is a thing, Harry, which thou hast often heard of, and it is known to many in our land by the name of pitch: this pitch, as ancient writers do report, doth defile; so doth the company thou keepest: for, Harry, now I do not speak to thee in drink, but in tears; not in pleasure, but in passion; not in words only, but in woes also:—and yet there is a virtuous man, whom I have often noted in thy company, but I know not his name.

*P. Henry.* What manner of man, an it like your majesty?

*Falstaff.* A goodly portly man, i'faith, and a corpulent; of a cheerful look, a pleasing eye, and a most noble carriage; and, as I think, his age some fifty, or, by'r-lady, inclining to threescore; and now I do remember me, his name is Falstaff: if that man should be lewdly given, he deceiveth me; for, Harry, I see virtue in his looks. If then the fruit may be known by the tree, as the tree by the fruit, then peremptorily I speak it, there is virtue in that Falstaff: him keep with, the rest banish. And tell me now, thou naughty varlet, tell me, where hast thou been this month?

*P. Henry.* Dost thou speak like a king? Do thou stand for me, and I'll play my father.

*Falstaff.* Depose me? if thou dost it half so gravely, so majestically, both in word and matter, hang me up by the heels for a rabbit-sucker, or a poulterer's hare.

*P. Henry.* Well, here I am set.

*Falstaff.* And here I stand:—judge, my masters.

*P. Henry.* Now, Harry, whence come you?

*Falstaff.* My noble lord, from Eastcheap.

*P. Henry.* The complaints I hear of thee are grievous.

*Falstaff.* S'blood, my lord, they are false:—nay, I'll tickle ye for a young prince, i'faith.

*P. Henry.* Swearest thou, ungracious boy? henceforth ne'er look on me. Thou art violently carried away from grace: there is a devil haunts thee, in the likeness of a fat old man; a tun of man is thy companion. Why dost thou converse with that trunk of humours, that bolting-hutch of beastliness, that swoln parcel of dropsies, that huge bombard of sack, that stuft cloak-bag of guts, that roasted Manning-tree ox with the pudding in his belly, that reverend vice, that grey iniquity, that father ruffian, that vanity in years? wherein is he good, but to taste sack and drink it? wherein neat and cleanly, but to carve a capon and eat it? wherein cunning, but in craft? wherein crafty, but in villainy? wherein villainous, but in all things? wherein worthy, but in nothing?

*Falstaff.* I would, your grace would take me with you; whom means your grace?

*P. Henry.* That villainous, abominable mis-leader of youth, Falstaff, that old white-bearded Satan.

*Falstaff.* My lord, the man I know.

*P. Henry.* I know thou dost.

*Falstaff.* But to say, I know more harm in him than in myself, were to say more than I know. That he is old (the more the pity) his white hairs do witness it: but that he is (saving your reverence) a whore-master, that I utterly deny. If sack and sugar be a fault, God help the wicked! if to be old and merry be a sin, then many an old host that I know is damned: if to be fat be to be hated, then Pharoah's lean kine are to be loved. No, my good lord; banish Peto, banish Bardolph, banish Poins:· but for sweet Jack Falstaff, kind Jack Falstaff, true Jack Falstaff, valiant Jack Falstaff, and therefore more valiant, being as he is, old Jack Falstaff, banish not him thy Harry's company; banish plump Jack, and banish all the world.

*P. Henry.* I do, I will.

[*Knocking; and Hostess and Bardolph go out.*

*Re-enter* BARDOLPH, *running.*

*Bardolph.* O, my lord, my lord; the sheriff, with a most monstrous watch, is at the door.

*Falstaff.* Out, you rogue! play out the play: I have much to say in the behalf of that Falstaff."

One of the most characteristic descriptions of Sir John is that which Mrs. Quickly gives of him when he asks her " What is the gross sum that I owe thee? "

" *Hostess.* Marry, if thou wert an honest man, thyself, and the money too. Thou didst swear to me upon a parcel-gilt goblet, sitting in my Dolphin-ҫhamber, at the round table, by a sea-coal fire on Wednesday in Whitsun-week, when the Prince broke thy head for likening his father to a singing man of Windsor; thou didst swear to me then, as I was washing thy wound, to marry me, and make me my lady thy wife. Canst thou deny it? Did not goodwife Keech, the butcher's wife, come in then, and call me gossip Quickly? coming in to borrow a mess of vinegar; telling us, she had a good dish of prawns; whereby thou didst desire to eat some; whereby I told thee they were ill for a green wound? And didst thou not, when she was gone down stairs, desire me to be no more so familiarity with such poor people; saying, that ere long they should call me madam? And didst thou not kiss me, and bid me fetch thee thirty shillings? I put thee now to thy book-oath; deny it, if thou canst."

This scene is to us the most convincing proof of Falstaff's power of gaining over the good will of those he was familiar with, except indeed Bardolph's somewhat profane exclamation on hearing the account of his death, "Would I were with him, wheresoe'er he is, whether in heaven or hell."

One of the topics of exulting superiority over others most common in Sir John's mouth is his corpulence and the exterior marks of good living which he carries about him, thus "turning his vices into commodity." He accounts for the friendship between the Prince and Poins, from "their legs being both of a bigness;" and compares Justice Shallow to "a man made after supper of a cheese-paring." There cannot be a more striking gradation of character than that beween Falstaff and Shallow, and Shallow and Silence. It seems difficult at first to fall lower than the squire; but this fool, great as he is, finds an admirer and humble foil in his cousin Silence. Vain of his acquaintance with Sir John, who makes a butt of him, he exclaims, "Would, cousin Silence, that thou had'st seen that which this knight and I have seen!"—"Aye, Master Shallow, we have heard the chimes at midnight," says Sir John. To Falstaff's observation, "I did not think Master Silence had been a man of this mettle," Silence answers, "Who, I? I have been merry twice and once ere now." What an idea is here conveyed of a prodigality of living? What good husbandry and economical self-denial in his pleasures? What a stock of lively recollections? It is curious that Shakspeare has ridiculed in Justice Shallow, who was "in some authority under the king," that disposition to unmeaning tautology which is the regal infirmity of later times, and which, it may be supposed, he acquired from talking to his cousin Silence, and receiving no answers.

"*Falstaff.* You have here a goodly dwelling, and a rich.
*Shallow.* Barren, barren, barren; beggars all, beggars all, Sir John: marry, good air. Spread Davy, spread Davy. Well said, Davy.

*Falstaff.* This Davy serves you for good uses.
*Shallow.* A good varlet, a good varlet, a very good varlet. By
the mass, I have drunk too much sack at supper. A good varlet.
Now sit down, now sit down. Come, cousin."

The true spirit of humanity, the thorough knowledge
of the stuff we are made of, the practical wisdom with
the seeming fooleries in the whole of the garden-scene at
Shallow's country-seat, and just before in the exquisite dialogue between him and Silence on the death of old Double,
have no parallel anywhere else. In one point of view, they
are laughable in the extreme; in another they are equally
affecting, if it is affecting to shew *what a little thing is
human life,* what a poor forked creature man is!

## TWELFTH NIGHT; OR, WHAT YOU WILL

This is justly considered as one of the most delightful
of Shakspeare's comedies. It is full of sweetness and pleasantry. It is perhaps too good-natured for comedy. It has
little satire, and no spleen. It aims at the ludicrous rather
than the ridiculous. It makes us laugh at the follies of
mankind, not despise them, and still less bear any ill-will
towards them. Shakspeare's comic genius resembles the
bee rather in its power of extracting sweets from weeds
or poisons, than in leaving a sting behind it. He gives the
most amusing exaggeration of the prevailing foibles of his
characters, but in a way that they themselves, instead of
being offended at, would almost join in to humour; he
rather contrives opportunities for them to shew themselves
off in the happiest lights, than renders them contemptible
in the perverse construction of the wit or malice of others.—
There is a certain stage of society in which people become
conscious of their peculiarities and absurdities, affect to
disguise what they are, and set up pretensions to what they

are not. This gives rise to a corresponding style of comedy, the object of which is to detect the disguises of self-love, and to make reprisals on these preposterous assumptions of vanity, by marking the contrast between the real and the affected character as severely as possible, and denying to those, who would impose on us for what they are not, even the merit which they have. This is the comedy of artificial life, of wit and satire, such as we see it in Congreve, Wycherley, Vanburgh, etc. To this succeeds a state of society from which the same sort of affectation and pretence are banished by a greater knowledge of the world or by their successful exposure on the stage; and which by neutralising the materials of comic character, both natural and artificial, leaves no comedy at all—but *the sentimental*. Such is our modern comedy. There is a period in the progress of manners anterior to both these, in which the foibles and follies of individuals are of nature's planting, not the growth of art or study; in which they are therefore unconscious of them themselves, or care not who knows them, if they can but have their whim out; and in which, as there is no attempt at imposition, the spectators rather receive pleasure from humouring the inclinations of the persons they laugh at, than wish to give them pain by exposing their absurdity. This may be called the comedy of nature, and it is the comedy which we generally find in Shakspeare.—Whether the analysis here given be just or not, the spirit of his comedies is evidently quite distinct from that of the authors above mentioned, as it is in its essence the same with that of Cervantes, and also very frequently of Molière, though he was more systematic in his extravagance than Shakspeare. Shakspeare's comedy is of a pastoral and poetical cast. Folly is indigenous to the soil, and shoots out with native, happy, unchecked luxuriance. Absurdity has every encouragement afforded

it; and nonsense has room to flourish in. Nothing is
stunted by the churlish, icy hand of indifference or severity.
The poet runs riot in a conceit, and idolises a quibble. His
whole object is to turn the meanest or rudest objects to
a pleasurable account. The relish which he has of a pun,
or of the quaint humour of a low character, does not inter-
fere with the delight with which he describes a beautiful
image, or the most refined love. The Clown's forced jests
do not spoil the sweetness of the character of Viola; the
same house is big enough to hold Malvolio, the Countess,
Maria, Sir Toby, and Sir Andrew Ague-cheek. For instance, nothing can fall much lower than this last character
in intellect or morals: yet how are his weaknesses nursed
and dandled by Sir Toby into something " high fantastical,"
when on Sir Andrew's commendation of himself for
dancing and fencing, Sir Toby answers—" Wherefore are
these things hid? Wherefore have these gifts a curtain
before them? Are they like to take dust like mistress
Moll's picture? Why dost thou not go to church in a
galliard, and come home in a coranto? My very walk
should be a jig! I would not so much as make water but
in a cinque-pace. What dost thou mean? Is this a world
to hide virtues in? I did think by the excellent constitution of thy leg, it was framed under the star of a galliard!"
—How Sir Toby, Sir Andrew, and the Clown afterwards
*chirp over their cups,* how they " rouse the night-owl in
a catch, able to draw three souls out of one weaver!"
What can be better than Sir Toby's unanswerable answer
to Malvolio, " Dost thou think because thou art virtuous,
there shall be no more cakes and ale?"—In a word, the
best turn is given to everything, instead of the worst.
There is a constant infusion of the romantic and enthusiastic, in proportion as the characters are natural and sincere: whereas, in the more artificial style of comedy, every-

thing gives way to ridicule and indifference, there being
nothing left but affectation on one side, and incredulity on
the other.—Much as we like Shakspeare's comedies, we
cannot agree with Dr. Johnson that they are better than
his tragedies; nor do we like them half so well.  If his
inclination to comedy sometimes led him to trifle with the
seriousness of tragedy, the poetical and impassioned passages are the best parts of his comedies.  The great and
secret charm of TWELFTH NIGHT is the character of Viola.
Much as we like catches and cakes and ale, there is something that we like better.  We have a friendship for Sir
Toby; we patronise Sir Andrew; we have an understanding
with the Clown, a sneaking kindness for Maria and her
rogueries; we feel a regard for Malvolio, and sympathise
with his gravity, his smiles, his cross garters, his yellow
stockings, and imprisonment in the stocks.  But there is
something that excites in us a stronger feeling than all
this—it is Viola's confession of her love.

> "*Duke.*  What's her history?
> *Viola.*  *A blank, my lord, she never told her love:*
> She let concealment, like a worm i' th' bud,
> Feed on her damask cheek: she pin'd in thought,
> And with a green and yellow melancholy,
> She sat like Patience on a monument,
> Smiling at grief. *Was not this love indeed?*
> We men may say more, swear more, but indeed,
> Our shews are more than will; for still we prove
> Much in our vows, but little in our love.
> *Duke.*  But died thy sister of her love, my boy?
> *Viola.*  I am all the daughters of my father's house,
> And all the brothers too;—and yet I know not."—

Shakspeare alone could describe the effect of his own
poetry.

> "Oh, it came o'er the ear like the sweet south
> That breathes upon a bank of violets,
> Stealing and giving odour."

What we so much admire here is not the image of Patience on a monument, which has been generally quoted, but the lines before and after it. " They give a very echo to the seat where love is throned." How long ago it is since we first learnt to repeat them; and still, still they vibrate on the heart, like the sounds which the passing wind draws from the trembling strings of a harp left on some desert shore! There are other passages of not less impassioned sweetness. Such is Olivia's address to Sebastian, whom she supposes to have already deceived her in a promise of marriage.

> " Blame not this haste of mine: if you mean well,
> Now go with me and with this holy man
> Into the chantry by: there before him,
> And underneath that consecrated roof,
> Plight me the full assurance of your faith,
> *That my most jealous and too doubtful soul*
> *May live at peace."*

# V

## MILTON

SHAKSPEARE discovers in his writings little religious enthusiasm, and an indifference to personal reputation; he
had none of the bigotry of his age, and his political prejudices were not very strong. In these respects, as well as
in every other, he formed a direct contrast to Milton. Milton's works are a perpetual invocation to the Muses; a
hymn to Fame. He had his thoughts constantly fixed on
the contemplation of the Hebrew theocracy, and of a perfect
commonwealth; and he seized the pen with a hand just
warm from the touch of the ark of faith. His religious
zeal infused its character into his imagination; so that he
devotes himself with the same sense of duty to the cultivation of his genius, as he did to the exercise of virtue, or
the good of his country. The spirit of the poet, the patriot,
and the prophet, vied with each other in his breast. His
mind appears to have held equal communion with the inspired writers, and with the bards and sages of ancient
Greece and Rome;—

> "Blind Thamyris, and blind Mæonides,
> And Tiresias, and Phineus, prophets old."

He had a high standard, with which he was always comparing himself, nothing short of which could satisfy his
jealous ambition. He thought of nobler forms and nobler
things than those he found about him. He lived apart, in
the solitude of his own thoughts, carefully excluding from

his mind whatever might distract its purposes, or alloy its
purity, or damp its zeal. "With darkness and with dangers
compassed round," he had the mighty models of antiquity
always present to his thoughts, and determined to raise a
monument of equal height and glory, "piling up every stone
of lustre from the brook," for the delight and wonder of
posterity. He had girded himself up, and as it were, sancti-
fied his genius to this service from his youth. "For after,"
he says, "I had from my first years, by the ceaseless dili-
gence and care of my father, been exercised to the tongues,
and some sciences as my age could suffer, by sundry masters and teachers, it was found that whether aught was
imposed upon me by them, or betaken to of my own choice,
the style by certain vital signs it had, was likely to live;
but much latelier, in the private academies of Italy, per-
ceiving that some trifles which I had in memory, composed
at under twenty or thereabout, met with acceptance above
what was looked for; I began thus far to assent both to
them and divers of my friends here at home, and not less
to an inward prompting which now grew daily upon me,
that by labour and intense study (which I take to be my
portion in this life), joined with the strong propensity of
nature, I might perhaps leave something so written to
after-times as they should not willingly let it die. The
accomplishment of these intentions which have lived within
me ever since I could conceive myself anything worth to
my country, lies not but in a power above man's to promise;
but that none hath by more studious ways endeavoured,
and with more unwearied spirit that none shall, that I dare
almost aver of myself, as far as life and free leisure will
extend. Neither do I think it shame to covenant with any
knowing reader, that for some few years yet, I may go on
trust with him toward the payment of what I am now
indebted, as being a work not to be raised from the heat

of youth or the vapours of wine; like that which flows
at waste from the pen of some vulgar amourist, or the
trencher fury of a rhyming parasite, nor to be obtained by
the invocation of Dame Memory and her Siren daughters,
but by devout prayer to that eternal spirit, who can enrich
with all utterance and knowledge, and sends out his
Seraphim with the hallowed fire of his altar, to touch and
purify the lips of whom he pleases: to this must be added
industrious and select reading, steady observation, and insight into all seemly and generous arts and affairs. Although it nothing content me to have disclosed thus much
beforehand; but that I trust hereby to make it manifest
with what small willingness I endure to interrupt the pursuit of no less hopes than these, and leave a calm and
pleasing solitariness, fed with cheerful and confident
thoughts, to embark in a troubled sea of noises and hoarse
disputes, from beholding the bright countenance of truth
in the quiet and still air of delightful studies."

So that of Spenser:

> " The noble heart that harbours virtuous thought,
>     And is with child of glorious great intent,
> Can never rest until it forth hath brought
>     The eternal brood of glory excellent."

Milton, therefore, did not write from casual impulse, but
after a severe examination of his own strength, and with
a resolution to leave nothing undone which it was in his
power to do. He always labours, and almost always succeeds. He strives hard to say the finest things in the
world, and he does say them. He adorns and dignifies his
subject to the utmost: he surrounds it with every possible
association of beauty or grandeur, whether moral, intellectual, or physical. He refines on his descriptions of
beauty; loading sweets on sweets, till the sense aches at

them; and raises his images of terror to a gigantic elevation, that "makes Ossa like a wart." In Milton there is always an appearance of effort: in Shakspeare, scarcely any.

Milton has borrowed more than any other writer, and exhausted every source of imitation, sacred or profane; yet he is perfectly distinct from every other writer. He is a writer of centos, and yet in originality scarcely inferior to Homer. The power of his mind is stamped on every line. The fervour of his imagination melts down and renders malleable, as in a furnace, the most contradictory materials. In reading his works, we feel ourselves under the influence of a mighty intellect, that the nearer it approaches to others, becomes more distinct from them. The quantity of art in him shews the strength of his genius: the weight of his intellectual obligations would have oppressed any other writer. Milton's learning has all the effect of intuition. He describes objects, of which he could only have read in books, with the vividness of actual observation. His imagination has the force of nature. He makes words tell as pictures.

> "Him followed Rimmon, whose delightful seat
> Was fair Damascus, on the fertile banks
> Of Abbana and Pharphar, lucid streams."

The word *lucid* here gives to the idea all the sparkling effect of the most perfect landscape.

And again:

> "As when a vulture on Imaus bred,
> Whose snowy ridge the roving Tartar bounds,
> Dislodging from a region scarce of prey,
> To gorge the flesh of lambs and yeanling kids
> On hills where flocks are fed, flies towards the springs
> Of Ganges or Hydaspes, Indian streams;
> But in his way lights on the barren plains
> Of Sericana, where Chineses drive
> With sails and wind their cany waggons light."

If Milton had taken a journey for the express purpose, he could not have described this scenery and mode of life better. Such passages are like demonstrations of natural history. Instances might be multiplied without end.

We might be tempted to suppose that the vividness with which he describes visible objects, was owing to their having acquired an unusual degree of strength in his mind, after the privation of his sight; but we find the same palpableness and truth in the descriptions which occur in his early poems. In Lycidas, he speaks of "the great vision of the guarded mount," with that preternatural weight of impression with which it would present itself suddenly to "the pilot of some small night-foundered skiff;" and the lines in the Penseroso, describing "the wandering moon,

> "Riding near her highest noon,
> Like one that had been led astray
> Through the heaven's wide pathless way,"

are as if he had gazed himself blind in looking at her. There is also the same depth of impression in his descriptions of the objects of all the different senses, whether colours, or sounds, or smells—the same absorption of his mind in whatever engaged his attention at the time. It has been indeed objected to Milton, by a common perversity of criticism, that his ideas were musical rather than picturesque, as if because they were in the highest degree musical, they must be (to keep the sage critical balance even, and to allow no one man to possess two qualities at the same time) proportionably deficient in other respects. But Milton's poetry is not cast in any such narrow, common-place mould; it is not so barren of resources. His worship of the Muse was not so simple or confined. A sound arises "like a steam of rich distilled perfumes;" we hear the pealing organ, but the incense on the altars is also there, and the statues of the gods are ranged around! The ear indeed predominates over the eye, because it is more immediately affected, and because the language of music blends more immediately with, and forms a more natural accompaniment to, the variable and indefinite associations of ideas conveyed by words. But where the associations of the imagination are not the principal thing, the individual object is given by Milton with equal force and beauty. The strongest and best proof of this, as a characteristic power of his mind, is, that the persons of Adam and Eve, of Satan, etc. are always accompanied, in our imagination, with the grandeur of the naked figure; they convey to us the ideas of sculpture. As an instance, take the following:

> "He soon
> Saw within ken a glorious Angel stand,
> The same whom John saw also in the sun:
> His back was turned, but not his brightness hid;
> Of beaming sunny rays a golden tiar
> Circled his head, nor less his locks behind
> Illustrious on his shoulders fledge with wings
> Lay waving round; on some great charge employ'd
> He seem'd, or fix'd in cogitation deep.
> Glad was the spirit impure, as now in hope
> To find who might direct his wand'ring flight
> To Paradise, the happy seat of man,
> His journey's end, and our beginning woe.
> But first he casts to change his proper shape,
> Which else might work him danger or delay:
> And now a stripling cherub he appears,
> Not of the prime, yet such as in his face
> Youth smiled celestial, and to every limb
> Suitable grace diffus'd, so well he feign'd:
> Under a coronet his flowing hair
> In curls on either cheek play'd; wings he wore
> Of many a colour'd plume sprinkled with gold,
> His habit fit for speed succinct, and held
> Before his decent steps a silver wand."

The figures introduced here have all the elegance and precision of a Greek statue; glossy and impurpled, tinged with golden light, and musical as the strings of Memnon's harp!

Again, nothing can be more magnificent than the portrait of Beelzebub:

> "With Atlantean shoulders fit to bear
> The weight of mightiest monarchies:"

Or the comparison of Satan, as he "lay floating many a rood," to "that sea beast,"

> "Leviathan, which God of all his works
> Created hugest that swim the ocean-stream!"

What a force of imagination is there in this last expression! What an idea it conveys of the size of that hugest of created beings, as if it shrunk up the ocean to a stream, and took up the sea in its nostrils as a very little thing! Force of style is one of Milton's greatest excellences. Hence, perhaps, he stimulates us more in the reading, and less afterwards. The way to defend Milton against all impugners, is to take down the book and read it.

Milton's blank verse is the only blank verse in the language (except Shakspeare's) that deserves the name of verse. Dr. Johnson, who had modelled his ideas of versification on the regular sing-song of Pope, condemns the Paradise Lost as harsh and unequal. I shall not pretend to say that this is not sometimes the case; for where a degree of excellence beyond the mechanical rules of art is attempted, the poet must sometimes fail. But I imagine that there are more perfect examples in Milton of musical expression, or of an adaptation of the sound and movement of the verse to the meaning of the passage, than in all our other writers, whether of rhyme or blank verse, put together, (with the exception already mentioned). Spenser is the most harmonious of our stanza writers, as Dryden

is the most sounding and varied of our rhymists.  But in
neither is there anything like the same ear for music, the
same power of approximating the varieties of poetical to
those of musical rhythm, as there is in our great epic poet.
The sound of his lines is moulded into the expression of the
sentiment, almost of the very image.  They rise or fall,
pause or hurry rapidly on, with exquisite art, but without
the least trick or affectation, as the occasion seems to
require.

The following are some of the finest instances:

> "His hand was known
> In Heaven by many a tower'd structure high;—
> Nor was his name unheard or unador'd
> In ancient Greece; and in the Ausonian land
> Men called him Mulciber; and how he fell
> From Heaven, they fabled, thrown by angry Jove
> Sheer o'er the crystal battlements; from morn
> To noon he fell, from noon to dewy eve,
> A summer's day; and with the setting sun
> Dropt from the zenith like a falling star
> On Lemnos, the Ægean isle: thus they relate,
> Erring."—

> "But chief the spacious hall
> Thick swarm'd, both on the ground and in the air,
> Brush'd with the hiss of rustling wings.  As bees
> In spring time, when the sun with Taurus rides,
> Pour forth their populous youth about the hive
> In clusters; they among fresh dews and flow'rs
> Fly to and fro; or on the smoothed plank,
> The suburb of their straw-built citadel,
> New rubb'd with balm, expatiate, and confer
> Their state affairs.  So thick the airy crowd
> Swarm'd and were straiten'd; till the signal giv'n,
> Behold a wonder!  They but now who seem'd
> In bigness to surpass earth's giant sons,
> Now less than smallest dwarfs, in narrow room
> Throng numberless, like that Pygmean race
> Beyond the Indian mount, or fairy elves,
> Whose midnight revels by a forest side
> Or fountain, some belated peasant sees,

Or dreams he sees, while over-head the moon
Sits arbitress, and nearer to the earth
Wheels her pale course: they on their mirth and dance
Intent, with jocund music charm his ear;
At once with joy and fear his heart rebounds."

I can give only another instance, though I have some
difficulty in leaving off.

" Round he surveys (and well might, where he stood
So high above the circling canopy
Of night's extended shade) from th' eastern point
Of Libra to the fleecy star that bears
Andromeda far off Atlantic seas
Beyond the horizon: then from pole to pole
He views in breadth, and without longer pause
Down right into the world's first region throws
His flight precipitant, and winds with ease
Through the pure marble air his oblique way
Amongst innumerable stars that shone
Stars distant, but nigh hand seem'd other worlds;
Or other worlds they seem'd or happy isles," etc.

The verse, in this exquisitely modulated passage, floats up
and down as if it had itself wings. Milton has himself
given us the theory of his versification—

" Such as the meeting soul may pierce
In notes with many a winding bout
Of linked sweetness long drawn out."

Dr. Johnson and Pope would have converted his vaulting
Pegasus into a rocking-horse. Read any other blank verse
but Milton's,—Thomson's, Young's, Cowper's, Wordsworth's,—and it will be found, from the want of the same
insight into " the hidden soul of harmony," to be mere
lumbering prose.

To proceed to a consideration of the merits of Paradise
Lost, in the most essential point of view, I mean as to the

poetry of character and passion. I shall say nothing of the fable, or of other technical objections or excellences; but I shall try to explain at once the foundation of the interest belonging to the poem. I am ready to give up the dialogues in Heaven, where, as Pope justly observes, "God the Father turns a school-divine;" nor do I consider the battle of the angels as the climax of sublimity, or the most successful effort of Milton's pen. In a word, the interest of the poem arises from the daring ambition and fierce passions of Satan, and from the account of the paradisaical happiness, and the loss of it by our first parents. Three-fourths of the work are taken up with these characters, and nearly all that relates to them is unmixed sublimity and beauty. The two first books alone are like too massy pillars of solid gold.

Satan is the most heroic subject that ever was chosen for a poem; and the execution is as perfect as the design is lofty. He was the first of created beings, who, for endeavouring to be equal with the highest, and to divide the empire of heaven with the Almighty, was hurled down to hell. His aim was no less than the throne of the universe; his means, myriads of angelic armies bright, the third part of the heavens, whom he lured after him with his countenance, and who durst defy the Omnipotent in arms. His ambition was the greatest, and his punishment was the greatest; but not so his despair, for his fortitude was as great as his sufferings. His strength of mind was matchless as his strength of body; the vastness of his designs did not surpass the firm, inflexible determination with which he submitted to his irreversible doom, and final loss of all good. His power of action and of suffering was equal. He was the greatest power that was ever overthrown, with the strongest will left to resist or to endure. He was baffled, not confounded. He stood like a tower; or

> "As when Heaven's fire
> Hath scathed the forest oaks or mountain pines!"

He is still surrounded with hosts of rebel angels, armèd warriors, who own him as their sovereign leader, and with whose fate he sympathises as he views them round, far as the eye can reach; though he keeps aloof from them in his own mind, and holds supreme counsel only with his own breast. An outcast from Heaven, Hell trembles beneath his feet, Sin and Death are at his heels, and mankind are his easy prey.

> "All is not lost; th' unconquerable will,
> And study of revenge, immortal hate,
> And courage never to submit or yield,
> And what else is not to be overcome,"

are still his. The sense of his punishment seems lost in the magnitude of it; the fierceness of tormenting flames, is qualified and made innoxious by the greater fierceness of his pride; the loss of infinite happiness to himself is compensated in thought, by the power of inflicting infinite misery on others. Yet Satan is not the principle of malignity, or of the abstract love of evil—but of the abstract love of power, of pride, of self-will personified, to which last principle all other good and evil, and even his own, are subordinate. From this principle he never once flinches. His love of power and contempt for suffering are never once relaxed from the highest pitch of intensity. His thoughts burn like a hell within him; but the power of thought holds dominion in his mind over every other consideration. The consciousness of a determined purpose, of "that intellectual being, those thought that wander through eternity," though accompanied with endless pain, he prefers to nonentity, to "being swallowed up and lost in the wide womb of uncreated night." He expresses the sum and substance of all ambition in one line: "Fallen cherub, to be weak is miserable, doing or suffering!" After such a conflict as his, and such a defeat, to retreat in order, to rally, to make terms, to exist at all, is something; but he does more than this—he founds a new empire in hell, and from it conquers this new world, whither he bends his undaunted flight, forcing his way through nether and surrounding fires. The poet has not in all this given us a mere shadowy outline; the strength is equal to the magnitude of the conception. The Achilles of Homer is not more distinct; the Titans were not more vast; Prometheus chained to his rock was not a more terrific example of suffering and of crime. Wherever the figure of Satan is introduced, whether he walks or flies, "rising aloft incumbent on the dusky air," it is illustrated with the most striking and appropriate images: so that we see it always before us, gigantic, irregular, portentous, uneasy, and disturbed—but dazzling in its faded splendour, the clouded ruins of a god. The deformity of Satan is only in the depravity of his will; he has no bodily deformity to excite our loathing or disgust. The horns and tail are not there, poor emblems of the unbending, unconquered spirit, of the writhing agonies within. Milton was too magnanimous and open an antagonist to support his argument by the bye-tricks of a hump and cloven foot; to bring into the fair field of controversy the good old catholic prejudices of which Tasso and Dante have availed themselves, and which the mystic German critics would restore. He relied on the justice of his cause, and did not scruple to give the devil his due. Some persons may think that he has carried his liberality too far, and injured the cause he professed to espouse by making him the chief person in his poem. Considering the nature of his subject, he would be equally in danger of running into this fault, from his faith in religion, and his love of rebellion; and perhaps each of these motives had its full share in determining the choice of his subject.

Not only the figure of Satan, but his speeches in council, his soliloquies, his address to Eve, his share in the war in heaven, or in the fall of man, show the same decided superiority of character. To give only one instance, almost the first speech he makes:

> "Is this the region, this the soil, the clime,
> Said then the lost archangel, this the seat
> That we must change for Heaven; this mournful gloom
> For that celestial light? Be it so, since he
> Who now is sov'rain can dispose and bid
> What shall be right: farthest from him is best,
> Whom reason hath equal'd, force hath made supreme
> Above his equals. Farewell happy fields,
> Where joy for ever dwells: Hail horrors, hail
> Infernal world, and thou profoundest Hell,
> Receive thy new possessor; one who brings
> A mind not to be chang'd by place or time.
> The mind is its own place, and in itself
> Can make a Heav'n of Hell, a Hell of Heav'n
> What matter where, if I be still the same,
> And what I should be, all but less than he
> Whom thunder hath made greater? Here at least
> We shall be free; th' Almighty hath not built
> Here for his envy, will not drive us hence:
> Here we may reign secure, and in my choice,
> To reign is worth ambition, though in Hell:
> Better to reign in Hell, than serve in Heaven."

The whole of the speeches and debates in Pandemonium are well worthy of the place and the occasion—with Gods for speakers, and angels and archangels for hearers. There is a decided manly tone in the arguments and sentiments, an eloquent dogmatism, as if each person spoke from thorough conviction; an excellence which Milton probably borrowed from his spirit of partisanship, or else his spirit of partisanship from the natural firmness and vigour of his mind. In this respect Milton resembles Dante, (the only modern writer with whom he has any thing in common) and it is remarkable that Dante, as well as Milton, was a political partisan. That approximation to the severity of impassioned prose which has been made an objection to Milton's poetry, and which is chiefly to be met with in these bitter invectives, is one of its great excellences. The author might here turn his philippics against Salmasius to good account. The rout in Heaven is like the fall of some mighty structure, nodding to its base, " with hideous ruin and combustion down." But, perhaps, of all the passages in Paradise Lost, the description of the employments of the angels during the absence of Satan, some of whom " retreated in a silent valley, sing with notes angelical to many a harp their own heroic deeds and hapless fall by doom of battle " is the most perfect example of mingled pathos and sublimity.—What proves the truth of this noble picture in every part, and that the frequent complaint of want of interest in it is the fault of the reader, not of the poet, is that when any interest of a practical kind takes a shape that can be at all turned into this, (and there is little doubt that Milton had some such in his eye in writing it,) each party converts it to its own purposes, feels the absolute identity of these abstracted and high speculations; and that, in fact, a noted political writer of the present day has exhausted nearly the whole account of Satan in the Paradise Lost, by applying it to a character whom he considered as after the devil, (though I do not know whether he would make even that exception) the greatest enemy of the human race. This may serve to show that Milton's Satan is not a very insipid personage.

Of Adam and Eve it has been said, that the ordinary reader can feel little interest in them, because they have none of the passions, pursuits, or even relations of human

life, except that of man and wife, the least interesting of
all others, if not to the parties concerned, at least to the
by-standers. The preference has on this account been given
to Homer, who, it is said, has left very vivid and infinitely
diversified pictures of all the passions and affections, public
and private, incident to human nature,—the relations of
son, of brother, parent, friend, citizen, and many others.
Longinus preferred the Iliad to the Odyssey, on account of
the greater number of battles it contains; but I can neither
agree to his criticism, nor assent to the present objection.
It is true, there is little action in this part of Milton's poem;
but there is much repose, and more enjoyment. There are
none of the every-day occurrences, contentions, disputes,
wars, fightings, feuds, jealousies, trades, professions, liv-
eries, and common handicrafts of life; " no kind of traffic;
letters are not known; no use of service, of riches, poverty,
contract, succession, bourn, bound of land, tilth, vineyard
none; no occupation, no treason, felony, sword, pike, knife,
gun, nor need of any engine." So much the better; thank
Heaven, all these were yet to come. But still the die was
cast, and in them our doom was sealed. In them

> "The generations were prepared; the pangs,
> The internal pangs, were ready, the dread strife
> Of poor humanity's afflicted will,
> Struggling in vain with ruthless destiny."

In their first false step we trace all our future woe, with
loss of Eden. But there was a short and precious interval
between, like the first blush of morning before the day
is overcast with tempest, the dawn of the world, the birth
of nature from " the unapparent deep," with its first dews
and freshness on its cheek, breathing odours. Theirs was
the first delicious taste of life, and on them depended all
that was to come of it. In them hung trembling all our

hopes and fears. They were as yet alone in the world, in the eye of nature, wondering at their new being, full of enjoyment and enraptured with one another, with the voice of their Maker walking in the garden, and ministering angels attendant on their steps, winged messengers from heaven like rosy clouds descending in their sight. Nature played around them her virgin fancies wild; and spread for them a repast where no crude surfeit reigned. Was there nothing in this scene, which God and nature alone witnessed, to interest a modern critic? What need was there of action, where the heart was full of bliss and innocence without it! They had nothing to do but feel their own happiness, and "know to know no more." "They toiled not, neither did they spin; yet Solomon in all his glory was not arrayed like one of these." All things seem to acquire fresh sweetness, and to be clothed with fresh beauty in their sight. They tasted as it were for themselves and us, of all that there ever was pure in human bliss. "In them the burthen of the mystery, the heavy and the weary weight of all this unintelligible world, is lightened." They stood awhile perfect, but they afterwards fell, and were driven out of Paradise, tasting the first fruits of bitterness as they had done of bliss. But their pangs were such as a pure spirit might feel at the sight—their tears "such as angels weep." The pathos is of that mild contemplative kind which arises from regret for the loss of unspeakable happiness, and resignation to inevitable fate. There is none of the fierceness of intemperate passion, none of the agony of mind and turbulence of action, which is the result of the habitual struggles of the will with circumstances, irritated by repeated disappointment, and constantly setting its desires most eagerly on that which there is an impossibility of attaining. This would have destroyed the beauty of the whole picture. They had received their unlooked-for happiness as a free gift from their Creator's hands, and they submitted to its loss, not without sorrow, but without impious and stubborn repining.

> "In either hand the hast'ning angel caught
> Our ling'ring parents, and to th' eastern gate
> Led them direct, and down the cliff as fast
> To the subjected plain; then disappear'd.
> They looking back, all th' eastern side beheld
> Of Paradise, so late their happy seat,
> Wav'd over by that flaming brand, the gate
> With dreadful faces throng'd, and fiery arms:
> Some natural tears they dropt, but wip'd them soon;
> The world was all before them, where to choose
> Their place of rest, and Providence their guide."

# VI

## POPE

THE question, whether Pope was a poet, has hardly yet been settled, and is hardly worth settling; for if he was not a great poet, he must have been a great prose-writer, that is, he was a great writer of some sort. He was a man of exquisite faculties, and of the most refined taste; and as he chose verse (the most obvious distinction of poetry) as the vehicle to express his ideas, he has generally passed for a poet, and a good one. If, indeed, by a great poet, we mean one who gives the utmost grandeur to our conceptions of nature, or the utmost force to the passions of the heart, Pope was not in this sense a great poet; for the bent, the characteristic power of his mind, lay the clean contrary way; namely, in representing things as they appear to the indifferent observer, stripped of prejudice and passion, as in his Critical Essays; or in representing them in the most contemptible and insignificant point of view, as in his Satires; or in clothing the little with mock-dignity, as in his poems of Fancy; or in adorning the trivial incidents and familiar relations of life with the utmost elegance of expression, and all the flattering illusions of friendship or self-love, as in his Epistles. He was not then distinguished as a poet of lofty enthusiasm, of strong imagination, with a passionate sense of the beauties of nature, or a deep insight into the workings of the heart; but he was a wit, and a critic, a man of sense, of observation, and the world, with a keen relish for the elegances of art, or of nature when embellished by art, a quick tact for propriety of

thought and manners as established by the forms and customs of society, a refined sympathy with the sentiments and
habitudes of human life, as he felt them within the little
circle of his family and friends. He was, in a word, the
poet, not of nature, but of art; and the distinction between
the two, as well as I can make it out, is this—The poet
of nature is one who, from the elements of beauty, of
power, and of passion in his own breast, sympathises with
whatever is beautiful, and grand, and impassioned in
nature, in its simple majesty, in its immediate appeal to
the senses, to the thoughts and hearts of all men; so that
the poet of nature, by the truth, and depth, and harmony
of his mind, may be said to hold communion with the very
soul of nature; to be identified with and to foreknow and to
record the feelings of all men at all times and places, as
they are liable to the same impressions; and to exert the
same power over the minds of his readers, that nature does.
He sees things in their eternal beauty, for he sees them as
they are; he feels them in their universal interest, for he
feels them as they affect the first principles of his and our
common nature. Such was Homer, such was Shakspeare,
whose works will last as long as nature, because they are
a copy of the indestructible forms and everlasting impulses
of nature, welling out from the bosom as from a perennial
spring, or stamped upon the senses by the hand of their
maker. The power of the imagination in them, is the representative power of all nature. It has its centre in the
human soul, and makes the circuit of the universe.

Pope was not assuredly a poet of this class, or in the
first rank of it. He saw nature only dressed by art; he
judged of beauty by fashion; he sought for truth in the
opinions of the world; he judged of the feelings of others
by his own. The capacious soul of Shakspeare had an
intuitive and mighty sympathy with whatever could enter

into the heart of man in all possible circumstances: Pope had an exact knowledge of all that he himself loved or hated, wished or wanted. Milton has winged his daring flight from heaven to earth, through Chaos and old Night. Pope's Muse never wandered with safety, but from his library to his grotto, or from his grotto into his library back again. His mind dwelt with greater pleasure on his own garden, than on the garden of Eden; he could describe the faultless whole-length mirror that reflected his own person, better than the smooth surface of the lake that reflects the face of heaven—a piece of cut-glass or a pair of paste buckles with more brilliance and effect, than a thousand dew-drops glittering in the sun. He would be more delighted with a patent lamp, than with "the pale reflex of Cynthia's brow," that fills the skies with its soft silent lustre, that trembles through the cottage window, and cheers the watchful mariner on the lonely wave. In short, he was the poet of personality and of polished life. That which was nearest to him, was the greatest; the fashion of the day bore sway in his mind over the immutable laws of nature. He preferred the artificial to the natural in external objects, because he had a stronger fellow-feeling with the self-love of the maker or proprietor of a gewgaw, than admiration of that which was interesting to all mankind. He preferred the artificial to the natural in passion, because the involuntary and uncalculating impulses of the one hurried him away with a force and vehemence with which he could not grapple; while he could trifle with the conventional and superficial modifications of mere sentiment at will, laugh at or admire, put them on or off like a masquerade dress, make much or little of them, indulge them for a longer or a shorter time, as he pleased; and because while they amused his fancy and exercised his ingenuity, they never once disturbed his vanity, his levity, or indifference. His mind

was the antithesis of strength and grandeur; its power was
the power of indifference. He had none of the enthusiasm
of poetry: he was in poetry what the sceptic is in religion.

It cannot be denied, that his chief excellence lay more
in diminishing, than in aggrandizing objects; in checking,
not in encouraging our enthusiasm; in sneering at the
extravagances of fancy or passion, instead of giving a
loose to them; in describing a row of pins and needles,
rather than the embattled spears of Greeks and Trojans;
in penning a lampoon or a compliment, and in praising
Martha Blount.

Shakspeare says,

> "In Fortune's ray and brightness
> The herd hath more annoyance by the brize
> Than by the tyger: but when the splitting wind
> Makes flexible the knees of knotted oaks,
> And flies fled under shade, why then
> The thing of courage,
> As roused with rage, with rage doth sympathise;
> And with an accent tuned in the self-same key,
> Replies to chiding Fortune."

There is none of this rough work in Pope. His Muse
was on a peace-establishment, and grew somewhat effeminate by long ease and indulgence. He lived in the smiles
of fortune, and basked in the favour of the great. In his
smooth and polished verse we meet with no prodigies of
nature, but with miracles of wit; the thunders of his pen
are whispered flatteries; its forked lightnings pointed sar-
casms; for "the gnarled oak," he gives us "the soft myrtle:" for rocks, and seas, and mountains, artificial grass-
plats, gravel-walks, and tinkling rills; for earthquakes and
tempests, the breaking of a flower-pot, or the fall of a
china jar; for the tug and war of the elements, or the
deadly strife of the passions, we have

> "Calm contemplation and poetic ease."

Yet within this retired and narrow circle how much, and that how exquisite, was contained! What discrimination, what wit, what delicacy, what fancy, what lurking spleen, what elegance of thought, what pampered refinement of sentiment! It is like looking at the world through a microscope, where everything assumes a new character and a new consequence, where things are seen in their minutest circumstances and slightest shades of difference; where the little becomes gigantic, the deformed beautiful, and the beautiful deformed. The wrong end of the magnifier is, to be sure, held to every thing, but still the exhibition is highly curious, and we know not whether to be most pleased or surprised. Such, at least, is the best account I am able to give of this extraordinary man, without doing injustice to him or others. It is time to refer to particular instances in his works.—The Rape of the Lock is the best or most ingenious of these. It is the most exquisite specimen of *fillagree* work ever invented. It is admirable in proportion as it is made of nothing.

> "More subtle web Arachne cannot spin,
>     Nor the fine nets, which oft we woven see
>     Of scorched dew, do not in th' air more lightly flee."

It is made of gauze and silver spangles. The most glittering appearance is given to every thing, to paste, pomatum, billet-doux, and patches. Airs, languid airs, breathe around;—the atmosphere is perfumed with affectation. A toilette is described with the solemnity of an altar raised to the goddess of vanity, and the history of a silver bodkin is given with all the pomp of heraldry. No pains are spared, no profusion of ornament, no splendour of poetic diction, to set off the meanest things. The balance between the concealed irony and the assumed gravity, is as nicely trimmed as the balance of power in Europe. The little

is made great, and the great little.  You hardly know
whether to laugh or weep.  It is the triumph of insignifi-
cance, the apotheosis of foppery and folly.  It is the perfection of the mock-heroic!  I will give only the two following passages in illustration of these remarks.  Can anything be more elegant and graceful than the description of
Belinda, in the beginning of the second canto?

> "Not with more glories, in the ethereal plain,
>  The sun first rises o'er the purpled main,
>  Than, issuing forth, the rival of his beams
>  Launch'd on the bosom of the silver Thames.
>  Fair nymphs, and well-drest youths around her shone,
>  But ev'ry eye was fix'd on her alone.
>  On her white breast a sparkling cross she wore,
>  Which Jews might kiss, and infidels adore.
>  Her lively looks a sprightly mind disclose,
>  Quick as her eyes, and as unfix'd as those:
>  Favours to none, to all she smiles extends;
>  Oft she rejects, but never once offends.
>  Bright as the sun, her eyes the gazers strike;
>  And like the sun, they shine on all alike.
>  Yet graceful ease, and sweetness void of pride,
>  Might hide her faults, if belles had faults to hide:
>  If to her share some female errors fall,
>  Look on her face, and you'll forget 'em all.
>     This nymph, to the destruction of mankind,
>  Nourish'd two locks, which graceful hung behind
>  In equal curls, and well conspir'd to deck
>  With shining ringlets the smooth iv'ry neck."

The following is the introduction to the account of
Belinda's assault upon the baron bold, who had dissevered
one of these locks " from her fair head for ever and for
ever."

> "Now meet thy fate, incens'd Belinda cry'd,
>  And drew a deadly bodkin from her side.
>  (The same his ancient personage to deck,
>  Her great, great grandsire wore about his neck,
>  In three seal-rings; which after, melted down,
>  Form'd a vast buckle for his widow's gown:

> Her infant grandame's whistle next it grew,
> The bells she jingled, and the whistle blew:
> Then in a bodkin grac'd her mother's hairs,
> Which long she wore, and now Belinda wears.)"

I do not know how far Pope was indebted for the original idea, or the delightful execution of this poem, to the Lutrin of Boileau.

The Rape of the Lock is a double-refined essence of wit and fancy, as the Essay on Criticism is of wit and sense. The quantity of thought and observation in this work, for so young a man as Pope was when he wrote it, is wonderful: unless we adopt the supposition, that most men of genius spend the rest of their lives in teaching others what they themselves have learned under twenty. The conciseness and felicity of the expression is equally remarkable. Thus in reasoning on the variety of men's opinions, he says—

> "'Tis with our judgments, as our watches; none
> Go just alike, yet each believes his own."

Nothing can be more original and happy than the general remarks and illustrations in the Essay: the critical rules laid down are too much those of a school, and of a confined one. There is one passage in the Essay on Criticism in which the author speaks with that eloquent enthusiasm of the fame of ancient writers, which those will always feel who have themselves any hope or chance of immortality. I have quoted the passage elsewhere, but I will repeat it here.

> " Still green with bays each ancient altar stands,
> Above the reach of sacrilegious hands;
> Secure from flames, from envy's fiercer rage,
> Destructive war, and all-involving age.
> Hail, bards triumphant, born in happier days,
> Immortal heirs of universal praise!

> Whose honours with increase of ages grow,
> As streams roll down, enlarging as they flow."

These lines come with double force and beauty on the reader as they were dictated by the writer's despair of ever attaining that lasting glory which he celebrates with such disinterested enthusiasm in others, from the lateness of the age in which he lived, and from his writing in a tongue, not understood by other nations, and that grows obsolete and unintelligible to ourselves at the end of every second century. But he needed not have thus antedated his own poetical doom—the loss and entire oblivion of that which can never die. If he had known, he might have boasted that his " little bark " wafted down the stream of time,

> "With *theirs* should sail,
> Pursue the triumph and partake the gale "—

if those who know how to set a due value on the blessing, were not the last to decide confidently on their own pretensions to it.

There is a cant in the present day about genius, as every thing in poetry: there was a cant in the time of Pope about sense, as performing all sorts of wonders. It was a kind of watchword, the shibboleth of a critical party of the day. As a proof of the exclusive attention which it occupied in their minds, it is remarkable that in the Essay on Criticism (not a very long poem) there are no less than half a score successive couplets rhyming to the word *sense*. This appears almost incredible without giving the instances, and no less so when they are given.

> " But of the two, less dangerous is the offence,
> To tire our patience than mislead our sense." *lines* 3, 4.

> " In search of wit these lose their common sense,
> And then turn critics in their own defence." *l.* 28, 29.

"Pride, where wit fails, steps in to our defence,
And fills up all the mighty void of sense." *l.* 209, 10.

"Some by old words to fame have made pretence,
Ancients in phrase, mere moderns in their sense." *l.* 324, 5.

"'Tis not enough no harshness gives offence;
The sound must seem an echo to the sense." *l.* 364, 5.

"At every trifle scorn to take offence;
That always shews great pride, or little sense." *l.* 386, 7.

"Be silent always, when you doubt your sense,
And speak, though sure, with seeming diffidence." *l.* 366, 7.

"Be niggards of advice on no pretence,
For the worst avarice is that of sense." *l.* 578, 9.

"Strain out the last dull dropping of their sense,
And rhyme with all the rage of impotence." *l.* 608, 9.

"Horace still charms with graceful negligence,
And without method talks us into sense." *l.* 653, 4.

I have mentioned this the more for the sake of those
critics who are bigotted idolisers of our author, chiefly on
the score of his correctness. These persons seem to be of
opinion that "there is but one perfect writer, even Pope."
This is, however, a mistake: his excellence is by no means
faultlessness. If he had no great faults, he is full of little
errors. His grammatical construction is often lame and
imperfect. In the Abelard and Eloise, he says—

"There died the best of passions, Love and Fame."

This is not a legitimate ellipsis. Fame is not a passion,
though love is: but his ear was evidently confused by
the meeting of the sounds "love and fame," as if they of
themselves immediately implied "love, and love of fame."
Pope's rhymes are constantly defective, being rhymes to
the eye instead of the ear; and this to a greater degree,

not only than in later, but than in preceding writers.  The
praise of his versification must be confined to its uniform
smoothness and harmony.  In the translation of the Iliad,
which has been considered as his masterpiece in style and
execution, he continually changes the tenses in the same
sentence for the purpose of the rhyme, which shews either
a want of technical resources, or great inattention to punctilious exactness.  But to have done with this.

The Epistle of Eloise to Abelard is the only exception
I can think of, to the general spirit of the foregoing remarks; and I should be disingenuous not to acknowledge
that it is an exception.  The foundation is in the letters
themselves of Abelard and Eloise, which are quite as impressive, but still in a different way.  It is fine as a poem:
it is finer as a piece of high-wrought eloquence.  No woman
could be supposed to write a finer love-letter in verse.  Besides the richness of the historical materials, the high *gusto*
of the original sentiments which Pope had to work upon,
there were perhaps circumstances in his own .ituation
which made him enter into the subject with even more
than a poet's feeling.  The tears shed are drops gushing
from the heart: the words are burning sighs breathed from
the soul of love.  Perhaps the poem to which it bears the
greatest similarity in our language, is Dryden's Tancred
and Sigismunda, taken from Boccaccio.  Pope's Eloise will
bear this comparison; and after such a test, with Boccaccio
for the original author, and Dryden for the translator, it
need shrink from no other.  There is something exceedingly
tender and beautiful in the sound of the concluding lines:

> "If ever chance two wandering lovers brings
>   To Paraclete's white walls and silver springs," etc.

The Essay on Man is not Pope's best work.  It is a
theory which Bolingbroke is supposed to have given him,

and which he expanded into verse. But "he spins the thread of his verbosity finer than the staple of his argument." All that he says, "the very words, and to the self-same tune," would prove just as well that whatever is, is *wrong,* as that whatever is, is *right.* The Dunciad has splendid passages, but in general it is dull, heavy, and mechanical. The sarcasm already quoted on Settle, the Lord Mayor's poet, (for at that time there was a city as well as a court poet)

> "Now night descending, the proud scene is o'er,
> But lives in Settle's numbers one day more"—

is the finest inversion of immortality conceivable. It is even better than his serious apostrophe to the great heirs of glory, the triumphant bards of antiquity!

The finest burst of severe moral invective in all Pope, is the prophetical conclusion of the epilogue to the Satires:

> "Virtue may chuse the high or low degree,
> 'Tis just alike to virtue, and to me;
> Dwell in a monk, or light upon a king,
> She's still the same belov'd, contented thing.
> Vice is undone if she forgets her birth,
> And stoops from angels to the dregs of earth.
> But 'tis the Fall degrades her to a whore:
> Let Greatness own her, and she's mean no more.
> Her birth, her beauty, crowds and courts confess,
> Chaste matrons praise her, and grave bishops bless;
> In golden chains the willing world she draws,
> And hers the gospel is, and hers the laws;
> Mounts the tribunal, lifts her scarlet head,
> And sees pale Virtue carted in her stead.
> Lo! at the wheels of her triumphal car,
> Old England's Genius, rough with many a scar,
> Dragged in the dust! his arms hang idly round,
> His flag inverted trails along the ground!
> Our youth, all livery'd o'er with foreign gold,
> Before her dance; behind her, crawl the old!
> See thronging millions to the Pagod run,
> And offer country, parent, wife, or son!

Hear her black trumpet through the land proclaim,
That *not to be corrupted is the shame.*
In soldier, churchman, patriot, man in pow'r,
'Tis av'rice all, ambition is no more!
See all our nobles begging to be slaves!
See all our fools aspiring to be knaves!
The wit of cheats, the courage of a whore,
Are what ten thousand envy and adore:
All, all look up with reverential awe,
At crimes that 'scape or triumph o'er the law;
While truth, worth, wisdom, daily they decry:
Nothing is sacred now but villainy.
Yet may this verse (if such a verse remain)
Show there was one who held it in disdain."

His Satires are not in general so good as his Epistles. His enmity is effeminate and petulant from a sense of weakness, as his friendship was tender from a sense of gratitude. I do not like, for instance, his character of Chartres, or his characters of women. His delicacy often borders upon sickliness; his fastidiousness makes others fastidious. But his compliments are divine; they are equal in value to a house or an estate. Take the following. In addressing Lord Mansfield, he speaks of the grave as a scene,

"Where Murray, long enough his country's pride,
Shall be no more than Tully, or than Hyde."

To Bolingbroke he says—

"Why rail they then if but one wreath of mine,
Oh all-accomplished St. John, deck thy shrine?"

Again, he has bequeathed this praise to Lord Cornbury—

"Despise low thoughts, low gains:
Disdain whatever Cornbury disdains;
Be virtuous and be happy for your pains."

One would think (though there is no knowing) that a descendant of this nobleman, if there be such a person living, could hardly be guilty of a mean or paltry action.

The finest piece of personal satire in Pope (perhaps in the world) is his character of Addison; and this, it may be observed, is of a mixed kind, made up of his respect for the man, and a cutting sense of his failings. The other finest one is that of Buckingham, and the best part of that is the pleasurable

> " Alas! how changed from him,
> That life of pleasure, and that soul of whim:
> Gallant and gay, in Cliveden's proud alcove,
> The bower of wanton Shrewsbury and love! "

Among his happiest and most inimitable effusions are the Epistles to Arbuthnot, and to Jervas the painter; amiable patterns of the delightful unconcerned life, blending ease with dignity, which poets and painters then led. Thus he says to Arbuthnot—

> " Why did I write? What sin to me unknown
> Dipp'd me in ink, my parents' or my own?
> As yet a child, nor yet a fool to fame,
> I lisped in numbers, for the numbers came.
> I left no calling for this idle trade,
> No duty broke, no father disobey'd:
> The Muse but served to ease some friend, not wife;
> To help me through this long disease, my life;
> To second, Arbuthnot! thy art and care,
> And teach the being you preserv'd to bear.
>   But why then publish? Granville the polite,
> And knowing Walsh, would tell me I could write;
> Well-natur'd Garth, inflam'd with early praise,
> And Congreve lov'd, and Swift endur'd my lays;
> The courtly Talbot, Somers, Sheffield read;
> E'en mitred Rochester would nod the head;
> And St. John's self (great Dryden's friend before)
> With open arms receiv'd one poet more.

Happy my studies, when by these approv'd!
Happier their author, when by these belov'd!
From these the world will judge of men and books,
Not from the Burnets, Oldmixons, and Cooks."

I cannot help giving also the conclusion of the Epistle to
Jervas.

"Oh, lasting as those colours may they shine,
Free as thy stroke, yet faultless as thy line;
New graces yearly like thy works display,
Soft without weakness, without glaring gay;
Led by some rule, that guides, but not constrains;
And finish'd more through happiness than pains.
The kindred arts shall in their praise conspire,
One dip the pencil, and one string the lyre.
Yet should the Graces all thy figures place,
And breathe an air divine on ev'ry face;
Yet should the Muses bid my numbers roll
Strong as their charms, and gentle as their soul;
With Zeuxis' Helen thy Bridgewater vie,
And these be sung till Granville's Myra die:
Alas! how little from the grave we claim!
Thou but preserv'st a face, and I a name."

And shall we cut ourselves off from beauties like these
with a theory? Shall we shut up our books, and seal up
our senses, to please the dull spite and inordinate vanity
of those "who have eyes, but they see not—ears, but they
hear not—and understandings, but they understand not,"—
and go about asking our blind guides, whether Pope was
a poet or not? It will never do. Such persons, when you
point out to them a fine passage in Pope, turn it off to
something of the same sort in some other writer. Thus
they say that the line, "I lisp'd in numbers, for the numbers
came," is pretty, but taken from that of Ovid—*Et quum
conabar scribere, versus erat.* They are safe in this mode
of criticism: there is no danger of any one's tracing their
writings to the classics.

Pope's letters and prose writings neither take away from, nor add to his poetical reputation. There is, occasionally, a littleness of manner, and an unnecessary degree of caution. He appears anxious to say a good thing in every word, as well as every sentence. They, however, give a very favourable idea of his moral character in all respects; and his letters to Atterbury, in his disgrace and exile, do equal honour to both. If I had to choose, there are one or two persons, and but one or two, that I should like to have been better than Pope!

# VII

## ON THE PERIODICAL ESSAYISTS

"The proper study of mankind is man."

I NOW come to speak of that sort of writing which has
been so successfully cultivated in this country by our periodical Essayists, and which consists in applying the talents
and resources of the mind to all that mixed mass of human
affairs, which, though not included under the head of any
regular art, science, or profession, falls under the cognisance
of the writer, and "comes home to the business and bosoms
of men." *Quicquid agunt homines nostri farrago libelli,*
is the general motto of this department of literature. It
does not treat of minerals or fossils, of the virtues of
plants, or the influence of planets; it does not meddle with
forms of belief or systems of philosophy, nor launch into
the world of spiritual existences; but it makes familiar
with the world of men and women, records theirs actions,
assigns their motives, exhibits their whims, characterises
their pursuits in all their singular and endless variety,
ridicules their absurdities, exposes their inconsistencies,
"holds the mirror up to nature, and shews the very age
and body of the time its form and pressure;" takes minutes of our dress, air, looks, words, thoughts, and actions;
shews us what we are, and what we are not; plays the
whole game of human life over before us, and by making
us enlightened spectators of its many-coloured scenes, en-
ables us (if possible) to become tolerably reasonable agents
in the one in which we have to perform a part. "The act

and practic part of life is thus made the mistress of our theorique." It is the best and most natural course of study. It is in morals and manners what the experimental is in natural philosophy, as opposed to the dogmatical method. It does not deal in sweeping clauses of proscription and anathema, but in nice distinction and liberal constructions. It makes up its general accounts from details, its few theories from many facts. It does not try to prove all black or all white as it wishes, but lays on the intermediate colours, (and most of them not unpleasing ones,) as it finds them blended with " the web of our life, which is of a mingled yarn, good and ill together." It inquires what human life is and has been, to shew what it ought to be. It follows it into courts and camps, into town and country, into rustic sports or learned disputations, into the various shades of prejudice or ignorance, of refinement or barbarism, into its private haunts or public pageants, into its weaknesses and littlenesses, its professions and its practices— before it pretends to distinguish right from wrong, or one thing from another. How, indeed, should it do so otherwise?

> " Quid sit pulchrum, quid turpe, quid utile, quid non,
>   Plenius et melius Chrysippo et Crantore dicit."

The writers I speak of are, if not moral philosophers, moral historians, and that's better: or if they are both, they found the one character upon the other; their premises precede their conclusions; and we put faith in their testimony, for we know that it is true.

Montaigne was the first person who in his Essays led the way to this kind of writing among the moderns. The great merit of Montaigne then was, that he may be said to have been the first who had the courage to say as an author what he felt as a man. And as courage is generally

the effect of conscious strength, he was probably led to
do so by the richness, truth, and force of his own observations on books and men. He was, in the truest sense, a
man of original mind, that is, he had the power of looking
at things for himself, or as they really were, instead of
blindly trusting to, and fondly repeating what others told
him that they were. He got rid of the go-cart of prejudice
and affectation, with the learned lumber that follows at
their heels, because he could do without them. In taking
up his pen he did not set up for a philosopher, wit, orator,
or moralist, but he became all these by merely daring to
tell us whatever passed through his mind, in its naked
simplicity and force, that he thought any ways worth communicating. He did not, in the abstract character of an
author, undertake to say all that could be said upon a subject, but what in his capacity as an inquirer after truth
he happened to know about it. He was neither a pedant nor
a bigot. He neither supposed that he was bound to know
all things, nor that all things were bound to conform to
what he had fancied or would have them to be. In treating
of men and manners, he spoke of them as he found them,
not according to preconceived notions and abstract dogmas;
and he began by teaching us what he himself was. In
criticising books he did not compare them with rules and
systems, but told us what he saw to like or dislike in them.
He did not take his standard of excellence " according to
an exact scale " of Aristotle, or fall out with a work that
was good for any thing, because " not one of the angles
at the four corners was a right one." He was, in a word,
the first author who was not a bookmaker, and who wrote
not to make converts of others to established creeds and
prejudices, but to satisfy his own mind of the truth of
things. In this respect we know not which to be most
charmed with, the author or the man. There is an inex-

pressible frankness and sincerity, as well as power, in what he writes. There is no attempt at imposition or conceal-ment, no juggling tricks or solemn mouthing, no laboured attempts at proving himself always in the right, and every body else in the wrong; he says what is uppermost, lays open what floats at the top or the bottom of his mind, and deserves Pope's character of him, where he professes to

> "——— pour out all as plain
> As downright Shippen, or as old Montaigne." *

He does not converse with us like a pedagogue with his pupil, whom he wishes to make as great a blockhead as himself, but like a philosopher and friend who has passed through life with thought and observation, and is willing to enable others to pass through it with pleasure and profit. A writer of this stamp, I confess, appears to me as much superior to a common bookworm, as a library of real books is superior to a mere book-case, painted and lettered on the outside with the names of celebrated works. As he was the first to attempt this new way of writing, so the same strong natural impulse which prompted the under-taking, carried him to the end of his career. The same force and honesty of mind which urged him to throw off the shackles of custom and prejudice, would enable him to complete his triumph over them. He has left little for his successors to atchieve in the way of just and original speculation on human life. Nearly all the thinking of the two last centuries of that kind which the French de-nominate *morale observatrice,* is to be found in Montaigne's Essays: there is the germ, at least, and generally much more. He sowed the seed and cleared away the rubbish, even where others have reaped the fruit, or cultivated and

---

* Why Pope should say in reference to him, "Or *more wise* Charron," is not easy to determine.

decorated the soil to a greater degree of nicety and perfection. There is no one to whom the old Latin adage is more applicable than to Montaigne, "*Pereant isti qui ante nos nostra dixerunt.*" There has been no new impulse given to thought since his time. Among the specimens of criticisms on authors which he has left us, are those on Virgil, Ovid, and Boccaccio, in the account of books which he thinks worth reading, or (which is the same thing) which he finds he can read in his old age, and which may be reckoned among the few criticisms which are worth reading at any age.*

* As an instance of his general power of reasoning, I shall give his chapter entitled *One Man's Profit is Another's Loss,* in which he has nearly anticipated Mandeville's celebrated paradox of private vices being public benefits :—

"Demades, the Athenian, condemned a fellow-citizen, who furnished out funerals, for demanding too great a price for his goods: and if he got an estate, it must be by the death of a great many people: but I think it a sentence ill grounded, forasmuch as no profit can be made, but at the expense of some other person, and that every kind of gain is by that rule liable to be condemned. The tradesman thrives by the debauchery of youth, and the farmer by the dearness of corn; the architect by the ruin of buildings, the officers of justice by quarrels and law-suits; nay, even the honour and functions of divines is owing to our mortality and vices. No physician takes pleasure in the health even of his best friends, said the ancient Greek comedian, nor soldier in the peace of his country; and so of the rest. And, what is yet worse, let every one but examine his own heart, and he will find, that his private wishes spring and grow up at the expense of some other person. Upon which consideration this thought came into my head, that nature does not hereby deviate from her general policy; for the naturalists hold, that the birth, nourishment, and increase of any one thing, is the decay and corruption of another:

> *Nam quodcunque suis mutatum finibus exit,*
> *Continuo hoc mors est illius, quod fuit ante.* i.e.

For what from its own confines chang'd doth pass,
Is straight the death of what before it was."

*Vol.* I, *Chap.* XXI.

Montaigne's Essays were translated into English by Charles Cotton, who was one of the wits and poets of the age of Charles II; and Lord Halifax, one of the noble critics of that day, declared it to be " the book in the world he was the best pleased with." This mode of familiar Essay-writing, free from the trammels of the schools, and the airs of professed authorship, was successfully imitated, about the same time, by Cowley and Sir William Temple, in their miscellaneous Essays, which are very agreeable and learned talking upon paper. Lord Shaftesbury, on the contrary, who aimed at the same easy, *dégagé* mode of communicating his thoughts to the world, has quite spoiled his matter, which is sometimes valuable, by his manner, in which he carries a certain flaunting, flowery, figurative, flirting style of amicable condescension to the reader, to an excess more tantalising than the most starched and ridiculous formality of the age of James I. There is nothing so tormenting as the affectation of ease and freedom from affectation.

The ice being thus thawed, and the barrier that kept authors at a distance from common-sense and feeling broken through, the transition was not difficult from Montaigne and his imitators, to our Periodical Essayists. These last applied the same unrestrained expression of their thoughts to the more immediate and passing scenes of life, to temporary and local matters; and in order to discharge the invidious office of *Censor Morum* more freely, and with less responsibility, assumed some fictitious and humorous disguise, which, however, in a great degree corresponded to their own peculiar habits and character. By thus concealing their own name and person under the title of the Tatler, Spectator, etc. they were enabled to inform us more fully of what was passing in the world, while the dramatic contrast and ironical point of view to which the whole is subjected, added a greater liveliness and *piquancy* to the descriptions. The philosopher and wit here commences newsmonger, makes himself master of "the perfect spy o' th' time," and from his various walks and turns through life, brings home little curious specimens of the humours, opinions, and manners of his contemporaries, as the botanist brings home different plants and weeds, or the mineralogist different shells and fossils, to illustrate their several theories, and be useful to mankind.

The first of these papers that was attempted in this country was set up by Steele in the beginning of the last century; and of all our Periodical Essayists, the Tatler (for that was the name he assumed) has always appeared to me the most amusing and agreeable. Montaigne, whom I have proposed to consider as the father of this kind of personal authorship among the moderns, in which the reader is admitted behind the curtain, and sits down with the writer in his gown and slippers, was a most magnanimous and undisguised egotist; but Isaac Bickerstaff, Esq. was the more disinterested gossip of the two. The French author is contented to describe the peculiarities of his own mind and constitution, which he does with a copious and unsparing hand. The English journalist good-naturedly lets you into the secret both of his own affairs and those of others. A young lady, on the other side Temple Bar, cannot be seen at her glass for half a day together, but Mr. Bickerstaff takes due notice of it; and he has the first intelligence of the symptoms of the *belle* passion appearing in any young gentleman at the West-end of the town. The departures and arrivals of widows with handsome jointures, either to bury their grief in the country, or to procure a second husband in town, are punctually recorded in his pages. He is well acquainted with the celebrated beauties of the preceding age at the court of Charles II; and the old gentleman (as he feigns himself) often grows romantic in recounting " the disastrous strokes which his youth suffered " from the glances of their bright eyes, and their unaccountable caprices. In particular, he dwells with a secret satisfaction on the recollection of one of his mistresses, who left him for a richer rival, and whose constant reproach to her husband, on occasion of any quarrel between them, was " I, that might have married the famous Mr. Bickerstaff, to be treated in this manner!" The club at the Trumpet consists of a set of persons almost as well worth knowing as himself. The cavalcade of the justice of the peace, the knight of the shire, the country squire, and the young gentleman, his nephew, who came to wait on him at his chambers, in such form and ceremony, seem not to have settled the order of their precedence to this hour; * and I should hope that the upholsterer and his companions, who used to sun themselves in the Green Park, and who broke their rest and fortunes to maintain the balance of power in Europe, stand as fair a chance for immortality as some modern politicians. Mr. Bickerstaff himself is a gentleman and a scholar, a humourist, and a man of the world; with a great deal of nice easy *naïveté* about him. If he walks out and is caught in a shower of rain, he makes amends for this unlucky accident by a criticism on the shower in Virgil, and concludes with a burlesque copy of verses on a city-shower. He entertains us, when he dates from his own apartment, with a quotation from Plutarch, or a moral reflection; from the Grecian coffee-house with politics; and from Wills', or the Temple, with the poets and players, the beaux and men of wit and pleasure about town. In reading the pages of the Tatler, we seem as if suddenly carried back to the age of Queen Anne, of toupees and full-bottomed periwigs. The whole

* No. 125.

appearance of our dress and manners undergoes a delightful metamorphosis. The beaux and the belles are of a quite different species from what they are at present; we distinguish the dappers, the smarts, and the pretty fellows, as they pass by Mr. Lilly's shop-windows in the Strand; we are introduced to Betterton and Mrs. Oldfield behind the scenes; are made familiar with the persons and performances of Will Estcourt or Tom Durfey; we listen to a dispute at a tavern, on the merits of the Duke of Marlborough, or Marshal Turenne; or are present at the first rehearsal of a play by Vanbrugh, or the reading of a new poem by Mr. Pope. The privilege of thus virtually transporting ourselves to past times, is even greater than that of visiting distant places in reality. London, a hundred years ago, would be much better worth seeing than Paris at the present moment.

It will be said, that all this is to be found, in the same or a greater degree, in the Spectator. For myself, I do not think so; or at least, there is in the last work a much greater proportion of commonplace matter. I have, on this account, always preferred the Tatler to the Spectator. Whether it is owing to my having been earlier or better acquainted with the one than the other, my pleasure in reading these two admirable works is not in proportion to their comparative reputation. The Tatler contains only half the number of volumes, and, I will venture to say, nearly an equal quantity of sterling wit and sense. "The first sprightly runnings" are there: it has more of the original spirit, more of the freshness and stamp of nature. The indications of character and strokes of humour are more true and frequent; the reflections that suggest themselves arise more from the occasion, and are less spun out into regular dissertations. They are more like the remarks which occur in sensible conversation, and less like a lecture.

Something is left to the understanding of the reader.  Steele seems to have gone into his closet chiefly to set down what he observed out of doors.  Addison seems to have spent most of his time in his study, and to have spun out and wire-drawn the hints, which he borrowed from Steele, or took from nature, to the utmost.  I am far from wishing to depreciate Addison's talents, but I am anxious to do justice to Steele, who was, I think, upon the whole, a less artificial and more original writer.  The humorous descriptions of Steele resemble loose sketches, or fragments of a comedy; those of Addison are rather comments or ingenious paraphrases on the genuine text.  The characters of the club, not only in the Tatler, but in the Spectator, were drawn by Steele.  That of Sir Roger de Coverley is among the number.  Addison has, however, gained himself immortal honour by his manner of filling up this last character.  Who is there that can forget, or be insensible to, the inimitable nameless graces and varied traits of nature and of old English character in it—to his unpretending virtues and amiable weaknesses—to his modesty, generosity, hospitality, and eccentric whims—to the respect of his neighbours, and the affection of his domestics—to his wayward, hopeless, secret passion for his fair enemy, the widow, in which there is more of real romance and true delicacy than in a thousand tales of knight-errantry—(we perceive the hectic flush of his cheek, the faltering of his tongue in speaking of her bewitching airs and " the whiteness of her hand ")—to the havoc he makes among the game in his neighbourhood—to his speech from the bench, to shew the Spectator what is thought of him in the country—to his unwillingness to be put up as a sign-post, and his having his own likeness turned into the Saracen's head—to his gentle reproof of the baggage of a gipsy that tells him " he has a widow in his line of life "—to his doubts as to the existence of witch-

craft, and protection of reputed witches—to his account of
the family pictures, and his choice of a chaplain—to his
falling asleep at church, and his reproof of John Williams,
as soon as he recovered from his nap, for talking in
sermon-time. The characters of Will. Wimble and Will.
Honeycomb are not a whit behind their friend, Sir Roger,
in delicacy and felicity. The delightful simplicity and
good-humoured officiousness in the one, are set off by the
graceful affectation and courtly pretension in the other.
How long since I first became acquainted with these two
characters in the Spectator! What old-fashioned friends
they seem, and yet I am not tired of them, like so many
other friends, nor they of me! How airy these abstractions
of the poet's pen stream over the dawn of our acquaintance
with human life! how they glance their fairest colours on
the prospect before us! how pure they remain in it to the
last, like the rainbow in the evening-cloud, which the rude
hand of time and experience can neither soil nor dissipate!
What a pity that we cannot find the reality, and yet if we
did, the dream would be over. I once thought I knew a
Will. Wimble, and a Will. Honeycomb, but they turned out
but indifferently; the originals in the Spectator still read,
word for word, the same that they always did. We have
only to turn to the page, and find them where we left them!
—Many of the most exquisite pieces in the Tatler, it is to
be observed, are Addison's, as the Court of Honour, and
the Personification of Musical Instruments, with almost all
those papers that form regular sets or series. I do not
know whether the picture of the family of an old college
acquaintance, in the Tatler, where the children run to let
Mr. Bickerstaff in at the door, and where the one that
loses the race that way, turns back to tell the father that
he is come; with the nice gradation of incredulity in the
little boy who is got into Guy of Warwick, and the Seven

Champions, and who shakes his head at the improbability of Æsop's Fables, is Steele's or Addison's, though I believe it belongs to the former. The account of the two sisters, one of whom held up her head higher than ordinary, from having on a pair of flowered garters, and that of the married lady who complained to the Tatler of the neglect of her husband, with her answers to some *home* questions that were put to her, are unquestionably Steele's.—If the Tatler is not inferior to the Spectator as a record of manners and character, it is superior to it in the interest of many of the stories. Several of the incidents related there by Steele have never been surpassed in the heart-rending pathos of private distress. I might refer to those of the lover and his mistress, when the theatre, in which they were, caught fire; of the bridegroom, who by accident kills his bride on the day of their marriage; the story of Mr. Eustace and his wife; and the fine dream about his own mistress when a youth. What has given its superior reputation to the Spectator, is the greater gravity of its pretensions, its moral dissertations and critical reasonings, by which I confess myself less edified than by other things, which are thought more lightly of. Systems and opinions change, but nature is always true. It is the moral and didactic tone of the Spectator which makes us apt to think of Addison (according to Mandeville's sarcasm) as "a parson in a tie-wig." Many of his moral Essays are, however, exquisitely beautiful and quite happy. Such are the reflections on cheerfulness, those in Westminster Abbey, on the Royal Exchange, and particularly some very affecting ones on the death of a young lady in the fourth volume. These, it must be allowed, are the perfection of elegant sermonising. His critical Essays are not so good. I prefer Steele's occasional selection of beautiful poetical passages, without any affectation of analysing their beauties, to Addison's finer-spun theories. The best criticism in the Spectator, that on the Cartoons of Raphael, of which Mr. Fuseli has availed himself with great spirit in his Lectures, is by Steele.* I owed this acknowledgment to a writer who has so often put me in good humour with myself, and every thing about me, when few things else could, and when the tomes of casuistry and ecclesiastical history, with which the little duodecimo volumes of the Tatler were overwhelmed and surrounded, in the only library to which I had access when a boy, had tried their tranquillising effects upon me in vain. I had not long ago in my hands, by favour of a friend, an original copy of the quarto edition of the Tatler, with a list of the subscribers. It is curious to see some names there which we should hardly think of (that of Sir Isaac Newton is among them,) and also to observe the degree of interest excited by those of the different persons, which is not determined according to the rules of the Herald's College. One literary name lasts as long as a whole race of heroes and their descendants! The Guardian, which followed the Spectator, was, as may be supposed, inferior to it.

The dramatic and conversational turn which forms the distinguishing feature and greatest charm of the Spectator and Tatler, is quite lost in the Rambler by Dr. Johnson. There is no reflected light thrown on human life from an assumed character, nor any direct one from a display of the author's own. The Tatler and Spectator are, as it were, made up of notes and memorandums of the events and incidents of the day, with finished studies after nature, and characters fresh from the life, which the writer moralises

---

* The antithetical style and verbal paradoxes which Burke was so fond of, in which the epithet is a seeming contradiction to the substantive, such as "proud submission and dignified obedience," are, I think, first to be found in the Tatler.

upon, and turns to account as they come before him: the Rambler is a collection of moral Essays, or scholastic theses, written on set subjects, and of which the individual characters and incidents are merely artificial illustrations, brought in to give a pretended relief to the dryness of didactic discussion. The Rambler is a splendid and imposing common-place-book of general topics, and rhetorical declamation on the conduct and business of human life. In this sense, there is hardly a reflection that has been suggested on such subjects which is not to be found in this celebrated work, and there is, perhaps, hardly a reflection to be found in it which had not been already suggested and developed by some other author, or in the common course of conversation. The mass of intellectual wealth here heaped together is immense, but it is rather the result of gradual accumulation, the produce of the general intellect, labouring in the mine of knowledge and reflection, than dug out of the quarry, and dragged into the light by the industry and sagacity of a single mind. I am not here saying that Dr. Johnson was a man without originality, compared with the ordinary run of men's minds, but he was not a man of original thought or genius, in the sense in which Montaigne or Lord Bacon was. He opened no new vein of precious ore, nor did he light upon any single pebbles of uncommon size and unrivalled lustre. We seldom meet with anything to " give us pause; " he does not set us thinking for the first time. His reflections present themselves like reminiscences; do not disturb the ordinary march of our thoughts; arrest our attention by the stateliness of their appearance, and the costliness of their garb, but pass on and mingle with the throng of our impressions. After closing the volumes of the Rambler, there is nothing that we remember as a new truth gained to the mind, nothing indelibly stamped upon the memory; nor is there any passage that we wish to turn to as embodying any known principle or observation, with such force and beauty that justice can only be done to the idea in the author's own words. Such, for instance, are many of the passages to be found in Burke, which shine by their own light, belong to no class, have neither equal nor counterpart, and of which we say that no one but the author could have written them! There is neither the same boldness of design, nor mastery of execution in Johnson. In the one, the spark of genius seems to have met with its congenial matter: the shaft is sped; the forked lightning dresses up the face of nature in ghastly smiles, and the loud thunder rolls far away from the ruin that is made. Dr. Johnson's style, on the contrary, resembles rather the rumbling of mimic thunder at one of our theatres; and the light he throws upon a subject is like the dazzling effect of phosphorus, or an *ignis fatuus* of words. There is a wide difference, however, between perfect originality and perfect common-place: neither ideas nor expressions are trite or vulgar because they are not quite new. They are valuable, and ought to be repeated, if they have not become quite common; and Johnson's style both of reasoning and imagery holds the middle rank between startling novelty and vapid common-place. Johnson has as much originality of thinking as Addison; but then he wants his familiarity of illustration, knowledge of character, and delightful humour. What most distinguishes Dr. Johnson from other writers is the pomp and uniformity of his style. All his periods are cast in the same mould, are of the same size and shape, and consequently have little fitness to the variety of things he professes to treat of. His subjects are familiar, but the author is always upon stilts. He has neither ease nor simplicity, and his efforts at playfulness, in part, remind one of the lines in Milton :—

> "——The elephant
> To make them sport wreath'd his proboscis lithe."

His Letters from Correspondents, in particular, are more pompous and unwieldy than what he writes in his own person. This want of relaxation and variety of manner has, I think, after the first effects of novelty and surprise were over, been prejudicial to the matter. It takes from the general power, not only to please, but to instruct. The monotony of style produces an apparent monotony of ideas. What is really striking and valuable, is lost in the vain ostentation and circumlocution of the expression; for when we find the same pains and pomp of diction bestowed upon the most trifling as upon the most important parts of a sentence or discourse, we grow tired of distinguishing between pretension and reality, and are disposed to confound the tinsel and bombast of the phraseology with want of weight in the thoughts. Thus, from the imposing and oracular nature of the style, people are tempted at first to imagine that our author's speculations are all wisdom and profundity: till having found out their mistake in some instances, they suppose that there is nothing but common-place in them, concealed under verbiage and pedantry; and in both they are wrong. The fault of Dr. Johnson's style is, that it reduces all things to the same artificial and unmeaning level. It destroys all shades of difference, the association between words and things. It is a perpetual paradox and innovation. He condescends to the familiar till we are ashamed of our interest in it: he expands the little till it looks big. "If he were to write a fable of little fishes," as Goldsmith said of him, "he would make them speak like great whales." We can no more distinguish the most familiar objects in his descriptions of them, than we can a well-known face under a huge painted mask. The structure of his sentences, which was his own invention, and which has been generally imitated since his time, is a species of rhyming in prose, where one clause answers to another in measure and quantity, like the tagging of syllables at the end of a verse; the close of the period follows as mechanically as the oscillation of a pendulum, the sense is balanced with the sound; each sentence, revolving round its centre of gravity, is contained with itself like a couplet, and each paragraph forms itself into a stanza. Dr. Johnson is also a complete balance-master in the topics of morality. He never encourages hope, but he counteracts it by fear; he never elicits a truth, but he suggests some objection in answer to it. He seizes and alternately quits the clue of reason, lest it should involve him in the labyrinths of endless error: he wants confidence in himself and his fellows. He dares not trust himself with the immediate impressions of things, for fear of compromising his dignity; or follow them into their consequences, for fear of committing his prejudices. His timidity is the result, not of ignorance, but of morbid apprehension. "He runs the great circle, and is still at home." No advance is made by his writings in any sentiment, or mode of reasoning. Out of the pale of established authority and received dogmas, all is sceptical, loose, and desultory: he seems in imagination to strengthen the dominion of prejudice, as he weakens and dissipates that of reason; and round the rock of faith and power, on the edge of which he slumbers blindfold and uneasy, the waves and billows of uncertain and dangerous opinion roar and heave for evermore. His Rasselas is the most melancholy and debilitating moral speculation that ever was put forth. Doubtful of the faculties of his mind, as of his organs of vision, Johnson trusted only to his feelings and his fears. He cultivated a belief in witches as an out-guard to the evidences of religion; and abused Milton, and patronised Lauder, in spite of his aversion to his countrymen, as a step to secure the existing establishment in church and state. This was neither right feeling nor sound logic.

The most triumphant record of the talents and character of Johnson is to be found in Boswell's Life of him. The man was superior to the author. When he threw aside his pen, which he regarded as an incumbrance, he became not only learned and thoughtful, but acute, witty, humorous, natural, honest; hearty and determined, "the king of good fellows and wale of old men." There are as many smart repartees, profound remarks, and keen invectives to be found in Boswell's "inventory of all he said," as are recorded of any celebrated man. The life and dramatic play of his conversation forms a contrast to his written works. His natural powers and undisguised opinions were called out in convivial intercourse. In public, he practised with the foils on: in private, he unsheathed the sword of controversy, and it was "the Ebro's temper." The eagerness of opposition roused him from his natural sluggishness and acquired timidity; he returned blow for blow; and whether the trial were of argument or wit, none of his rivals could boast much of the encounter. Burke seems to have been the only person who had a chance with him; and it is the unpardonable sin of Boswell's work, that he has purposely omitted their combats of strength and skill. Goldsmith asked, " Does he wind into a subject like a serpent, as Burke does? " And when exhausted with sickness, he himself said, " If that fellow Burke were here now, he would kill me." It is to be observed, that Johnson's colloquial style was as blunt, direct, and downright, as his style of studied composition was involved and circuitous. As when Topham Beauclerc and Langton knocked him up at his chambers, at three in the morning, and he came to the door with the poker in his hand, but seeing them, exclaimed, " What, is it you, my lads? then I'll have a frisk with you! " and

he afterwards reproaches Langton, who was a literary
milksop, for leaving them to go to an engagement " with
some *un-idead* girls." What words to come from the mouth
of the great moralist and lexicographer! His good deeds
were as many as his good sayings. His domestic habits,
his tenderness to servants, and readiness to oblige his
friends; the quantity of strong tea that he drank to keep
down sad thoughts; his many labours reluctantly begun,
and irresolutely laid aside; his honest acknowledgment of
his own, and indulgence to the weaknesses of others; his
throwing himself back in the post-chaise with Boswell, and
saying, " Now I think I am a good-humoured fellow,"
though nobody thought him so, and yet he was; his quitting
the society of Garrick and his actresses, and his reason
for it; his dining with Wilkes, and his kindness to Goldsmith; his sitting with the young ladies on his knee at the
Mitre, to give them good advice, in which situation, if not
explained, he might be taken for Falstaff; and last and
noblest, his carrying the unfortunate victim of disease and
dissipation on his back up through Fleet Street, (an act
which realises the parable of the good Samaritan)—all
these, and innumerable others, endear him to the reader,
and must be remembered to his lasting honour. He had
faults, but they lie buried with him. He had his prejudices
and his intolerant feelings; but he suffered enough in the
conflict of his own mind with them. For if no man can
be happy in the free exercise of his reason, no wise man
can be happy without it. His were not time-serving, heart-
less, hypocritical prejudices; but deep, inwoven, not to be
rooted out but with life and hope, which he found from
old habit necessary to his own peace of mind, and thought
so to the peace of mankind. I do not hate, but love him
for them. They were between himself and his conscience;
and should be left to that higher tribunal, " where they in

trembling hope repose, the bosom of his Father and his God." In a word, he has left behind him few wiser or better men.

The herd of his imitators shewed what he was by their disproportionate effects. The Periodical Essayists, that succeeded the Rambler, are, and deserve to be, little read at present. The Adventurer, by Hawksworth, is completely trite and vapid, aping all the faults of Johnson's style, without any thing to atone for them. The sentences are often absolutely unmeaning; and one half of each might regularly be left blank. The World, and Connoisseur, which followed, are a little better; and in the last of these there is one·good idea, that of a man in indifferent health, who judges of every one's title to respect from their possession of this blessing, and bows to a sturdy beggar with sound limbs and a florid complexion, while he turns his back upon a lord who is a valetudinarian.

Goldsmith's Citizen of the World, like all his works, bears the stamp of the author's mind. It does not " go about to cozen reputation without the stamp of merit." He is more observing, more original, more natural and picturesque than Johnson. His work is written on the model of the Persian Letters; and contrives to give an abstracted and somewhat perplexing view of things, by opposing foreign prepossessions to our own, and thus stripping objects of their customary disguises. Whether truth is elicited in this collision of contrary absurdities, I do not know; but I confess the process is too ambiguous and full of intricacy to be very amusing to my plain understanding. For light summer reading, it is like walking in a garden full of traps and pitfalls. It necessarily gives rise to paradoxes, and there are some very bold ones in the Essays, which would subject an author less established to no very agreeable sort of *censura literaria*. Thus the Chinese philosopher exclaims very unadvisedly, " The bonzes and priests of all religions keep up superstition and imposture: all reformations begin with the laity." Goldsmith, however, was staunch in his practical creed, and might bolt speculative extravagances with impunity. There is a striking difference in this respect between him and Addison, who, if he attacked authority, took care to have common sense on his side, and never hazarded anything offensive to the feelings of others, or on the strength of his own discretional opinion. There is another inconvenience in this assumption of an exotic character and tone of sentiment, that it produces an inconsistency between the knowledge which the individual has time to acquire, and which the author is bound to communicate. Thus the Chinese has not been in England three days before he is acquainted with the characters of the three countries which compose this kingdom, and describes them to his friend at Canton, by extracts from the newspapers of each metropolis. The nationality of Scotchmen is thus ridiculed:—" *Edinburgh.* We are positive when we say, that Sanders Macgregor, lately executed for horse-stealing, is not a native of Scotland, but born at Carrickfergus." Now this is very good; but how should our Chinese philosopher find it out by instinct? Beau Tibbs, a prominent character in this little work, is the best comic sketch since the time of Addison; unrivalled in his finery, his vanity, and his poverty.

I have only to mention the names of the Lounger and the Mirror, which are ranked by the author's admirers with Sterne for sentiment, and with Addison for humour. I shall not enter into that: but I know that the story of La Roche is not like the story of Le Fevre, nor one hundredth part so good. Do I say this from prejudice to the author? No: for I have read his novels. Of the Man of the World I cannot think so favourably as some others; nor shall I here dwell on the picturesque and romantic beauties of Julia de Roubigné, the early favourite of the author of Rosamond Gray; but of the Man of Feeling I would speak with grateful recollections: nor is it possible to forget the sensitive, irresolute, interesting Harley; and that lone figure of Miss Walton in it, that floats in the horizon, dim and ethereal, the day-dream of her lover's youthful fancy—better, far better than all the realities of life!

# VIII

## THE ENGLISH NOVELISTS

THERE is an exclamation in one of Gray's Letters—"Be mine to read eternal new romances of Marivaux and Crebillon!"—If I did not utter a similar aspiration at the conclusion of the last new novel which I read (I would not give offence by being more particular as to the name) it was not from any want of affection for the class of writing to which it belongs: for, without going so far as the celebrated French philosopher, who thought that more was to be learnt from good novels and romances than from the gravest treatises on history and morality, yet there are few works to which I am oftener tempted to turn for profit or delight, than to the standard productions in this species of composition. We find there a close imitation of men and manners; we see the very web and texture of society as it really exists, and as we meet with it when we come into the world. If poetry has " something more divine in it," this savours more of humanity. We are brought acquainted with the motives and characters of mankind, imbibe our notions of virtue and vice from practical examples, and are taught a knowledge of the world through the airy medium of romance. As a record of past manners and opinions, too, such writings afford the best and fullest information. For example, I should be at a loss where to find in any authentic documents of the same period so satisfactory an account of the general state of society, and of moral, political, and religious feeling in the reign of

George II, as we meet with in the Adventures of Joseph Andrews and his friend Mr. Abraham Adams. This work, indeed, I take to be a perfect piece of statistics in its kind. In looking into any regular history of that period, into a learned and eloquent charge to a grand jury or the clergy of a diocese, or into a tract on controversial divinity, we should hear only of the ascendancy of the Protestant succession, the horrors of Popery, the triumph of civil and religious liberty, the wisdom and moderation of the sovereign, the happiness of the subject, and the flourishing state of manufactures and commerce. But if we really wish to know what all these fine-sounding names come to, we cannot do better than turn to the works of those, who having no other object than to imitate nature, could only hope for success from the fidelity of their pictures; and were bound (in self-defence) to reduce the boasts of vague theorists and the exaggerations of angry disputants to the mortifying standard of reality. Extremes are said to meet: and the works of imagination, as they are called, sometimes come the nearest to truth and nature. Fielding in speaking on this subject, and vindicating the use and dignity of the style of writing in which he excelled against the loftier pretensions of professed historians, says that in their productions nothing is true but the names and dates, whereas in his everything is true but the names and dates. If so, he has the advantage on his side.

I will here confess, however, that I am a little prejudiced on the point in question; and that the effect of many fine speculations has been lost upon me, from an early familiarity with the most striking passages in the work to which I have just alluded. Thus nothing can be more captivating than the description somewhere given by Mr. Burke of the indissoluble connection between learning and nobility; and of the respect universally paid by wealth to piety and morals. But the effect of this ideal representation has always been spoiled by my recollection of Parson Adams sitting over his cup of ale in Sir Thomas Booby's kitchen. Echard "On the Contempt of the Clergy" is, in like manner, a very good book, and "worthy of all acceptation:" but, somehow, an unlucky impression of the reality of Parson Trulliber involuntarily checks the emotions of respect, to which it might otherwise give rise: while, on the other hand, the lecture which Lady Booby reads to Lawyer Scout on the immediate expulsion of Joseph and Fanny from the parish casts no very favourable light on the flattering accounts of our practical jurisprudence which are to be found in Blackstone or De Lolme. The most moral writers, after all, are those who do not pretend to inculcate any moral. The professed moralist almost unavoidably degenerates into the partisan of a system; and the philosopher is too apt to warp the evidence to his own purpose. But the painter of manners gives the facts of human nature, and leaves us to draw the inference: if we are not able to do this, or do it ill, at least it is our own fault.

The first-rate writers in this class, of course, are few; but those few we may reckon among the greatest ornaments and best benefactors of our kind. There is a certain set of them who, as it were, take their rank by the side of reality, and are appealed to as evidence on all questions concerning human nature. The principal of these are Cervantes and Le Sage, who may be considered as having been naturalised among ourselves; and, of native English growth, Fielding, Smollett, Richardson, and Sterne.* As

---

* It is not to be forgotten that the author of Robinson Crusoe was also an Englishman. His other works, such as the Life of Colonel Jack, &c., are of the same cast, and leave an impression on the mind more like that of things than words.

this is a department of criticism which deserves more attention than has been usually bestowed upon it, I shall here
venture to recur (not from choice, but necessity) to what
I have said upon it in a well-known periodical publication;
and endeavour to contribute my mite towards settling the
standard of excellence, both as to degree and kind, in these
several writers. . . .

There is very little to warrant the common idea that
Fielding was an imitator of Cervantes, except his own
declaration of such an intention in the title-page of Joseph
Andrews, the romantic turn of the character of Parson
Adams (the only romantic character in his works), and
the proverbial humour of Partridge, which is kept up only
for a few pages.  Fielding's novels are, in general, thoroughly his own; and they are thoroughly English.  What
they are most remarkable for, is neither sentiment, nor
imagination, nor wit, nor even humour, though there is an
immense deal of this last quality; but profound knowledge
of human nature, at least of English nature; and masterly
pictures of the characters of men as he saw them existing.
This quality distinguishes all his works, and is shown almost
equally in all of them.  As a painter of real life, he was
equal to Hogarth; as a mere observer of human nature, he
was little inferior to Shakspeare, though without any of the
genius and poetical qualities of his mind.  His humour is
less rich and laughable than Smollett's; his wit as often
misses as hits; he has none of the fine pathos of Richardson
or Sterne; but he has brought together a greater variety
of characters in common life, marked with more distinct
peculiarities, and without an atom of caricature, than any
other novel writer whatever.  The extreme subtlety of observation on the springs of human conduct in ordinary
characters, is only equalled by the ingenuity of contrivance
in bringing those springs into play, in such a manner as

to lay open their smallest irregularity. The detection is
always complete, and made with the certainty and skill of
a philosophical experiment, and the obviousness and familiarity of a casual observation. The truth of the imitation
is indeed so great, that it has been argued that Fielding
must have had his materials ready-made to his hands, and
was merely a transcriber of local manners and individual
habits. For this conjecture, however, there seems to be no
foundation. His representations, it is true, are local and
individual; but they are not the less profound and conclusive. The feeling of the general principles of human
nature, operating in particular circumstances, is always intense, and uppermost in his mind; and he makes use of
incident and situation only to bring out character.

It is scarcely necessary to give any illustrations. Tom
Jones is full of them. There is the account, for example,
of the gratitude of the elder Blifil to his brother, for
assisting him to obtain the fortune of Miss Bridget Alworthy by marriage; and of the gratitude of the poor in
his neighbourhood to Alworthy himself, who had done so
much good in the country that he had made every one in
it his enemy. There is the account of the Latin dialogues
between Partridge and his maid, of the assault made on
him during one of these by Mrs. Partridge, and the severe
bruises he patiently received on that occasion, after which
the parish of Little Baddington rung with the story, that
the school-master had killed his wife. There is the exquisite
keeping in the character of Blifil, and the want of it in that
of Jones. There is the gradation in the lovers of Molly
Seagrim; the philosopher Square succeeding to Tom Jones,
who again finds that he himself had succeeded to the accomplished Will. Barnes, who had the first possession of her
person, and had still possession of her heart, Jones being
only the instrument of her vanity, as Square was of her

interest.  Then there is the discreet honesty of Black
George, the learning of Thwackum and Square, and the
profundity of Squire Western, who considered it as a
physical impossibility that his daughter should fall in love
with Tom Jones.  We have also that gentleman's disputes
with his sister, and the inimitable appeal of that lady to
her niece.—" I was never so handsome as you, Sophy: yet
I had something of you formerly.  I was called the cruel
Parthenissa.  Kingdoms and states, as Tully Cicero says,
undergo alteration, and so must the human form! "  The
adventure of the same lady with the highwayman, who
robbed her of her jewels while he complimented her beauty,
ought not to be passed over, nor that of Sophia and her
muff, nor the reserved coquetry of her cousin Fitzpatrick,
nor the description of Lady Bellaston, nor the modest overtures of the pretty widow Hunt, nor the indiscreet babblings
of Mrs. Honour.  The moral of this book has been objected to, without much reason; but a more serious objection has been made to the want of refinement and elegance
in two principal characters.  We never feel this objection,
indeed, while we are reading the book; but at other times
we have something like a lurking suspicion that Jones was
but an awkward fellow, and Sophia a pretty simpleton.  I
do not know how to account for this effect, unless it is that
Fielding's constantly assuring us of the beauty of his hero,
and the good sense of his heroine, at last produces a distrust
of both.  The story of Tom Jones is allowed to be unrivalled: and it is this circumstance, together with the vast
variety of characters, that has given the History of a
Foundling so decided a preference over Fielding's other
novels.  The characters themselves, both in Amelia and
Joseph Andrews, are quite equal to any of those in Tom
Jones.  The account of Miss Matthews and Ensign Hibbert,
in the former of these; the way in which that lady recon-

ciles herself to the death of her father; the inflexible Colonel
Bath; the insipid Mrs. James, the complaisant Colonel
Trent, the demure, sly, intriguing, equivocal Mrs. Bennet,
the lord who is her seducer, and who attempts afterwards
to seduce Amelia by the same mechanical process of a
concert-ticket, a book, and the disguise of a great-coat; his
little, fat, short-nosed, red-faced, good-humoured accom-
plice, the keeper of the lodging-house, who, having no
pretensions to gallantry herself, has a disinterested delight
in forwarding the intrigues and pleasures of others (to say
nothing of honest Atkinson, the story of the miniature-
picture of Amelia, and the hashed mutton, which are in
a different style,) are masterpieces of description. The
whole scene at the lodging-house, the masquerade, etc., in
Amelia, are equal in interest to the parallel scenes in Tom
Jones, and even more refined in the knowledge of character.
For instance, Mrs. Bennet is superior to Mrs. Fitzpatrick
in her own way. The uncertainty, in which the event of
her interview with her former seducer is left, is admirable.
Fielding was a master of what may be called the *double
entendre* of character, and surprises you no less by what
he leaves in the dark, (hardly known to the persons themselves) than by the unexpected discoveries he makes of
the real traits and circumstances in a character with which,
till then, you find you were unacquainted. There is nothing
at all heroic, however, in the usual style of his delineations.
He does not draw lofty characters or strong passions; all
his persons are of the ordinary stature as to intellect; and
possess little elevation of fancy, or energy of purpose. Perhaps, after all, Parson Adams is his finest character. It
is equally true to nature, and more ideal than any of the
others. Its unsuspecting simplicity makes it not only more
amiable, but doubly amusing, by gratifying the sense of
superior sagacity in the reader. Our laughing at him does

not once lessen our respect for him. His declaring that he would willingly walk ten miles to fetch his sermon on vanity, merely to convince Wilson of his thorough contempt of this vice, and his consoling himself for the loss of his Æschylus, by suddenly recollecting that he could not read it if he had it, because it is dark, are among the finest touches of *naïveté*. The night-adventures at Lady Booby's with Beau Didapper, and the amiable Slipslop, are the most ludicrous; and that with the huntsman, who draws off the hounds from the poor Parson, because they would be spoiled by following *vermin*, the most profound. Fielding did not often repeat himself; but Dr. Harrison, in Amelia, may be considered as a variation of the character of Adams: so also is Goldsmith's Vicar of Wakefield; and the latter part of that work, which sets out so delightfully, an almost entire plagiarism from Wilson's account of himself, and Adams's domestic history.

Smollett's first novel, Roderick Random, which is also his best, appeared about the same time as Fielding's Tom Jones; and yet it has a much more modern air with it: but this may be accounted for from the circumstance that Smollett was quite a young man at the time, whereas Fielding's manner must have been formed long before. The style of Roderick Random is more easy and flowing than that of Tom Jones; the incidents follow one another more rapidly (though, it must be confessed, they never come in such a throng, or are brought out with the same dramatic effect); the humour is broader, and as effectual; and there is very nearly, if not quite, an equal interest excited by the story. What, then, is it that gives the superiority to Fielding? It is the superior insight into the springs of human character, and the constant developement of that character through every change of circumstance. Smollett's humour often arises from the situation of the persons, or the pecul-

iarity of their external appearance; as, from Roderick
Random's carrotty locks, which hung down over his shoulders like a pound of candles, or Strap's ignorance of
London, and the blunders that follow from it. There is a
tone of vulgarity about all his productions. The incidents
frequently resemble detached anecdotes taken from a newspaper or magazine; and, like those in Gil Blas, might
happen to a hundred other characters. He exhibits the
ridiculous accidents and reverses to which human life is
liable, not " the stuff " of which it is composed. He seldom
probes to the quick, or penetrates beyond the surface; and,
therefore, he leaves no stings in the minds of his readers,
and in this respect is far less interesting than Fielding.
His novels. always enliven, and never tire us: we take them
up with pleasure, and lay them down without any strong
feeling of regret. We look on and laugh, as spectators of
a highly amusing scene, without closing in with the combatants, or being made parties in the event. We read
Roderick Random as an entertaining story; for the particular accidents and modes of life which it describes have
ceased to exist : but we regard Tom Jones as a real history;
because the author never stops short of those essential principles which lie at the bottom of all our actions, and in
which we feel an immediate interest—*intus et in cute.*
Smollett excels most as the lively caricaturist: Fielding as
the exact painter and profound metaphysician. I am far
from maintaining that this account applies uniformly to the
productions of these two writers; but I think that, as far
as they essentially differ, what I have stated is the general
distinction between them. Roderick Random is the purest
of Smollett's novels: I mean in point of style and description. Most of the incidents and characters are supposed
to have been taken from the events of his own life; and
are, therefore, truer to nature. There is a rude conception

of generosity in some of his characters, of which Fielding seems to have been incapable, his amiable persons being merely good-natured. It is owing to this that Strap is superior to Partridge; as there is a heartiness and warmth of feeling in some of the scenes between Lieutenant Bowling and his nephew, which is beyond Fielding's power of impassioned writing. The whole of the scene on ship-board is a most admirable and striking picture, and, I imagine, very little if at all exaggerated, though the interest it excites is of a very unpleasant kind, because the irritation and resistance to petty oppression can be of no avail. The picture of the little profligate French friar, who was Roderick's travelling companion, and of whom he always kept to the windward, is one of Smollett's most masterly sketches. Peregrine Pickle is no great favourite of mine, and Launcelot Greaves was not worthy of the genius of the author.

Humphry Clinker and Count Fathom are both equally admirable in their way. Perhaps the former is the most pleasant gossiping novel that ever was written; that which gives the most pleasure with the least effort to the reader. It is quite as amusing as going the journey could have been; and we have just as good an idea of what happened on the road, as if we had been of the party. Humphry Clinker himself is exquisite; and his sweetheart, Winifred Jenkins, not much behind him. Matthew Bramble, though not altogether original, is excellently supported, and seems to have been the prototype of Sir Anthony Absolute in the Rivals. But Lismahago is the flower of the flock. His tenaciousness in argument is not so delightful as the relaxation of his logical severity, when he finds his fortune mellowing in the wintry smiles of Mrs. Tabitha Bramble. This is the best-preserved and most severe of all Smollett's characters. The resemblance to Don Quixote is only just enough to make it

interesting to the critical reader, without giving offence to
any body else. The indecency and filth in this novel are
what must be allowed to all Smollett's writings.—The subject and characters in Count Fathom are, in general, exceedingly disgusting: the story is also spun out to a degree of
tediousness in the serious and sentimental parts; but there
is more power of writing occasionally shewn in it than in
any of his works. I need only refer to the fine and bitter
irony of the Count's address to the country of his ancestors
on his landing in England; to the robber-scene in the forest,
which has never been surpassed; to the Parisian swindler
who personates a raw English country squire (Western is
tame in the comparison); and to the story of the seduction
in the west of England. It would be difficult to point out,
in any author, passages written with more force and mastery than these.

It is not a very difficult undertaking to class Fielding or
Smollett;—the one as an observer of the characters of
human life, the other as a describer of its various eccen-
tricities. But it is by no means so easy to dispose of
Richardson, who was neither an observer of the one, nor
a describer of the other; but who seemed to spin his materials entirely out of his own brain, as if there had been
nothing existing in the world beyond the little room in
which he sat writing. There is an artificial reality about
his works, which is no where else to be met with. They
have the romantic air of a pure fiction, with the literal
minuteness of a common diary. The author had the strongest matter-of-fact imagination that ever existed, and wrote
the oddest mixture of poetry and prose. He does not
appear to have taken advantage of anything in actual nature,
from one end of his works to the other; and yet, throughout
all his works, voluminous as they are—(and this, to be sure,
is one reason why they are so,)—he sets about describing

every object and transaction, as if the whole had been given in on evidence by an eye-witness. This kind of high finishing from imagination is an anomaly in the history of human genius; and, certainly, nothing so fine was ever produced by the same accumulation of minute parts. There is not the least distraction, the least forgetfulness of the end: every circumstance is made to tell. I cannot agree that this exactness of detail produces heaviness; on the contrary, it gives an appearance of truth, and a positive interest to the story; and we listen with the same attention as we should to the particulars of a confidential communication. I at one time used to think some parts of Sir Charles Grandison rather trifling and tedious, especially the long description of Miss Harriet Byron's wedding-clothes, till I was told of two young ladies who had severally copied out the whole of that very description for their own private gratification. After that, I could not blame the author.

The effect of reading this work is like an increase of kindred. You find yourself all of a sudden introduced into the midst of a large family, with aunts and cousins to the third and fourth generation, and grandmothers both by the father's and mother's side;—and a very odd set of people they are, but people whose real existence and personal identity you can no more dispute than your own senses, for you see and hear all that they do or say. What is still more extraordinary, all this extreme elaborateness in working out the story, seems to have cost the author nothing; for it is said, that the published works are mere abridgments. I have heard (though this I suspect must be a pleasant exaggeration) that Sir Charles Grandison was originally written in eight and twenty volumes.

Pamela is the first of Richardson's productions, and the very child of his brain. Taking the general idea of the character of a modest and beautiful country girl, and of

the ordinary situation in which she is placed, he makes out
all the rest, even to the smallest circumstance, by the mere
force of a reasoning imagination. It would seem as if
a step lost, would be as fatal here as in a mathematical
demonstration. The development of the character is the
most simple, and comes the nearest to nature that it can
do, without being the same thing. The interest of the story
increases with the dawn of understanding and reflection in
the heroine: her sentiments gradually expand themselves,
like opening flowers. She writes better every time, and
acquires a confidence in herself, just as a girl would do,
writing such letters in such circumstances; and yet it is
certain *that no girl would write such letters in such circumstances.* What I mean is this:—Richardson's nature is
always the nature of sentiment and reflection, not of impulse
or situation. He furnishes his characters, on every occasion, with the presence of mind of the author. He makes
them act, not as they would from the impulse of the moment, but as they might upon reflection, and upon a careful
review of every motive and circumstance in their situation.
They regularly sit down to write letters: and if the business
of life consisted in letter-writing, and was carried on by
the post (like a Spanish game at chess), human nature
would be what Richardson represents it. All actual objects
and feelings are blunted and deadened by being presented
through a medium which may be true to reason, but is
false in nature. He confounds his own point of view with
that of the immediate actors in the scene; and hence presents you with a conventional and factitious nature, instead
of that which is real. Dr. Johnson seems to have preferred
this truth of reflection to the truth of nature, when he said
that there was more knowledge of the human heart in a
page of Richardson, than in all Fielding. Fielding, however, saw more of the practical results, and understood

thé principles as well; but he had not the same power of speculating upon their possible results, and combining them in certain ideal forms of passion and imagination, which was Richardson's real excellence.

It must be observed, however, that it is this mutual good understanding, and comparing of notes between the author and the persons he describes; his infinite circumspection, his exact process of ratiocination and calculation, which gives such an appearance of coldness and formality to most of his characters,—which makes prudes of his women, and coxcombs of his men. Every thing is too conscious in his works. Every thing is distinctly brought home to the mind of the actors in the scene, which is a fault undoubtedly: but then it must be confessed, every thing is brought home in its full force to the mind of the reader also; and we feel the same interest in the story as if it were our own. Can anything be more beautiful or more affecting than Pamela's reproaches to her "lumpish heart," when she is sent away from her master's at her own request; its lightness, when she is sent for back; the joy which the conviction of the sincerity of his love diffuses in her heart, like the coming on of spring; the artifice of the stuff gown; the meeting with Lady Davers after her marriage; and the trial-scene with her husband? Who ever remained insensible to the passion of Lady Clementina, except Sir Charles Grandison himself, who was the object of it? Clarissa is, however, his masterpiece, if we except Lovelace. If she is fine in herself, she is still finer in his account of her. With that foil, her purity is dazzling indeed: and she who could triumph by her virtue, and the force of her love, over the regality of Lovelace's mind, his wit, his person, his accomplishments, and his spirit, conquers all hearts. I should suppose that never sympathy more deep or sincere was excited than by the heroine of Richardson's romance, except by the calamities of real life. The links in this wonderful chain of interest are not more finely wrought, than their whole weight is overwhelming and irresistible. Who can forget the exquisite gradations of her long dying-scene, or the closing of the coffin-lid, when Miss Howe comes to take her last leave of her friend; or the heart-breaking reflection that Clarissa makes on what was to have been her wedding-day? Well does a certain writer exclaim—

> "Books are a real world, both pure and good,
>     Round which, with tendrils strong as flesh and blood,
>     Our pastime and our happiness may grow!"

Richardson's wit was unlike that of any other writer—his humour was so too. Both were the effect of intense activity of mind—laboured, and yet completely effectual. I might refer to Lovelace's reception and description of Hickman, when he calls out Death in his ear, as the name of the person with whom Clarissa had fallen in love; and to the scene at the glove-shop. What can be more magnificent than his enumeration of his companions—"Belton, so pert and so pimply—Tourville, so fair and so foppish!" etc. In casuistry this author is quite at home; and, with a boldness greater even than his puritanical severity, has exhausted every topic on virtue and vice. There is another peculiarity in Richardson, not perhaps so uncommon, which is, his systematically preferring his most insipid characters to his finest, though both were equally his own invention, and he must be supposed to have understood something of their qualities. Thus he preferred the little, selfish, affected, insignificant Miss Byron, to the divine Clementina; and again, Sir Charles Grandison, to the nobler Lovelace. I have nothing to say in favour of Lovelace's morality; but Sir Charles is the prince of coxcombs,—whose eye was never once taken from his own person, and his own virtues; and there is nothing which excites so little sympathy as this excessive egotism.

It remains to speak of Sterne; and I shall do it in few words. There is more of *mannerism* and affectation in him, and a more immediate reference to preceding authors; but his excellences, where he is excellent, are of the first order. His characters are intellectual and inventive, like Richardson's; but totally opposite in the execution. The one are made out by continuity, and patient repetition of touches: the others, by glancing transitions and graceful apposition. His style is equally different from Richardson's: it is at times the most rapid, the most happy, the most idomatic of any that is to be found. It is the pure essence of English conversational style. His works consist only of *morceaux*—of brilliant passages. I wonder that Goldsmith, who ought to have known better, should call him "a dull fellow." His wit is poignant, though artificial; and his characters (though the groundwork of some of them had been laid before) have yet invaluable original differences; and the spirit of the execution, the masterstrokes constantly thrown into them, are not to be surpassed. It is sufficient to name them;—Yorick, Dr. Slop, Mr. Shandy, My Uncle Toby, Trim, Susanna, and the Widow Wadman. In these he has contrived to oppose, with equal felicity and originality, two characters, one of pure intellect, and the other of pure good nature, in My Father and My Uncle Toby. There appears to have been in Sterne a vein of dry, sarcastic humour, and of extreme tenderness of feeling; the latter sometimes carried to affectation, as in the tale of Maria, and the apostrophe to the recording angel: but at other times pure, and without blemish. The story of Le Fevre is perhaps the finest in the English language. My Father's restlessness, both of body and mind, is inimitable. It is the model from which all those despicable performances against modern philosophy ought to have been copied, if their authors had known any thing of the subject they were writing about. My Uncle Toby is one of the finest compliments ever paid to human nature. He is the most unoffending of God's creatures; or, as the French express it, *un tel petit bon homme!* Of his bowling-green, his sieges, and his amours, who would say or think any thing amiss!

## IX

## CHARACTER OF MR. BURKE, 1807 *

THE following speech is perhaps the fairest specimen I could give of Mr. Burke's various talents as a speaker. The subject itself is not the most interesting, nor does it admit of that weight and closeness of reasoning which he displayed on other occasions. But there is no single speech which can convey a satisfactory idea of his powers of mind: to do him justice, it would be necessary to quote all his works; the only specimen of Burke is, *all that he wrote*. With respect to most other speakers, a specimen is generally enough, or more than enough. When you are acquainted with their manner, and see what proficiency they have made in the mechanical exercise of their profession, with what facility they can borrow a simile, or round a period, how dexterously they can argue, and object, and rejoin, you are satisfied; there is no other difference in their speeches than what arises from the difference of the subjects. But this was not the case with Burke. He brought his subjects along with him; he drew his materials from himself. The only limits which circumscribed his variety were the stores of his own mind. His stock of ideas did not consist of a few meagre facts, meagrely stated, of half a dozen common-places tortured in a thousand different ways: but his mine of wealth was a profound understanding, inexhaustible as the human heart, and various as

* This character was written in a fit of extravagant candour, at a time when I thought I could do justice, or more than justice, to an enemy, without betraying a cause.

the sources of nature. He therefore enriched every subject to which he applied himself, and new subjects were
only the occasions of calling forth fresh powers of mind
which had not been before exerted. It would therefore
be in vain to look for the proof of his powers in any one
of his speeches or writings: they all contain some additional
proof of power. In speaking of Burke, then, I shall speak
of the whole compass and circuit of his mind—not of that
small part or section of him which I have been able to give:
to do otherwise would be like the story of the man who
put the brick in his pocket, thinking to shew it as the model
of a house. I have been able to manage pretty well with
respect to all my other speakers, and curtailed them down
without remorse. It was easy to reduce them within certain limits, to fix their spirit, and condense their variety;
by having a certain quantity given, you might infer all the
rest; it was only the same thing over again. But who can
bind Proteus, or confine the roving flight of genius?

Burke's writings are better than his speeches, and indeed
his speeches are writings. But he seemed to feel himself
more at ease, to have a fuller possession of his faculties in
addressing the public, than in addressing the House of
Commons. Burke was *raised* into public life: and he seems
to have been prouder of this new dignity than became so
great a man. For this reason, most of his speeches have
a sort of parliamentary preamble to them: there is an air
of affected modesty, and ostentatious trifling in them: he
seems fond of coqueting with the House of Commons, and
is perpetually calling the Speaker out to dance a minuet
with him, before he begins. There is also something like
an attempt to stimulate the superficial dulness of his hearers
by exciting their surprise, by running into extravagance:
and he sometimes demeans himself by condescending to
what may be considered as bordering too much upon buf-

foonery, for the amusement of the company. Those lines of Milton were admirably applied to him by some one— " The elephant to make them sport wreathed his proboscis lithe." The truth is, that he was out of his place in the House of Commons; he was eminently qualified to shine as a man of genius, as the instructor of mankind, as the brightest luminary of his age: but he had nothing in common with that motley crew of knights, citizens, and burgesses. He could not be said to be " native and endued unto that element." He was above it; and never appeared like himself, but when, forgetful of the idle clamours of party, and of the little views of little men, he appealed to his country, and the enlightened judgment of mankind.

I am not going to make an idle panegyric on Burke (he has no need of it) ; but I cannot help looking upon him as the chief boast and ornament of the English House of Commons. What has been said of him is, I think, strictly true, that " he was the most eloquent man of his time: his wisdom was greater than his eloquence." The only public man that in my opinion can be put in any competition with him, is Lord Chatham: and he moved in a sphere so very remote, that it is almost impossible to compare them. But though it would perhaps be difficult to determine which of them excelled most in his particular way, there is nothing in the world more easy than to point out in what their peculiar excellences consisted. They were in every respect the reverse of each other. Chatham's eloquence was popular: his wisdom was altogether plain and practical. Burke's eloquence was that of the poet; of the man of high and unbounded fancy: his wisdom was profound and contemplative. Chatham's eloquence was calculated to make men *act;* Burke's was calculated to make them *think*. Chatham could have roused the fury of a multitude, and wielded their physical energy as he pleased: Burke's eloquence carried conviction into the mind of the retired and lonely student, opened the recesses of the human breast, and lighted up the face of nature around him. Chatham supplied his hearers with motives to immediate action: Burke furnished them with *reasons* for action which might have little effect upon them at the time, but for which they would be the wiser and better all their lives after. In research, in originality, in variety of knowledge, in richness of invention, in depth and comprehension of mind, Burke had as much the advantage of Lord Chatham as he was excelled by him in plain common sense, in strong feeling, in steadiness of purpose, in vehemence, in warmth, in enthusiasm, and energy of mind. Burke was the man of genius, of fine sense, and subtle reasoning; Chatham was a man of clear understanding, of strong sense, and violent passions. Burke's mind was satisfied with speculation: Chatham's was essentially *active:* it could not rest without an object. The power which governed Burke's mind was his Imagination; that which gave its *impetus* to Chatham's was Will. The one was almost the creature of pure intellect, the other of physical temperament.

There are two very different ends which a man of genius may propose to himself either in writing or speaking, and which will accordingly give birth to very different styles. He can have but one of these two objects; either to enrich or strengthen the mind; either to furnish us with new ideas, to lead the mind into new trains of thought, to which it was before unused, and which it was incapable of striking out for itself; or else to collect and embody what we already knew, to rivet our old impressions more deeply; to make what was before plain still plainer, and to give to that which was familiar all the effect of novelty. In the one case we receive an accession to the stock of our ideas; in the other, an additional degree of life and energy is infused into them: our thoughts continue to flow in the same channels, but their pulse is quickened and invigorated. I do not know how to distinguish these different styles better than by calling them severally the inventive and refined, or the impressive and vigorous styles. It is only the subject-matter of eloquence, however, which is allowed to be remote or obscure. The things in themselves may be subtle and recondite, but they must be dragged out of their obscurity and brought struggling to the light; they must be rendered plain and palpable, (as far as it is in the wit of man to do so) or they are no longer eloquence. That which by its natural impenetrability, and in spite of every effort, remains dark and difficult, which is impervious to every ray, on which the imagination can shed no lustre, which can be clothed with no beauty, is not a subject for the orator or poet. At the same time it cannot be expected that abstract truths or profound observations should ever be placed in the same strong and dazzling points of view as natural objects and mere matters of fact. It is enough if they receive a reflex and borrowed lustre, like that which cheers the first dawn of morning, where the effect of surprise and novelty gilds every object, and the joy of beholding another world gradually emerging out of the gloom of night, " a new creation rescued from his reign," fills the mind with a sober rapture. Philosophical eloquence is in writing what *chiaro scuro* is in painting; he would be a fool who should object that the colours in the shaded part of a picture were not so bright as those on the opposite side; the eye of the connoisseur receives an equal delight from both, balancing the want of brilliancy and effect with the greater delicacy of the tints, and difficulty of the execution. In judging of Burke, therefore, we are to consider first the style of eloquence which he adopted, and secondly the effects which he produced with it. If he did not produce the same effects on vulgar minds, as some others have done, it was not for want of power, but from the turn and direction of his mind.* It was because his subjects, his ideas, his arguments, were less vulgar. The question is not whether he brought certain truths equally home to us, but how much nearer he brought them than they were before. In my opinion, he united the two extremes of refinement and strength in a higher degree than any other writer whatever.

The subtlety of his mind was undoubtedly that which rendered Burke a less popular writer and speaker than he otherwise would have been. It weakened the impression of his observations upon others, but I cannot admit that it weakened the observations themselves; that it took anything from their real weight and solidity. Coarse minds think all that is subtle, futile: that because it is not gross and obvious and palpable to the senses, it is therefore light and frivolous, and of no importance in the real affairs of life; thus making their own confined understandings the measure of truth, and supposing that whatever they do not distinctly perceive, is nothing. Seneca, who was not one of the vulgar, also says, that subtle truths are those which have the least substance in them, and consequently approach nearest to nonentity. But for my own part I cannot help thinking that the most important truths must be the most refined and subtle; for that very reason, that they must comprehend a great number of particulars, and instead of referring to any distinct or positive fact, must point out the combined effects of an extensive chain of causes, operating gradually, remotely, and collectively, and therefore imperceptibly. General principles are not the less true or im-

---

* For instance: he produced less effect on the mob that compose the English House of Commons than Chatham or Fox, or even Pitt.

portant because from their nature they elude immediate observation; they are like the air, which is not the less necessary because we neither see nor feel it, or like that secret influence which binds the world together, and holds the planets in their orbits. The very same persons who are the most forward to laugh at all systematic reasoning as idle and impertinent, you will the next moment hear exclaiming bitterly against the baleful effects of new-fangled systems of philosophy, or gravely descanting on the immense importance of instilling sound principles of morality into the mind. It would not be a bold conjecture, but an obvious truism to say, that all the great changes which have been brought about in the moral world, either for the better or worse, have been introduced not by the bare statement of facts, which are things already known, and which must always operate nearly in the same manner, but by the development of certain opinions and abstract principles of reasoning on life and manners, on the origin of society and man's nature in general, which being obscure and uncertain, vary from time to time, and produce correspondent changes in the human mind. They are the wholesome dew and rain, or the mildew and pestilence that silently destroy. To this principle of generalization all religious creeds, the institutions of wise lawgivers, and the systems of philosophers, owe their influence.

It has always been with me a test of the sense and candour of any one belonging to the opposite party, whether he allowed Burke to be a great man. Of all the persons of this description that I have ever known, I never met with above one or two who would make this concession; whether it was that party feelings ran too high to admit of any real candour, or whether it was owing to an essential vulgarity in their habits of thinking, they all seemed to be of opinion that he was a wild enthusiast, or a hollow sophist, who was to be answered by bits of facts, by smart logic, by shrewd questions, and idle songs. They looked upon him as a man of disordered intellects, because he reasoned in a style to which they had not been used and which confounded their dim perceptions. If you said that though you differed with him in sentiment, yet you thought him an admirable reasoner, and a close observer of human nature, you were answered with a loud laugh, and some hackneyed quotation. "Alas! Leviathan was not so tamed!" They did not know whom they had to contend with. The corner stone, which the builders rejected, became the head-corner, though to the Jews a stumbling block, and to the Greeks foolishness; for indeed I cannot discover that he was much better understood by those of his own party, if we may judge from the little affinity there is between his mode of reasoning and theirs.—The simple clue to all his reasonings on politics is, I think, as follows. He did not agree with some writers, that that mode of government is necessarily the best which is the cheapest. He saw in the construction of society other principles at work, and other capacities of fulfilling the desires, and perfecting the nature of man, besides those of securing the equal enjoyment of the means of animal life, and doing this at as little expense as possible. He thought that the wants and happiness of men were not to be provided for, as we provide for those of a herd of cattle, merely by attending to their physical necessities. He thought more nobly of his fellows. He knew that man had affections and passions and powers of imagination, as well as hunger and thirst and the sense of heat and cold. He took his idea of political society from the pattern of private life, wishing, as he himself expresses it, to incorporate the domestic charities with the orders of the state, and to blend them together. He strove to establish an analogy between the compact that binds together the community at large, and that which binds together the several families that compose it. He knew that the rules that form the basis of private morality are not founded in reason, that is, in the abstract properties of those things which are the subjects of them, but in the nature of man, and his capacity of being affected by certain things from habit, from imagination, and sentiment, as well as from reason.

Thus, the reason why a man ought to be attached to his wife and children is not, surely, that they are better than others, (for in this case every one else ought to be of the same opinion) but because he must be chiefly interested in those things which are nearest to him, and with which he is best acquainted, since his understanding cannot reach equally to every thing; because he must be most attached to those objects which he has known the longest, and which by their situation have actually affected him the most, not those which in themselves are the most affecting, whether they have ever made any impression on him or no; that is, because he is by his nature the creature of habit and feeling, and because it is reasonable that he should act in conformity to his nature. Burke was so far right in saying that it is no objection to an institution that it is founded in *prejudice,* but the contrary, if that prejudice is natural and right; that is, if it arises from those circumstances which are properly subjects of feeling and association, not from any defect or perversion of the understanding in those things which fall strictly under its jurisdiction. On this profound maxim he took his stand. Thus he contended, that the prejudice in favour of nobility was natural and proper, and fit to be encouraged by the positive institutions of society; not on account of the real or personal merit of the individuals, but because such an institution has a tendency to enlarge and raise the mind, to keep alive the memory of past greatness, to connect the different ages of the world together, to carry back the imagination over a long tract of time, and feed it with the contemplation of remote events: because it is natural to think highly of that which inspires us with high thoughts, which has been connected for many generations with splendour, and affluence, and dignity, and power, and privilege. He also conceived, that by transferring the respect from the person to the thing, and thus rendering it steady and permanent, the mind would be habitually formed to sentiments of deference, attachment, and fealty, to whatever else demanded its respect: that it would be led to fix its view on what was elevated and lofty, and be weaned from that low and narrow jealousy which never willingly or heartily admits of any superiority in others, and is glad of every opportunity to bring down all excellence to a level with its own miserable standard. Nobility did not therefore exist to the prejudice of the other orders of the state, but by, and for them. The inequality of the different orders of society did not destroy the unity and harmony of the whole. The health and well-being of the moral world was to be promoted by the same means as the beauty of the natural world; by contrast, by change, by light and shade, by variety of parts, by order and proportion. To think of reducing all mankind to the same insipid level, seemed to him the same absurdity as to destroy the inequalities of surface in a country, for the benefit of agriculture and commerce. In short, he believed that the interests of men in society should be consulted, and their several stations and employments assigned, with a view to their nature, not as physical, but as moral beings, so as to nourish their hopes, to lift their imagination, to enliven their fancy, to rouse their activity, to strengthen their virtue, and to furnish the greatest number of objects of pursuit and means of enjoyment to beings constituted as man is, consistently with the order and stability of the whole.

The same reasoning might be extended farther. I do not say that his arguments are conclusive; but they are profound and *true*, as far as they go. There may be disadvantages and abuses necessarily interwoven with his scheme, or opposite advantages of infinitely greater value, to be derived from another order of things and state of society. This however does not invalidate either the truth or importance of Burke's reasoning; since the advantages he points out as connected with the mixed form of government are really and necessarily inherent in it: since they are compatible in the same degree with no other; since the principle itself on which he rests his argument (whatever we may think of the application) is of the utmost weight and moment; and since on whichever side the truth lies, it is impossible to make a fair decision without having the opposite side of the question clearly and fully stated to us. This Burke has done in a masterly manner. He presents to you one view or face of society. Let him, who thinks he can, give the reverse side with equal force, beauty, and clearness. It is said, I know, that truth is *one;* but to this I cannot subscribe, for it appears to me that truth is *many*. There are as many truths as there are things and causes of action and contradictory principles at work in society. In making up the account of good and evil, indeed, the final result must be one way or the other; but the particulars on which that result depends are infinite and various.

It will be seen from what I have said, that I am very far from agreeing with those who think that Burke was a man without understanding, and a merely florid writer. There are two causes which have given rise to this calumny; namely, that narrowness of mind which leads men to suppose that the truth lies entirely on the side of their own opinions, and that whatever does not make for them is absurd and irrational; secondly, a trick we have of confounding reason with judgment, and supposing that it is merely the province of the understanding to pronounce sentence, and not to give in evidence, or argue the case; in short, that it is a passive, not an active faculty. Thus there are persons who never run into any extravagance, because they are so buttressed up with the opinions of others on all sides, that they cannot lean much to one side or the other; they are so little moved with any kind of reasoning, that they remain at an equal distance from every extreme, and are never very far from the truth, because the slowness of their faculties will not suffer them to make much progress in error. These are persons of great judgment. The scales of the mind are pretty sure to remain even, when there is nothing in them. In this sense of the word, Burke must be allowed to have wanted judgment, by all those who think that he was wrong in his conclusions. The accusation of want of judgment, in fact, only means that you yourself are of a different opinion. But if in arriving at one error he discovered a hundred truths, I should consider myself a hundred times more indebted to him than if, stumbling on that which I consider as the right side of the question, he had committed a hundred absurdities in striving to establish his point. I speak of him now merely as an author, or as far as I and other readers are concerned with him; at the same time, I should not differ from any one who may be disposed to contend that the consequences of his writings as instruments of political power have been tremendous, fatal, such as no exertion of wit or knowledge or genius can ever counteract or atone for.

Burke also gave a hold to his antagonists by mixing up

sentiment and imagery with his reasoning; so that being
unused to such a sight in the region of politics, they were
deceived, and could not discern the fruit from the flowers.
Gravity is the cloke of wisdom; and those who have nothing else think it an insult to affect the one without the
other, because it destroys the only foundation on which
their pretensions are built. The easiest part of reason is
dulness; the generality of the world are therefore concerned in discouraging any example of unnecessary brilliancy that might tend to show that the two things do not
always go together. Burke in some measure dissolved the
spell. It was discovered, that his gold was not the less
valuable for being wrought into elegant shapes, and richly
embossed with curious figures; that the solidity of a building is not destroyed by adding to it beauty and ornament;
and that the strength of a man's understanding is not always to be estimated in exact proportion to his want of
imagination. His understanding was not the less real, because it was not the only faculty he possessed. He justified
the description of the poet,—

> "How charming is divine philosophy!
> Not harsh and crabbed as dull fools suppose,
> But musical as is Apollo's lute!"

Those who object to this union of grace and beauty with
reason, are in fact weak-sighted people, who cannot distinguish the noble and majestic form of Truth from that
of her sister Folly, if they are dressed both alike! But
there is always a difference even in the adventitious ornaments they wear, which is sufficient to distinguish them.

Burke was so far from being a gaudy or flowery writer,
that he was one of the severest writers we have. His
words are the most like things; his style is the most strictly
suited to the subject. He unites every extreme and every

variety of composition; the lowest and the meanest words
and descriptions with the highest. He exults in the display
of power, in shewing the extent, the force, and intensity
of his ideas; he is led on by the mere impulse and vehemence of his fancy, not by the affectation of dazzling his
readers by gaudy conceits or pompous images. He was
completely carried away by his subject. He had no other
object but to produce the strongest impression on his
reader, by giving the truest, the most characteristic, the
fullest, and most forcible description of things, trusting to
the power of his own mind to mould them into grace and
beauty. He did not produce a splendid effect by setting
fire to the light vapours that float in the regions of fancy,
as the chemists make fine colours with phosphorus, but
by the eagerness of his blows struck fire from the flint,
and melted the hardest substances in the furnace of his
imagination. The wheels of his imagination did not catch
fire from the rottenness of the materials, but from the
rapidity of their motion. One would suppose, to hear
people talk of Burke, that his style was such as would have
suited the " Lady's Magazine "; soft, smooth, showy, tender,
insipid, full of fine words, without any meaning. The
essence of the gaudy or glittering style consists in producing a momentary effect by fine words and images
brought together, without order or connexion. Burke most
frequently produced an effect by the remoteness and novelty
of his combinations, by the force of contrast, by the striking
manner in which the most opposite and unpromising materials were harmoniously blended together; not by laying
his hands on all the fine things he could think of, but by
bringing together those things which he knew would blaze
out into glorious light by their collision. The florid style
is a mixture of affectation and common-place. Burke's
was an union of untameable vigour and originality.

Burke was not a verbose writer. If he sometimes multiplies words, it is not for want of ideas, but because there are no words that fully express his ideas, and he tries to do it as well as he can by different ones. He had nothing of the *set* or formal style, the measured cadence, and stately phraseology of Johnson, and most of our modern writers. This style, which is what we understand by the *artificial,* is all in one key. It selects a certain set of words to represent all ideas whatever, as the most dignified and elegant, and excludes all others as low and vulgar. The words are not fitted to the things, but the things to the words. Every thing is seen through a false medium. It is putting a mask on the face of nature, which may indeed hide some specks and blemishes, but takes away all beauty, delicacy, and variety. It destroys all dignity or elevation, because nothing can be raised where all is on a level, and completely destroys all force, expression, truth, and character, by arbitrarily confounding the differences of things, and reducing every thing to the same insipid standard. To suppose that this stiff uniformity can add any thing to real grace or dignity, is like supposing that the human body in order to be perfectly graceful, should never deviate from its upright posture. Another mischief of this method is, that it confounds all ranks in literature. Where there is no room for variety, no discrimination, no nicety to be shewn in matching the idea with its proper word, there can be no room for taste or elegance. A man must easily learn the art of writing, when every sentence is to be cast in the same mould: where he is only allowed the use of one word, he cannot choose wrong, nor will he be in much danger of making himself ridiculous by affectation or false glitter, when, whatever subject he treats of, he must treat of it in the same way. This indeed is to wear golden chains for the sake of ornament.

Burke was altogether free from the pedantry which I have here endeavoured to expose. His style was as original, as expressive, as rich and varied, as it was possible; his combinations were as exquisite, as playful, as happy, as unexpected, as bold and daring, as his fancy. If any thing, he ran into the opposite extreme of too great an inequality, if truth and nature could ever be carried to an extreme.

Those who are best acquainted with the writings and speeches of Burke will not think the praise I have here bestowed on them exaggerated. Some proof will be found of this in the following extracts. But the full proof must be sought in his works at large, and particularly in the " Thoughts on the Discontents"; in his " Reflections on the French Revolution "; in his " Letter to the Duke of Bedford "; and in the " Regicide Peace." The two last of these are perhaps the most remarkable of all his writings, from the contrast they afford to each other. The one is the most delightful exhibition of wild and brilliant fancy, that is to be found in English prose, but it is too much like a beautiful picture painted upon gauze; it wants something to support it: the other is without ornament, but it has all the solidity, the weight, the gravity of a judicial record. It seems to have been written with a certain constraint upon himself, and to shew those who said he could not *reason,* that his arguments might be stripped of their ornaments without losing any thing of their force. It is certainly, of all his works, that in which he has shewn most power of logical deduction, and the only one in which he has made any important use of facts. In general he certainly paid little attention to them: they were the playthings of his mind. He saw them as he pleased, not as they were; with the eye of the philosopher or the poet, regarding them only in their general principle, or as they might serve to decorate his subject. This is the natural consequence of much imagination: things that are probable are elevated into the rank of realities. To those who can reason on the essences of things, or who can invent according to nature, the experimental proof is of little value. This was the case with Burke. In the present instance, however, he seems to have forced his mind into the service of facts: and he succeeded completely. His comparison between our connection with France or Algiers, and his account of the conduct of the war, are as clear, as convincing, as forcible examples of this kind of reasoning, as are any where to be met with. Indeed I do not think there is any thing in Fox (whose mind was purely historical) or in Chatham, (who attended to feelings more than facts) that will bear a comparison with them.

Burke has been compared to Cicero—I do not know for what reason. Their excellences are as different, and indeed as opposite, as they well can be. Burke had not the polished elegance, the glossy neatness, the artful regularity, the exquisite modulation of Cicero: he had a thousand time more richness and originality of mind, more strength and pomp of diction.

It has been well observed, that the ancients had no word that properly expresses what we mean by the word *genius*. They perhaps had not the thing. Their minds appear to have been too exact, too retentive, too minute and subtle, too sensible to the external differences of things, too passive under their impressions, to admit of those bold and rapid combinations, those lofty flights of fancy, which, glancing from heaven to earth, unite the most opposite extremes, and draw the happiest illustrations from things the most remote. Their ideas were kept too confined and distinct by the material form or vehicle in which they were conveyed, to unite cordially together, or be melted down in the imagination. Their metaphors are taken from things of the same class, not from things of different classes; the general analogy, not the individual feeling, directs them in their choice. Hence, as Dr. Johnson observed, their similes are either repetitions of the same idea, or so obvious and general as not to lend any additional force to it; as when a huntress is compared to Diana, or a warrior rushing into battle to a lion rushing on his prey. Their *forte* was exquisite art and perfect imitation. Witness their statues and other things of the same kind. But they had not that high and enthusiastic fancy which some of our own writers have shewn. For the proof of this, let any one compare Milton and Shakspeare with Homer and Sophocles, or Burke with Cicero.

It may be asked whether Burke was a poet. He was so only in the general vividness of his fancy, and in richness of invention. There may be poetical passages in his works, but I certainly think that his writings in general are quite distinct from poetry; and that for the reason before given, namely, that the subject-matter of them is not poetical. The finest part of them are illustrations or personifications of dry abstract ideas; * and the union between the idea and the illustration is not of that perfect and pleasing kind as to constitute poetry, or indeed to be admissible, but for the effect intended to be produced by it; that is, by every means in our power to give animation and attraction to subjects in themselves. barren of ornament, but which at the same time are pregnant with the most important consequences, and in which the understanding and the passions are equally interested.

I have heard it remarked by a person, to whose opinion I would sooner submit than to a general council of critics, that the sound of Burke's prose is not musical; that it

* As in the comparison of the British Constitution to the "proud keep of Windsor," etc., the most splendid passage in his works.

wants cadence; and that instead of being so lavish of his imagery as is generally supposed, he seemed to him to be rather parsimonious in the use of it, always expanding and making the most of his ideas. This may be true if we compare him with some of our poets, or perhaps with some of our early prose writers, but not if we compare him with any of our political writers or parliamentary speakers. There are some very fine things of Lord Bolingbroke's on the same subjects, but not equal to Burke's. As for Junius, he is at the head of his class; but that class is not the highest. He has been said to have more dignity than Burke. Yes—if the stalk of a giant is less dignified than the strut of a *petit-maître*. I do not mean to speak disrespectfully of Junius, but grandeur is not the character of his composition; and if it is not to be found in Burke, it is to be found nowhere.

# X

## MR. WORDSWORTH

Mr. Wordsworth's genius is a pure emanation of the Spirit of the Age. Had he lived in any other period of the world, he would never have been heard of. As it is, he has some difficulty to contend with the hebetude of his intellect, and the meanness of his subject. With him "lowliness is young ambition's ladder;" but he finds it a toil to climb in this way the steep of Fame. His homely Muse can hardly raise her wing from the ground, nor spread her hidden glories to the sun. He has " no figures nor no fantasies, which busy *passion* draws in the brains of men:" neither the gorgeous machinery of mythologic lore, nor the splendid colours of poetic diction. His style is vernacular: he delivers household truths. He sees nothing loftier than human hopes; nothing deeper than the human heart. This he probes, this he tampers with, this he poises, with all its incalculable weight of thought and feeling, in his hands, and at the same time calms the throbbing pulses of his own heart, by keeping his eye ever fixed on the face of nature. If he can make the life-blood flow from the wounded breast, this is the living colouring with which he paints his verse: if he can assuage the pain or close up the wound with the balm of solitary musing, or the healing power of plants and herbs and " skyey influences," this is the sole triumph of his art. He takes the simplest elements of nature and of the human mind, the mere abstract conditions inseparable from our being, and tries to compound a new system of poetry from them; and has perhaps succeeded as well as any one could. " *Nihil humani a me alienum puto* "—is the motto of his works. He thinks nothing low or indifferent of which this can be affirmed: every thing that professes to be more than this, that is not an absolute essence of truth and feeling, he holds to be vitiated, false, and spurious. In a word, his poetry is founded on setting up an opposition (and pushing it to the utmost length) between the natural and the artificial; between the spirit of humanity, and the spirit of fashion and of the world!

It is one of the innovations of the time. It partakes of, and is carried along with, the revolutionary movement of our age: the political changes of the day were the model on which he formed and conducted his poetical experiments. His Muse (it cannot be denied, and without this we cannot explain its character at all) is a levelling one. It proceeds on a principle of equality, and strives to reduce all things to the same standard. It is distinguished by a proud humility. It relies upon its own resources, and disdains external show and relief. It takes the commonest events and objects, as a test to prove that nature is always interesting from its inherent truth and beauty, without any of the ornaments of dress or pomp of circumstances to set it off. Hence the unaccountable mixture of seeming simplicity and real abstruseness in the *Lyrical Ballads*. Fools have laughed at, wise men scarcely understand them. He takes a subject or a story merely as pegs or loops to hang thought and feeling on; the incidents are trifling, in proportion to his contempt for imposing appearances; the reflections are profound, according to the gravity and aspiring pretensions of his mind.

His popular, inartificial style gets rid (at a blow) of all the trappings of verse, of all the high places of poetry: " the cloud-capt towers, the solemn temples, the gorgeous palaces," are swept to the ground, and "like the baseless fabric of a vision, leave not a wreck behind." All the traditions of learning, all the superstitions of age, are obliterated and effaced. We begin *de novo*, on a *tabula rasa* of poetry. The purple pall, the nodding plume of tragedy, are exploded as mere pantomime and trick, to return to the simplicity of truth and nature. Kings, queens, priests, nobles, the altar and the throne, the distinctions of rank, birth, wealth, power, "the judge's robe, the marshal's truncheon, the ceremony that to great ones 'longs," are not to be found here. The author tramples on the pride of art with greater pride. The Ode and Epode, the Strophe and the Antistrophe, he laughs to scorn. The harp of Homer, the trump of Pindar and of Alcæus are still. The decencies of costume, the decorations of vanity are stripped off without mercy as barbarous, idle, and Gothic. The jewels in the crisped hair, the diadem on the polished brow are thought meretricious, theatrical, vulgar; and nothing contents his fastidious taste beyond a simple garland of flowers. Neither does he avail himself of the advantages which nature or accident holds out to him. He chooses to have his subject a foil to his invention, to owe nothing but to himself. He gathers manna in the wilderness, he strikes the barren rock for the gushing moisture. He elevates the mean by the strength of his own aspirations; he clothes the naked with beauty and grandeur from the stores of his own recollections. No cypress grove loads his verse with funeral pomp: but his imagination lends " a sense of joy

> "To the bare trees and mountains bare,
>    And grass in the green field."

No storm, no shipwreck startles us by its horrors: but the rainbow lifts its head in the cloud, and the breeze sighs through the withered fern. No sad vicissitude of fate, no overwhelming catastrophe in nature deforms his page: but the dewdrop glitters on the bending flower, the tear collects in the glistening eye.

> "Beneath the hills, along the flowery vales,
> The generations are prepared; the pangs,
> The internal pangs are ready; the dread strife
> Of poor humanity's afflicted will,
> Struggling in vain with ruthless destiny."

As the lark ascends from its low bed on fluttering wing, and salutes the morning skies; so Mr. Wordsworth's unpretending Muse, in russet guise, scales the summits of reflection, while it makes the round earth its footstool, and its home!

Possibly a good deal of this may be regarded as the effect of disappointed views and an inverted ambition. Prevented by native pride and indolence from climbing the ascent of learning or greatness, taught by political opinions to say to the vain pomp and glory of the world, " I hate ye," seeing the path of classical and artificial poetry blocked up by the cumbrous ornaments of style and turgid *commonplaces,* so that nothing more could be achieved in that direction but by the most ridiculous bombast or the tamest servility; he has turned back partly from the bias of his mind, partly perhaps from a judicious policy—has struck into the sequestered vale of humble life, sought out the Muse among sheep-cotes and hamlets and the peasant's mountain-haunts, has discarded all the tinsel pageantry of verse, and endeavoured (not in vain) to aggrandise the trivial and add the charm of novelty to the familiar. No one has shown the same imagination in raising trifles into importance: no one has displayed the same pathos in treating of the simplest feelings of the heart. Reserved, yet haughty, having no unruly or violent passions, (or those

passions having been early suppressed,) Mr. Wordsworth
has passed his life in solitary musing, or in daily converse
with the face of nature. He exemplifies in an eminent
degree the power of *association;* for his poetry has no
other source or character. He has dwelt among pastoral
scenes, till each object has become connected with a thousand feelings, a link in the chain of thought, a fibre of his
own heart. Every one is by habit and familiarity strongly
attached to the place of his birth, or to objects that recall
the most pleasing and eventful circumstances of his life.
But to the author of the *Lyrical Ballads,* nature is a kind
of home; and he may be said to take a personal interest in
the universe. There is no image so insignificant that it
has not in some mood or other found the way into his
heart: no sound that does not awaken the memory of
other years—

> " To him the meanest flower that blows can give
> Thoughts that do often lie too deep for tears."

The daisy looks up to him with sparkling eye as an old
acquaintance: the cuckoo haunts him with sounds of early
youth not to be expressed: a linnet's nest startles him with
boyish delight: an old withered thorn is weighed down
with a heap of recollections: a grey cloak, seen on some
wild moor, torn by the wind, or drenched in the rain,
afterwards becomes an object of imagination to him: even
the lichens on the rock have a life and being in his thoughts.
He has described all these objects in a way and with an
intensity of feeling that no one else had done before him,
and has given a new view or aspect of nature. He is in
this sense the most original poet now living, and the one
whose writings could the least be spared: for they have no
substitute elsewhere. The vulgar do not read them, the
learned, who see all things through books, do not under-

stand them, the great despise, the fashionable may ridicule them: but the author has created himself an interest in the heart of the retired and lonely student of nature, which can never die. Persons of this class will still continue to feel what he has felt: he has expressed what they might in vain wish to express, except with glistening eye and faultering tongue! There is a lofty philosophic tone, a thoughtful humanity, infused into his pastoral vein. Remote from the passions and events of the great world, he has communicated interest and dignity to the primal movements of the heart of man, and ingrafted his own conscious reflections on the casual thoughts of hinds and shepherds. Nursed amidst the grandeur of mountain scenery, he has stooped to have a nearer view of the daisy under his feet, or plucked a branch of white-thorn from the spray: but in describing it, his mind seems imbued with the majesty and solemnity of the objects around him—the tall rock lifts its head in the erectness of his spirit; the cataract roars in the sound of his verse; and in its dim and mysterious meaning, the mists seem to gather in the hollows of Helvellyn, and the forked Skiddaw hovers in the distance. There is little mention of mountainous scenery in Mr. Wordsworth's poetry; but by internal evidence one might be almost sure that it is written in a mountainous country, from its bareness, its simplicity, its loftiness, and its depth!

His later philosophic productions have a somewhat different character. They are a departure from, a dereliction of his first principles. They are classical and courtly. They are polished in style, without being gaudy; dignified in subject, without affectation. They seem to have been composed not in a cottage at Grasmere, but among the half-inspired groves and stately recollections of Cole-Orton. We might allude in particular, for examples of what we mean, to the lines on a Picture by Claude Lorraine, and to the exquisite poem, entitled *Laodamia*. The last of these breathes the pure spirit of the finest fragments of antiquity —the sweetness, the gravity, the strength, the beauty and the languor of death—

"Calm contemplation and majestic pains."

Its glossy brilliancy arises from the perfection of the finishing, like that of careful sculpture, not from gaudy colouring—the texture of the thoughts has the smoothness and solidity of marble. It is a poem that might be read aloud in Elysium, and the spirits of departed heroes and sages would gather round to listen to it! Mr. Wordsworth's philosophic poetry, with a less glowing aspect and less tumult in the veins than Lord Byron's on similar occasions, bends a calmer and keener eye on mortality; the impression, if less vivid, is more pleasing and permanent; and we confess it (perhaps it is a want of taste and proper feeling) that there are lines and poems of our author's, that we think of ten times for once that we recur to any of Lord Byron's. Or if there are any of the latter's writings, that we can dwell upon in the same way, that is, as lasting and heart-felt sentiments, it is when, laying aside his usual pomp and pretension, he descends with Mr. Wordsworth to the common ground of a disinterested humanity. It may be considered as characteristic of our poet's writings, that they either make no impression on the mind at all, seem mere *nonsense-verses,* or that they leave a mark behind them that never wears out. They either

"Fall blunted from the indurated breast"—

without any perceptible result, or they absorb it like a passion. To one class of readers he appears sublime, to another (and we fear the largest) ridiculous. He has probably realised Milton's wish,—" and fit audience found, though few:" but we suspect he is not reconciled to the alternative. There are delightful passages in the EXCUR-SION, both of natural description and of inspired reflectio.1 (passages of the latter kind that in the sound of the thoughts and of the swelling language resemble heavenly symphonies, mournful *requiems* over the grave of human hopes); but we must add, in justice and in sincerity, that we think it impossible that this work should ever become popular, even in the same degree as the *Lyrical Ballads.* It affects a system without having any intelligible clue to one; and instead of unfolding a principle in various and striking lights, repeats the same conclusions till they become flat and insipid. Mr. Wordsworth's mind is obtuse, except as it is the organ and the receptacle of accumulated feelings: it is not analytic, but synthetic; it is reflecting, rather than theoretical. The EXCURSION, we believe, fell still-born from the press. There was something abortive, and clumsy, and ill-judged in the attempt. It was long and laboured. The personages, for the most part, were low, the fare rustic: the plan raised expectations which were not ful-filled, and the effect was like being ushered into a stately hall and invited to sit down to a splendid banquet in the company of clowns, and with nothing but successive courses of apple-dumplings served up. It was not even *toujours perdrix!*

Mr. Wordsworth, in his person, is above the middle size, with marked features, and an air somewhat stately and Quixotic. He reminds one of some of Holbein's heads, grave, saturnine, with a slight indication of sly humour, kept under by the manners of the age or by the pretensions of the person. He has a peculiar sweetness in his smile, and great depth and manliness and a rugged harmony, in the tones of his voice. His manner of reading his own poetry is particularly imposing; and in his favourite passages his eye beams with preternatural lustre, and the meaning labours slowly up from his swelling breast. No one who has seen him at these moments could go away with an impression that he was a " man of no mark or likelihood." Perhaps the comment of his face and voice is necessary to convey a full idea of his poetry. His language may not be intelligible, but his manner is not to be mistaken. It is clear that he is either mad or inspired. In company, even in a *tête-à-tête,* Mr. Wordsworth is often silent, indolent, and reserved. If he is become verbose and oracular of late years, he was not so in his better days. He threw out a bold or an indifferent remark without either effort or pretension, and relapsed into musing again. He shone most (because he seemed most roused and animated) in reciting his own poetry, or in talking about it. He sometimes gave striking views of his feelings and trains of association in composing certain passages ; or if one did not always understand his distinctions, still there was no want of interest— there was a latent meaning worth inquiring into, like a vein of ore that one cannot exactly hit upon at the moment, but of which there are sure indications. His standard of poetry is high and severe, almost to exclusiveness. He admits of nothing below, scarcely of any thing above himself. It is fine to hear him talk of the way in which certain subjects should have been treated by eminent poets, according to his notions of the art. Thus he finds fault with Dryden's description of Bacchus in the *Alexander's Feast,* as if he were a mere good-looking youth, or boon companion—

> " Flushed with a purple grace,
> He shows his honest face "—

instead of representing the God returning from the conquest of India, crowned with vine-leaves, and drawn by panthers, and followed by troops of satyrs, of wild men and animals that he had tamed. You would think, in hearing him speak on this subject, that you saw Titian's picture of the meeting of *Bacchus* and *Ariadne*—so classic were his conceptions, so glowing his style. Milton is his great idol, and he sometimes dares to compare himself with him. His Sonnets, indeed, have something of the same high-raised tone and prophetic spirit. Chaucer is another prime favourite of his, and he has been at the pains to modernize some of the Canterbury Tales. Those persons who look upon Mr. Wordsworth as a merely puerile writer, must be rather at a loss to account for his strong predilection for such geniuses as Dante and Michael Angelo. We do not think our author has any very cordial sympathy with Shakspeare. How should he? Shakspeare was the least of an egotist of anybody in the world. He does not much relish the variety and scope of dramatic composition. " He hates those interlocutions between Lucius and Caius." Yet Mr. Wordsworth himself wrote a tragedy when he was young; and we have heard the following energetic lines quoted from it, as put into the mouth of a person smit with remorse for some rash crime:

> " Action is momentary,
> The motion of a muscle this way or that;
> Suffering is long, obscure, and infinite ! "

Perhaps for want of light and shade, and the unshackled spirit of the drama, this performance was never brought forward. Our critic has a great dislike to Gray, and a fondness for Thomson and Collins. It is mortifying to hear him speak of Pope and Dryden, whom, because they have been supposed to have all the possible excellences of poetry, he will allow to have none. Nothing, however, can be fairer, or more amusing, than the way in which he sometimes exposes the unmeaning verbiage of modern poetry. Thus, in the beginning of Dr. Johnson's *Vanity of Human Wishes*—

"Let observation with extensive view
Survey mankind from China to Peru"—

he says there is a total want of imagination accompanying the words, the same idea is repeated three times under the disguise of a different phraseology: it comes to this—" let *observation*, with extensive *observation, observe* mankind; " or take away the first line, and the second,

"Survey mankind from China to Peru,"

literally conveys the whole. Mr. Wordsworth is, we must say, a perfect Drawcansir as to prose writers. He complains of the dry reasoners and matter-of-fact people for their want of *passion;* and he is jealous of the rhetorical declaimers and rhapsodists as trenching on the province of poetry. He condemns all French writers (as well of poetry as prose) in the lump. His list in this way is indeed small. He approves of Walton's Angler, Paley, and some other writers of an inoffensive modesty of pretension. He also likes books of voyages and travels, and Robinson Crusoe. In art, he greatly esteems Bewick's woodcuts, and Waterloo's sylvan etchings. But he sometimes takes a higher tone, and gives his mind fair play. We have known him enlarge with a noble intelligence and enthusiasm on Nicolas Poussin's fine landscape-compositions, pointing out the unity of design that pervades them, the superintending mind, the imaginative principle that brings all to bear on the same end; and declaring he would not give a rush for any landscape that did not express the time of day, the climate, the period of the world it was meant to illustrate,

or had not this character of *wholeness* in it. His eye also
does justice to Rembrandt's fine and masterly effects. In
the way in which that artist works something out of nothing, and transforms the stump of a tree, a common figure
into an *ideal* object, by the gorgeous light and shade thrown
upon it, he perceives an analogy to his own mode of invest-
ing the minute details of nature with an atmosphere of
sentiment; and in pronouncing Rembrandt to be a man of
genius, feels that he strengthens his own claim to the title.
It has been said of Mr. Wordsworth, that " he hates conchology, that he hates the Venus of Medicis." But these,
we hope, are mere epigrams and *jeux-d'esprit,* as far from
truth as they are free from malice; a sort of running satire
or critical clenches—

> "Where one for sense and one for rhyme
> Is quite sufficient at one time."

We think, however, that if Mr. Wordsworth had been a
more liberal and candid critic, he would have been a more
sterling writer. If a greater number of sources of pleasure
had been open to him, he would have communicated pleasure
to the world more frequently. Had he been less fastidious
in pronouncing sentence on the works of others, his own
would have been received more favourably, and treated
more leniently. The current of his feelings is deep, but
narrow; the range of his understanding is lofty and aspiring rather than discursive. The force, the originality, the
absolute truth and identity with which he feels some things,
makes him indifferent to so many others. The simplicity
and enthusiasm of his feelings, with respect to nature, renders him bigotted and intolerant in his judgments of men
and things. But it happens to him, as to others, that his
strength lies in his weakness; and perhaps we have no
right to complain. We might get rid of the cynic and

the egotist, and find in his stead a common-place man. We should "take the good the Gods provide us:" a fine and original vein of poetry is not one of their most contemptible gifts, and the rest is scarcely worth thinking of, except as it may be a mortification to those who expect perfection from human nature; or who have been idle enough at some period of their lives, to deify men of genius as possessing claims above it. But this is a chord that jars, and we shall not dwell upon it.

Lord Byron we have called, according to the old proverb, "the spoiled child of fortune:" Mr. Wordsworth might plead, in mitigation of some peculiarities, that he is "the spoiled child of disappointment." We are convinced, if he had been early a popular poet, he would have borne his honours meekly, and would have been a person of great *bonhommie* and frankness of disposition. But the sense of injustice and of undeserved ridicule sours the temper and narrows the views. To have produced works of genius, and to find them neglected or treated with scorn is one of the heaviest trials of human patience. We exaggerate our own merits when they are denied by others, and are apt to grudge and cavil at every particle of praise bestowed on those to whom we feel a conscious superiority. In mere self-defence we turn against the world, when it turns against us; brood over the undeserved slights we receive; and thus the genial current of the soul is stopped, or vents itself in effusions of petulance and self-conceit. Mr. Wordsworth has thought too much of contemporary critics and criticism; and less than he ought of the award of posterity, and of the opinion, we do not say of private friends, but of those who were made so by their admiration of his genius. He did not court popularity by a conformity to established models, and he ought not to have been surprised that his originality was not understood as a matter of course.　He has *gnawed too much on the bridle;* and has often thrown out crusts to the critics, in mere defiance or as a point of honour when he was challenged, which otherwise his own good sense would have withheld.　We suspect that Mr. Wordsworth's feelings are a little morbid in this respect, or that he resents censure more than he is gratified by praise.　Otherwise, the tide has turned much in his favour of late years—he has a large body of determined partisans—and is at present sufficiently in request with the public to save or relieve him from the last necessity to which a man of genius can be reduced—that of becoming the God of his own idolatry!

# XI

## MR. COLERIDGE

THE present is an age of talkers, and not of doers; and the reason is, that the world is growing old. We are so far advanced in the Arts and Sciences, that we live in retrospect, and doat on past achievements. The accumulation of knowledge has been so great, that we are lost in wonder at the height it has reached, instead of attempting to climb or add to it; while the variety of objects distracts and dazzles the looker-on. What *niche* remains unoccupied? What path untried? What is the use of doing anything, unless we could do better than all those who have gone before us? What hope is there of this? We are like those who have been to see some noble monument of art, who are content to admire without thinking of rivalling it; or like guests after a feast, who praise the hospitality of the donor "and thank the bounteous Pan" —perhaps carrying away some trifling fragments; or like the spectators of a mighty battle, who still hear its sound afar off, and the clashing of armour and the neighing of the war-horse and the shout of victory is in their ears, like the rushing of innumerable waters!

MR. COLERIDGE has "a mind reflecting ages past:" his voice is like the echo of the congregated roar of the "dark rearward and abyss" of thought. He who has seen a mouldering tower by the side of a chrystal lake, hid by the mist, but glittering in the wave below, may conceive the dim, gleaming, uncertain intelligence of his eye: he who has marked the evening clouds uprolled (a world of vapours), has seen the picture of his mind, unearthly, unsubstantial, with gorgeous tints and ever-varying forms—

"That which was now a horse, even with a thought
The rack dislimns, and makes it indistinct
As water is in water."

Our author's mind is (as he himself might express it) *tangential*. There is no subject on which he has not touched, none on which he has rested. With an understanding fertile, subtle, expansive, "quick, forgetive, apprehensive," beyond all living precedent, few traces of it will perhaps remain. He lends himself to all impressions alike; he gives up his mind and liberty of thought to none. He is a general lover of art and science, and wedded to no one in particular. He pursues knowledge as a mistress, with outstretched hands and winged speed; but as he is about to embrace her, his Daphne turns—alas! not to a laurel! Hardly a speculation has been left on record from the earliest time, but it is loosely folded up in Mr. Coleridge's memory, like a rich, but somewhat tattered piece of tapestry: we might add (with more seeming than real extravagance), that scarce a thought can pass through the mind of man, but its sound has at some time or other passed over his head with rustling pinions. On whatever question or author you speak, he is prepared to take up the theme with advantage—from Peter Abelard down to Thomas Moore, from the subtlest metaphysics to the politics of the *Courier*. There is no man of genius, in whose praise he descants, but the critic seems to stand above the author, and " what in him is weak, to strengthen, what is low, to raise and support: " nor is there any work of genius that does not come out of his hands like an illuminated Missal, sparkling even in its defects. If Mr. Coleridge had not been the most impressive

talker of his age, he would probably have been the finest
writer; but he lays down his pen to make sure of an auditor,
and mortgages the admiration of posterity for the stare of
an idler. If he had not been a poet, he would have been
a powerful logician; if he had not dipped his wing in the
Unitarian controversy, he might have soared to the very
summit of fancy. But in writing verse, he is trying to
subject the Muse to *transcendental* theories: in his abstract
reasoning, he misses his way by strewing it with flowers.
All that he has done of moment, he had done twenty years
ago: since then, he may be said to have lived on the sound
of his own voice. Mr. Coleridge is too rich in intellectual
wealth, to need to task himself to any drudgery: he has
only to draw the sliders of his imagination, and a thousand
subjects expand before him, startling him with their brilliancy, or losing themselves in endless obscurity—

> " And by the force of blear illusion,
>   They draw him on to his confusion."

What is the little he could add to the stock, compared with
the countless stores that lie about him, that he should
stoop to pick up a name, or to polish an idle fancy? He
walks abroad in the majesty of an universal understanding,
eyeing the " rich strond," or golden sky above him, and
" goes sounding on his way," in eloquent accents, uncom-
pelled and free!

Persons of the greatest capacity are often those, who
for this reason do the least; for surveying themselves from
the highest point of view, amidst the infinite variety of the
universe, their own share in it seems trifling, and scarce
worth a thought, and they prefer the contemplation of all
that is, or has been, or can be, to the making a coil about
doing what, when done, is no better than vanity. It is
hard to concentrate all our attention and efforts on one

pursuit, except from ignorance of others; and without this concentration of our faculties, no great progress can be made in any one thing. It is not merely that the mind is not capable of the effort; it does not think the effort worth making. Action is one; but thought is manifold. He whose restless eye glances through the wide compass of nature and art, will not consent to have " his own nothings monstered:" but he must do this, before he can give his whole soul to them. The mind, after " letting contemplation have its fill," or

> " Sailing with supreme dominion
> Through the azure deep of air,"

sinks down on the ground, breathless, exhausted, powerless, inactive; or if it must have some vent to its feelings, seeks the most easy and obvious; is soothed by friendly flattery, lulled by the murmur of immediate applause, thinks as it were aloud, and babbles in its dreams! A scholar (so to speak) is a more disinterested and abstracted character than a mere author. The first looks at the numberless volumes of a library, and says, " All these are mine:" the other points to a single volume (perhaps it may be an immortal one) and says, " My name is written on the back of it." This is a puny and groveling ambition, beneath the lofty amplitude of Mr. Coleridge's mind. No, he revolves in his wayward soul, or utters to the passing wind, or discourses to his own shadow, things mightier and more various!—Let us draw the curtain, and unlock the shrine.

Learning rocked him in his cradle, and while yet a child,

> He lisped in numbers, for the numbers came."

At sixteen he wrote his *Ode on Chatterton,* and he still reverts to that period with delight, not so much as it relates

to himself (for that string of his own early promise of
fame rather jars than otherwise) but as exemplifying the
youth of a poet. Mr. Coleridge talks of himself, without
being an egotist, for in him the individual is always merged
in the abstract and general. He distinguished himself at
school and at the University by his knowledge of the
classics, and gained several prizes for Greek epigrams.
How many men are there (great scholars, celebrated names
in literature) who having done the same thing in their
youth, have no other idea all the rest of their lives but of
this achievement, of a fellowship and dinner, and who,
installed in academic honours, would look down on our
author as a mere strolling bard! At Christ's Hospital,
where he was brought up, he was the idol of those among
his schoolfellows, who mingled with their bookish studies
the music of thought and of humanity; and he was usually
attended round the cloisters by a group of these (inspiring
and inspired) whose hearts, even then, burnt within them
as he talked, and where the sounds yet linger to mock Elia
on his way, still turning pensive to the past! One of the
finest and rarest parts of Mr. Coleridge's conversation, is
when he expatiates on the Greek tragedians (not that he
is not well acquainted, when he pleases, with the epic poets,
or the philosophers, or orators, or historians of antiquity)
—on the subtle reasonings and melting pathos of Euripides,
on the harmonious gracefulness of Sophocles, tuning his
love-laboured song, like sweetest warblings from a sacred
grove; on the high-wrought, trumpet-tongued eloquence of
Æschylus, whose Prometheus, above all, is like an Ode to
Fate, and a pleading with Providence, his thoughts being
let loose as his body is chained on his solitary rock, and his
afflicted will (the emblem of mortality)

"Struggling in vain with ruthless destiny."

As the impassioned critic speaks and rises in his theme, you would think you heard the voice of the Man hated by the Gods, contending with the wild winds as they roar, and his eye glitters with the spirit of Antiquity!

Next, he was engaged with Hartley's tribes of mind, "etherial braid, thought-woven,"—and he busied himself for a year or two with vibrations and vibratiuncles, and the great law of association that binds all things in its mystic chain, and the doctrine of Necessity (the mild teacher of Charity) and the Millernium, anticipative of a life to come—and he plunged deep into the controversy on Matter and Spirit, and, as an escape from Dr. Priestley's Materialism, where he felt himself imprisoned by the logician's spell, like Ariel in the cloven pine-tree, he became suddenly enamoured of Bishop Berkeley's fairy-world,* and used in all companies to build the universe, like a brave poetical fiction, of fine words—and he was deep-read in Malebranche, and in Cudworth's Intellectual System (a huge pile of learning, unwieldy, enormous) and in Lord Brook's hieroglyphic theories, and in Bishop Butler's Sermons, and in the Duchess of Newcastle's fantastic folios, and in Clarke and South and Tillotson, and all the fine thinkers and masculine reasoners of that age—and Leibnitz's *Pre-established Harmony* reared its arch above his head, like the rainbow in the cloud, covenanting with the hopes of man—and then he fell plump, ten thousand fathoms

---

* Mr. Coleridge named his eldest son (the writer of some beautiful sonnets) after Hartley, and the second after Berkeley. The third was called Derwent, after the river of that name. Nothing can be more characteristic of his mind than this circumstance. All his ideas indeed are like a river, flowing on for ever, and still murmuring as it flows, discharging its waters and still replenished—

"And so by many winding nooks it strays,
With willing sport to the wild ocean!"

down (but his wings saved him harmless) into the *hortus siccus* of Dissent, where he pared religion down to the standard of reason, and stripped faith of mystery, and preached Christ crucified and the Unity of the Godhead, and so dwelt for a while in the spirit of John Huss and Jerome of Prague and Socinus and old John Zisca, and ran through Neal's History of the Puritans, and Calamy's Non-Conformists' Memorial, having like thoughts and passions with them—but then Spinoza became his God, and he took up the vast chain of being in his hand, and the round world became the centre and the soul of all things in some shadowy sense, forlorn of meaning, and around him he beheld the living traces and the sky-pointing proportions of the mighty Pan—but poetry redeemed him from this spectral philosophy, and he bathed his heart in beauty, and gazed at the golden light of heaven, and drank of the spirit of the universe, and wandered at eve by fairy-stream or fountain,

> ——" When he saw nought but beauty,
> When he heard the voice of that Almighty. One
> In every breeze that blew, or wave that murmured "—

and wedded with truth in Plato's shade, and in the writings of Proclus and Plotinus saw the ideas of things in the eternal mind, and unfolded all mysteries with the School-men and fathomed the depths of Duns Scotus and Thomas Aquinas, and entered the third heaven with Jacob Behmen, and walked hand in hand with Swedenborg through the pavilions of the New Jerusalem, and sung his faith in the promise and in the word in his *Religious Musings*—and lowering himself from that dizzy height, poised himself on Milton's wings, and spread out his thoughts in charity with the glad prose of Jeremy Taylor, and wept over Bowles's Sonnets, and studied Cowper's blank verse, and betook him-

self to Thomson's Castle of Indolence, and sported with
the wits of Charles the Second's days and of Queen Anne,
and relished Swift's style and that of the John Bull (Arbuthnot's we mean, not Mr. Croker's), and dallied with the
British Essayists and Novelists, and knew all qualities of
more modern writers with a learned spirit, Johnson, and
Goldsmith, and Junius, and Burke, and Godwin, and the
Sorrows of Werter, and Jean Jacques Rousseau, and Voltaire, and Marivaux, and Crebillon, and thousands more —
now "laughed with Rabelais in his easy chair" or pointed
to Hogarth, or afterwards dwelt on Claude's classic scenes,
or spoke with rapture of Raphael, and compared the women
at Rome to figures that had walked out of his pictures, or
visited the Oratory of Pisa, and described the works of
Giotto and Ghirlandaio and Massaccio, and gave the moral
of the picture of the Triumph of Death, where the beggars
and the wretched invoke his dreadful dart, but the rich
and mighty of the earth quail and shrink before it; and in
.that land of siren sights and sounds, saw a dance of peasant
girls, and was charmed with lutes and gondolas,—or wandered into Germany and lost himself in the labyrinths of the
Hartz Forest and of the Kantean philosophy, and amongst
the cabalistic names of Fichtè and Schelling and Lessing,
and God knows who—this was long after, but all the former
while he had nerved his heart and filled his eyes with tears,
as he hailed the rising orb of liberty, since quenched in
darkness and in blood, and had kindled his affections at the
blaze of the French Revolution, and sang for joy when the
towers of the Bastile and the proud places of the insolent
and the oppressor fell, and would have floated his bark,
freighted with fondest fancies, across the Atlantic wave
with Southey and others to seek for peace and freedom—

"In Philarmonia's undivided dale!"

Alas! " Frailty, thy name is *Genius!* "—What is become of
all this mighty heap of hope, of thought, of learning, and
humanity? It has ended in swallowing doses of oblivion
and in writing paragraphs in the *Courier.*—Such and so
little is the mind of man!

It was not to be supposed that Mr. Coleridge could keep
on at the rate he set off; he could not realize all he knew
or thought, and less could not fix his desultory ambition;
other stimulants supplied the place, and kept up the intoxicating dream, the fever and the madness of his early impressions. Liberty (the philosopher's and the poet's bride)
had fallen a victim, meanwhile, to the murderous practice
of the hag, Legitimacy. Proscribed by court-hirelings, too
romantic for the herd of vulgar politicians, our enthusiast
stood at bay, and at last turned on the pivot of a subtle
casuistry to the *unclean side:* but his discursive reason
would not let him trammel himself into a poet-laureate or
stamp-distributor, and he stopped, ere he had quite passed
that well-known " bourne from whence no traveller returns "
—and so has sunk into torpid, uneasy repose, tantalized by
useless resources, haunted by vain imaginings, his lips idly
moving, but his heart for ever still, or, as the shattered
chords vibrate of themselves, making melancholy music to
the ear of memory! Such is the fate of genius in an age,
when in the unequal contest with sovereign wrong, every
man is ground to powder who is not either a born slave,
or who does not willingly and at once offer up the yearnings of humanity and the dictates of reason as a welcome
sacrifice to besotted prejudice and loathsome power.

Of all Mr. Coleridge's productions, the *Ancient Mariner*
is the only one that we could with confidence put into
any person's hands, on whom we wished to impress a favourable idea of his extraordinary powers. Let whatever
other objections be made to it, it is unquestionably a work

of genius—of wild, irregular, overwhelming imagination, and has that rich, varied movement in the verse, which gives a distant idea of the lofty or changeful tones of Mr. Coleridge's voice. In the *Christobel,* there is one splendid passage on divided friendship. The *Translation of Schiller's Wallenstein* is also a masterly production in its kind, faithful and spirited. Among his smaller pieces there are occasional bursts of pathos and fancy, equal to what we might expect from him; but these form the exception, and not the rule. Such, for instance, is his affecting Sonnet to the author of the Robbers.

> "Schiller! that hour I would have wish'd to die,
>   If through the shudd'ring midnight I had sent
>   From the dark dungeon of the tower time-rent,
> That fearful voice, a famish'd father's cry—
> That in no after-moment aught less vast
>   Might stamp me mortal! A triumphant shout
>   Black horror scream'd, and all her goblin rout
> From the more with'ring scene diminish'd pass'd.
> Ah! Bard tremendous in sublimity!
>   Could I behold thee in thy loftier mood,
> Wand'ring at eve, with finely frenzied eye,
>   Beneath some vast old tempest-swinging wood!
>   Awhile, with mute awe gazing, I would brood,
> Then weep aloud in a wild ecstasy."

His Tragedy, entitled *Remorse,* is full of beautiful and striking passages, but it does not place the author in the first rank of dramatic writers. But if Mr. Coleridge's works do not place him in that rank, they injure instead of conveying a just idea of the man, for he himself is certainly in the first class of general intellect.

If our author's poetry is inferior to his conversation, his prose is utterly abortive. Hardly a gleam is to be found in it of the brilliancy and richness of those stores of thought and language that he pours out incessantly, when they are lost like drops of water in the ground. The principal work, in which he has attempted to embody his general view of things, is the FRIEND, of which, though it contains some noble passages and fine trains of thought, prolixity and obscurity are the most frequent characteristics.

# XII

## MR. SOUTHEY

Perhaps the most pleasing and striking of all Mr.
Southey's poems are not his triumphant taunts hurled
against oppression, are not his glowing effusions to Liberty,
but those in which, with a mild melancholy, he seems conscious of his own infirmities of temper, and to feel a wish
to correct by thought and time the precocity and sharpness
of his disposition. May the quaint but affecting aspiration
expressed in one of these be fulfilled, that as he mellows
into maturer age, all such asperities may wear off, and
he himself become

"Like the high leaves upon the holly-tree!"

Mr. Southey's prose-style can hardly be too much praised.
It is plain, clear, pointed, familiar, perfectly modern in its
texture, but with a grave and sparkling admixture of
*archaisms* in its ornaments and occasional phraseology.
He is the best and most natural prose-writer of any poet of
the day; we mean that he is far better than Lord Byron,
Mr. Wordsworth, or Mr. Coleridge, for instance. The
manner is perhaps superior to the matter, that is, in his
Essays and Reviews. There is rather a want of originality
and even of *impetus:* but there is no want of playful or
biting satire, of ingenuity, of casuistry, of learning and of
information. He is " full of wise saws and modern " (as
well as ancient) " instances." Mr. Southey may not always
convince his opponents; but he seldom fails to stagger,

never to gall them. In a word, we may describe his style by saying that it has not the body or thickness of port wine, but it is like clear sherry, with kernels of old authors thrown into it!—He also excels as an historian and prose-translator. His histories abound in information, and exhibit proofs of the most indefatigable patience and industry. By no uncommon process of the mind, Mr. Southey seems willing to steady the extreme levity of his opinions and feelings by an appeal to facts. His translations of the Spanish and French romances are also executed *con amore,* and with the literary fidelity of a mere linguist. That of the *Cid,* in particular, is a masterpiece. Not a word could be altered for the better in the old scriptural style which it adopts in conformity to the original. It is no less interesting in itself, or as a record of high and chivalrous feelings and manners, than it is worthy of perusal as a literary curiosity.

Mr. Southey's conversation has a little resemblance to a common-place book; his habitual deportment to a piece of clock-work. He is not remarkable either as a reasoner or an observer: but he is quick, unaffected, replete with anecdote, various and retentive in his reading, and exceedingly happy in his play upon words, as most scholars are who give their minds this sportive turn. We have chiefly seen Mr. Southey in company where few people appear to advantage, we mean in that of Mr. Coleridge. He has not certainly the same range of speculation, nor the same flow of sounding words, but he makes up by the details of knowledge and by a scrupulous correctness of statement for what he wants in originality of thought, or impetuous declamation. The tones of Mr. Coleridge's voice are eloquence: those of Mr. Southey are meagre, shrill, and dry. Mr. Coleridge's *forte* is conversation, and he is conscious of this: Mr. Southey evidently considers writing as

his stronghold, and if gravelled in an argument, or at a
loss for an explanation, refers to something he has written
on the subject, or brings out his port-folio, doubled down
in dog-ears, in confirmation of some fact. He is scholastic
and professional in his ideas. He sets more value on what
he writes than on what he says: he is perhaps prouder
of his library than of his own productions—themselves a
library! He is more simple in his manners than his friend
Mr. Coleridge; but at the same time less cordial or con-
ciliating. He is less vain, or has less hope of pleasing,
and therefore lays himself less out to please. There is an
air of condescension in his civility. With a tall, loose
figure, a peaked austerity of countenance, and no inclination to *embonpoint*, you would say he has something puritanical, something ascetic in his appearance. He answers
to Mandeville's description of Addison, " a parson in a
tye-wig." He is not a boon companion, nor does he indulge
in the pleasures of the table, nor in any other vice; nor are
we aware that Mr. Southey is chargeable with any human
frailty but—*want of charity!* Having fewer errors to plead
guilty to, he is less lenient to those of others. He was
born an age too late. Had he lived a century or two ago,
he would have been a happy as well as blameless character. But the distraction of the time has unsettled him,
and the multiplicity of his pretensions have jostled with
each other. No man in our day (at least no man of
genius) has led so uniformly and entirely the life of a
scholar from boyhood to the present hour, devoting himself
to learning with the enthusiasm of an early love, with the
severity and constancy of a religious vow—and well would
it have been for him if he had confined himself to this, and
not undertaken to pull down or to patch up the State!
However irregular in his opinions, Mr. Southey is constant,
unremitting, mechanical in his studies, and the performance

of his duties.  There is nothing Pindaric or Shandean here.
In all the relations and charities of private life, he is correct,
exemplary, generous, just.  We never heard a single impropriety laid to his charge; and if he has many enemies,
few men can boast more numerous or stauncher friends.—
The variety and piquancy of his writings form a striking
contrast to the mode in which they are produced.  He
rises early, and writes or reads till breakfast-time.  He
writes or reads after breakfast till dinner, after dinner till
tea, and from tea till bed-time—

> "And follows so the ever-running year
> With profitable labour to his grave.—"

on Derwent's banks, beneath the foot of Skiddaw.  Study
serves him for business, exercise, recreation.  He passes
from verse to prose, from history to poetry, from reading
to writing, by a stop-watch.  He writes a fair hand without
blots, sitting upright in his chair, leaves off when he comes
to the bottom of the page, and changes the subject for
another, as opposite as the Antipodes.  His mind is after
all rather the recipient and transmitter of knowledge, than
the originator of it.  He has hardly grasp of thought
enough to arrive at any great leading truth.  His passions
do not amount to more than irritability.  With some gall
in his pen, and coldness in his manner, he has a great deal
of kindness in his heart.  Rash in his opinions, he is steady
in his attachments—and is a man, in many particulars admirable, in all respectable—his political inconsistency alone
excepted!

# XIII

## ELIA

So Mr. Charles Lamb chooses to designate himself; and as his lucubrations under this *nom de guerre* have gained considerable notice from the public, we shall here attempt to describe his style and manner, and to point out his beauties and defects.

Mr. Lamb, though he has borrowed from previous sources, instead of availing himself of the most popular and admired, has groped out his way, and made his most successful researches among the more obscure and intricate, though certainly not the least pithy or pleasant of our writers. He has raked among the dust and cobwebs of a remote period, has exhibited specimens of curious relics, and pored over moth-eaten, decayed manuscripts, for the benefit of the more inquisitive and discerning part of the public. Antiquity after a time has the grace of novelty, as old fashions revived are mistaken for new ones; and a certain quaintness and singularity of style is an agreeable relief to the smooth and insipid monotony of modern composition. Mr. Lamb has succeeded not by conforming to the *Spirit of the Age,* but in opposition to it. He does not march boldly along with the crowd, but steals off the pavement to pick his way in the contrary direction. He prefers *bye-ways* to *highways.* When the full tide of human life pours along to some festive show, to some pageant of a day, Elia would stand on one side to look over an old book-stall, or stroll down some deserted pathway in search of a pensive description over a tottering door-way, or some

quaint device in architecture, illustrative of embryo art
and ancient manners. Mr. Lamb has the very soul of an
antiquarian, as this implies a reflecting humanity; the film
of the past hovers for ever before him. He is shy, sensitive, the reverse of every thing coarse, vulgar, obtrusive, and
*common-place.* He would fain "shuffle off this mortal
coil," and his spirit clothes itself in the garb of elder time,
homelier, but more durable. He is borne along with no
pompous paradoxes, shines in no glittering tinsel of a fashionable phraseology; is neither fop nor sophist. He has
none of the turbulence or froth of new-fangled opinions.
His style runs pure and clear, though it may often take
an underground course, or be conveyed through old-fashioned conduit-pipes. Mr. Lamb does not court popularity,
nor strut in gaudy plumes, but shrinks from every kind of
ostentatious and obvious pretension into the retirement of
his own mind.

> " The self-applauding bird, the peacock see :—
> Mark what a sumptuous pharisee is he !
> Meridian sun-beams tempt him to unfold
> His radiant glories, azure, green, and gold :
> He treads as if, some solemn music near,
> His measured step were governed by his ear :
> And seems to say—' Ye meaner fowl, give place,
> I am all splendour, dignity, and grace !'
> Not so the pheasant on his charms presumes,
> Though he too has a glory in his plumes.
> He, Christian-like, retreats with modest mien
> To the close copse or far sequestered green,
> And shines without desiring to be seen."

These lines well describe the modest and delicate beauties
of Mr. Lamb's writings, contrasted with the lofty and vain-
glorious pretensions of some of his contemporaries. This
gentleman is not one of those who pay all their homage
to the prevailing idol: he thinks that

"Newborn gauds are made and moulded of things past,"

nor does he

> "Give to dust that is a little gilt
> More laud than gilt o'er-dusted."

His convictions " do not in broad rumor lie," nor are they
" set off to the world in the glistering foil" of fashion;
but " live and breathe aloft in those pure eyes, and perfect
judgment of all-seeing *time*." Mr. Lamb rather affects
and is tenacious of the obscure and remote: of that which
rests on its own intrinsic and silent merit; which scorns
all alliance, or even the suspicion of owing any thing to
noisy clamour, to the glare of circumstances. There is a
fine tone of *chiaro-scuro,* a moral perspective in his
writings. He delights to dwell on that which is fresh to the
eye of memory; he yearns after and covets what soothes the
frailty of human nature. That touches him most nearly
which is withdrawn to a certain distance, which verges on
the borders of oblivion:—that piques and provokes his fancy
most, which is hid from a superficial glance. That which,
though gone by, is still remembered, is in his view more
genuine, and has given more " vital signs that it will live,"
than a thing of yesterday, that may be forgotten to-morrow.
Death has in this sense the spirit of life in it; and the
shadowy has to our author something substantial in it.
Ideas savour most of reality in his mind; or rather his
imagination loiters on the edge of each, and a page of his
writings recalls to our fancy the *stranger* on the grate, fluttering in its dusky tenuity, with its idle superstition and
hospitable welcome!

Mr. Lamb has a distate to new faces, to new books, to
new buildings, to new customs. He is shy of all imposing
appearances, of all assumptions of self-importance, of all

adventitious ornaments, of all mechanical advantages, even
to a nervous excess. It is not merely that he does not
rely upon or ordinarily avail himself of them; he holds
them in abhorrence, he utterly abjures and discards them,
and places a great gulph between him and them. He disdains all the vulgar artifices of authorship, all the cant of
criticism, and helps to notoriety. He has no grand swelling theories to attract the visionary and the enthusiast, no
passing topics to allure the thoughtless and the vain. He
evades the present, he mocks the future. His affections
revert to and settle on the past, but then, even this must
have something personal and local in it to interest him
deeply and thoroughly; he pitches his tent in the suburbs
of existing manners; brings down the account of character to the few straggling remains of the last generation;
seldom ventures beyond the bills of mortality, and occupies
that nice point between egotism and disinterested humanity. No one makes the tour of our southern metropolis,
or describes the manners of the last age, so well as Mr.
Lamb—with so fine, and yet so formal an air—with such
vivid obscurity, with such arch piquancy, such picturesque
quaintness, such smiling pathos. How admirably he has
sketched the former inmates of the South-Sea House;
what "fine fretwork he makes of their double and single
entries!" With what a firm, yet subtle pencil he has embodied *Mrs. Battle's Opinions on Whist!* How notably he
embalms a battered *beau;* how delightfully an amour, that
was cold forty years ago, revives in his pages! With what
well-disguised humour, he introduces us to his relations, and
how freely he serves up his friends! Certainly, some of
his portraits are *fixtures,* and will do to hang up as lasting
and lively emblems of human infirmity. Then there is no
one who has so sure an ear for " the chimes at midnight,"
not even excepting Mr. Justice Shallow; nor could Master

Silence himself take his "cheese and pippins" with a more
significant and satisfactory air.  With what a gusto Mr.
Lamb describes the inns and courts of law, the Temple and
Gray's-Inn, as if he had been a student there for the last
two hundred years, and had been as well acquainted with
the person of Sir Francis Bacon as he is with his portrait
or writings!  It is hard to say whether St. John's Gate is
connected with more intense and authentic associations in
his mind, as a part of old London Wall, or as the frontis-
piece (time out of mind) of the Gentleman's Magazine.
He haunts Watling-street like a gentle spirit; the avenues
to the play-houses are thick with panting recollections, and
Christ's-Hospital still breathes the balmy breath of infancy
in his description of it!  Whittington and his Cat are a
fine hallucination for Mr. Lamb's historic Muse, and we
believe he never heartily forgave a certain writer who took
the subject of Guy Faux out of his hands.  The streets
of London are his fairy-land, teeming with wonder, with
life and interest to his retrospective glance, as it did to the
eager eye of childhood; he has contrived to weave its tritest
traditions into a bright and endless romance!

Mr. Lamb's taste in books is also fine, and it is peculiar.
It is not the worse for a little *idiosyncrasy*.  He does not
go deep into the Scotch novels, but he is at home in
Smollett or Fielding.  He is little read in Junius or Gibbon,
but no man can give a better account of Burton's Anatomy
of Melancholy, or Sir Thomas Brown's Urn-Burial, or
Fuller's Worthies, or John Bunyan's Holy War.  No one
is more unimpressible to a specious declamation; no one
relishes a recondite beauty more.  His admiration of Shakspeare and Milton does not make him despise Pope; and
he can read Parnell with patience, and Gay with delight.
His taste in French and German literature is somewhat
defective; nor has he made much progress in the science

of Political Economy or other abstruse studies, though
he has read vast folios of controversial divinity, merely
for the sake of the intricacy of style, and to save himself
the pain of thinking. Mr. Lamb is a good judge of prints
and pictures. His admiration of Hogarth does credit to
both, particularly when it is considered that Leonardo da
Vinci is his next greatest favourite, and that his love of
the *actual* does not proceed from a want of taste for the
*ideal*. His worst fault is an over-eagerness of enthusiasm,
which occasionally makes him take a surfeit of his highest
favourites.—Mr. Lamb excels in familiar conversation almost as much as in writing, when his modesty does not
overpower his self-possession. He is as little of a proser
as possible, but he *blurts* out the finest wit and sense in the
world. He keeps a good deal in the back-ground at first,
till some excellent conceit pushes him forward, and then
he abounds in whim and pleasantry. There is a primitive
simplicity and self-denial about his manners; and a Quakerism in his personal appearance, which is, however, relieved
by a fine Titian head, full of dumb eloquence! Mr. Lamb
is a general favourite with those who know him. His
character is equally singular and amiable. He is endeared
to his friends not less by his foibles than his virtues; he
ensures their esteem by the one, and does not wound their
self-love by the other. He gains ground in the opinion
of others, by making no advances in his own. We easily
admire genius where the diffidence of the possessor makes
our acknowledgment of merit seem like a sort of patronage,
or act of condescension, as we willingly extend our good
offices where they are not exacted as obligations, or repaid
with sullen indifference.—The style of the Essays of Elia
is liable to the charge of a certain *mannerism*. His sentences are cast in the mould of old authors; his expressions
are borrowed from them; but his feelings and observations

are genuine and original, taken from actual life, or from his own breast; and he may be said (if any one can) " to have coined his heart for *jests,*" and to have split his brain for fine distinctions!  Mr. Lamb, from the peculiarity of his exterior and address as an author, would probably never have made his way by detached and independent efforts; but, fortunately for himself and others, he has taken advantage of the Periodical Press, where he has been stuck into notice, and the texture of his compositions is assuredly fine enough to bear the broadest glare of popularity that has hitherto shone upon them.  Mr. Lamb's literary efforts have procured him civic honours (a thing unheard of in our times), and he has been invited, in his character of ELIA, to dine at a select party with the Lord Mayor.  We should prefer this distinction to that of being poet-laureat.  We would recommend to Mr. Waithman's perusal (if Mr. Lamb has not anticipated us) the *Rosamond Gray* and the *John Woodvil* of the same author, as an agreeable relief to the noise of a City feast, and the heat of city elections.  A friend, a short time ago, quoted some lines * from the last-mentioned of these works, which meeting Mr. Godwin's eye, he was so struck with the beauty of the passage, and with a consciousness of having seen it before, that he was uneasy till he could recollect where, and after hunting in vain for it in Ben Jonson, Beaumont and Fletcher, and other not unlikely places, sent to Mr. Lamb to know if he could help him to the author!

* The description of the sports in the forest:

"To see the sun to bed and to arise,
Like some hot amourist with glowing eyes," etc.

# XIV

## SIR WALTER SCOTT

SIR WALTER has found out (oh, rare discovery!) that facts are better than fiction; that there is no romance like the romance of real life; and that if we can but arrive at what men feel, do, and say in striking and singular situations, the result will be " more lively, audible, and full of vent," than the fine-spun cobwebs of the brain. With reverence be it spoken, he is like the man who having to imitate the squeaking of a pig upon the stage, brought the animal under his coat with him. Our author has conjured up the actual people he has to deal with, or as much as he could get of them, in " their habits as they lived." He has ransacked old chronicles, and poured the contents upon his page; he has squeezed out musty records; he has consulted wayfaring pilgrims, bed-rid sybils; he has invoked the spirits of the air; he has conversed with the living and the dead, and let them tell their story their own way; and by borrowing of others, has enriched his own genius with everlasting variety, truth, and freedom. He has taken his materials from the original, authentic sources, in large concrete masses, and not tampered with or too much frittered them away. He is only the amanuensis of truth and history. It is impossible to say how fine his writings in consequence are, unless we could describe how fine nature is. All that portion of the history of his country that he has touched upon (wide as the scope is) the manners, the personages, the events, the scenery, lives over again in his volumes. Nothing is wanting—the illusion is complete. There is a hurtling in the air, a trampling of feet upon the ground, as these perfect representations of human character or fanciful belief come thronging back upon our imaginations. We will merely recall a few of the subjects of his pencil to the reader's recollection; for nothing we could add, by way of note or commendation, could make the impression more vivid.

There is (first and foremost, because the earliest of our acquaintance) the Baron of Bradwardine, stately, kind-hearted, whimsical, pedantic; and Flora MacIvor (whom even *we* forgive for her Jacobitism), the fierce Vich Ian Vohr, and Evan Dhu, constant in death, and Davie Gellatly roasting his eggs or turning his rhymes with restless volubility, and the two stag-hounds that met Waverley, as fine as ever Titian painted, or Paul Veronese:—then there is old Balfour of Burley, brandishing his sword and his Bible with fire-eyed fury, trying a fall with the insolent, gigantic Bothwell at the 'Change-house, and vanquishing him at the noble battle of Loudon-hill; there is Bothwell himself, drawn to the life, proud, cruel, selfish, profligate, but with the love-letters of the gentle Alice (written thirty years before), and his verses to her memory found in his pocket after his death: in the same volume of *Old Mortality* is that lone figure, like a figure in Scripture, of the woman sitting on the stone at the turning to the mountain, to warn Burley that there is a lion in his path; and the fawning Claverhouse, beautiful as a panther, smooth-looking, blood-spotted; and the fanatics, Macbriar and Mucklewrath, crazed with zeal and sufferings; and the inflexible Morton, and the faithful Edith, who refused to " give her hand to another while her heart was with her lover in the deep and dead sea." And in the *Heart of Mid Lothian* we have Effie Deans (that sweet, faded flower) and Jeanie, her more than

sister, and old David Deans, the patriarch of St. Leonard's
Crags, and Butler, and Dumbiedikes, eloquent in his silence,
and Mr. Bartoline Saddle-tree and his prudent helpmate,
and Porteous swinging in the wind, and Madge Wildfire,
full of finery and madness, and her ghastly mother.—Again,
there is Meg Merrilies, standing on her rock, stretched on
her bier with " her head to the east," and Dirk Hatterick
(equal to Shakspeare's Master Barnardine), and Glossin,
the soul of an attorney, and Dandy Dinmont, with his
terrier-pack and his pony Dumple, and the fiery Colonel
Mannering, and the modish old counsellor Pleydell, and
Dominie Sampson,* and Rob Roy (like the eagle in his
eyry), and Baillie Nicol Jarvie, and the inimitable Major
Galbraith, and Rashleigh Osbaldistone, and Die Vernon, the
best of secret-keepers; and in the *Antiquary,* the ingenious
and abstruse Mr. Jonathan Oldbuck, and the old beadsman
Edie Ochiltree, and that preternatural figure of old Edith
Elspeith, a living shadow, in whom the lamp of life had
been long extinguished, had it not been fed by remorse and
" thick-coming " recollections; and that striking picture of
the effects of feudal tyranny and fiendish pride, the unhappy Earl of Glenallan; and the Black Dwarf, and his
friend Habbie of the Heughfoot (the cheerful hunter), and
his cousin Grace Armstrong, fresh and laughing like the
morning; and the *Children of the Mist,* and the baying of
the bloodhound that tracks their steps at a distance (the
hollow echoes are in our ears now), and Amy and her hapless love, and the villain Varney, and the deep voice of
George of Douglas—and the immoveable Balafre, and
Master Oliver the Barber in Quentin Durward—and the
quaint humour of the Fortunes of Nigel, and the comic

* Perhaps the finest scene in all these novels, is that where the
Dominie meets his pupil, Miss Lucy, the morning after her brother's
arrival.

spirit of Peveril of the Peak—and the fine old English romance of Ivanhoe. What a list of names! What a host of associations! What a thing is human life! What a power is that of genius! What a world of thought and feeling is thus rescued from oblivion! How many hours of heartfelt satisfaction has our author given to the gay and thoughtless! How many sad hearts has he soothed in pain and solitude! It is no wonder that the public repay with lengthened applause and gratitude the pleasure they receive. He writes as fast as they can read, and he does not write himself down. He is always in the public eye, and we do not tire of him. His worst is better than any other person's best. His *back-grounds* (and his later works are little else but back-grounds capitally made out) are more attractive than the principal figures and most complicated actions of other writers. His works (taken together) are almost like a new edition of human nature. This is indeed to be an author!

The political bearing of the *Scotch Novels* has been a considerable recommendation to them. They are a relief to the mind, rarefied as it has been with modern philosophy, and heated with ultra-radicalism. At a time also, when we bid fair to revive the principles of the Stuarts, it is interesting to bring us acquainted with their persons and misfortunes. The candour of Sir Walter's historic pen levels our bristling prejudices on this score, and sees fair play between Roundheads and Cavaliers, between Protestant and Papist. He is a writer reconciling all the diversities of human nature to the reader. He does not enter into the distinctions of hostile sects or parties, but treats of the strength or the infirmity of the human mind, of the virtues or vices of the human breast, as they are to be found blended in the whole race of mankind. Nothing can show more handsomely or be more gallantly executed. There

was a talk at one time that our author was about to take
Guy Faux for the subject of one of his novels, in order to
put a more liberal and humane construction on the Gunpowder Plot than our " No Popery " prejudices have hitherto permitted.  Sir Walter is a professed *clarifier* of the
age from the vulgar and still lurking old-English antipathy
to Popery and Slavery.  Through some odd process of
*servile* logic, it should seem, that in restoring the claims of
the Stuarts by the courtesy of romance, the House of
Brunswick are more firmly seated in point of fact, and the
Bourbons, by collateral reasoning, become legitimate!  In
any other point of view, we cannot possibly conceive how
Sir Walter imagines " he has done something to revive the
declining spirit of loyalty " by these novels.  His loyalty is
founded on *would-be* treason: he props the actual throne
by the shadow of rebellion.  Does he really think of making
us enamoured of the " good old times " by the faithful and
harrowing portraits he has drawn of them?  Would he
carry us back to the early stages of barbarism, of clanship,
of the feudal system as " a consummation devoutly to be
wished? "  Is he infatuated enough, or does he so dote
and drivel over his own slothful and self-willed prejudices,
as to believe that he will make a single convert to the
beauty of Legitimacy, that is, of lawless power and savage
bigotry, when he himself is obliged to apologize for the
horrors he describes, and even render his descriptions credi-
ble to the modern reader by referring to the authentic history of these delectable times?  He is indeed so besotted
as to the moral of his own story, that he has even the blind-
ness to go out of his way to have a fling at *flints* and *dungs*
(the contemptible ingredients, as he would have us believe, of a modern rabble) at the very time when he is
describing a mob of the twelfth century—a mob (one
should think) after the writer's own heart, without one

particle of modern philosophy or revolutionary politics in
their composition, who were to a man, to a hair, just what
priests, and kings, and nobles *let* them be, and who were
collected to witness (a spectacle proper to the times) the
burning of the lovely Rebecca at a stake for a sorceress,
because she was a Jewess, beautiful and innocent, and the
consequent victim of insane bigotry and unbridled prof-
ligacy. And it is at this moment (when the heart is kindled
and bursting with indignation at the revolting abuses of
self-constituted power) that Sir Walter *stops the press* to
have a sneer at the people, and to put a spoke (as he
thinks) in the wheel of upstart innovation! This is what
he "calls backing his friends"—it is thus he administers
charms and philtres to our love of Legitimacy, makes us
conceive a horror of all reform, civil, political, or religious,
and would fain put down the *Spirit of the Age*. The author
of Waverley might just as well get up and make a speech
at a dinner at Edinburgh, abusing Mr. Mac-Adam for his
improvements in the roads, on the ground that they were
nearly *impassable* in many places "sixty years since;" or
object to Mr. Peel's *Police-Bill,* by insisting that Hounslow-
Heath was formerly a scene of greater interest and terror
to highwaymen and travellers, and cut a greater figure in
the Newgate Calendar than it does at present.—Oh! Wickliff, Luther, Hampden, Sidney, Somers, mistaken Whigs,
and thoughtless Reformers in religion and politics, and all
ye, whether poets or philosophers, heroes or sages, in-
ventors of arts or sciences, patriots, benefactors of the
human race, enlighteners and civilisers of the world, who
have (so far) reduced opinion to reason, and power to law,
who are the cause that we no longer burn witches and
heretics at slow fires, that the thumb-screws are no longer
applied by ghastly, smiling judges, to extort confession of
imputed crimes from sufferers for conscience sake; that

men are no longer strung up like acorns on trees without
judge or jury, or hunted like wild beasts through thickets
and glens, who have abated the cruelty of priests, the pride
of nobles, the divinity of kings in former times; to whom
we owe it, that we no longer wear round our necks the
collar of Gurth the swineherd, and of Wamba the jester;
that the castles of great lords are no longer the dens of
banditti, whence they issue with fire and sword to lay waste
the land; that we no longer expire in loathsome dungeons
without knowing the cause, or have our right hands struck
off for raising them in self-defence against wanton insult;
that we can sleep without fear of being burnt in our beds,
or travel without making our wills; that no Amy Robsarts
are thrown down trap-doors by Richard Varneys with impunity; that no Red-Reiver of Westburn-Flat sets fire to
peaceful cottages; that no Claverhouse signs cold-blooded
death-warrants in sport; that we have no Tristan the Hermit, or Petit-André, crawling near us, like spiders, and
making our flesh creep, and our hearts sicken within us at
every movement of our lives—ye who have produced this
change in the face of nature and society, return to earth
once more, and beg pardon of Sir Walter and his patrons,
who sigh at not being able to undo all that you have done!
Leaving this question, there are two other remarks which
we wished to make on the Novels. The one was, to express
our admiration of the good-nature of the mottos, in which
the author has taken occasion to remember and quote almost
every living author (whether illustrious or obscure) but
himself—an indirect argument in favour of the general
opinion as to the source from which they spring—and the
other was, to hint our astonishment at the innumerable and
incessant instances of bad and slovenly English in them,
more, we believe, than in any other works now printed.
We should think the writer could not possibly read the

manuscript after he has once written it, or overlook the press.

If there were a writer, who " born for the universe "—

> "——Narrow'd his mind,
> And to party gave up what was meant for mankind——"

who, from the height of his genius looking abroad into nature, and scanning the recesses of the human heart, " winked and shut his apprehension up " to every thought and purpose that tended to the future good of mankind—who, raised by affluence, the reward of successful industry, and by the voice of fame above the want of any but the most honourable patronage, stooped to the unworthy arts of adulation, and abetted the views of the great with the pettifogging feelings of the meanest dependant on office—who, having secured the admiration of the public (with the probable reversion of immortality), showed no respect for himself, for that genius that had raised him to distinction, for that nature which he trampled under foot—who, amiable, frank, friendly, manly in private life, was seized with the dotage of age and the fury of a woman, the instant politics were concerned—who reserved all his candour and comprehensiveness of view for history, and vented his littleness, pique, resentment, bigotry, and intolerance on his contemporaries—who took the wrong side, and defended it by unfair means—who, the moment his own interest or the prejudices of others interfered, seemed to forget all that was due to the pride of intellect, to the sense of manhood—who, praised, admired by men of all parties alike, repaid the public liberality by striking a secret and envenomed blow at the reputation of every one who was not the ready tool of power—who strewed the slime of rankling malice and mercenary scorn over the bud and promise of genius, because it was not fostered in the hot-

bed of corruption, or warped by the trammels of servility—
who supported the worst abuses of authority in the worst
spirit—who joined a gang of desperadoes to spread
calumny, contempt, infamy, wherever they were merited
by honesty or talent on a different side—who officiously
undertook to decide public questions by private insinuations, to prop the throne by nicknames, and the altar by
lies—who being (by common consent), the finest, the most
humane and accomplished writer of his age, associated himself with and encouraged the lowest panders of a venal
press; deluging, nauseating the public mind with the offal
and garbage of Billingsgate abuse and vulgar *slang;* showing no remorse, no relenting or compassion towards the
victims of this nefarious and organized system of party-
proscription, carried on under the mask of literary criticism and fair discussion, insulting the misfortunes of some,
and trampling on the early grave of others—

"Who would not grieve if such a man there be?
Who would not weep if Atticus were he?"

But we believe there is no other age or country in the
world (but ours), in which such genius could have been
so degraded!

# XV

## LORD BYRON

Lord Byron and Sir Walter Scott are among writers now living * the two, who would carry away a majority of suffrages as the greatest geniuses of the age. The former would, perhaps, obtain the preference with fine gentlemen and ladies (squeamishness apart)—the latter with the critics and the vulgar. We shall treat of them in the same connection, partly on account of their distinguished pre-eminence, and partly because they afford a complete contrast to each other. In their poetry, in their prose, in their politics, and in their tempers, no two men can be more unlike.

If Sir Walter Scott may be thought by some to have been

"Born universal heir to all humanity,"

it is plain Lord Byron can set up no such pretension. He is, in a striking degree, the creature of his own will. He holds no communion with his kind; but stands alone, without mate or fellow—

"As if a man were author of himself,
And owned no other kin."

He is like a solitary peak, all access to which is cut off not more by elevation than distance. He is seated on a lofty eminence, " cloud-capt," or reflecting the last rays of setting suns; and in his poetical moods reminds us of the

* This essay was written just before Lord Byron's death.

236

fabled Titans, retired to a ridgy steep, playing on their Pan's-pipes, and taking up ordinary men and things in their hands with haughty indifference. He raises his subject to himself, or tramples on it; he neither stoops to, nor loses himself in it. He exists not by sympathy, but by antipathy. He scorns all things, even himself. Nature must come to him to sit for her picture—he does not go to her. She must consult his time, his convenience, and his humour; and wear a *sombre* or a fantastic garb, or his Lordship turns his back upon her. There is no ease, no unaffected simplicity of manner, no "golden mean." All is strained, or petulant in the extreme. His thoughts are sphered and crystalline; his style "prouder than when blue Iris bends;" his spirit fiery, impatient, wayward, indefatigable. Instead of taking his impressions from without, in entire and almost unimpaired masses, he moulds them according to his own temperament, and heats the materials of his imagination in the furnace of his passions.—Lord Byron's verse glows like a flame, consuming everything in its way; Sir Walter Scott's glides like a river, clear, gentle, harmless. The poetry of the first scorches, that of the last scarcely warms. The light of the one proceeds from an internal source, ensanguined, sullen, fixed; the other reflects the hues of Heaven, or the face of nature, glancing vivid and various. The productions of the Northern Bard have the rust and the freshness of antiquity about them; those of the Noble Poet cease to startle from their extreme ambition of novelty, both in style and matter. Sir Walter's rhymes are "silly sooth"—

> "And dally with the innocence of thought,
> Like the old age"—

his Lordship's Muse spurns *the olden time,* and affects all the supercilious airs of a modern fine lady and an upstart.

The object of the one writer is to restore us to truth and nature: the other chiefly thinks how he shall display his own power, or vent his spleen, or astonish the reader either by starting new subjects and trains of speculation, or by expressing old ones in a more striking and emphatic manner than they have been expressed before. He cares little what it is he says, so that he can say it differently from others. This may account for the charges of plagiarism which have been repeatedly brought against the Noble Poet—if he can borrow an image or sentiment from another, and heighten it by an epithet or an allusion of greater force and beauty than is to be found in the original passage, he thinks he shows his superiority of execution in this in a more marked manner than if the first suggestion had been his own. It is not the value of the observation itself he is solicitous about; but he wishes to shine by contrast—even nature only serves as a foil to set off his style. He therefore takes the thoughts of others (whether contemporaries or not) out of their mouths, and is content to make them his own, to set his stamp upon them, by imparting to them a more meretricious gloss, a higher relief, a greater loftiness of tone, and a characteristic inveteracy of purpose. Even in those collateral ornaments of modern style, slovenliness, abruptness, and eccentricity (as well as in terseness and significance), Lord Byron, when he pleases, defies competition and surpasses all his contemporaries. Whatever he does, he must do in a more decided and daring manner than any one else—he lounges with extravagance, and yawns so as to alarm the reader! Self-will, passion, the love of singularity, a disdain of himself and of others (with a conscious sense that this is among the ways and means of procuring admiration) are the proper categories of his mind: he is a lordly writer, is above his own reputation, and condescends to the Muses with a scornful grace!

Lord Byron, who in his politics is a *liberal,* in his genius is haughty and aristocratic: Walter Scott, who is an aristocrat in principle, is popular in his writings, and is (as it were) equally *servile* to nature and to opinion. The genius of Sir Walter is essentially imitative, or " denotes a foregone conclusion:" that of Lord Byron is self-dependent; or at least requires no aid, is governed by no law, but the impulses of its own will. We confess, however much we may admire independence of feeling and erectness of spirit in general or practical questions, yet in works of genius we prefer him who bows to the authority of nature, who appeals to actual objects, to mouldering superstitions, to history, observation, and tradition, before him who only consults the pragmatical and restless workings of his own breast, and gives them out as oracles to the world. We like a writer (whether poet or prose-writer) who takes in (or is willing to take in) the range of half the universe in feeling, character, description, much better than we do one who obstinately and invariably shuts himself up in the Bastile of his own ruling passions. In short, we had rather be Sir Walter Scott (meaning thereby the Author of Waverley) than Lord Byron, a hundred times over. And for the reason just given, namely, that he casts his descriptions in the mould of nature, ever-varying, never tiresome, always interesting and always instructive, instead of casting them constantly in the mould of his own individual impressions. He gives us man as he is, or as he was, in almost every variety of situation, action, and feeling. Lord Byron makes man after his own image, woman after his own heart; the one is a capricious tyrant, the other a yielding slave; he gives us the misanthrope and the voluptuary by turns; and with these two characters, burning or melting in their own fires, he makes out everlasting centos of himself. He hangs the cloud, the film of his existence over all out-

ward things—sits in the centre of his thoughts, and enjoys
dark night, bright day, the glitter and the gloom " in cell
monastic"—we see the mournful pall, the crucifix, the
death's-heads, the faded chaplet of flowers, the gleaming
tapers, the agonized brow of genius, the wasted form of
beauty—but we are still imprisoned in a dungeon, a curtain
intercepts our view, we do not breathe freely the air of
nature or of our own thoughts—the other admired author
draws aside the curtain, and the veil of egotism is rent,
and he shows us the crowd of living men and women, the
endless groups, the landscape back-ground, the cloud and
the rainbow, and enriches our imaginations and relieves
one passion by another, and expands and lightens reflection, and takes away that tightness at the breast which
arises from thinking or wishing to think that there is nothing in the world out of a man's self!—In this point of view,
the Author of Waverley is one of the greatest teachers of
morality that ever lived, by emancipating the mind from
petty, narrow, and bigotted prejudices: Lord Byron is the
greatest pamperer of those prejudices, by seeming to think
there is nothing else worth encouraging but the seeds or
the full luxuriant growth of dogmatism and self-conceit.
In reading the *Scotch Novels,* we never think about the
author, except from a feeling of curiosity respecting our
unknown benefactor: in reading Lord Byron's works, he
himself is never absent from our minds.  The colouring of
Lord Byron's style, however rich and dipped in Tyrian
dyes, is nevertheless opaque, is in itself an object of delight
and wonder: Sir Walter Scott's is perfectly transparent.
In studying the one, you seem to gaze at the figures cut in
stained glass, which exclude the view beyond, and where
the pure light of Heaven is only a means of setting off the
gorgeousness of art: in reading the other, you look through
a noble window at the clear and varied landscape without.

Or to sum up the distinction in one word, Sir Walter Scott is the most *dramatic* writer now living; and Lord Byron is the least so.—It would be difficult to imagine that the Author of Waverley is in the smallest degree a pedant; as it would be hard to persuade ourselves that the Author of Childe Harold and Don Juan is not a coxcomb, though a provoking and sublime one. In this decided preference given to Sir Walter Scott over Lord Byron, we distinctly include the prose-works of the former; for we do not think his poetry alone by any means entitles him to that precedence. Sir Walter in his poetry, though pleasing and natural, is a comparative trifler: it is in his anonymous productions that he has shown himself for what he is!—

*Intensity* is the great and prominent distinction of Lord Byron's writings. He seldom gets beyond force of style, nor has he produced any regular work or masterly whole. He does not prepare any plan beforehand, nor revise and retouch what he has written with polished accuracy. His only object seems to be to stimulate himself and his readers for the moment—to keep both alive, to drive away *ennui,* to substitute a feverish and irritable state of excitement for listless indolence or even calm enjoyment. For this purpose he pitches on any subject at random without much thought or delicacy—he is only impatient to begin—and takes care to adorn and enrich it as he proceeds with "thoughts that breathe and words that burn." He composes (as he himself has said) whether he is in the bath, in his study, or on horseback—he writes as habitually as others talk or think—and whether we have the inspiration of the Muse or not, we always find the spirit of the man of genius breathing from his verse. He grapples with his subject, and moves, penetrates, and animates it by the electric force of his own feelings. He is often monotonous, extravagant, offensive; but he is never dull, or tedious, but when he writes prose.  Lord Byron does not exhibit a new view of nature, or raise insignificant objects into importance by the romantic associations with which he surrounds them; but generally (at least) takes common-place thoughts and events and endeavours to express them in stronger and statelier language than others.  His poetry stands like a Martello tower by the side of his subject.  He does not, like Mr. Wordsworth, lift poetry from the ground, or create a sentiment out of nothing.  He does not describe a daisy or a periwinkle, but the cedar or the cypress: not "poor men's cottages, but princes' palaces."  His Childe Harold contains a lofty and impassioned review of the great events of history, of the mighty objects left as wrecks of time, but he dwells chiefly on what is familiar to the mind of every schoolboy; has brought out few new traits of feeling or thought; and has done no more than justice to the reader's preconceptions by the sustained force and brilliancy of his style and imagery.

Lord Byron's earlier productions, *Lara,* the *Corsair,* etc. were wild and gloomy romances, put into rapid and shining verse.  They discover the madness of poetry, together with the inspiration: sullen, moody, capricious, fierce, inexorable, gloating on beauty, thirsting for revenge, hurrying from the extremes of pleasure to pain, but with nothing permanent, nothing healthy or natural.  The gaudy decorations and the morbid sentiments remind one of flowers strewed over the face of death!  In his *Childe Harold* (as has been just observed) he assumes a lofty and philosophic tone, and "reasons high of providence, fore-knowledge, will, and fate."  He takes the highest points in the history of the world, and comments on them from a more commanding eminence: he shows us the crumbling monuments of time, he invokes the great names, the mighty spirit of antiquity. The universe is changed into a stately mausoleum:—in sol-

emn measures he chaunts a hymn to fame. Lord Byron
has strength and elevation enough to fill up the moulds of
our classical and time-hallowed recollections, and to re-
kindle the earliest aspirations of the mind after greatness
and true glory with a pen of fire. The names of Tasso,
of Ariosto, of Dante, of Cincinnatus, of Cæsar, of Scipio,
lose nothing of their pomp or their lustre in his hands,
and when he begins and continues a strain of panegyric on
such subjects, we indeed sit down with him to a banquet
of rich praise, brooding over imperishable glories,

" Till Contemplation has her fill."

Lord Byron seems to cast himself indignantly from " this
bank and shoal of time," or the frail tottering bark that
bears up modern reputation, into the huge sea of ancient
renown, and to revel there with untired, outspread plume.
Even this in him is spleen—his contempt of his contemporaries makes him turn back to the lustrous past, or project
himself forward to the dim future!—Lord Byron's tragedies, Faliero,* Sardanapalus, etc. are not equal to his other
works. They want the essence of the drama. They abound
in speeches and descriptions, such as he himself might
make either to himself or others, lolling on his couch of
a morning, but do not carry the reader out of the poet's
mind to the scenes and events recorded. They have neither
action, character, nor interest, but are a sort of *gossamer*
tragedies, spun out, and glittering, and spreading a flimsy
veil over the face of nature. Yet he spins them on. Of
all that he has done in this way, the *Heaven and Earth* (the
same subject as Mr. Moore's *Loves of the Angels*) is the

* " Don Juan was my Moscow, and Faliero
  My Leipsic, and my Mont St. Jean seems Cain."
  *Don Juan,* Canto XI.

best.  We prefer it even to *Manfred*.  *Manfred* is merely himself with a fancy-drapery on: but in the dramatic fragment published in the *Liberal,* the space between Heaven and Earth, the stage on which his characters have to pass to and fro, seems to fill his Lordship's imagination; and the Deluge, which he has so finely described, may be said to have drowned all his own idle humours.

We must say we think little of our author's turn for satire.  His "English Bards and Scotch Reviewers" is dogmatical and insolent, but without refinement or point. He calls people names, and tries to transfix a character with an epithet, which does not stick, because it has no other foundation than his own petulance and spite; or he endeavours to degrade by alluding to some circumstance of external situation.  He says of Mr. Wordsworth's poetry, that "it is his aversion."  That may be: but whose fault is it?  This is the satire of a lord, who is accustomed to have all his whims or dislikes taken for gospel, and who cannot be at the pains to do more than signify his contempt or displeasure.  If a great man meets with a rebuff which he does not like, he turns on his heel, and this passes for a repartee.  The Noble Author says of a celebrated barrister and critic, that he was "born in a garret sixteen stories high."  The insinuation is not true; or if it were, it is low. The allusion degrades the person who makes it, not him to whom it is applied.  This is also the satire of a person of birth and quality, who measures all merit by external rank, that is, by his own standard.  So his Lordship, in a "Letter to the Editor of my Grandmother's Review," addresses him fifty times as "*my dear Robarts;*" nor is there any other wit in the article.  This is surely a mere assumption of superiority from his Lordship's rank, and is the sort of *quizzing* he might use to a person who came to hire himself as a valet to him at *Long's*—the waiters might laugh, the public will not. In like manner, in the controversy about Pope, he claps Mr. Bowles on the back with a coarse facetious familiarity, as if he were his chaplain whom he had invited to dine with him, or was about to present to a benefice. The reverend divine might submit to the obligation, but he has no occasion to subscribe to the jest. If it is a jest that Mr. Bowles should be a parson, and Lord Byron a peer, the world knew this before; there was no need to write a pamphlet to prove it.

The *Don Juan* indeed has great power; but its power is owing to the force of the serious writing, and to the oddity of the contrast between that and the flashy passages with which it is interlarded. From the sublime to the ridiculous there is but one step. You laugh and are surprised that any one should turn round and *travestie* himself: the drollery is in the utter discontinuity of ideas and feelings. He makes virtue serve as a foil to vice; *dandyism* is (for want of any other) a variety of genius. A classical intoxication is followed by the splashing of soda-water, by frothy effusions of ordinary bile. After the lightning and the hurricane, we are introduced to the interior of the cabin and the contents of the wash-hand basins. The solemn hero of tragedy plays *Scrub* in the farce. This is " very tolerable and not to be endured." The Noble Lord is almost the only writer who has prostituted his talents in this way. He hallows in order to desecrate; takes a pleasure in defacing the images of beauty his hands have wrought; and raises our hopes and our belief in goodness to Heaven only to dash them to the earth again, and break them in pieces the more effectually from the very height they have fallen. Our enthusiasm for genius or virtue is thus turned into a jest by the very person who has kindled it, and who thus fatally quenches the spark of both. It is not that Lord Byron is sometimes serious and sometimes trifling, sometimes profligate, and sometimes moral—but when he is most serious and most moral, he is only preparing to mortify the unsuspecting reader by putting a pitiful *hoax* upon him. This is a most unaccountable anomaly. It is as if the eagle were to build its eyry in a common sewer, or the owl were seen soaring to the mid-day sun. Such a sight might make one laugh, but one would not wish or expect it to occur more than once! *

In fact, Lord Byron is the spoiled child of fame as well as fortune. He has taken a surfeit of popularity, and is not contented to delight, unless he can shock the public. He would force them to admire in spite of decency and common-sense—he would have them read what they would read in no one but himself, or he would not give a rush for their applause. He is to be " a chartered libertine," from whom insults are favours, whose contempt is to be a new incentive to admiration. His Lordship is hard to please: he is equally averse to notice or neglect, enraged at censure and scorning praise. He tries the patience of the town to the very utmost, and when they show signs of weariness or disgust, threatens to *discard* them. He says he will write on, whether he is read or not. He would never write another page, if it were not to court popular applause, or to affect a superiority over it. In this respect also, Lord Byron presents a striking contrast to Sir Walter Scott. The latter takes what part of the public favour falls to his share, without grumbling (to be sure, he has no reason to complain) ; the former is always quarrelling with the world about his *modicum* of applause, the *spolia opima* of vanity, and ungraciously throwing the offerings of incense heaped on his shrine back in the faces of his admirers. Again, there is no taint in the writings of the Author of

* This censure applies to the first cantos of Don Juan much more than to the last. It has been called a Tristram Shandy in rhyme: it is rather a poem written about itself.

Waverley, all is fair and natural and *above-board:* he never outrages the public mind. He introduces no anomalous character: broaches no staggering opinion. If he goes back to old prejudices and superstitions as a relief to the modern reader, while Lord Byron floats on swelling paradoxes—

"Like proud seas under him;"

if the one defers too much to the spirit of antiquity, the other panders to the spirit of the age, goes to the very edge of extreme and licentious speculation, and breaks his neck over it. Grossness and levity are the playthings of his pen. It is a ludicrous circumstance that he should have dedicated his *Cain* to the worthy Baronet! Did the latter ever acknowledge the obligation? We are not nice, not very nice; but we do not particularly approve those subjects that shine chiefly from their rottenness: nor do we wish to see the Muses dressed out in the flounces of a false or questionable philosophy, like *Portia* and *Nerissa* in the garb of Doctors of Law. We like metaphysics as well as Lord Byron; but not to see them making flowery speeches, nor dancing a measure in the fetters of verse. We have as good as hinted, that his Lordship's poetry consists mostly of a tissue of superb common-places; even his paradoxes are *common-place.* They are familiar in the schools: they are only new and striking in his dramas and stanzas, by being out of place. In a word, we think that poetry moves best within the circle of nature and received opinion: speculative theory and subtle casuistry are forbidden ground to it. But Lord Byron often wanders into this ground wantonly, wilfully, and unwarrantably. The only apology we can conceive for the spirit of some of Lord Byron's writings, is the spirit of some of those opposed to him. They would provoke a man to write anything. " Farthest from them is best." The extravagance and license of the one seems a proper antidote to the bigotry and narrowness of the other. The first *Vision of Judgment* was a set-off to the second, though

"None but itself could be its parallel."

Perhaps the chief cause of most of Lord Byron's errors is, that he is that anomaly in letters and in society, a Noble Poet. It is a double privilege, almost too much for humanity. He has all the pride of birth and genius. The strength of his imagination leads him to indulge in fantastic opinions; the elevation of his rank sets censure at defiance. He becomes a pampered egotist. He has a seat in the House of Lords, a niche in the Temple of Fame. Everyday mortals, opinions, things, are not good enough for him to touch or think of. A mere nobleman is, in his estimation, but "the tenth transmitter of a foolish face:" a mere man of genius is no better than a worm. His Muse is also a lady of quality. The people are not polite enough for him: the Court is not sufficiently intellectual. He hates the one and despises the other. By hating and despising others, he does not learn to be satisfied with himself. A fastidious man soon grows querulous and splenetic. If there is nobody but ourselves to come up to our idea of fancied perfection, we easily get tired of our idol. When a man is tired of what he is, by a natural perversity he sets up for what he is not. If he is a poet, he pretends to be a metaphysician: if he is a patrician in rank and feeling, he would fain be one of the people. His ruling motive is not the love of the people, but of distinction;—not of truth, but of singularity. He patronises men of letters out of vanity, and deserts them from caprice, or from the advice of friends. He embarks in an obnoxious publication to provoke censure, and leaves it to shift for itself for fear of scandal. We do not like

Sir Walter's gratuitous servility: we like Lord Byron's preposterous *liberalism* little better. He may affect the principles of equality, but he resumes his privilege of peerage, upon occasion. His Lordship has made great offers of service to the Greeks—money and horses. He is at present in Cephalonia, waiting the event!

.    .    .    .    .    .    .

We had written thus far when news came of the death of Lord Byron, and put an end at once to a strain of somewhat peevish invective, which was intended to meet his eye, not to insult his memory. Had we known that we were writing his epitaph, we must have done it with a different feeling. As it is, we think it better and more like himself, to let what we had written stand, than to take up our leaden shafts, and try to melt them into " tears of sensibility," or mould them into dull praise, and an affected show of candour. We were not silent during the author's life-time, either for his reproof or encouragement (such as we could give, and *he* did not disdain to accept) nor can we now turn undertakers' men to fix the glittering plate upon his coffin, or fall into the procession of popular woe.—Death cancels every thing but truth; and strips a man of every thing but genius and virtue. It is a sort of natural canonization. It makes the meanest of us sacred—it installs the poet in his immortality, and lifts him to the skies. Death is the great assayer of the sterling ore of talent. At his touch the drossy particles fall off, the irritable, the personal, the gross, and mingle with the dust—the finer and more ethereal part mounts with the winged spirit to watch over our latest memory, and protect our bones from insult. We consign the least worthy qualities to oblivion, and cherish the nobler and imperishable nature with double pride and fondness. Nothing could show the real superiority of genius in a more striking point of view than the idle contests and the public indifference about the place of Lord Byron's interment, whether in Westminster Abbey or his own family-vault. A king must have a coronation—a nobleman a funeral-procession.—The man is nothing without the pageant. The poet's cemetery is the human mind, in which he sows the seeds of never-ending thought—his monument is to be found in his works:

> " Nothing can cover his high fame but Heaven;
> No pyramids set off his memory,
> But the eternal substance of his greatness."

Lord Byron is dead: he also died a martyr to his zeal in the cause of freedom, for the last, best hopes of man. Let that be his excuse and his epitaph!

# XVI

## ON POETRY IN GENERAL

THE best general notion which I can give of poetry is, that it is the natural impression of any object or event, by its vividness exciting an involuntary movement of imagination and passion, and producing, by sympathy, a certain modulation of the voice, or sounds, expressing it.

In treating of poetry, I shall speak first of the subject-matter of it, next of the forms of expression to which it gives birth, and afterwards of its connection with harmony of sound.

Poetry is the language of the imagination and the passions. It relates to whatever gives immediate pleasure or pain to the human mind. It comes home to the bosoms and businesses of men; for nothing but what so comes home to them in the most general and intelligible shape, can be a subject for poetry. Poetry is the universal language which the heart holds with nature and itself. He who has a contempt for poetry, cannot have much respect for himself, or for any thing else. It is not a mere frivolous accomplishment, (as some persons have been led to imagine) the trifling amusement of a few idle readers or leisure hours—it has been the study and delight of mankind in all ages. Many people suppose that poetry is something to be found only in books, contained in lines of ten syllables with like endings: but wherever there is a sense of beauty, or power, or harmony, as in the motion of a wave of the sea, in the growth of a flower that " spreads its sweet leaves to the air and dedicates its beauty to the sun."—

*there* is poetry, in its birth. If history is a grave study, poetry may be said to be a graver: its materials lie deeper, and are spread wider. History treats, for the most part, of the cumbrous and unwieldy masses of things, the empty cases in which the affairs of the world are packed, under the heads of intrigue or war, in different states, and from century to century: but there is no thought or feeling that can have entered into the mind of man, which he would be eager to communicate to others, or which they would listen to with delight, that is not a fit subject for poetry. It is not a branch of authorship: it is " the stuff of which our life is made." The rest is " mere oblivion," a dead letter: for all that is worth remembering in life, is the poetry of it. Fear is poetry, hope is poetry, love is poetry, hatred is poetry; contempt, jealousy, remorse, admiration, wonder, pity, despair, or madness, are all poetry. Poetry is that fine particle within us, that expands, rarefies, refines, raises our whole being: without it " man's life is poor as beast's." Man is a poetical animal: and those of us who do not study the principles of poetry, act upon them all our lives, like Molière's *Bourgeois Gentilhomme,* who had always spoken prose without knowing it. The child is a poet in fact, when he first plays at hide-and-seek, or repeats the story of Jack the Giant-killer; the shepherd-boy is a poet, when he first crowns his mistress with a garland of flowers; the countryman, when he stops to look at the rainbow; the city-apprentice, when he gazes after the Lord-Mayor's show; the miser, when he hugs his gold; the courtier, who builds his hopes upon a smile; the savage, who paints his idol with blood; the slave, who worships a tyrant, or the tyrant, who fancies himself a god;—the vain, the ambitious, the proud, the choleric man, the hero and the coward, the beggar and the king, the rich and the poor, the young and the old, all live in a world of their own

making; and the poet does no more than describe what all
the others think and act. If his art is folly and madness,
it is folly and madness at second hand. "There is warrant
for it." Poets alone have not "such seething brains, such
shaping fantasies, that apprehend more than cooler reason"
can.

> "The lunatic, the lover, and the poet
> Are of imagination all compact.
> One sees more devils than vast hell can hold;
> The madman. While the lover, all as frantic,
> Sees Helen's beauty in a brow of Egypt.
> The poet's eye in a fine frenzy rolling,
> Doth glance from heav'n to earth, from earth to heav'n;
> And as imagination bodies forth
> The forms of things unknown, the poet's pen
> Turns them to shape, and gives to airy nothing
> A local habitation and a name.
> Such tricks hath strong imagination."

If poetry is a dream, the business of life is much the
same. If it is a fiction, made up of what we wish things
to be, and fancy that they are, because we wish them so,
there is no other nor better reality. Ariosto has described
the loves of Angelica and Medoro: but was not Medoro,
who carved the name of his mistress on the barks of trees,
as much enamoured of her charms as he? Homer has
celebrated the anger of Achilles: but was not the hero as
mad as the poet? Plato banished the poets from his Commonwealth, lest their descriptions of the natural man should
spoil his mathematical man, who was to be without passions
and affections, who was neither to laugh nor weep, to feel
sorrow nor anger, to be cast down nor elated by any thing.
This was a chimera, however, which never existed but in
the brain of the inventor; and Homer's poetical world has
outlived Plato's philosophical Republic.

Poetry then is an imitation of nature, but the imagination

and the passions are a part of man's nature. We shape things according to our wishes and fancies, without poetry; but poetry is the most emphatical language that can be found for those creations of the mind "which ecstacy is very cunning in." Neither a mere description of natural objects, nor a mere delineation of natural feelings, however distinct or forcible, constitutes the ultimate end and aim of poetry, without the heightenings of the imagination. The light of poetry is not only a direct but also a reflected light, that while it shows us the object, throws a sparkling radiance on all around it: the flame of the passions, communicated to the imagination, reveals to us, as with a flash of lightning, the inmost recesses of thought, and penetrates our whole being. Poetry represents forms chiefly as they suggest other forms; feelings, as they suggest forms or other feelings. Poetry puts a spirit of life and motion into the universe. It describes the flowing, not the fixed. It does not define the limits of sense, or analyze the distinctions of the understanding, but signifies the excess of the imagination beyond the actual or ordinary impression of any object or feeling. The poetical impression of any object is that uneasy, exquisite sense of beauty or power that cannot be contained within itself; that is impatient of all limit; that (as flame bends to flame) strives to link itself to some other image of kindred beauty or grandeur; to enshrine itself, as it were, in the highest forms of fancy, and to relieve the aching sense of pleasure by expressing it in the boldest manner, and by the most striking examples of the same quality in other instances. Poetry, according to Lord Bacon, for this reason "has something divine in it, because it raises the mind and hurries it into sublimity, by conforming the shows of things to the desires of the soul, instead of subjecting the soul to external things, as reason and history do." It is strictly the language of the imagination; and the imagination is that faculty which represents objects, not as they are in themselves, but as they are moulded by other thoughts and feelings, into an infinite variety of shapes and combinations of power. This language is not the less true to nature, because it is false in point of fact; but so much the more true and natural, if it conveys the impression which the object under the influence of passion makes on the mind. Let an object, for instance, be presented to the senses in a state of agitation or fear—and the imagination will distort or magnify the object, and convert it into the likeness of whatever is most proper to encourage the fear. "Our eyes are made the fools" of our other faculties. This is the universal law of the imagination,

> "That if it would but apprehend some joy,
> It comprehends some bringer of that joy:
> Or in the night imagining some fear,
> How easy is a bush suppos'd a bear!"

When Iachimo says of Imogen,

> "The flame o' th' taper
> Bows toward her, and would under-peep her lids
> To see the enclosed lights"—

this passionate interpretation of the motion of the flame to accord with the speaker's own feelings, is true poetry. The lover, equally with the poet, speaks of the auburn tresses of his mistress as locks of shining gold, because the least tinge of yellow in the hair has, from novelty and a sense of personal beauty, a more lustrous effect to the imagination than the purest gold. We compare a man of gigantic stature to a tower: not that he is any thing like so large, but because the excess of his size beyond what we are accustomed to expect, or the usual size of things of the same class, produces by contrast a greater feeling of magnitude and ponderous strength than another object of ten times the same dimensions. The intensity of the feeling makes up for the disproportion of the objects. Things are equal to the imagination, which have the power of affecting the mind with an equal degree of terror, admiration, delight, or love. When Lear calls upon the heavens to avenge his cause, " for they are old like him," there is nothing extravagant or impious in this sublime identification of his age with theirs; for there is no other image which could do justice to the agonising sense of his wrongs and his despair!

Poetry is the high-wrought enthusiasm of fancy and feeling. As in describing natural objects, it impregnates sensible impressions with the forms of fancy, so it describes the feelings of pleasure or pain, by blending them with the strongest movements of passion, and the most striking forms of nature. Tragic poetry, which is the most impassioned species of it, strives to carry on the feeling to the utmost point of sublimity or pathos, by all the force of comparison or contrast; loses the sense of present suffering in the imaginary exaggeration of it; exhausts the terror or pity by an unlimited indulgence of it; grapples with impossibilities in its desperate impatience of restraint; throws us back upon the past, forward into the future; brings every moment of our being or object of nature in startling review before us; and in the rapid whirl of events, lifts us from the depths of woe to the highest contemplations on human life. When Lear says, of Edgar, " Nothing but his unkind daughters could have brought him to this; " what a bewildered amazement, what a wrench of the imagination, that cannot be brought to conceive of any other cause of misery than that which has bowed it down, and absorbs all other sorrow in its own! His sorrow, like a flood, supplies the sources of all

other sorrow. Again, when he exclaims in the mad scene,
"The little dogs and all, Tray, Blanche, and Sweetheart,
see, they bark at me!" it is passion lending occasion to
imagination to make every creature in league against him,
conjuring up ingratitude and insult in their least looked-for
and most galling shapes, searching every thread and fibre
of his heart, and finding out the last remaining image of
respect or attachment in the bottom of his breast, only to
torture and kill it! In like manner the "So I am" of
Cordelia gushes from her heart like a torrent of tears,
relieving it of a weight of love and of supposed ingratitude,
which had pressed upon it for years. What a fine return
of the passion upon itself is that in Othello—with what a
mingled agony of regret and despair he clings to the last
traces of departed happiness—when he exclaims,

> "Oh now, for ever
> Farewel the tranquil mind. Farewel content;
> Farewel the plumed troops and the big wars,
> That make ambition virtue! Oh farewel!
> Farewel the neighing steed, and the shrill trump,
> The spirit-stirring drum, th' ear-piercing fife,
> The royal banner, and all quality,
> Pride, pomp, and circumstance of glorious war:
> And O you mortal engines, whose rude throats
> Th' immortal Jove's dread clamours counterfeit,
> Farewel! Othello's occupation's gone!"

How his passion lashes itself up and swells and rages like
a tide in its sounding course, when, in answer to the doubts
expressed of his returning love, he says,

> "Never, Iago. Like to the Pontic sea,
> Whose icy current and compulsive course
> Ne'er feels retiring ebb, but keeps due on
> To the Propontic and the Hellespont:
> Even so my bloody thoughts, with violent pace,
> Shall ne'er look back, ne'er ebb to humble love,
> Till that a capable and wide revenge
> Swallow them up."—

The climax of his expostulation afterwards with Desdemona is at that line,

"But there where I had garner'd up my heart,
To be discarded thence!"—

One mode in which the dramatic exhibition of passion excites our sympathy without raising our disgust is, that in proportion as it sharpens the edge of calamity and disappointment, it strengthens the desire of good. It enhances our consciousness of the blessing, by making us sensible of the magnitude of the loss. The storm of passion lays bare and shews us the rich depths of the human soul: the whole of our existence, the sum total of our passions and pursuits, of that which we desire and that which we dread, is brought before us by contrast; the action and re-action are equal; the keenness of immediate suffering only gives us a more intense aspiration after, and a more intimate participation with the antagonist world of good; makes us drink deeper of the cup of human life; tugs at the heart-strings; loosens the pressure about them; and calls the springs of thought and feeling into play with tenfold force.

Impassioned poetry is an emanation of the moral and intellectual part of our nature, as well as of the sensitive— of the desire to know, the will to act, and the power to feel; and ought to appeal to these different parts of our constitution, in order to be perfect. The domestic or prose tragedy, which is thought to be the most natural, is in this sense the least so, because it appeals almost exclusively to one of these faculties, our sensibility. The tragedies of Moore and Lillo, for this reason, however affecting at the time, oppress and lie like a dead weight upon the mind, a load of misery which it is unable to throw off: the tragedy of Shakspeare, which is true poetry, stirs our inmost af-

fections; abstracts evil from itself by combining it with all
the forms of imagination, and with the deepest workings of
the heart, and rouses the whole man within us.

The pleasure, however, derived from tragic poetry, is not
anything peculiar to it as poetry, as a fictitious and fanciful
thing. It is not an anomaly of the imagination. It has
its source and ground-work in the common love of strong
excitement. As Mr. Burke observes, people flock to see
a tragedy; but if there were a public execution in the next
street, the theatre would very soon be empty. It is not then
the difference between fiction and reality that solves the
difficulty. Children are satisfied with the stories of ghosts
and witches in plain prose: nor do the hawkers of full, true,
and particular accounts of murders and executions about
the streets, find it necessary to have them turned into penny
ballads, before they can dispose of these interesting and
authentic documents. The grave politician drives a thriving
trade of abuse and calumnies poured out against those
whom he makes his enemies for no other end than that he
may live by them. The popular preacher makes less frequent mention of heaven than of hell. Oaths and nicknames
are only a more vulgar sort of poetry or rhetoric. We are
as fond of indulging our violent passions as of reading
a description of those of others. We are as prone to make
a torment of our fears, as to luxuriate in our hopes of good.
If it be asked, Why we do so? the best answer will be,
Because we cannot help it. The sense of power is as strong
a principle in the mind as the love of pleasure. Objects
of terror and pity exercise the same despotic control over
it as those of love or beauty. It is as natural to hate as
to love, to despise as to admire, to express our hatred or
contempt, as our love or admiration.

> "Masterless passion sways us to the mood
> Of what it likes or loathes."

Not that we like what we loathe; but we like to indulge our hatred and scorn of·it; to dwell upon it, to exasperate our idea of it by every refinement of ingenuity and extravagance of illustration; to make it a bugbear to ourselves, to point it out to others in all the splendour of deformity, to embody it to the senses, to stigmatise it by name, to grapple with it in thought, in action, to sharpen our intellect, to arm our will against it, to know the worst we have to contend with, and to contend with it to the utmost. Poetry is only the highest eloquence of passion, the most vivid form of expression that can be given to our conception of any thing, whether pleasurable or painful, mean or dignified, delightful or distressing. It is the perfect coincidence of the image and the words with the feeling we have, and of which we cannot get rid in any other way, that gives an instant " satisfaction to the thought." This is equally the origin of wit and fancy, of comedy and tragedy, of the sublime and pathetic. When Pope says of the Lord Mayor's shew,—

> " Now night descending, the proud scene is o'er,
> But lives in Settle's numbers one day more! "

when Collins makes Danger, with " limbs of giant mould,"

> " Throw him on the steep
> Of some loose hanging rock, asleep : "

when Lear calls out in extreme anguish,

> "Ingratitude, thou marble-hearted fiend,
> How much more hideous shew'st in a child
> Than the sea-monster ! "

—the passion of contempt in the one case, of terror in the other, and of indignation in the last, is perfectly satisfied. We see the thing ourselves, and shew it to others as we feel it to exist, and as, in spite of ourselves, we are compelled to think of it. The imagination, by thus embodying and turning them to shape, gives an obvious relief to the indistinct and importunate cravings of the will.—We do not wish the thing to be so; but we wish it to appear such as it is. For knowledge is conscious power; and the mind is no longer, in this case, the dupe, though it may be the victim of vice or folly.

Poetry is in all its shapes the language of the imagination and the passions, of fancy and will. Nothing, therefore, can be more absurd than the outcry which has been sometimes raised by frigid and pedantic critics, for reducing the language of poetry to the standard of common sense and reason: for the end and use of poetry, "both at the first and now, was and is to hold the mirror up to nature," seen through the medium of passion and imagination, not divested of that medium by means of literal truth or abstract reason. The painter of history might as well be required to represent the face of a person who has just trod upon a serpent with the still-life expression of a common portrait, as the poet to describe the most striking and vivid impressions which things can be supposed to make upon the mind, in the language of common conversation. Let who will strip nature of the colours and the shapes of fancy, the poet is not bound to do so; the impressions of common sense and strong imagination, that is, of passion and indifference, cannot be the same, and they must have a separate language to do justice to either. Objects must strike differently upon the mind, independently of what they are in themselves, as long as we have a different interest in them, as we see them in a different point of view, nearer or at a greater distance (morally or physically speaking) from novelty, from old acquaintance, from our ignorance of them, from our fear of their consequences, from contrast, from unexpected likeness. We can no more take away the faculty of the imagination, than we can see all objects without light or shade. Some things must dazzle us by their preternatural light; others must hold us in suspense, and tempt our curiosity to explore their obscurity. Those who would dispel these various illusions, to give us their drab-coloured creation in their stead, are not very wise. Let the naturalist, if he will, catch the glow-worm, carry it home with him in a box, and find it next morning nothing but a little grey worm; let the poet or the lover of poetry visit it at evening, when beneath the scented hawthorn and the crescent moon it has built itself a palace of emerald light. This is also one part of nature, one appearance which the glow-worm presents, and that not the least interesting; so poetry is one part of the history of the human mind, though it is neither science nor philosophy. It cannot be concealed, however, that the progress of knowledge and refinement has a tendency to circumscribe the limits of the imagination, and to clip the wings of poetry. The province of the imagination is principally visionary, the unknown and undefined: the understanding restores things to their natural boundaries, and strips them of their fanciful pretensions. Hence the history of religious and poetical enthusiasm is much the same; and both have received a sensible shock from the progress of experimental philosophy. It is the undefined and uncommon that gives birth and scope to the imagination: we can only fancy what we do not know. As in looking into the mazes of a tangled wood we fill them with what shapes we please, with ravenous beasts, with caverns vast, and drear enchantments, so, in our ignorance of the world about us, we make gods or devils of the first object we see, and set no bounds to the wilful suggestions of our hopes and fears.

> " And visions, as poetic eyes avow,
> Hang on each leaf and cling to every bough."

There can never be another Jacob's dream. Since that
time, the heavens have gone farther off, and grown astro-
nomical. They have become averse to the imagination, nor
will they return to us on the squares of the distances, or
on Doctor Chalmers's Discourses. Rembrandt's picture
brings the matter nearer to us.—It is not only the progress
of mechanical knowledge, but the necessary advances of
civilization that are unfavourable to the spirit of poetry.
We not only stand in less awe of the preternatural world,
but we can calculate more surely, and look with more indifference, upon the regular routine of this. The heroes of
the fabulous ages rid the world of monsters and giants. At
present we are less exposed to the vicissitudes of good or
evil, to the incursions of wild beasts or "bandit fierce," or
to the unmitigated fury of the elements. The time has
been that "our fell of hair would at a dismal treatise rouse
and stir as life were in it." But the police spoils all; and
we now hardly so much as dream of a midnight murder.
Macbeth is only tolerated in this country for the sake of
the music; and in the United States of America, where the
philosophical principles of government are carried still farther in theory and practice, we find that the Beggar's Opera
is hooted from the stage. Society, by degrees, is con-
structed into a machine that carries us safely and insipidly
from one end of life to the other, in a very comfortable
prose style.

> "Obscurity her curtain round them drew,
> And siren Sloth a dull quietus sung."

The remarks which have been here made, would, in some
measure, lead to a solution of the question of the comparative merits of painting and poetry. I do not mean to
give any preference, but it should seem that the argument
which has been sometimes set up, that painting must affect

the imagination more strongly, because it represents the image more distinctly, is not well founded. We may assume without much temerity, that poetry is more poetical than painting. When artists or connoisseurs talk on stilts about the poetry of painting, they shew that they know little about poetry, and have little love for the art. Painting gives the object itself; poetry what it implies. Painting embodies what a thing contains in itself: poetry suggests what exists out of it, in any manner connected with it. But this last is the proper province of the imagination. Again, as it relates to passion, painting gives the event, poetry the progress of events: but it is during the progress, in the interval of expectation and suspense, while our hopes and fears are strained to the highest pitch of breathless agony, that the pinch of the interest lies

> "Between the acting of a dreadful thing
> And the first motion, all the interim is
> Like a phantasma or a hideous dream.
> The mortal instruments are then in council;
> And the state of man, like to a little kingdom,
> Suffers then the nature of an insurrection."

But by the time that the picture is painted, all is over. Faces are the best part of a picture; but even faces are not what we chiefly remember in what interests us most.— But it may be asked then, Is there any thing better than Claude Lorraine's landscapes, than Titian's portraits, than Raphael's cartoons, or the Greek statues? Of the two first I shall say nothing, as they are evidently picturesque, rather than imaginative. Raphael's cartoons are certainly the finest comments that ever were made on the Scriptures. Would their effect be the same if we were not acquainted with the text? But the New Testament existed before the cartoons. There is one subject of which there is no cartoon, Christ washing the feet of the disciples the night before his death.  But that chapter does not need a commentary!  It is for want of some such resting-place for the imagination that the Greek statues are little else than specious forms.  They are marble to the touch and to the heart.  They have not an informing principle within them.  In their faultless excellence they appear sufficient to themselves.  By their beauty they are raised above the frailties of passion or suffering.  By their beauty they are deified.  But they are not objects of religious faith to us, and their forms are a reproach to common humanity.  They seem to have no sympathy with us, and not to want our admiration.

Poetry in its matter and form is natural imagery or feeling, combined with passion and fancy.  In its mode of conveyance, it combines the ordinary use of language, with musical expression.  There is a question of long standing in what the essence of poetry consists; or what it is that determines why one set of ideas should be expressed in prose, another in verse.  Milton has told us his idea of poetry in a single line—

> "Thoughts that voluntary move
> Harmonious numbers."

As there are certain sounds that excite certain movements, and the song and dance go together, so there are, no doubt, certain thoughts that lead to certain tones of voice, or modulations of sound, and change " the words of Mercury into the songs of Apollo."  There is a striking instance of this adaptation of the movement of sound and rhythm to the subject, in Spenser's description of the Satyrs accompanying Una to the cave of Sylvanus.

> " So from the ground she fearless doth arise
> And walketh forth without suspect of crime.

They, all as glad as birds of joyous prime,
    Thence lead her forth, about her dancing round,
Shouting and singing all a shepherd's rhyme;
    And with green branches strewing all the ground,
Do worship her as queen with olive garland crown'd.

And all the way their merry pipes they sound,
    That all the woods with doubled echo ring;
And with their horned feet do wear the ground,
    Leaping like wanton kids in pleasant spring;
So towards old Sylvanus they her bring,
    Who with the noise awaked, cometh out."

*Faery Queen,* b. i.  c. vi.

On the contrary, there is nothing either musical or natural
in the ordinary construction of language. It is a thing
altogether arbitrary and conventional. Neither in the
sounds themselves, which are the voluntary signs of certain
ideas, nor in their grammatical arrangements in common
speech, is there any principle of natural imitation, or correspondence to the individual ideas, or to the tone of feeling
with which they are conveyed to others. The jerks, the
breaks, the inequalities, and harshnesses of prose are fatal
to the flow of a poetical imagination, as a jolting road or
a stumbling horse disturbs the reverie of an absent man.
But poetry makes these odds all even. It is the music of
language, answering to the music of the mind, untying as
it were "the secret soul of harmony." Wherever any
object takes such a hold of the mind as to make us dwell
upon it, and brood over it, melting the heart in tenderness,
or kindling it to a sentiment of enthusiasm;—wherever a
movement of imagination or passion is impressed on the
mind, by which it seeks to prolong and repeat the emotion,
to bring all other objects into accord with it, and to give
the same movement of harmony, sustained and continuous,
or gradually varied according to the occasion, to the sounds
that express it—this is poetry. The musical in sound is the
sustained and continuous; the musical in thought is the

sustained and continuous also. There is a near connection between music and deep-rooted passion. Mad people sing. As often as articulation passes naturally into intonation, there poetry begins. Where one idea gives a tone and colour to others, where one feeling melts others into it, there can be no reason why the same principle should not be extended to the sounds by which the voice utters these emotions of the soul, and blends syllables and lines into each other. It is to supply the inherent defect of harmony in the customary mechanism of language, to make the sound an echo to the sense, when the sense becomes a sort of echo to itself—to mingle the tide of verse, "the golden cadences of poetry," with the tide of feeling, flowing and murmuring as it flows—in short, to take the language of the imagination from off the ground, and enable it to spread its wings where it may indulge its own impulses—

> "Sailing with supreme dominion
> Through the azure deep of air"—

without being stopped, or fretted, or diverted with the abruptnesses and petty obstacles, and discordant flats and sharps of prose, that poetry was invented. It is to common language, what springs are to a carriage, or wings to feet. In ordinary speech we arrive at a certain harmony by the modulations of voice: in poetry the same thing is done systematically by a regular collocation of syllables. It has been well observed, that every one who declaims warmly, or grows intent upon a subject, rises into a sort of blank verse or measured prose. The merchant, as described in Chaucer, went on his way "sounding always the increase of his winning." Every prose-writer has more or less of rhythmical adaptation, except poets, who, when deprived of the regular mechanism of verse, seem to have no principle of modulation left in their writings.

An excuse might be made for rhyme in the same manner. It is but fair that the ear should linger on the sounds that delight it, or avail itself of the same brilliant coincidence and unexpected recurrence of syllables, that have been displayed in the invention and collocation of images. It is allowed that rhyme assists the memory; and a man of wit and shrewdness has been heard to say, that the only four good lines of poetry are the well-known ones which tell the number of days in the months of the year.

"Thirty days hath September," etc.

But if the jingle of names assists the memory, may it not also quicken the fancy? and there are other things worth having at our fingers' ends, besides the contents of the almanac.—Pope's versification is tiresome, from its excessive sweetness and uniformity. Shakspeare's blank verse is the perfection of dramatic dialogue.

All is not poetry that passes for such: nor does verse make the whole difference between poetry and prose. The Iliad does not cease to be poetry in a literal translation; and Addison's Campaign has been very properly denominated a Gazette in rhyme. Common prose differs from poetry, as treating for the most part either of such trite, familiar, and irksome matters of fact, as convey no extraordinary impulse to the imagination, or else of such difficult and laborious processes of the understanding, as do not admit of the wayward or violent movements either of the imagination or the passions.

I will mention three works which come as near to poetry as possible without absolutely being so, namely, the Pilgrim's Progress, Robinson Crusoe, and the Tales of Boccaccio. Chaucer and Dryden have translated some of the last into English rhyme, but the essence and the power of poetry was there before. That which lifts the spirit above the earth, which draws the soul out of itself with indescribable longings, is poetry in kind, and generally fit to become so in name, by being "married to immortal verse." If it is of the essence of poetry to strike and fix the imagination, whether we will or no, to make the eye of childhood glisten with the starting tear, to be never thought of afterwards with indifference, John Bunyan and Daniel Defoe may be permitted to pass for poets in their way. The mixture of fancy and reality in the Pilgrim's Progress was never equalled in any allegory. His pilgrims walk above the earth, and yet are on it. What zeal, what beauty, what truth of fiction! What deep feeling in the description of Christian's swimming across the water at last, and in the picture of the Shining Ones within the gates, with wings at their backs and garlands on their heads, who are to wipe all tears from his eyes! The writer's genius, though not "dipped in dews of Castalie," was baptised with the Holy Spirit and with fire. The prints in this book are no small part of it. If the confinement of Philoctetes in the island of Lemnos was a subject for the most beautiful of all the Greek tragedies, what shall we say to Robinson Crusoe in his? Take the speech of the Greek hero on leaving his cave, beautiful as it is, and compare it with the reflections of the English adventurer in his solitary place of confinement. The thoughts of home, and of all from which he is for ever cut off, swell and press against his bosom, as the heaving ocean rolls its ceaseless tide against the rocky shore, and the very beatings of his heart become audible in the eternal silence that surrounds him. Thus he says,

"As I walked about, either in my hunting, or for viewing the country, the anguish of my soul at my condition would break out upon me on a sudden, and my very heart would die within me to think of the woods, the mountains, the deserts I was in; and how

I was a prisoner, locked up with the eternal bars and bolts of the ocean, in an uninhabited wilderness, without redemption. In the midst of the greatest composures of my mind, this would break out upon me like a storm, and make me wring my hands, and weep like a child. Sometimes it would take me in the middle of my work, and I would immediately sit down and sigh, and look upon the ground for an hour or two together, and this was still worse to me, for if I could burst out into tears, or vent myself in words, it would go off, and the grief having exhausted itself would abate."

The story of his adventures would not make a poem like the Odyssey, it is true; but the relator had the true genius of a poet. It has been made a question whether Richardson's romances are poetry; and the answer perhaps is, that they are not poetry, because they are not romance. The interest is worked up to an inconceivable height; but it is by an infinite number of little things, by incessant labour and calls upon the attention, by a repetition of blows that have no rebound in them. The sympathy excited is not a voluntary contribution, but a tax. Nothing is unforced and spontaneous. There is a want of elasticity and motion. The story does not " give an echo to the seat where love is throned." The heart does not answer of itself like a chord in music. The fancy does not run on before the writer with breathless expectation, but is dragged along with an infinite number of pins and wheels, like those with which the Lilliputians dragged Gulliver pinioned to the royal palace.—Sir Charles Grandison is a coxcomb. What sort of a figure would he cut, translated into an epic poem, by the side of Achilles? Clarissa, the divine Clarissa, is too interesting by half. She is interesting in her ruffles, in her gloves, her samplers, her aunts and uncles—she is interesting in all that is uninteresting. Such things, however intensely they may be brought home to us, are not conductors to the imagination. There is infinite truth and feeling in Richardson; but it is extracted from a *caput mortuum* of circumstances: it does not evaporate of itself. His poetical genius is like Ariel confined in a pine-tree, and requires an artificial process to let it out. Shakspeare says—

> " Our poesy is as a gum
> Which issues whence 'tis nourished, our gentle flame
> Provokes itself, and like the current flies
> Each bound it chafes.*

I shall conclude this general account with some remarks on four of the principal works of poetry in the world, at different periods of history—Homer, the Bible, Dante, and let me add, Ossian. In Homer, the principle of action or life is predominant; in the Bible, the principle of faith and the idea of Providence; Dante is a personification of blind will; and in Ossian we see the decay of life, and the lag end of the world. Homer's poetry is the heroic: it is full of life and action: it is bright as the day, strong as a river. In the vigour of his intellect, he grapples with all the objects of nature, and enters into all the relations of social life. He saw many countries, and the manners of many men; and he has brought them all together in his poem. He describes his heroes going to battle with a prodigality of life, arising from an exuberance of animal

---

* Burke's writings are not poetry, notwithstanding the vividness of the fancy, because the subject matter is abstruse and dry, not natural, but artificial. The difference between poetry and eloquence is, that the one is the eloquence of the imagination, and the other of the understanding. Eloquence tries to persuade the will, and convince the reason: poetry produces its effects by instantaneous sympathy. Nothing is a subject for poetry that admits of a dispute. Poets are in general bad prose-writers, because their images, though fine in themselves, are not to the purpose, and do not carry on the argument. The French poetry wants the forms of the imagination. It is didactic more than dramatic. And some of our own poetry, which has been most admired, is only poetry in the rhyme, and in the studied use of poetic diction.

spirits: we see them before us, their number, and their
order of battle, poured out upon the plain, "all plumed
like estriches, like eagles newly bathed, wanton as goats,
wild as young bulls, youthful as May, and gorgeous as
the sun at midsummer," covered with glittering armour,
with dust and blood; while the Gods quaff their nectar in
golden cups, or mingle in the fray; and the old men assem-
bled on the walls of Troy rise up with reverence as Helen
passes by them. The multitude of things in Homer is
wonderful; their splendour, their truth, their force, and
variety. His poetry is, like his religion, the poetry of
number and form: he describes the bodies as well as the
souls of men.

The poetry of the Bible is that of imagination and of
faith: it is abstract and disembodied: it is not the poetry
of form, but of power; not of multitude, but of immensity.
It does not divide into many, but aggrandizes into one. Its
ideas of nature are like its ideas of God. It is not the
poetry of social life, but of solitude: each man seems alone
in the world with the original forms of nature, the rocks,
the earth, and the sky. It is not the poetry of action or
heroic enterprise, but of faith in a supreme Providence,
and resignation to the power that governs the universe.
As the idea of God was removed farther from humanity,
and a scattered polytheism, it became more profound and
intense as it became more universal, for the Infinite is
present to every thing: "If we fly into the uttermost parts
of the earth, it is there also; if we turn to the east or
the west, we cannot escape from it." Man is thus aggrandised in the image of his Maker. The history of the
patriarchs is of this kind; they are founders of the chosen
race of people, the inheritors of the earth; they exist in
the generations which are to come after them. Their
poetry, like their religious creed, is vast, unformed, ob-

scure, and infinite; a vision is upon it—an invisible hand is suspended over it. The spirit of the Christian religion consists in the glory hereafter to be revealed; but in the Hebrew dispensation, Providence took an immediate share in the affairs of this life. Jacob's dream arose out of this intimate communion between heaven and earth: it was this that let down, in the sight of the youthful patriarch, a golden ladder from the sky to the earth, with angels ascending and descending upon it, and shed a light upon the lonely place, which can never pass away. The story of Ruth, again, is as if all the depth of natural affection in the human race was involved in her breast. There are descriptions in the book of Job more prodigal of imagery, more intense in passion, than anything in Homer, as that of the state of his prosperity, and of the vision that came upon him by night. The metaphors in the Old Testament are more boldly figurative. Things were collected more into masses, and gave a greater *momentum* to the imagination.

Dante was the father of modern poetry, and he may therefore claim a place in this connection. His poem is the first great step from Gothic darkness and barbarism; and the struggle of thought in it to burst the thraldom in which the human mind had been so long held, is felt in every page. He stood bewildered, not appalled, on that dark shore which separates the ancient and the modern world; and saw the glories of antiquity dawning through the abyss of time, while revelation opened its passage to the other world. He was lost in wonder at what had been done before him, and he dared to emulate it. Dante seems to have been indebted to the Bible for the gloomy tone of his mind, as well as for the prophetic fury which exalts and kindles his poetry; but he is utterly unlike Homer. His genius is not a sparkling flame, but the sullen heat of a furnace. He is power, passion, self-will personified. In all that relates to the descriptive or fanciful part of poetry, he bears no comparison to many who had gone before, or who have come after him; but there is a gloomy abstraction in his conceptions, which lies like a dead weight upon the mind; a benumbing stupor, a breathless awe, from the intensity of the impression; a terrible obscurity, like that which oppresses us in dreams; an identity of interest, which moulds every object to its own purposes, and clothes all things with the passions and imaginations of the human soul,—that make amends for all other deficiencies. The immediate objects he presents to the mind are not much in themselves, they want grandeur, beauty, and order; but they become every thing by the force of the character he impresses upon them. His mind lends its own power to the objects which it contemplates, instead of borrowing it from them. He takes advantage even of the nakedness and dreary vacuity of his subject. His imagination peoples the shades of death, and broods over the silent air. He is the severest of all writers, the most hard and impenetrable, the most opposite to the flowery and glittering; who relies most on his own power, and the sense of it in others, and who leaves most room to the imagination of his readers. Dante's only endeavour is to interest; and he interests by exciting our sympathy with the emotion by which he is himself possessed. He does not place before us the objects by which that emotion has been created; but he seizes on the attention, by shewing us the effect they produce on his feelings; and his poetry accordingly gives the same thrilling and overwhelming sensation, which is caught by gazing on the face of a person who has seen some object of horror. The improbability of the events, the abruptness and monotony in the Inferno, are excessive: but the interest never flags, from the continued earnestness of the author's mind.

Dante's great power is in combining internal feelings with external objects. Thus the gate of hell, on which that withering inscription is written, seems to be endowed with speech and consciousness, and to utter its dread warning, not without a sense of mortal woes. This author habitually unites the absolutely local and individual with the greatest wildness and mysticism. In the midst of the obscure and shadowy regions of the lower world, a tomb suddenly rises up with the inscription, "I am the tomb of Pope Anastasius the Sixth": and half the personages whom he has crowded into the Inferno are his own acquaintance. All this, perhaps, tends to heighten the effect by the bold intermixture of realities, and by an appeal, as it were, to the individual knowledge and experience of the reader. He affords few subjects for picture. There is, indeed, one gigantic .one, that of Count Ugolino, of which Michael Angelo made a bas-relief, and which Sir Joshua Reynolds ought not to have painted.

Another writer whom I shall mention last, and whom I cannot persuade myself to think a mere modern in the groundwork, is Ossian. He is a feeling and a name that can never be destroyed in the minds of his readers. As Homer is the first vigour and lustihed, Ossian is the decay and old age of poetry. He lives only in the recollection and regret of the past. There is one impression which he conveys more entirely than all other poets, namely, the sense of privation, the loss of all things, of friends, of good name, of country—he is even without God in the world. He converses only with the spirits of the departed; with the motionless and silent clouds. The cold moonlight sheds its faint lustre on his head; the fox peeps out of the ruined tower; the thistle waves its beard to the wandering gale; and the strings of his harp seem, as the hand of age, as the tale of other times, passes over them, to sigh and rustle like the dry reeds in the winter's wind! The feeling of cheerless desolation, of the loss of the pith and sap of existence, of the annihilation of the substance, and the clinging to the shadow of all things as in a mock embrace, is here perfect. In this way the lamentation of Selma for the loss of Salgar is the finest of all. If it were indeed possible to shew that this writer was nothing, it would only be another instance of mutability, another blank made, another void left in the heart, another confirmation of that feeling which makes him so often complain, " Roll on, ye dark brown years, ye bring no joy on your wing to Ossian! "

## XVII

## MY FIRST ACQUAINTANCE WITH POETS

My father was a Dissenting Minister at W—m in
Shropshire; and in the year 1798 (the figures that compose
that date are to me like the "dreaded name of Demo-
gorgon") Mr. Coleridge came to Shrewsbury, to succeed
Mr. Rowe in the spiritual charge of a Unitarian Congregation there. He did not come till late on the Saturday
afternoon before he was to preach; and Mr. Rowe, who
himself went down to the coach in a state of anxiety and
expectation, to look for the arrival of his successor, could
find no one at all answering the description but a round-
faced man in a short black coat (like a shooting jacket)
which hardly seemed to have been made for him, but who
seemed to be talking at a great rate to his fellow-pas-
sengers. Mr. Rowe had scarce returned to give an account
of his disappointment, when the round-faced man in black
entered, and dissipated all doubts on the subject, by beginning to talk. He did not cease while he staid; nor has
he since, that I know of. He held the good town of
Shrewsbury in delightful suspense for three weeks that he
remained there, "fluttering the *proud Salopians* like an
eagle in a dove-cote;" and the Welch mountains that skirt
the horizon with their tempestuous confusion, agree to
have heard no such mystic sounds since the days of

"High-born Hoel's harp or soft Llewellyn's lay!"

As we passed along between W—m and Shrewsbury, and
I eyed their blue tops seen through the wintry branches,

or the red rustling leaves of the sturdy oak-trees by the road-side, a sound was in my ears as of a Siren's song; I was stunned, startled with it, as from deep sleep; but I had no notion then that I should ever be able to express my admiration to others in motley imagery or quaint allusion, till the light of his genius shone into my soul, like the sun's rays glittering in the puddles of the road. I was at that time dumb, inarticulate, helpless, like a worm by the way-side, crushed, bleeding, lifeless; but now, bursting the deadly bands that " bound them,

"With Styx nine times round them,"

my ideas float on winged words, and as they expand their plumes, catch the golden light of other years. My soul has indeed remained in its original bondage, dark, obscure, with longings infinite and unsatisfied; my heart, shut up in the prison-house of this' rude clay, has never found, nor will it ever find, a heart to speak to; but that my understanding also did not remain dumb and brutish, or at length found a language to express itself, I owe to Coleridge. But this is not to my purpose.

My father lived ten miles from Shrewsbury, and was in the habit of exchanging visits with Mr. Rowe, and with Mr. Jenkins of Whitchurch (nine miles farther on) according to the custom of Dissenting Ministers in each other's neighbourhood. A line of communication is thus established, by which the flame of civil and religious liberty is kept alive, and nourishes its smouldering fire unquenchable, like the fires in the Agamemnon of Æschylus, placed at different stations, that waited for ten long years to announce with their blazing pyramids the destruction of Troy. Coleridge had agreed to come over to see my father, according to the courtesy of the country, as Mr. Rowe's probable successor; but in the meantime I had gone

to hear him preach the Sunday after his arrival.  A poet
and a philosopher getting up into a Unitarian pulpit to
preach the Gospel, was a romance in these degenerate days,
a sort of revival of the primitive spirit of Christianity,
which was not to be resisted.

It was in January, 1798, that I rose one morning before
day-light, to walk ten miles in the mud, and went to hear this
celebrated person preach.  Never, the longest day I have to
live, shall I have such another walk as this cold, raw,
comfortless one, in the winter of the year 1798.—*Il y a
des impressions que ni le tems ni les circonstances peuvent
effacer.  Dusse-je vivre des siècles entiers, le doux tems de
ma jeunesse ne peut renaître pour moi, ni s'effacer jamais
dans ma mémoire.*  When I got there, the organ was playing the 100th psalm, and, when it was done, Mr. Coleridge
rose and gave out his text, " And he went up into the mountain to pray, HIMSELF, ALONE."  As he gave out this text,
his voice " rose like a steam of rich distilled perfumes,"
and when he came to the two last words, which he pronounced loud, deep, and distinct, it seemed to me, who was
then young, as if the sounds had echoed from the bottom
of the human heart, and as if that prayer might have
floated in solemn silence through the universe.  The idea
of St. John came into my mind, " of one crying in the
wilderness, who had his loins girt about, and whose food
was locusts and wild honey."  The preacher then launched
into his subject, like an eagle dallying with the wind.  The
sermon was upon peace and war ; upon church and state —
not their alliance, but their separation — on the spirit of the
world and the spirit of Christianity, not as the same, but
as opposed to one another.  He talked of those who had
" inscribed the cross of Christ on banners dripping with
human gore."  He made a poetical and pastoral excursion,
—and to shew the fatal effects of war, drew a striking con-

trast between the simple shepherd boy, driving his team
afield, or sitting under the hawthorn, piping to his flock,
"as though he should never be old," and the same poor
country-lad, crimped, kidnapped, brought into town, made
drunk at an alehouse, turned into a wretched drummer-boy,
with his hair sticking on end with powder and pomatum,
a long cue at his back, and tricked out in the loathsome
finery of the profession of blood.

> "Such were the notes our once-lov'd poet sung."

And for myself, I could not have been more delighted if
I had heard the music of the spheres. Poetry and Philosophy had met together, Truth and Genius had embraced,
under the eye and with the sanction of Religion. This
was even beyond my hopes. I returned home well satisfied.
The sun that was still labouring pale and wan through
the sky, obscured by thick mists, seemed an emblem of
the *good cause;* and the cold dank drops of dew that hung
half melted on the beard of the thistle, had something
genial and refreshing in them; for there was a spirit of
hope and youth in all nature, that turned everything into
good. The face of nature had not then the brand of Jus
Divinum on it:

> "Like to that sanguine flower inscrib'd with woe."

On the Tuesday following, the half-inspired speaker
came. I was called down into the room where he was,
and went half-hoping, half-afraid. He received me very
graciously, and I listened for a long time without uttering
a word. I did not suffer in his opinion by my silence. "For
those two hours," he afterwards was pleased to say, "he
was conversing with W. H.'s forehead!" His appearance
was different from what I had anticipated from seeing him

before. At a distance, and in the dim light of the chapel,
there was to me a strange wildness in his aspect, a dusky
obscurity, and I thought him pitted with the small-pox.
His complexion was at that time clear, and even bright—

"As are the children of yon azure sheen."

His forehead was broad and high, light as if built of
ivory, with large projecting eyebrows, and his eyes rolling
beneath them like a sea with darkened lustre. "A certain
tender bloom his face o'erspread," a purple tinge as we see
it in the pale thoughtful complexions of the Spanish por-
trait-painters, Murillo and Velasquez. His mouth was
gross, voluptuous, open, eloquent; his chin good-humoured
and round; but his nose, the rudder of the face, the index
of the will, was small, feeble, nothing—like what he has
done. It might seem that the genius of his face as from
a height surveyed and projected him (with sufficient capacity and huge aspiration) into the world unknown of thought
and imagination, with nothing to support or guide his
veering purpose, as if Columbus had launched his adventurous course for the New World in a scallop, without
oars or compass. So at least I comment on it after the
event. Coleridge in his person was rather above the
common size, inclining to the corpulent, or like Lord Hamlet, "somewhat fat and pursy." His hair (now, alas! grey)
was then black and glossy as the raven's, and fell in smooth
masses over his forehead. This long pendulous hair is
peculiar to enthusiasts, to those whose minds tend heaven-
ward; and is traditionally inseparable (though of a different
colour) from the pictures of Christ. It ought to belong,
as a character, to all who preach *Christ crucified*, and
Coleridge was at that time one of those!
It was curious to observe the contrast between him and
my father, who was a veteran in the cause, and then

declining into the vale of years. He had been a poor
Irish lad, carefully brought up by his parents, and sent
to the University of Glasgow (where he studied under
Adam Smith) to prepare him for his future destination.
It was his mother's proudest wish to see her son a Dissenting Minister. So if we look back to past generations
(as far as eye can reach) we see the same hopes, fears,
wishes, followed by the same disappointments, throbbing
in the human heart; and so we may see them (if we look
forward) rising up for ever, and disappearing, like vapour-
ish bubbles, in the human breast! After being tossed
about from congregation to congregation in the heats of
the Unitarian controversy, and squabbles about the American war, he had been relegated to an obscure village, where
he was to spend the last thirty years of his life, far from
the only converse that he loved, the talk about disputed
texts of Scripture and the cause of civil and religious
liberty. Here he passed his days, repining but resigned,
in the study of the Bible, and the perusal of the Commentators,—huge folios, not easily got through, one of
which would outlast a winter! Why did he pore on these
from morn to night (with the exception of a walk in the
fields or a turn in the garden to gather brocoli-plants or
kidney beans of his own rearing, with no small degree of
pride and pleasure)?—Here were " no figures nor no fantasies,"—neither poetry nor philosophy—nothing to dazzle,
nothing to excite modern curiosity; but to his lack-lustre
eyes there appeared, within the pages of the ponderous,
unwieldy, neglected tomes, the sacred name of JEHOVAH
in Hebrew capitals: pressed down by the weight of the style,
worn to the last fading thinness of the understanding,
there were glimpses, glimmering notions of the patriarchal
wanderings, with palm-trees hovering in the horizon, and
processions of camels at the distance of three thousand

years; there was Moses with the Burning Bush, the number of the Twelve Tribes, types, shadows, glosses on the law and the prophets; there were discussions (dull enough) on the age of Methuselah, a mighty speculation! there were outlines, rude guesses at the shape of Noah's Ark and of the riches of Solomon's Temple; questions as to the date of the creation, predictions of the end of all things; the great lapses of time, the strange mutations of the globe were unfolded with the voluminous leaf, as it turned over; and though the soul might slumber with an hieroglyphic veil of inscrutable mysteries drawn over it, yet it was in a slumber ill-exchanged for all the sharpened realities of sense, wit, fancy, or reason. My father's life was comparatively a dream; but it was a dream of infinity and eternity, of death, the resurrection, and a judgment to come!

No two individuals were ever more unlike than were the host and his guest. A poet was to my father a sort of nondescript: yet whatever added grace to the Unitarian cause was to him welcome. He could hardly have been more surprised or pleased, if our visitor had worn wings. Indeed, his thoughts had wings; and as the silken sounds rustled round our little wainscoted parlour, my father threw back his spectacles over his forehead, his white hairs mixing with its sanguine hue; and a smile of delight beamed across his rugged cordial face, to think that Truth had found a new ally in Fancy!* Besides, Coleridge seemed to take considerable notice of me, and that of itself was enough. He talked very familiarly, but agreeably, and glanced over a variety of subjects. At dinner-time he grew more ani-

* My father was one of those who mistook his talent after all. He used to be very much dissatisfied that I preferred his Letters to his Sermons. The last were forced and dry; the first came naturally from him. For ease, half-plays on words, and a supine, monkish, indolent pleasantry, I have never seen them equalled.

mated, and dilated in a very edifying manner on Mary
Wolstonecraft and Mackintosh. The last, he said, he considered (on my father's speaking of his *Vindiciæ Gallicæ* as a capital performance) as a clever scholastic man
—a master of the topics,—or as the ready warehouseman
of letters, who knew exactly where to lay his hand on what
he wanted, though the goods were not his own. He thought
him no match for Burke, either in style or matter. Burke
was a metaphysician, Mackintosh a mere logician. Burke
was an orator (almost a poet) who reasoned in figures,
because he had an eye for nature: Mackintosh, on the other
hand, was a rhetorician, who had only an eye to common-
places. On this I ventured to say that I had always entertained a great opinion of Burke, and that (as far as I
could find) the speaking of him with contempt might be
made the test of a vulgar democratical mind. This was
the first observation I ever made to Coleridge, and he
said it was a very just and striking one. I remember the
leg of Welsh mutton and the turnips on the table that day
had the finest flavour imaginable. Coleridge added that
Mackintosh and Tom. Wedgwood (of whom, however, he
spoke highly) had expressed a very indifferent opinion of
his friend Mr. Wordsworth, on which he remarked to them—
" He strides on so far before you, that he dwindles in the
distance ! " Godwin had once boasted to him of having
carried on an argument with Mackintosh for three hours
with dubious success; Coleridge told him—" If there had
been a man of genius in the room, he would have settled
the question in five minutes." He asked me if I had ever
seen Mary Wolstonecraft, and I said, I had once for a
few moments, and that she seemed to me to turn off Godwin's objections to something she advanced with quite a
playful, easy air. He replied, that " this was only one
instance of the ascendancy which people of imagination

exercised over those of mere intellect." He did not rate
Godwin very high * (this was caprice or prejudice, real
or affected) but he had a great idea of Mrs. Wolstonecraft's
powers of conversation, none at all of her talent for book-
making. We talked a little about Holcroft. He had been
asked if he was not much struck *with* him, and he said, he
thought himself in more danger of being struck *by* him.
I complained that he would not let me get on at all, for
he required a definition of every the commonest word,
exclaiming, "What do you mean by a *sensation*, Sir?
What do you mean by an *idea?*" This, Coleridge said, was
barricadoing the road to truth: it was setting up a turnpike-
gate at every step we took. I forget a great number of
things, many more than I remember; but the day passed
off pleasantly, and the next morning Mr. Coleridge was to
return to Shrewsbury. When I came down to breakfast,
I found that he had just received a letter from his friend,
T. Wedgwood, making him an offer of 150 *l.* a-year if he
chose to wave his present pursuit, and devote himself
entirely to the study of poetry and philosophy. Coleridge
seemed to make up his mind to close with this' proposal
in the act of tying on one of his shoes. It threw an additional damp on his departure. It took the wayward enthusiast quite from us to cast him into Deva's winding
vales, or by the shores of old romance. Instead of living
at ten miles distance, of being the pastor of a Dissenting
congregation at Shrewsbury, he was henceforth to inhabit
the Hill of Parnassus, to be a Shepherd on the Delectable
Mountains. Alas! I knew not the way thither, and felt very
little gratitude for Mr. Wedgwood's bounty. I was pres-

* He complained in particular of the presumption of his attempting to establish the future immortality of man, "without" (as he
said) "knowing what Death was or what Life was"—and the tone
in which he pronounced these two words seemed to convey a complete image of both.

ently relieved from this dilemma; for Mr. Coleridge, asking
for a pen and ink, and going to a table to write something
on a bit of card, advanced towards me with undulating
step, and giving me the precious document, said that that
was his address, *Mr. Coleridge, Nether-Stowey, Somerset-
shire;* and that he should be glad to see me there in a few
weeks' time, and, if I chose, would come half-way to meet
me.    I was not less surprised than the shepherd-boy (this
simile is to be found in Cassandra) when he sees a thunder-
bolt fall close at his feet.    I stammered out my acknowl-
edgments and acceptance of this offer (I thought Mr.
Wedgwood's annuity a trifle to it) as well as I could; and
this mighty business being settled, the poet-preacher took
leave, and I accompanied him six miles on the road.    It
was a fine morning in the middle of winter, and he talked
the whole way.    The scholar in Chaucer is described as
going

——" Sounding on his way."

So Coleridge went on his.    In digressing, in dilating, in
passing from subject to subject, he appeared to me to float
in air, to slide on ice.    He told me in confidence (going
along) that he should have preached two sermons before
he accepted the situation at Shrewsbury, one on Infant
Baptism, the other on the Lord's Supper, shewing that
he could not administer either, which would have effectually
disqualified him for the object in view.    'I observed that he
continually crossed me on the way by shifting from one
side of the foot-path to the other.    This struck me as an
odd movement; but I did not at that time connect it with
any instability of purpose or involuntary change of principle, as I have done since.    He seemed unable to keep
on in a strait line.    He spoke slightingly of Hume
(whose Essay on Miracles he said was stolen from an

objection started in one of South's sermons—*Credat Judæus Appella!*) I was not very much pleased at this account of Hume, for I had just been reading, with infinite relish, that completest of all metaphysical *choke-pears,* his *Treatise on Human Nature,* to which the *Essays,* in point of scholastic subtlety and close reasoning, are mere elegant trifling, light summer-reading. Coleridge even denied the excellence of Hume's general style, which I think betrayed a want of taste or candour. He however made me amends by the manner in which he spoke of Berkeley. He dwelt particularly on his *Essay on Vision* as a masterpiece of analytical reasoning. So it undoubtedly is. He was exceedingly angry with Dr. Johnson for striking the stone with his foot, in allusion to this author's Theory of Matter and Spirit, and saying, "Thus I confute him, Sir." Coleridge drew a parallel (I don't know how he brought about the connection) between Bishop Berkeley and Tom Paine. He said the one was an instance of a subtle, the other of an acute mind, than which no two things could be more distinct. The one was a shop-boy's quality, the other the characteristic of a philosopher. He considered Bishop Butler as a true philosopher, a profound and conscientious thinker, a genuine reader of nature and of his own mind. He did not speak of his *Analogy,* but of his *Sermons at the Rolls' Chapel,* of which I had never heard. Coleridge somehow always contrived to prefer the *unknown* to the *known.* In this instance he was right. The *Analogy* is a tissue of sophistry, of wire-drawn, theological special-pleading; the *Sermons* (with the Preface to them) are in a fine vein of deep, matured reflection, a candid appeal to our observation of human nature, without pedantry and without bias. I told Coleridge I had written a few remarks, and was sometimes foolish enough to believe that I had made a discovery on the same subject (the *Natural Disinter-*

*estedness of the Human Mind*)—and I tried to explain my
view of it to Coleridge, who listened with great willingness,
but I did not succeed in making myself understood. I sat
down to the task shortly afterwards for the twentieth time,
got new pens and paper, determined to make clear work of
it, wrote a few meagre sentences in the skeleton-style of a
mathematical demonstration, stopped half-way down the
second page; and, after trying in vain to pump up any
words, images, notions, apprehensions, facts, or observations, from that gulph of abstraction in which I had plunged
myself for four or five years preceding, gave up the attempt
as labour in vain, and shed tears of helpless despondency
on the blank unfinished paper. I can write fast enough
now. Am I better than I was then? Oh no! One truth
discovered, one pang of regret at not being able to express
it, is better than all the fluency and flippancy in the world.
Would that I could go back to what I then was! Why
can we not revive past times as we can revisit old places?
If I had the quaint Muse of Sir Philip Sidney to assist
me, I would write a *Sonnet to the Road between W—m and
Shrewsbury,* and immortalise every step of it by some fond
enigmatical conceit. I would swear that the very mile-
stones had ears, and that Harmer-hill stooped with all its
pines, to listen to a poet, as he passed! I remember but
one other topic of discourse in this walk. He mentioned
Paley, praised the naturalness and clearness of his style,
but condemned his sentiments, thought him a mere time-
serving casuist, and said that "the fact of his work on
Moral and Political Philosophy being made a text-book in
our Universities was a disgrace to the national character."
We parted at the six-mile stone; and I returned homeward
pensive but much pleased. I had met with unexpected
notice from a person, whom I believed to have been prejudiced against me. "Kind and affable to me had been his

condescension, and should be honoured ever with suitable regard." He was the first poet I had known, and he certainly answered to that inspired name. I had heard a great deal of his powers of conversation, and was not disappointed. In fact, I never met with any thing at all like them, either before or since. I could easily credit the accounts which were circulated of his holding forth to a large party of ladies and gentlemen, an evening or two before, on the Berkeleian Theory, when he made the whole material universe look like a transparency of fine words; and another story (which I believe he has somewhere told himself) of his being asked to a party at Birmingham, of his smoking tobacco and going to sleep after dinner on a sofa, where the company found him to their no small surprise, which was increased to wonder when he started up of a sudden, and rubbing his eyes, looked about him, and launched into a three-hours' description of the third heaven, of which he had had a dream, very different from Mr. Southey's Vision of Judgment, and also from that other Vision of Judgment, which Mr. Murray, the Secretary of the Bridge-street Junto, has taken into his especial keeping!

On my way back, I had a sound in my ears, it was the voice of Fancy: I had a light before me, it was the face of Poetry. The one still lingers there, the other has not quitted my side! Coleridge in truth met me half-way on the ground of philosophy, or I should not have been won over to his imaginative creed. I had an uneasy, pleasurable sensation all the time, till I was to visit him. During those months the chill breath of winter gave me a welcoming; the vernal air was balm and inspiration to me. The golden sun-sets, the silver star of evening, lighted me on my way to new hopes and prospects. *I was to visit Coleridge in the spring.* This circumstance was never absent from my thoughts, and mingled with all my feelings. I wrote to him at the time proposed, and received an answer postponing my intended visit for a week or two, but very cordially urging me to complete my promise then. This delay did not damp, but rather increase my ardour. In the mean time, I went to Llangollen Vale, by way of initiating myself in the mysteries of natural scenery; and I must say I was enchanted with it. I had been reading Coleridge's description of England, in his fine *Ode on the Departing Year,* and I applied it, *con amore,* to the objects before me. That valley was to me (in a manner) the cradle of a new existence: in the river that winds through it, my spirit was baptised in the waters of Helicon!

I returned home, and soon after set out on my journey with unworn heart and untired feet. My way lay through Worcester and Gloucester, and by Upton, where I thought of Tom Jones and the adventure of the muff. I remember getting completely wet through one day, and stopping at an inn (I think it was at Tewkesbury) where I sat up all night to read Paul and Virginia. Sweet were the showers in early youth that drenched my body, and sweet the drops of pity that fell upon the books I read! I recollect a remark of Coleridge's upon this very book, that nothing could shew the gross indelicacy of French manners and the entire corruption of their imagination more strongly than the behaviour of the heroine in the last fatal scene, who turns away from a person on board the sinking vessel, that offers to save her life, because he has thrown off his clothes to assist him in swimming. Was this a time to think of such a circumstance? I once hinted to Wordsworth, as we were sailing in his boat on Grasmere lake, that I thought he had borrowed the idea of his *Poems on the Naming of Places* from the local inscriptions of the same kind in Paul and Virginia. He did not own the obligation, and stated some distinction without a difference, in defence of his claim to originality. Any the slightest variation would be sufficient for this purpose in his mind; for whatever *he* added or omitted would inevitably be worth all that any one else had done, and contain the marrow of the sentiment.—I was still two days before the time fixed for my arrival, for I had taken care to set out early enough. I stopped these two days at Bridgewater, and when I was tired of sauntering on the banks of its muddy river, returned to the inn, and read Camilla. So have I loitered my life away, reading books, looking at pictures, going to plays, hearing, thinking, writing on what pleased me best. I have wanted only one thing to make me happy; but wanting that, have wanted every thing!

I arrived, and was well received. The country about Nether Stowey is beautiful, green and hilly, and near the sea-shore. I saw it but the other day, after an interval of twenty years, from a hill near Taunton. How was the map of my life spread out before me, as the map of the country lay at my feet! In the afternoon, Coleridge took me over to All-Foxden, a romantic old family-mansion of the St. Aubins, where Wordsworth lived. It was then in the possession of a friend of the poet's, who gave him the free use of it. Somehow that period (the time just after the French Revolution) was not a time when *nothing was given for nothing*. The mind opened, and a softness might be perceived coming over the heart of individuals, beneath "the scales that fence" our self-interest. Wordsworth himself was from home, but his sister kept house, and set before us a frugal repast; and we had free access to her brother's poems, the *Lyrical Ballads,* which were still in manuscript, or in the form of *Sybilline Leaves.* I dipped into a few of these with great satisfaction, and with the faith of a novice. I slept that night in an old room with blue hangings, and covered with the round-faced family-

portraits of the age of George I. and II. and from the
wooded declivity of the adjoining park that overlooked my
window, at the dawn of day, could

——" hear the loud stag speak."

In the outset of life (and particularly at this time I felt
it so) our imagination has a body to it. We are in a state
between sleeping and waking, and have indistinct but glorious glimpses of strange shapes, and there is always something to come better than what we see. As in our dreams
the fulness of the blood gives warmth and reality to the
coinage of the brain, so in youth our ideas are clothed, and
fed, and pampered with our good spirits; we breathe thick
with thoughtless happiness, the weight of future years
presses on the strong pulses of the heart, and we repose
with undisturbed faith in truth and good. As we advance,
we exhaust our fund of enjoyment and of hope. We are
no longer wrapped in *lamb's-wool,* lulled in Elysium. As
we taste the pleasures of life, their spirit evaporates, the
sense palls; and nothing is left but the phantoms, the lifeless shadows of what *has been!*

That morning, as soon as breakfast was over, we strolled
out into the park, and seating ourselves on the trunk of an
old ash-tree that stretched along the ground, Coleridge read
aloud with a sonorous and musical voice, the ballad of
*Betty Foy.* I was not critically or sceptically inclined. I
saw touches of truth and nature, and took the rest for
granted. But in the *Thorn,* the *Mad Mother,* and the *Complaint of a Poor Indian Woman,* I felt that deeper power
and pathos which have been since acknowledged,

"In spite of pride, in erring reason's spite,"

as the characteristics of this author; and the sense of a
new style and a new spirit in poetry came over me. It had

to me something of the effect that arises from the turning
up of the fresh soil, or of the first welcome breath of
Spring,

"While yet the trembling year is unconfirmed."

Coleridge and myself walked back to Stowey that evening,
and his voice sounded high

"Of Providence, foreknowledge, will, and fate,
    Fix'd fate, free-will, foreknowledge absolute,"

as we passed through echoing grove, by fairy stream or
waterfall, gleaming in the summer moonlight! He la-
mented that Wordsworth was not prone enough to belief
in the traditional superstitions of the place, and that there
was a something corporeal, a *matter-of-fact-ness,* a clinging
to the palpable, or often to the petty, in his poetry, in consequence. His genius was not a spirit that descended to
him through the air; it sprung out of the ground like a
flower, or unfolded itself from a green spray, on which the
gold-finch sang. He said, however (if I remember right),
that this objection must be confined to his descriptive pieces,
that his philosophic poetry had a grand and comprehensive
spirit in it, so that his soul seemed to inhabit the universe
like a palace, and to discover truth by intuition, rather than
by deduction. The next day Wordsworth arrived from
Bristol at Coleridge's cottage. I think I see him now. He
answered in some degree to his friend's description of him,
but was more gaunt and Don Quixote-like. He was quaintly
dressed (according to the *costume* of that unconstrained
period) in a brown fustian jacket and striped pantaloons.
There was something of a roll, a lounge in his gait, not
unlike his own Peter Bell. There was a severe, worn
pressure of thought about his temples, a fire in his eye

(as if he saw something in objects more than the outward appearance) an intense high narrow forehead, a Roman nose, cheeks furrowed by strong purpose and feeling, and a convulsive inclination to laughter about the mouth, a good deal at variance with the solemn, stately expression of the rest of his face. Chantrey's bust wants the marking traits; but he was teazed into making it regular and heavy: Haydon's head of him, introduced into the *Entrance of Christ into Jerusalem,* is the most like his drooping weight of thought and expression. He sat down and talked very naturally and freely, with a mixture of clear gushing accents in his voice, a deep guttural intonation, and a strong tincture of the northern *burr,* like the crust on wine. He instantly began to make havoc of the half of a Cheshire cheese on the table, and said triumphantly that " his marriage with experience had not been so unproductive as Mr. Southey's in teaching him a knowledge of the good things of this life." He had been to see the *Castle Spectre* by Monk Lewis, while at Bristol, and described it very well. He said " it fitted the taste of the audience like a glove." This *ad captandum* merit was however by no means a recommendation of it, according to the severe principles of the new school, which reject rather than court popular effect. Wordsworth, looking out of the low, latticed window, said, " How beautifully the sun sets on that yellow bank!" I thought within myself, " With what eyes these poets see nature!" and ever after, when I saw the sun-set stream upon the objects facing it, conceived I had made a discovery, or thanked Mr. Wordsworth for having made one for me! We went over to All-Foxden again the day following, and Wordsworth read us the story of Peter Bell in the open air; and the comment upon it by his face and voice was very different from that of some later critics! Whatever might be thought of the poem, " his face was as

a book where men might read strange matters," and he
announced the fate of his hero in prophetic tones. There
is a *chaunt* in the recitation both of Coleridge and Wordsworth, which acts as a spell upon the hearer, and disarms
the judgment. Perhaps they have deceived themselves by
making habitual use of this ambiguous accompaniment.
Coleridge's manner is more full, animated, and varied;
Wordsworth's more equable, sustained, and internal. The
one might be termed more *dramatic,* the other more *lyrical.*
Coleridge has told me that he himself liked to compose in
walking over uneven ground, or breaking through the straggling branches of a copse wood; whereas Wordsworth always wrote (if he could) walking up and down a strait
gravel-walk, or in some spot where the continuity of his
verse met with no collateral interruption. Returning that
same evening, I got into a metaphysical argument with
Wordsworth, while Coleridge was explaining the different
notes of the nightingale to his sister, in which we neither
of us succeeded in making ourselves perfectly clear and
intelligible. Thus I passed three weeks at Nether Stowey
and in the neighbourhood, generally devoting the after-
noons to a delightful chat in an arbour made of bark by
the poet's friend Tom Poole, sitting under two fine elm-
trees, and listening to the bees humming round us, while
we quaffed our *flip.* It was agreed, among other things,
that we should make a jaunt down the Bristol-Channel, as
far as Linton. We set off together on foot, Coleridge,
John Chester, and I. This Chester was a native of Nether
Stowey, one of those who were attracted to Coleridge's
discourse as flies are to honey, or bees in swarming-time
to the sound of a brass pan. He " followed in the chace,
like a dog who hunts, not like one that made up the cry."
He had on a brown cloth coat, boots, and corduroy breeches,
was low in stature, bow-legged, had a drag in his walk

like a drover, which he assisted by a hazel switch, and kept
on a sort of trot by the side of Coleridge, like a running
footman by a state coach, that he might not lose a syllable
or sound, that fell from Coleridge's lips. He. told me his
private opinion, that Coleridge was a wonderful man. He
scarcely opened his lips, much less offered an opinion the
whole way: yet of the three, had I to chuse during that
journey, I would be John Chester. He afterwards followed
Coleridge into Germany, where the Kantean philosophers
were puzzled how to bring him under any of their categories. When he sat down at table with his idol, John's
felicity was complete; Sir Walter Scott's or Mr. Blackwood's, when they sat down at the same table with the
King, was not more so. We passed Dunster on our right,
a small town between the brow of a hill and the sea. I
remember eyeing it wistfully as it lay below us: contrasted
with the woody scene around, it looked as clear, as pure,
as *embrowned* and ideal as any landscape I have seen since,
of Gaspar Poussin's or Domenichino's. We had a long
day's march—(our feet kept time to the echoes of
Coleridge's tongue)—through Minehead and by the Blue
Anchor, and on to Linton, which we did not reach till near
midnight, and where we had some difficulty in making a
lodgment. We however knocked the people of the house
up at last, and we were repaid for our apprehensions and
fatigue by some excellent rashers of fried bacon and eggs.
The view in coming along had been splendid. We walked
for miles and miles on dark brown heaths overlooking the
channel, with the Welsh hills beyond, and at times descended into little sheltered valleys close by the sea-side,
with a smuggler's face scowling by us, and then had to
ascend conical hills with a path winding up through a cop-
pice to a barren top, like a monk's shaven crown, from
one of which I pointed out to Coleridge's notice the bare

masts of a vessel on the very edge of the horizon and within the red-orbed disk of the setting sun, like his own spectre-ship in the *Ancient Mariner*. At Linton the char·acter of the sea-coast becomes more marked and rugged. There is a place called the *Valley of Rocks* (I suspect this was only the poetical name for it) bedded among precipices overhanging the sea, with rocky caverns beneath, into which the waves dash, and where the sea-gull for ever wheels its screaming flight. On the tops of these are huge stones thrown transverse, as if an earthquake had tossed them there, and behind these is a fretwork of perpendicular rocks, something like the *Giant's Causeway*. A thunderstorm came on while we were at the inn, and Coleridge was running out bareheaded to enjoy the commotion of the elements in the *Valley of Rocks,* but as if in spite, the clouds only muttered a few angry sounds, and let fall a few refreshing drops. Coleridge told me that he and Wordsworth were to have made this place the scene of a prose-tale, which was to have been in the manner of, but far superior to, the *Death of Abel,* but they had relinquished the design. In the morning of the second day, we breakfasted luxuriously in an old-fashioned parlour, on tea, toast, eggs, and honey, in the very sight of the bee-hives from which it had been taken, and a garden full of thyme and wild flowers that had produced it. On this occasion Coleridge spoke of Virgil's Georgics, but not well. I do not think he had much feeling for the classical or elegant. It was in this room that we found a little worn-out copy of the *Seasons,* lying in a window-seat, on which Coleridge exclaimed, "*That* is true fame!" He said Thomson was a great poet, rather than a good one; his style was as meretricious as his thoughts were natural. He spoke of Cowper as the best modern poet. He said the *Lyrical Ballads* were an experiment about to be tried by him and Wordsworth, to

see how far the public taste would endure poetry written
in a more natural and simple style than had hitherto been
attempted; totally discarding the artifices of poetical diction,
and making use only of such words as had probably been
common in the most' ordinary language since the days of
Henry II. Some comparison was introduced between
Shakspeare and Milton. He said " he hardly knew which
to prefer. Shakspeare appeared to him a mere stripling,
in the art; he was as tall and as strong, with infinitely more
activity than Milton, but he never appeared to have come
to man's estate; or if he had, he would not have been a
man, but a monster." He spoke with contempt of Gray,
and with intolerance of Pope. He did not like the versification of the latter. He observed that " the ears of these
couplet-writers might be charged with having short memories, that could not retain the harmony of whole passages."
He thought little of Junius as a writer; he had a dislike of
Dr. Johnson; and a much higher opinion of Burke as an
orator and politician, than of Fox or Pitt. He however
thought him very inferior in richness of style and imagery
to some of our elder prose-writers, particularly Jeremy
Taylor. He liked Richardson, but not Fielding; nor could
I get him to enter into the merits of *Caleb Williams*.* In
short, he was profound and discriminating with respect to
those authors whom he liked, and where he gave his judgment fair play; capricious, perverse, and prejudiced in his
antipathies and distastes. We loitered on the " ribbed sea-

---

*He had no idea of pictures, of Claude or Raphael, and at this
time I had as little as he. He sometimes gives a striking account
at present of the cartoons at Pisa, by .Buffamalco and others; of
one in particular, where Death is seen in the air brandishing his
scythe, and the great and mighty of the earth shudder at his
approach, while the beggars and the wretched kneel to him as their
deliverer. He would of course understand so broad and fine a
moral as this at any time.

sands," in such talk as this, a whole morning, and I recollect
met with a curious sea-weed, of which John Chester told
us the country name! A fisherman gave Coleridge an
account of a boy that had been drowned the day before,
and that they had tried to save him at the risk of their
own lives. He said " he did not know how it was that they
ventured, but, Sir, we have a *nature* towards one another."
This expression, Coleridge remarked to me, was a fine
illustration of that theory of disinterestedness which I (in
common with Butler) had adopted. I broached to him an
argument of mine to prove that *likeness* was not mere
association of ideas. I said that the mark in the sand put
one in mind of a man's foot, not because it was part of
a former impression of a man's foot (for it was quite
new) but because it was like the shape of a man's foot.
He assented to the justness of this distinction (which I have
explained at length elsewhere, for the benefit of the curious)
and John Chester listened; not from any interest in the
subject, but because he was astonished that I should be
able to suggest any thing to Coleridge that he did not
already know. We returned on the third morning, and
Coleridge remarked the silent cottage-smoke curling up the
valleys where, a few evenings before, we had seen the
lights gleaming through the dark

In a day or two after we arrived at Stowey we set out,
I on my return home, and he for Germany. It was a
Sunday morning, and he was to preach that day for Dr.
Toulmin of Taunton. I asked him if he had prepared any
thing for the occasion? He said he had not even thought
of the text, but should as soon as we parted. I did not
go to hear him,—this was a fault,—but we met in the evening at Bridgewater. The next day we had a long day's
walk to Bristol, and sat down, I recollect, by a well-side
on the road, to cool ourselves and satisfy our thirst, when

Coleridge repeated to me some descriptive lines from his tragedy of Remorse; which I must say became his mouth and that occasion better than they, some years after, did Mr. Elliston's and the Drury-lane boards,—

"Oh memory! shield me from the world's poor strife,
And give those scenes thine everlasting life."

I saw no more of him for a year or two, during which period he had been wandering in the Hartz Forest in Germany; and his return was cometary, meteorous, unlike his setting out. It was not till some time after that I knew his friends Lamb and Southey. The last always appears to me (as I first saw him) with a common-place book under his arm, and the first with a *bon-mot* in his mouth. It was at Godwin's that I met him with Holcroft and Coleridge, where they were disputing fiercely which was the best— *Man as he was, or man as he is to be.* "Give me," says Lamb, "man as he is *not* to be." This saying was the beginning of a friendship between us, which I believe still continues.—Enough of this for the present.

"But there is matter for another rhyme,
And I to this may add a second tale."

# XVIII

## ON THE CONVERSATION OF AUTHORS

THE soul of conversation is sympathy.—Authors should converse chiefly with authors, and their talk should be of books. " When Greek meets Greek, then comes the tug of war." There is nothing so pedantic as pretending not to be pedantic. No man can get above his pursuit in life: it is getting above himself, which is impossible. There is a Free-masonry in all things. You can only speak to be understood, but this you cannot be, except by those who are in the secret. Hence an argument has been drawn to supersede the necessity of conversation altogether; for it has been said, that there is no use in talking to people of sense, who know all that you can tell them, nor to fools, who will not be instructed. There is, however, the smallest encouragement to proceed, when you are conscious that the more you really enter into a subject, the farther you will be from the comprehension of your hearers—and that the more proofs you give of any position, the more odd and out-of-the-way they will think your notions. C—— is the only person who can talk to all sorts of people, on all sorts of subjects, without caring a farthing for their understanding one word he says—and *he* talks only for admiration and to be listened to, and accordingly the least interruption puts him out. I firmly believe he would make just the same impression on half his audiences, if he purposely repeated absolute nonsense with the same voice and manner and inexhaustible flow of undulating speech! In general,

wit shines only by reflection. You must take your cue
from your company—must rise as they rise, and sink as
they fall. You must see that your good things, your
knowing allusions, are not flung away, like the pearls
in the adage. What a check it is to be asked a foolish
question; to find that the first principles are not understood! You are thrown on your back immediately, the
conversation is stopped like a country-dance by those who
do not know the figure. But when a set of adepts, of
*illuminati,* get about a question, it is worth while to hear
them talk. They may snarl and quarrel over it, like dogs;
but they pick it bare to the bone, they masticate it
thoroughly.

This was the case formerly at L——'s—where we used
to have many lively skirmishes at their Thursday evening
parties. I doubt whether the Small-coal man's musical
parties could exceed them. Oh! for the pen of John Buncle
to consecrate a *petit souvenir* to their memory!—There was
L—— himself, the most delightful, the most provoking,
the most witty and sensible of men. He always made the
best pun, and the best remark in the course of the evening.
His serious conversation, like his serious writing, is his
best. No one ever stammered out such fine, piquant, deep,
eloquent things in half a dozen half sentences as he does.
His jests scald like tears: and he probes a question with a
play upon words. What a keen, laughing, hair-brained
vein of home-felt truth! What choice venom! How often
did we cut into the haunch of letters, while we discussed
the haunch of mutton on the table! How we skimmed the
cream of criticism! How we got into the heart of controversy! How we picked out the marrow of authors!
"And, in our flowing cups, many a good name and true
was freshly remembered." Recollect (most sage and
critical reader) that in all this I was but a guest! Need

I go over the names? They were but the old everlasting set—Milton and Shakespeare, Pope and Dryden, Steele and Addison, Swift and Gay, Fielding, Smollett, Sterne, Richardson, Hogarth's prints, Claude's landscapes, the Cartoons at Hampton-court, and all those things, that, having once been, must ever be. The Scotch Novels had not then been heard of: so we said nothing about them. In general, we were hard upon the moderns. The author of the Rambler was only tolerated in Boswell's Life of him; and it was as much as anyone could do to edge in a word for Junius. L—— could not bear Gil Blas. This was a fault. I remember the greatest triumph I ever had was in persuading him, after some years' difficulty, that Fielding was better than Smollett. On one occasion, he was for making out a list of persons famous in history that one would wish to see again—at the head of whom were Pontius Pilate, Sir Thomas Browne, and Dr. Faustus—but we black-balled most of his list! But with what a gusto would he describe his favourite authors, Donne, or Sir Philip Sidney, and call their most crabbed passages *delicious!* He tried them on his palate as epicures taste olives, and his observations had a smack in them, like a roughness on the tongue. With what discrimination he hinted a defect in what he admired most—as in saying that the display of the sumptuous banquet in Paradise Regained was not in true keeping, as the simplest fare was all that was necessary to tempt the extremity of hunger—and stating that Adam and Eve in Paradise Lost were too much like married people. He has furnished many a text for C—— to preach upon. There was no fuss or cant about him: nor were his sweets or his sours ever diluted with one particle of affectation. I cannot say that the party at L——'s were all of one description. There were honorary members, lay-brothers. Wit and good fellowship was the motto inscribed over the door. When a stranger came in, it was not asked, " Has he written anything? "—we were above that pedantry; but we waited to see what he could do. If he could take a hand at piquet, he was welcome to sit down. If a person liked any thing, if he took snuff heartily, it was sufficient. He would understand, by analogy, the pungency of other things, besides Irish blackguard or Scotch rappee. A character was good any where, in a room or on paper. But we abhorred insipidity, affectation, and fine gentlemen. There was one of our party who never failed to mark " two for his Nob " at cribbage, and he was thought no mean person. This was Ned P——, and a better fellow in his way breathes not. There was ——, who asserted some incredible matter of fact as a likely paradox, and settled all controversies by an *ipse dixit,* a fiat of his will, hammering out many a hard theory on the anvil of his brain— the Baron Munchausen of politics and practical philosophy: —there was Captain ——, who had you at an advantage by never understanding you:—there was Jem White, the author of Falstaff's Letters, who the other day left this dull world to go in search of more kindred spirits, " turning like the latter end of a lover's lute: "—there was A——, who sometimes dropped in, the Will Honeycomb of our set—and Mrs. R——, who being of a quiet turn, loved to hear a noisy debate. An utterly uninformed person might have supposed this a scene of vulgar confusion and uproar. While the most critical question was pending, while the most difficult problem in philosophy was solving, P—— cried out, " That's game," and M. B. muttered a quotation over the last remains of a veal-pie at a side-table. Once, and once only, the literary interest overcame the general. For C—— was riding the high German horse, and demonstrating the Categories of the Transcendental philosophy to the author of the Road to Ruin; who insisted on his knowl-

edge of German, and German metaphysics, having read the
*Critique of Pure Reason* in the original. "My dear Mr.
Holcroft," said C——, in a tone of infinitely provoking
conciliation, "you really put me in mind of a sweet pretty
German girl, about fifteen, that I met with in the Hartz
forest in Germany—and who one day, as I was reading the
Limits of the Knowable and the Unknowable, the pro-
foundest of all his works, with great attention, came behind
my chair, and leaning over, said, What, *you* read Kant?
Why, *I* that am a German born, don't understand him!"
This was too much to bear, and Holcroft, starting up,
called out in no measured tone, "Mr. C——, you are the
most eloquent man I ever met with, and the most trouble-
some with your eloquence!" P—— held the cribbage-peg
that was to mark him game, suspended in his hand; and
the whist table was silent for a moment. I saw Holcroft
down stairs, and, on coming to the landing-place in Mitre-
court, he stopped me to observe, that "he thought Mr.
C—— a very clever man, with a great command of language, but that he feared he did not always affix very
precise ideas to the words he used." After he was gone,
we had our laugh out, and went on with the argument on
the nature of Reason, the Imagination, and the Will. I
wish I could find a publisher for it : it would make a supple-
ment to the *Biographia Literaria* in a volume and a half
octavo.

Those days are over! An event, the name of which I
wish never to mention, broke up our party, like a bomb-
shell thrown into the room : and now we seldom meet——

"Like angels' visits, short and far between."

There is no longer the same set of persons, nor of associations. L—— does not live where he did. By shifting
his abode, his notions seem less fixed. He does not wear

his old snuff-coloured coat and breeches. It looks like an alteration in his style. An author and a wit should have a separate costume, a particular cloth: he should present something positive and singular to the mind, like Mr. Douce of the Museum. Our faith in the religion of letters will not bear to be taken to pieces, and put together again by caprice or accident. L. H—— goes there sometimes. He has a fine vinous spirit about him, and tropical blood in his veins: but he is better at his own table. He has a great flow of pleasantry and delightful animal spirits: but his hits do not tell like L——'s; you cannot repeat them the next day. He requires not only to be appreciated, but to have a select circle of admirers and devotees, to feel himself quite at home. He sits at the head of a party with great gaiety and grace; has an elegant manner and turn of features; is never at a loss—*aliquando sufflaminandus erat*—has continual sportive sallies of wit or fancy; tells a story capitally; mimics an actor, or an acquaintance to admiration; laughs with great glee and good-humour at his own or other people's jokes; understands the point of an equivoque, or an observation immediately; has a taste and knowledge of books, of music, of medals; manages an argument adroitly; is genteel and gallant, and has a set of bye-phrases and quaint allusions always at hand to produce a laugh:—if he has a fault, it is that he does not listen so well as he speaks, is impatient of interruption, and is fond of being looked up to, without considering by whom. I believe, however, he has pretty well seen the folly of this. Neither is his ready display of personal accomplishment and variety of resources an advantage to his writings. They sometimes present a desultory and slipshod appearance, owing to this very circumstance. The same things that tell, perhaps, best, to a private circle round the fireside, are not always intelligible to the public, nor does he take pains to make them so. He is too confident and secure of his audience. That which may be entertaining enough with the assistance of a certain liveliness of manner, may read very flat on paper, because it is abstracted from all the circumstances that had set it off to advantage. A writer should recollect that he has only to trust to the immediate impression of words, like a musician who sings without the accompaniment of an instrument. There is nothing to help out, or slubber over, the defects of the voice in the one case, nor of the style in the other. The reader may, if he pleases, get a very good idea of .L. H——'s conversation from a very agreeable paper he has lately published, called the *Indicator,* than which nothing can be more happily conceived or executed.

The art .of conversation is the art of hearing as well as of being heard. Authors in general are not good listeners. Some of the best talkers are, on this account, the worst company; and some who are very indifferent, but very great talkers, are as bad. It is sometimes wonderful to see how a person, who has been entertaining or tiring a company by the hour together, drops his countenance as if he had been shot, or had been seized with a sudden lock-jaw, the moment anyone interposes a single observation. The best converser I know is, however, the best listener. I mean Mr. Northcote, the painter. Painters by their profession are not bound to shine in conversation, and they shine the more. He lends his ear to an observation, as if you had brought him a piece of news, and enters into it with as much avidity and earnestness, as if it interested himself personally. If he repeats an old remark or story, it is with the same freshness and point as for the first time. It always arises out of the occasion, and has the stamp of originality. There is no parroting of himself. His look is a continual, ever-varying history-piece of what passes in his mind. His face is as a book. There need no marks of interjection or interrogation to what he says. His manner is quite picturesque. There is an excess of character and *naïveté* that never tires. His thoughts bubble up and sparkle, like beads on old wine. The fund of anecdote, the collection of curious particulars, is enough to set up any common retailer of jests, that dines out every day; but these are not strung together like a row of galley-slaves, but are always introduced to illustrate some argument or bring out some fine distinction of character. The mixture of spleen adds to the sharpness of the point, like poisoned arrows. Mr. Northcote enlarges with enthusiasm on the old painters, and tells good things of the new. The only thing he ever vexed me in was his liking the *Catalogue Raisonnée*. I had almost as soon hear him talk of Titian's pictures (which he does with tears in his eyes, and looking just like them) as see the originals, and I had rather hear him talk of Sir Joshua's than see them. He is the last of that school who knew Goldsmith and Johnson. How finely he describes Pope! His elegance of mind, his figure, his character were not unlike his own. He does not resemble a modern Englishman, but puts one in mind of a Roman Cardinal or Spanish Inquisitor. I never ate or drank with Mr. Northcote; but I have lived on his conversation with undiminished relish ever since I can remember,—and when I leave it, I come out into the street with feelings lighter and more etherial than I have at any other time.—One of his *tête-à-têtes* would at any time make an Essay; but he cannot write himself, because he loses himself in the connecting passages, is fearful of the effect, and wants the habit of bringing his ideas into one focus or point of view. A *lens* is necessary to collect the diverging rays, the refracted and broken angular lights of conversation on paper. Contradiction is half the battle in talking—the being startled by what others say, and having to answer on the spot. You have to defend yourself, paragraph by paragraph, parenthesis within parenthesis. Perhaps it might be supposed that a person who excels in conversation and cannot write, would succeed better in dialogue. But the stimulus, the immediate irritation would be wanting; and the work would read flatter than ever, from not having the very thing it pretended to have.

Lively sallies and connected discourse are very different things. There are many persons of that impatient and restless turn of mind, that they cannot wait a moment for a conclusion, or follow up the thread of any argument. In the hurry of conversation their ideas are somehow huddled into sense; but in the intervals of thought, leave a great gap between. Montesquieu said, he often lost an idea before he could find words for it: yet he dictated, by way of saving time, to an amanuensis. This last is, in my opinion, a vile method, and a solecism in authorship. Horne Tooke, among other paradoxes, used to maintain, that no one could write a good style who was not in the habit of talking and hearing the sound of his own voice. He might as well have said that no one could relish a good style without reading it aloud, as we find common people do to assist their apprehension. But there is a method of trying periods on the ear, or weighing them with the scales of the breath, without any articulate sound. Authors, as they write, may be said to " hear a sound so fine, there's nothing lives 'twixt it and silence." Even musicians generally compose in their heads. I agree that no style is good that is not fit to be spoken or read aloud with effect. This holds true not only of emphasis and cadence, but also with regard to natural idiom and colloquial freedom. Sterne's was in this respect the best style that ever was written. You fancy that you hear the people talking. For a contrary reason, no college-man writes a good style, or understands it when written. Fine writing is with him all verbiage and monotony—a translation into classical centos or hexameter lines.

That which I have just mentioned is among many instances I could give of ingenious absurdities advanced by Mr. Tooke in the heat and pride of controversy. A person who knew him well, and greatly admired his talents, said of him that he never (to his recollection) heard him defend an opinion which he thought right, or in which he believed him to be himself sincere. He indeed provoked his antagonists into the toils by the very extravagance of his assertions, and the teasing sophistry by which he rendered them plausible. His temper was prompter to his skill. He had the manners of a man of the world, with great scholastic resources. He flung everyone else off his guard, and was himself immovable. I never knew anyone who did not admit his superiority in this kind of warfare. He put a full stop to one of C——'s long-winded prefatory apologies for his youth and inexperience, by saying abruptly, " Speak up, young man! " and, at another time, silenced a learned professor, by desiring an explanation of a word which the other frequently used, and which, he said, he had been many years trying to get at the meaning of,—the copulative Is! He was the best intellectual fencer of his day. He made strange havoc of Fuseli's fantastic hieroglyphics, violent humours, and oddity of dialect.—Curran, who was sometimes of the same party, was lively and animated in convivial conversation, but dull in argument; nay, averse to anything like reasoning or serious observation, and had the worst taste I ever knew. His favourite critical topics were to abuse Milton's Paradise Lost, and Romeo and Juliet. Indeed, he confessed a want of sufficient acquaintance with books when he found himself in literary society in London. He and Sheridan once dined at John Kemble's with Mrs.

Inchbald and Mary Woolstonecroft, when the discourse almost wholly turned on Love, " from noon to dewy eve, a summer's day!" What a subject! What speakers, and what hearers! What would I not give to have been there, had I not learned it all from the bright eyes of Amaryllis, and may one day make a *Table-talk* of it!—Peter Pindar was rich in anecdote and grotesque humour, and profound in technical knowledge both of music, poetry, and painting, but he was gross and overbearing. Wordsworth sometimes talks like a man inspired on subjects of poetry (his own out of the question)—Coleridge well on every subject, and G—dwin on none. To finish this subject—Mrs. M——'s conversation is as fine-cut as her features, and I like to sit in the room with that sort of coronet face. What she said leaves a flavour, like fine green tea. H—t's is like champagne, and N——'s like anchovy sandwiches. H—yd—n's is like a game at trap-ball: L——'s like snap-dragon: and my own (if I do not mistake the matter) is not very much unlike a game at nine-pins! . . . . . One source of the conversation of authors, is the character of other authors, and on that they are rich indeed. What things they say! What stories they tell of one another, more particularly of their friends! If I durst only give some of these confidential communications! . . . The reader may perhaps think the foregoing a specimen of them:—but indeed he is mistaken.

I do not know of any greater impertinence, than for an obscure individual to set about pumping a character of celebrity. " Bring him to me," said a Doctor Tronchin, speaking of Rousseau, " that I may see whether he has anything in him." Before you can take measure of the capacity of others, you ought to be sure that they have not taken measure of yours. They may think you a spy on them, and may not like their company. If you really want to know whether another person can talk well, begin by saying a good thing yourself, and you will have a right to look for a rejoinder. " The best tennis-players," says Sir Fopling Flutter, "make the best matches."

> ————————For wit is like a rest
> Held up at tennis, which men do the best
> With the best players.

We hear it often said of a great author, or a great actress, that they are very stupid people in private. But he was a fool that said so. *Tell me your company, and I'll tell you your manners.* In conversation, as in other things, the action and reaction should bear a certain proportion to each other.—Authors may, in some sense, be looked upon as foreigners, who are not naturalised even in their native soil. L—— once came down into the country to see us. He was " like the most capricious poet Ovid among the Goths." The country people thought him an oddity, and did not understand his jokes. It would be strange if they had; for he did not make any, while he staid. But when he crossed the country to Oxford, then he spoke a little. He and the old colleges were hail-fellow well met; and in the quadrangles, he " walked gowned."

There is a character of a· gentleman; so there is a character of a scholar, which is no less easily recognised. The one has an air of books about him, as the other has of good-breeding. The one wears his thoughts as the other does his clothes, gracefully; and even if they are a little old-fashioned, they are not ridiculous: they have had their day. The gentleman shows, by his manner, that he has been used to respect from others: the. scholar that he lays claim to self-respect and to a certain independence of opinion. The one has been accustomed to the best company; the other has passed his time in cultivating an inti-

macy with the best authors. There is nothing forward or
vulgar in the behaviour of the one; nothing shrewd or
petulant in the observations of the other, as if he should
astonish the bye-standers, or was astonished himself at his
own discoveries. Good taste and good sense, like common
politeness, are, or are supposed to be, matters of course.
One is distinguished by an appearance of marked attention
to every one present; the other manifests an habitual air of
abstraction and absence of mind. The one is not an upstart
with all the self-important airs of the founder of his own
fortune; nor the other a self-taught man, with the repulsive
self-sufficiency which arises from an ignorance of what
hundreds have known before him. We must excuse perhaps a little conscious family-pride in the one, and a little
harmless pedantry in the other.—As there is a class of the
first character which sinks into the mere gentleman, that
is, which has nothing but this sense of respectability and
propriety to support it—so the character of a scholar not
unfrequently dwindles down into the shadow of a shade,
till nothing is left of it but the mere book-worm. There
is often something amiable as well as enviable in this last
character. I know one such instance, at least. The person
I mean has an admiration for learning, if he is only dazzled
by its light. He lives among old authors, if he does not
enter much into their spirit. He handles the covers, and
turns over the page, and is familiar with the names and
dates. He is busy and self-involved. He hangs like a film
and cobweb upon letters, or is like the dust upon the outside
of knowledge, which should not be rudely brushed aside.
He follows learning as its shadow; but as such, he is respectable. He browzes on the husk and leaves of books,
as the young fawn browzes on the bark and leaves of trees.
Such a one lives all his life in a dream of learning, and has
never once had his sleep broken by a real sense of things.

He believes implicitly in genius, truth, virtue, liberty, because he finds the names of these things in books. He thinks that love and friendship are the finest things imaginable, both in practice and theory. The legend of good women is to him no fiction. When he steals from the twilight of his cell, the scene breaks upon him like an illuminated missal, and all the people he sees are but so many figures in a *camera obscura*. He reads the world, like a favourite volume, only to find beauties in it, or like an edition of some old work which he is preparing for the press, only to make emendations in it, and correct the errors that have inadvertently slipt in. He and his dog Tray are much the same honest, simple-hearted, faithful, affectionate creatures—if Tray could but read! His mind cannot take the impression of vice: but the gentleness of his nature turns gall to milk. He would not hurt a fly. He draws the picture of mankind from the guileless simplicity of his own heart: and when he dies, his spirit will take its smiling leave, without having ever had an ill thought of others, or the consciousness of one in itself!

# XIX

## OF PERSONS ONE WOULD WISH TO HAVE SEEN

" Come like shadows—so depart."

B—— it was, I think, who suggested this subject, as
well as the defence of Guy Faux, which I urged him to
execute. As, however, he would undertake neither, I suppose I must do both—a task for which he would have been
much fitter, no less from the temerity than the felicity of
his pen—

> "Never so sure our rapture to create
> As when it touch'd the brink of all we hate."

Compared with him, I shall, I fear, make but a common-
place piece of business of it; but I should be loth the idea
was entirely lost, and besides I may avail myself of some
hints of his in the progress of it. I am sometimes, I suspect, a better reporter of the ideas of other people than
expounder of my own. I pursue the one too far into
paradox or mysticism; the others I am not bound to follow
farther than I like, or than seems fair and reasonable.

On the question being started, A—— said, " I suppose
the two first persons you would choose to see would be
the two greatest names in English literature, Sir Isaac
Newton and Mr. Locke?" In this A——, as usual,
reckoned without his host. Every one burst out a laughing at the expression of B——'s face, in which impatience
was restrained by courtesy. " Yes, the greatest names," he
stammered out hastily, " but they were not persons—not

persons."—"Not persons?" said A——, looking wise and foolish at the same time, afraid his triumph might be premature. "That is," rejoined B——, "not characters, you know. By Mr. Locke and Sir Isaac Newton, you mean the Essay on the Human Understanding, and the *Principia,* which we have to this day. Beyond their contents there is nothing personally interesting in the men. But what we want to see any one *bodily* for, is when there is something peculiar, striking in the individuals, more than we can learn from their writings, and yet are curious to know. I dare say Locke and Newton were very like Kneller's portraits of them. But who could paint Shakspeare?"—"Ay," retorted A——, "there it is; then I suppose you would prefer seeing him and Milton instead?"—"No," said B——, "neither. I have seen so much of Shakspeare on the stage and on book-stalls, in frontispieces and on mantle-pieces, that I am quite tired of the everlasting repetition: and as to Milton's face, the impressions that have come down to us of it I do not like; it is too starched and puritanical; and I should be afraid of losing some of the manna of his poetry in the leaven of his countenance and the precisian's band and gown."—"I shall guess no more," said A——. "Who is it, then, you would like to see 'in his habit as he lived,' if you had your choice of the whole range of English literature?" B—— then named Sir Thomas Brown and Fulke Greville, the friend of Sir Philip Sidney, as the two worthies whom he should feel the greatest pleasure to encounter on the floor of his apartment in their night-gown and slippers, and to exchange friendly greeting with them. At this A—— laughed outright, and conceived B—— was jesting with him; but as no one followed his example, he thought there might be something in it, and waited for an explanation in a state of whimsical suspense. B—— then (as well as I can remember a con-

versation that passed twenty years ago—how time slips!)
went on as follows. "The reason why I pitch upon these
two authors is, that their writings are riddles, and they
themselves the most mysterious of personages. They resemble the soothsayers of old, who dealt in dark hints and
doubtful oracles; and I should like to ask them the meaning
of what no mortal but themselves, I should suppose, can
fathom. There is Dr. Johnson, I have no curiosity, no
strange uncertainty about him: he and Boswell together
have pretty well let me into the secret of what passed
through his mind. He and other writers like him are sufficiently explicit: my friends, whose repose I should be
tempted to disturb, (were it in my power) are implicit,
inextricable, inscrutable.

> "And call up him who left half-told
> The story of Cambuscan bold."

"When I look at that obscure but gorgeous prose-com-
position (the *Urn-burial*) I seem to myself to look into a
deep abyss, at the bottom of which are hid pearls and rich
treasure; or it is like a stately labyrinth of doubt and
withering speculation, and I would invoke the spirit of the
author to lead me through it. Besides, who would not be
curious to see the lineaments of a man who, having himself
been twice married, wished that mankind were propagated
like trees! As to Fulke Greville, he is like nothing but one
of his own 'Prologues spoken by the ghost of an old king
of Ormus,' a truly formidable and inviting personage: his
style is apocalyptical, cabalistical, a knot worthy of such an
apparition to untie; and for the unravelling a passage or
two, I would stand the brunt of an encounter with so portentous a commentator!"—"I am afraid in that case," said
A——, "that if the mystery were once cleared up, the
merit might be lost;"—and turning to me, whispered a

friendly apprehension, that while B—— continued to admire these old crabbed authors, he would never become a popular writer. Dr. Donne was mentioned as a writer of the same period, with a very interesting countenance, whose history was singular, and whose meaning was often quite as *uncomeatable,* without a personal citation from the dead, as that of any of his contemporaries. The volume was produced; and while some one was expatiating on the exquisite simplicity and beauty of the portrait prefixed to the old edition, A—— got hold of the poetry, and exclaiming, " What have we here? " read the following :—

> " Here lies a She-Sun and a He-Moon there,
> She gives the best light to his sphere,
> Or each is both and all, and so
> They unto one another nothing owe."

There was no resisting this, till B——, seizing the volume, turned to the beautiful " Lines to his Mistress," dissuading her from accompanying him abroad, and read them with suffused features and a faltering tongue.

> " By our first strange and fatal interview,
> By all desires which thereof did ensue,
> By our long starving hopes, by that remorse
> Which my words' masculine persuasive force
> Begot in thee, and by the memory
> Of hurts, which spies and rivals threaten'd me,
> I calmly beg. But by thy father's wrath,
> By all pains which want and divorcement hath,
> I conjure thee; and all the oaths which I
> And thou have sworn to seal joint constancy
> Here I unswear, and overswear them thus,
> Thou shalt not love by ways so dangerous.
> Temper, oh fair Love! love's impetuous rage,
> Be my true mistress still, not my feign'd Page;
> I'll go, and, by thy kind leave, leave behind
> Thee! only worthy to nurse it in my mind.
> Thirst to come back; oh, if thou die before,
> My soul from other lands to thee shall soar.

Thy (else Almighty) beauty cannot move
Rage from the seas, nor thy love teach them love,
Nor tame wild Boreas' harshness; thou hast read
How roughly he in pieces shivered
Fair Orithea, whom he swore he lov'd.
Fall ill or good, 'tis madness to have prov'd
Dangers unurg'd: Feed on this flattery,
That absent lovers one with th' other be.
Dissemble nothing, not a boy; nor change
Thy body's habit, nor mind; be not strange
To thyself only. All will spy in thy face
A blushing, womanly, discovering grace.
Richly cloth'd apes are called apes, and as soon
Eclips'd as bright we call the moon the moon.
Men of France, changeable cameleons,
Spittles of diseases, shops of fashions,
Love's fuellers, and the rightest company
Of players, which upon the world's stage be,
Will quickly know thee. . . . O stay here! for thee
England is only a worthy gallery,
To walk in expectation; till from thence
Our greatest King call thee to his presence.
When I am gone, dream me some happiness,
Nor let thy looks our long hid love confess,
Nor praise, nor dispraise me; nor bless, nor curse
Openly love's force, nor in bed fright thy nurse
With midnight startings, crying out, Oh, oh,
Nurse, oh, my love is slain, I saw him go
O'er the white Alps alone; I saw him, I,
Assail'd, fight, taken, stabb'd, bleed, fall, and die.
Augur me better chance, except dread Jove
Think it enough for me to have had thy love."

Some one then inquired of B—— if we could not see
from the window the Temple-walk in which Chaucer used
to take his exercise; and on his name being put to the vote,
I was pleased to find that there was a general sensation in
his favour in all but A——, who said something about the
ruggedness of the metre, and even objected to the quaintness of the orthography. I was vexed at this superficial
gloss, pertinaciously reducing every thing to its own trite
level, and asked " if he did not think it would be worth

while to scan the eye that had first greeted the Muse in
that dim twilight and early dawn of English literature;
to see the head, round which the visions of fancy must
have played like gleams of inspiration or a sudden glory;
to watch those lips that "lisped in numbers, for the numbers came"—as by a miracle, or as if the dumb should
speak? Nor was it alone that he had been the first to
tune his native tongue (however imperfectly to modern
ears); but he was himself a noble, manly character, standing before his age and striving to advance it; a pleasant
humourist withal, who has not only handed down to us the
living manners of his time, but had, no doubt, store of
curious and quaint devices, and would make as hearty a
companion as Mine Host of Tabard. His interview
with Petrarch is fraught with interest. Yet I would rather
have seen Chaucer in company with the author of the
Decameron, and have heard them exchange their best
stories together,—the Squire's Tale against the Story of
the Falcon, the Wife of Bath's Prologue against the Adventures of Friar Albert. How fine to see the high mysterious brow which learning then wore, relieved by the gay,
familiar tone of men of the world, and by the courtesies.
of genius. Surely, the thoughts and feelings which passed
through the minds of these great revivers of learning, these
Cadmuses who sowed the teeth of letters, must have
stamped an expression on their features, as different from
the moderns as their books, and well worth the perusal.
Dante," I continued, " is as interesting a person as his own
Ugolino, one whose lineaments curiosity would as eagerly
devour in order to penetrate his spirit, and the only one
of the Italian poets I should care much to see. There is
a fine portrait of Ariosto by no less a hand than Titian's;
light, Moorish, spirited, but not answering our idea. The
same artist's large colossal profile of Peter Aretine is the

only likeness of the kind that has the effect of conversing with ' the mighty dead,' and this is truly spectral, ghastly, necromantic." B—— put it to me if I should like to see Spenser as well as Chaucer; and I answered without hesitation, "No; for that his beauties were ideal, visionary, not palpable or personal, and therefore connected with less curiosity about the man. His poetry was the essence of romance, a very halo round the bright orb of fancy; and the bringing in the individual might dissolve the charm. No tones of voice could come up to the mellifluous cadence of his verse; no form but of a winged angel could vie with the airy shapes he has described. He was (to our apprehensions) rather a " creature of the element, that lived in the rainbow and played in the plighted clouds," than an ordinary mortal. Or if he did appear, I should wish it to be as a mere vision, like one of his own pageants, and that he should pass by unquestioned like a dream or sound—

> ——" *That* was Arion crown'd:
> So went he playing on the wat'ry plain!"

Captain C. muttered something about Columbus, and M. C. hinted at the Wandering Jew; but the last was set aside as spurious, and the first made over to the New World.

"I should like," said Miss D——, "to have seen Pope talking with Patty Blount; and I *have* seen Goldsmith." Every one turned round to look at Miss D——, as if by so doing they too could get a sight of Goldsmith.

"Where," asked a harsh croaking voice, "was Dr. Johnson in the years 1745-6? He did not write anything that we know of, nor is there any account of him in Boswell during those two years. Was he in Scotland with the Pretender? He seems to have passed through the scenes in the Highlands in company with Boswell many years after ' with lack-lustre eye,' yet as if they were familiar to him, or associated in his mind with interests that he durst not explain. If so, it would be an additional reason for my liking him; and I would give something to have seen him seated in the tent with the youthful Majesty of Britain, and penning the Proclamation to all true subjects and adherents of the legitimate Government."

"I thought," said A——, turning short round upon B——, "that you of the Lake School did not like Pope?" —"Not like Pope! My dear sir, you must be under a mistake—I can read him over and over for ever!"—"Why certainly, the Essay on Man must be allowed to be a master-piece."—"It may be so, but I seldom look into it."— "Oh! then it's his Satires you admire?"—"No, not his Satires, but his friendly Epistles and his compliments."— "Compliments! I did not know he ever made any."—"The finest," said B——, "that were ever paid by the wit of man. Each of them is worth an estate for life—nay, is an immortality. There is that superb one to Lord Cornbury:

> "Despise low joys, low gains:
> Disdain whatever Cornbury disdains;
> Be virtuous, and be happy for your pains.

"Was there ever more artful insinuation of idolatrous praise? And then that noble apotheosis of his friend Lord Mansfield (however little deserved), when, speaking of the House of Lords, he adds—

> "Conspicuous scene! another yet is nigh,
> (More silent far) where kings and poets lie;
> Where Murray (long enough his Country's pride)
> Shall be no more than Tully or than Hyde!

"And with what a fine turn of indignant flattery he addresses Lord Bolingbroke—

> "Why rail they then, if but one wreath of mine,
> Oh! all-accomplish'd St. John, deck thy shrine?

"Or turn," continued B——, with a slight hectic on his cheek and his eye glistening, "to his list of early friends:

> "But why then publish?  Granville the polite,
> And knowing Walsh, would tell me I could write;
> Well-natured Garth inflamed with early praise,
> And Congreve loved and Swift endured my lays:
> The courtly Talbot, Somers, Sheffield read,
> Ev'n mitred Rochester would nod the head;
> And St. John's self (great Dryden's friend before)
> Received with open arms one poet more.
> Happy my studies, if by these approved!
> Happier their author, if by these beloved!
> From these the world will judge of men and books,
> Not from the Burnets, Oldmixons, and Cooks."

Here his voice totally failed him, and throwing down the book, he said, "Do you think I would not wish to have been friends with such a man as this?"

"What say you to Dryden?"—"He rather made a show of himself, and courted popularity in that lowest temple of Fame, a coffee-house, so as in some measure to vulgarize one's idea of him.  Pope, on the contrary, reached the very *beau ideal* of what a poet's life should be; and his fame while living seemed to be an emanation from that which was to circle his name after death.  He was so far enviable (and one would feel proud to have witnessed the rare spectacle in him) that he was almost the only poet and man of genius who met with his reward on this side of the tomb, who realized in friends, fortune, the esteem of the world, the most sanguine hopes of a youthful ambition, and who found that sort of patronage from the great during his lifetime which they would be thought anxious to bestow upon him after his death.  Read Gay's verses to him on his supposed return from Greece, after his translation of Homer was finished, and say if you would not gladly join the bright procession that welcomed him home, or see it once more land at Whitehall-stairs."—"Still," said Miss

D——, " I would rather have seen him talking with Patty
Blount, or riding by in a coronet-coach with Lady Mary
Wortley Montagu! "

E——, who was deep in a game of piquet at the other
end of the room, whispered to M. C. to ask if Junius would
not be a fit person to invoke from the dead. " Yes," said
B——, " provided he would agree to lay aside his mask."

We were now at a stand for a short time, when Fielding
was mentioned as a candidate: only one, however, seconded
the proposition. " Richardson? "—" By all means, but only
to look at him through the glass-door of his back-shop,
hard at work upon one of his novels (the most extraordinary contrast that ever was presented between an author
and his works), but not to let him come behind his counter
lest he should want you to turn customer, nor to go upstairs
with him, lest he should offer to read the first manuscript of
Sir Charles Grandison, which was originally written in
eight and twenty volumes octavo, or get out the letters of
his female correspondents, to prove that Joseph Andrews
was low."

There was but one statesman in the whole of English
history that any one expressed the least desire to see—
Oliver Cromwell, with his fine, frank, rough, pimply face,
and wily policy; and one enthusiast, John Bunyan, the immortal author of the Pilgrim's Progress. It seemed that
if he came into the room, dreams would follow him, and
that each person would nod under his golden cloud, " nigh-
sphered in Heaven," a canopy as strange and stately as any
in Homer.

Of all persons near our own time, Garrick's name was
received with the greatest enthusiasm, who was proposed
by J. F——. He presently superseded both Hogarth and
Handel, who had been talked of, but then it was on condition that he should act in tragedy and comedy, in the

play and the farce, Lear and Wildair and Abel Drugger.
What a *sight for sore eyes* that would be! Who would
not part with a year's income at least, almost with a year
of his natural life, to be present at it? Besides, as he could
not act alone, and recitations are unsatisfactory things,
what a troop he must bring with him—the silver-tongued
Barry, and Quin, and Shuter and Weston, and Mrs. Clive
and Mrs. Pritchard, of whom I have heard my father speak
as so great a favourite when he was young! This would
indeed be a revival of the dead, the restoring of art; and
so much the more desirable, as such is the lurking scep-
ticism mingled with our overstrained admiration of past
excellence, that though we have the speeches of Burke, the
portraits of Reynolds, the writings of Goldsmith, and the
conversation of Johnson, to show what people could do at
that period, and to confirm the universal testimony to the
merits of Garrick; yet, as it was before our time, we have
our misgivings, as if he was probably after all little better
than a Bartlemy-fair actor, dressed out to play Macbeth in
a scarlet coat and laced cocked-hat. For one, I should like
to have seen and heard with my own eyes and ears. Certainly, by all accounts, if any one was ever moved by the
true histrionic *æstus,* it was Garrick. When he followed
the Ghost in Hamlet, he did not drop the sword as most
actors do behind the scenes, but kept the point raised the
whole way round, so fully was he possessed with the idea,
or so anxious not to lose sight of his part for a moment.
Once at a splendid dinner-party at Lord ——'s, they suddenly missed Garrick, and could not imagine what was
become of him, till they were drawn to the window by the
convulsive screams and peals of laughter of a young negro-
boy, who was rolling on the ground in an ecstasy of delight
to see Garrick mimicking a turkey-cock in the court-yard,
with his coat-tail stuck out behind, and in a seeming flutter

of feathered rage and pride. Of our party only two persons present had seen the British Roscius; and they seemed as willing as the rest to renew their acquaintance with their old favourite.

We were interrupted in the hey-day and mid-career of this fanciful speculation, by a grumbler in a corner, who declared it was a shame to make all this rout about a mere player and farce-writer, to the neglect and exclusion of the fine old dramatists, the contemporaries and rivals of Shakspeare. B—— said he had anticipated this objection when he had named the author of Mustapha and Alaham; and out of caprice insisted upon keeping him to represent the set, in preference to the wild hair-brained enthusiast Kit Marlowe; to the sexton of St. Ann's, Webster, with his melancholy yew-trees and death's-heads; to Deckar, who was but a garrulous proser; to the voluminous Heywood; and even to Beaumont and Fletcher, whom we might offend by complimenting the wrong author on their joint productions. Lord Brook, on the contrary, stood quite by himself, or in Cowley's words, was "a vast species alone." Some one hinted at the circumstance of his being a lord, which rather startled B——, but he said a *ghost* would perhaps dispense with strict etiquette, on being regularly addressed by his title. Ben Jonson divided our suffrages pretty equally. Some were afraid he would begin to traduce Shakspeare, who was not present to defend himself. "If he grows disagreeable," it was whispered aloud, "there is G—— can match him." At length his romantic visit to Drummond of Hawthornden was mentioned, and turned the scale in his favour.

B—— inquired if there was any one that was hanged that I would choose to mention? And I answered, Eugene Aram.* The name of the "Admirable Crichton" was sud-

* See Newgate Calendar for 1758.

denly started as a splendid example of *waste* talents, so different from the generality of his countrymen. This choice was mightily approved by a North-Briton present, who declared himself descended from that prodigy of learning and accomplishment, and said he had family-plate in his possession as vouchers for the fact, with the initials A. C.— *Admirable Crichton!* H—— laughed or rather roared as heartily at this as I should think he has done for many years.

The last-named Mitre-courtier * then wished to know whether there were any metaphysicians to whom one might be tempted to apply the wizard spell? I replied, there were only six in modern times deserving the name—Hobbes, Berkeley, Butler, Hartley, Hume, Leibnitz; and perhaps Jonathan Edwards, a Massachusetts man.† As to the French, who talked fluently of having *created* this science, there was not a tittle in any of their writings, that was not to be found literally in the authors I had mentioned. [Horne Tooke, who might have a claim to come in under the head of Grammar, was still living.] None of these names seemed to excite much interest, and I did not plead for the re-appearance of those who might be thought best fitted by the abstracted nature of their studies for their present spiritual and disembodied state, and who, even while

* B—— at this time occupied chambers in Mitre-court, Fleet-street.

† Lord Bacon is not included in this list, nor do I know where he should come in. It is not easy to make room for him and his reputation together. This great and celebrated man in some of his works recommends it to pour a bottle of claret into the ground of a morning, and to stand over it, inhaling the perfumes. So he sometimes enriched the dry and barren soil of speculation with the fine aromatic spirit of his genius. His "Essays" and his "Advancement of Learning" are works of vast depth and scope of observation. The last, though it contains no positive discoveries, is a noble chart of the human intellect, and a guide to all future inquirers.

on this living stage, were nearly divested of common flesh and blood. As A—— with an uneasy fidgetty face was about to put some question about Mr. Locke and Dugald Stewart, he was prevented by M. C., who observed, " If J—— was here, he would undoubtedly be for having up those profound and redoubted scholiasts, Thomas Aquinas and Duns Scotus." I said; this might be fair enough in him who had read or fancied he had read the original works, but I did not see how we could have any right to call up these authors to give an account of themselves in person, till we had looked into their writings.

By this time it should seem that some rumour of our whimsical deliberation had got wind, and had disturbed the *irritable genus* in their shadowy abodes, for we received messages from several candidates that we had just been thinking of. Gray declined our invitation, though he had not yet been asked: Gay offered to come and bring in his hand the Duchess of Bolton, the original Polly: Steele and Addison left their cards as Captain Sentry and Sir Roger de Coverley: Swift came in and sat down without speaking a word, and quitted the room as abruptly: Otway and Chatterton were seen lingering on the opposite side of the Styx, but could not muster enough between them to pay Charon his fare: Thomson fell asleep in the boat, and was rowed back again—and Burns sent a low fellow, one John Barleycorn, an old companion of his who had conducted him to the other world, to say that he had during his lifetime been drawn out of his retirement as a show, only to be made an exciseman of, and that he would rather remain where he was. He desired, however, to shake hands by his representative—the hand, thus held out, was in a burning fever, and shook prodigiously.

The room was hung round with several portraits of

eminent painters. While we were debating whether we
should demand speech with these masters of mute eloquence,
whose features were so familiar to us, it seemed that all
at once they glided from their frames, and seated themselves at some little distance from us. There was Leonardo
with his majestic beard and watchful eye, having a bust
of Archimedes before him; next him was Raphael's graceful head turned round to the Fornarina; and on his other
side was Lucretia Borgia, with calm, golden locks; Michael
Angelo had placed the model of St. Peter's on the table
before him; Correggio had an angel at his side; Titian
was seated with his Mistress between himself and Giorgioni;
Guido was accompanied by his own Aurora, who took a
dice-box from him; Claude held a mirror in his hand;
Rubens patted a beautiful panther (led in by a satyr) on
the head; Vandyke appeared as his own Paris, and Rembrandt was hid under furs, gold chains and jewels, which
Sir Joshua eyed closely, holding his hand so as to shade his
forehead. Not a word was spoken; and as we rose to do
them homage, they still presented the same surface to the
view. Not being *bonâ-fide* representations of living people,
we got rid of the splendid apparitions by signs and dumb
show. As soon as they had melted into thin air, there
was a loud noise at the outer door, and we found it was
Giotto, Cimabue, and Ghirlandaio, who had been raised
from the dead by their earnest desire to see their illustrious
successors—

> "Whose names on earth
> In Fame's eternal records live for aye!"

Finding them gone, they had no ambition to be seen after
them, and mournfully withdrew. "Egad!" said B——,
" those are the very fellows I should like to have had some

talk with, to know how they could see to paint when all was
dark around them?"

"But shall we have nothing to say," interrogated G.
J——, "to the Legend of Good Women?"—"Name,
name, Mr. J——," cried H—— in a boisterous tone of
friendly exultation, "name as many as you please, without
reserve or fear of molestation!" J—— was perplexed between so many amiable recollections, that the name of the
lady of his choice expired in a pensive whiff of his pipe;
and B—— impatiently declared for the Duchess of Newcastle. Mrs. Hutchinson was no sooner mentioned, than
she carried the day from the Duchess. We were the less
solicitous on this subject of filling up the posthumous lists
of Good Women, as there was already one in the room as
good, as sensible, and in all respects as exemplary, as the
best of them could be for their lives! "I should like vastly
to have seen Ninon de l'Enclos," said that incomparable
person; and this immediately put us in mind that we had
neglected to pay honour due to our friends on the other
side of the Channel: Voltaire, the patriarch of levity, and
Rousseau, the father of sentiment, Montaigne and Rabelais
(great in wisdom and in wit), Molière and that illustrious
group that are collected round him (in the print of that
subject) to hear him read his comedy of the Tartuffe at
the house of Ninon; Racine, La Fontaine, Rochefoucault,
St. Evremont, etc.

"There is one person," said a shrill, querulous voice, "I
would rather see than all these—Don Quixote!"

"Come, come!" said H——; "I thought we should have
no heroes, real or fabulous. What say you, Mr. B——?
Are you for eking out your shadowy list with such names
as Alexander, Julius Cæsar, Tamerlane, or Ghengis Khan?"

—"Excuse me," said B——, "on the subject of characters
in active life, plotters and disturbers of the world, I have

a crotchet of my own, which I beg leave to reserve."—
" No, no! come, out with your worthies!"—" What do you
think of Guy Faux and Judas Iscariot?" H—— turned
an eye upon him like a wild Indian, but cordial and full of
smothered glee. "Your most exquisite reason!" was
echoed on all sides; and A—— thought that B—— had now
fairly entangled himself. "Why, I cannot but think," retorted he of the wistful countenance, "that Guy Faux,
that poor fluttering annual scare-crow of straw and rags, is
an ill-used gentleman. I would give something to see him
sitting pale and emaciated, surrounded by his matches and
his barrels of gunpowder, and expecting the moment that
was to transport him to Paradise for his heroic self-devo-
tion; but if I say any more, there is that fellow G—— will
make something of it.—And as to Judas Iscariot, my reason
is different. I would fain see the face of him, who, having
dipped his hand in the same dish with the Son of Man,
could afterwards betray him. I have no conception of such
a thing; nor have I ever seen any picture (not even
Leonardo's very fine one) that gave me the least idea of
it."—" You have said enough, Mr. B——, to justify your
choice."

"Oh! ever right, Menenius,—ever right!"

" There is only one other person I can ever think of after
this," continued H——; but without mentioning a name
that once put on a semblance of mortality. "If Shakspeare
was to come into the room, we should all rise up to meet
him; but if that person was to come into it, we should all
fall down and try to kiss the hem of his garment!"

As a lady present seemed now to get uneasy at the turn
the conversation had taken, we rose up to go. The morning
broke with that dim, dubious light by which Giotto, Cimabue, and Ghirlandaio must have seen to paint their earliest
works; and we parted to meet again and renew similar

topics at night, the next night, and the night after that, till that night overspread Europe which saw no dawn. The same event, in truth, broke up our little Congress that broke up the great one. But that was to meet again: our deliberations have never been resumed.

# XX

## ON READING OLD BOOKS

I HATE to read new books. There are twenty or thirty
volumes that I have read over and over again, and these
are the only ones that I have any desire ever to read at
all. It was a long time before I could bring myself to sit
down to the Tales of My Landlord, but now that author's
works have made a considerable addition to my scanty
library. I am told that some of Lady Morgan's are good,
and have been recommended to look into Anastasius; but I
have not yet ventured upon that task. A lady, the other
day, could not refrain from expressing her surprise to a
friend, who said he had been reading Delphine:—she
asked,—If it had not been published some time back?
Women judge of books as they do of fashions or complexions, which are admired only " in their newest gloss."
That is not my way. I am not one of those who trouble
the circulating libraries much, or pester the booksellers for
mail-coach copies of standard periodical publications. I
cannot say that I am greatly addicted to black-letter, but
I profess myself well versed in the marble bindings of
Andrew Millar, in the middle of the last century; nor does
my taste revolt at Thurloe's State Papers, in Russia leather;
or an ample impression of Sir William Temple's Essays,
with a portrait after Sir Godfrey Kneller in front. I do
not think altogether the worse of a book for having survived the author a generation or two. I have more confidence in the dead than the living. Contemporary writers

may generally be divided into two classes—one's friends or one's foes. Of the first we are compelled to think too well, and of the last we are disposed to think too ill, to receive much genuine pleasure from the perusal, or to judge fairly of the merits of either. One candidate for literary fame, who happens to be of our acquaintance, writes finely, and like a man of genius; but unfortunately has a foolish face, which spoils a delicate passage:—another inspires us with the highest respect for his personal talents and character, but does not quite come up to our expectations in print. All these contradictions and petty details interrupt the calm current of our reflections. If you want to know what any of the authors were who lived before our time, and are still objects of anxious inquiry, you have only to look into their works. But the dust and smoke and noise of modern literature have nothing in common with the pure, silent air of immortality.

When I take up a work that I have read before (the oftener the better) I know what I have to expect. The satisfaction is not lessened by being anticipated. When the entertainment is altogether new, I sit down to it as I should to a strange dish,—turn and pick out a bit here and there, and am in doubt what to think of the composition. There is a want of confidence and security to second appetite. New-fangled books are also like made-dishes in this respect, that they are generally little else than hashes and *rifaccimentos* of what has been served up entire and in a more natural state at other times. Besides, in thus turning to a well-known author, there is not only an assurance that my time will not be thrown away, or my palate nauseated with the most insipid or vilest trash,—but I shake hands with, and look an old, tried, and valued friend in the face,—compare notes, and chat the hours away. It is true, we form dear friendships with such ideal guests—dearer,

alas! and more lasting, than those with our most intimate
acquaintance. In reading a book which is an old favourite
with me (say the first novel I ever read) I not only have
the pleasure of imagination and of a critical relish of the
work, but the pleasures of memory added to it. It recalls
the same feelings and associations which I had in first
reading it, and which I can never have again in any other
way. Standard productions of this kind are links in the
chain of our conscious being. They bind together the different scattered divisions of our personal identity. They
are land-marks and guides in our journey through life.
They are pegs and loops on which we can hang up, or
from which we can take down, at pleasure, the wardrobe of
a moral imagination, the relics of our best affections, the
tokens and records of our happiest hours. They are " for
thoughts and for remembrance!" They are like Fortunatus's Wishing-Cap—they give us the best riches—those
of Fancy; and transport us, not over half the globe, but
(which is better) over half our lives, at a word's notice!

My father Shandy solaced himself with Bruscambille.
Give me for this purpose a volume of Peregrine Pickle or
Tom Jones. Open either of them anywhere—at the Memoirs of Lady Vane, or the adventures at the masquerade
with Lady Bellaston, or the disputes between Thwackum
and Square, or the escape of Molly Seagrim, or the incident.
of Sophia and her muff, or the edifying prolixity of her
aunt's lecture—and there I find the same delightful, busy,
bustling scene as ever, and feel myself the same as when I
was first introduced into the midst of it. Nay, sometimes
the sight of an odd volume of these good old English
authors on a stall, or the name lettered on the back among
others on the shelves of a library, answers the purpose,
revives the whole train of ideas, and sets " the puppets
dallying." Twenty years are struck off the list, and I am

a child again.   A sage philosopher, who was not a very
wise man, said, that he should like very well to be young
again, if he could take his experience along with him.
This ingenious person did not seem to be aware, by the
gravity of his remark, that the great advantage of being
young is to be without this weight of experience, which he
would fain place upon the shoulders of youth, and which
never comes too late with years.   Oh! what a privilege to
be able to let this hump, like Christian's burthen, drop
from off one's back, and transport one's-self, by the help
of a little musty duodecimo, to the time when "ignorance
was bliss," and when we first got a peep at the rarée-show
of the world, through the glass of fiction—gazing at mankind, as we do at wild beasts in a menagerie, through the
bars of their cages,—or at curiosities in a museum, that
we must not touch!   For myself, not only are the old ideas
of the contents of the work brought back to my mind in
all their vividness, but the old associations of the faces and
persons of those I then knew, as they were in their lifetime—the place where I sat to read the volume, the day
when I got it, the feeling of the air, the fields, the sky—
return, and all my early impressions with them.   This is
better to me—those places, those times, those persons, and
those feelings that come across me as I retrace the story
and devour the page, are to me better far than the wet
sheets of the last new novel from the Ballantyne press, to
say nothing of the Minerva press in Leadenhall-street.   It
is like visiting the scenes of early youth.   I think of the
time "when I was in my father's house, and my path ran
down with butter and honey,"—when I was a little, thoughtless child, and had no other wish or care but to con my
daily task, and be happy!—Tom Jones, I remember, was
the first work that broke the spell.   It came down in numbers once a fortnight, in Cooke's pocket-edition, embel-

lished with cuts. I had hitherto read only in school-books, and a tiresome ecclesiastical history (with the exception of Mrs. Radcliffe's Romance of the Forest) : but this had a different relish with it,—" sweet in the mouth," though not " bitter in the belly." It smacked of the world I lived in, and in which I was to live—and shewed me groups, " gay creatures " not " of the element," but of the earth; not " living in the clouds," but travelling the same road that I did;—some that had passed on before me, and others that might soon overtake me. My heart had palpitated at the thoughts of a boarding-school ball, or gala-day at Midsummer or Christmas: but the world I had found out in Cooke's edition of the British Novelists was to me a dance through life, a perpetual gala-day. The six-penny numbers of this work regularly contrived to leave off just in the middle of a sentence, and in the nick of a story, where Tom Jones discovers Square behind the blanket; or where Parson Adams, in the inextricable confusion of events, very undesignedly gets to bed to Mrs. Slip-slop. Let me caution the reader against this impression of Joseph Andrews; for there is a picture of Fanny in it which he should not set his heart on, lest he should never meet with anything like it; or if he should, it would, perhaps, be better for him that he had not. It was just like —— ——! With what eagerness I used to look forward to the next number, and open the prints! Ah! never again shall I feel the enthusiastic delight with which I gazed at the figures, and anticipated the story and adventures of Major Bath and Commodore Trunnion, of Trim and my Uncle Toby, of Don Quixote and Sancho and Dapple, of Gil Blas and Dame Lorenza Sephora, of Laura and the fair Lucretia, whose lips open and shut like buds of roses. To what nameless ideas did they give rise,—with what airy delights I filled up the outlines, as I hung in silence over the page!—Let me still

recal them, that they may breathe fresh life into me, and
that I may live that birthday of thought and romantic
pleasure over again! Talk of the *ideal!* This is the only
true ideal—the heavenly tints of Fancy reflected in the
bubbles that float upon the spring-tide of human life.

> Oh! Memory! shield me from the world's poor strife,
> And give those scenes thine everlasting life!

The paradox with which I set out is, I hope, less startling
than it was; the reader will, by this time, have been let
into my secret.   Much about the same time, or I believe
rather earlier, I took a particular satisfaction in reading
Chubb's Tracts, and I often think I will get them again
to wade through.   There is a high gusto of polemical
divinity in them; and you fancy that you hear a club of
shoemakers at Salisbury, debating a disputable text from
one of St. Paul's Epistles in a workmanlike style, with equal
shrewdness and pertinacity.   I cannot say much for my
metaphysical studies, into which I launched shortly after
with great ardour, so as to make a toil of a pleasure.   I
was presently entangled in the briars and thorns of subtle
distinctions,—of " fate, free-will, fore-knowledge absolute,"
though I cannot add that " in their wandering mazes I
found no end; " for I did arrive at some very satisfactory
and potent conclusions; nor will I go so far, however ungrateful the subject might seem, as to exclaim with Marlowe's Faustus—" Would I 'had never seen Wittenberg,
never read book "—that is, never studied such authors as
Hartley, Hume, Berkeley, etc.   Locke's Essay on the
Human Understanding is, however, a work from which I
never derived either pleasure or profit; and Hobbes, dry
and powerful as he is, I did not read till long afterwards.
I read a few poets, which did not much hit my taste,—for
I would have the reader understand, I am deficient in the

faculty of imagination; but I fell early upon French romances and philosophy, and devoured them tooth-and-nail.
Many a dainty repast have I made of the New Eloise;—
the description of the kiss; the excursion on the water;
the letter of St. Preux, recalling the time of their first
loves; and the account of Julia's death; these I read over
and over again with unspeakable delight and wonder. Some
years after, when I met with this work again, I found I
had lost nearly my whole relish for it (except some few
parts) and was, I remember, very much mortified with the
change in my taste, which I sought to attribute to the small-
ness and gilt edges of the edition I had bought, and its
being perfumed with rose-leaves. Nothing could exceed
the gravity, the solemnity with which I carried home and
read the Dedication to the Social Contract, with some other
pieces of the same author, which I had picked up at a stall
in a coarse leathern cover. Of the Confessions I have
spoken elsewhere, and may repeat what I have said—
" Sweet is the dew of their memory, and pleasant the balm
of their recollection! " Their beauties are not " scattered
like stray-gifts o'er the earth," but sown thick on the page,
rich and rare. I wish I had never read the Emilius, or
read it with less implicit faith. I had no occasion to pamper
my natural aversion to affectation or pretence, by romantic
and artificial means. I had better have formed myself on
the model of Sir Fopling Flutter. There is a class of
persons whose virtues and most shining qualities sink in,
and are concealed by, an absorbent ground of modesty and
reserve; and such a one I do, without vanity, profess
myself.* Now these are the very persons who are likely

* Nearly the same sentiment was wittily and happily expressed by
a friend, who had some lottery puffs, which he had been employed
to write, returned on his hands for their too great severity of
thought and classical terseness of style, and who observed on that
occasion, that " Modest merit never can succeed! "

to attach themselves to the character of Emilius, and of whom it is sure to be the bane. This dull, phlegmatic, retiring humour is not in a fair way to be corrected, but confirmed and rendered desperate, by being in that work held up as an object of imitation, as an example of simplicity and magnanimity—by coming upon us with all the recommendations of novelty, surprise, and superiority to the prejudices of the world—by being stuck upon a pedestal, made amiable, dazzling, a *leurre de dupe!* The reliance on solid worth which' it inculcates, the preference of sober truth to gaudy tinsel, hangs like a mill-stone round the neck of the imagination—" a load to sink a navy "—impedes our progress, and blocks up every prospect in life. A man, to get on, to be successful, conspicuous, applauded, should not retire upon the centre of his conscious resources, but be always at the circumference of appearances. He must envelop himself in a halo of mystery—he must ride in an equipage of opinion—he must walk with a train of self-conceit following him—he must not strip himself to a buff-jerkin, to the doublet and hose of his real merits, but must surround himself with a *cortege* of prejudices, like the signs of the Zodiac—he must seem any thing but what he is, and then he may pass for any thing he pleases. The world love to be amused by hollow professions, to be deceived by flattering appearances, to live in a state of hallucination; and can forgive every thing but the plain, downright, simple honest truth—such as we see it chalked out in the character of Emilius.—To return from this digression, which is a little out of place here.

Books have in a great measure lost their power over me; nor can I revive the same interest in them as formerly. I perceive when a thing is good, rather than feel it. It is true,

Marcian Colonna is a dainty book;

and the reading of Mr. Keats's Eve of St. Agnes lately made me regret that I was not young again. The beautiful and tender images there conjured up, " come like shadows —so depart." The " tiger-moth's wings," which he has spread over his rich poetic blazonry, just flit across my fancy; the gorgeous twilight window which he has painted over again in his verse, to me " blushes " almost in vain " with blood of queens and kings." I know how I should have felt at one time in reading such passages; and that is all. The sharp luscious flavour, the fine *àroma* is fled, and nothing but the stalk, the bran, the husk of literature is left. If any one were to ask me what I read now, I might answer with my Lord Hamlet in the play—" Words, words, words."—" What is the matter?"—" *Nothing!* "— They have scarce a meaning. But it was not always so. There was a time when to my thinking, every word was a flower or a pearl, like those which dropped from the mouth of the little peasant-girl in the Fairy tale, or like those that fall from the 'great preacher in the Caledonian Chapel! I drank of the stream of knowledge that tempted, but did not mock my lips, as of the river of life, freely. How eagerly I slaked my thirst of German sentiment, " as the hart that panteth for the water-springs; " how I bathed and revelled, and added my floods of tears to Goëthe's Sorrows of Werter, and to Schiller's Robbers—

Giving my stock of more to that which had too much!

I read and assented with all my soul to Coleridge's fine Sonnet, begininng—

Schiller! that hour I would have wish'd to die,
If through the shuddering midnight I had sent,
From the dark dungeon of the tow'r time-rent,
That fearful voice, a famish'd father's cry!

I believe I may date my insight into the mysteries of poetry from the commencement of my acquaintance with the authors of the Lyrical Ballads; at least, my discrimination of the higher sorts—not my predilection for such writers as Goldsmith or Pope: nor do I imagine they will say I got my liking for the Novelists, or the comic writers, —for the characters of Valentine, Tattle, or Miss Prue, from them. If so, I must have got from them what they never had themselves. In points where poetic diction and conception are concerned, I may be at a loss, and liable to be imposed upon: but in forming an estimate of passages relating to common life and manners, I cannot think I am a plagiarist from any man. I there "know my cue without a prompter." I may say of such studies—*Intus et in cute*. I am just able to admire those literal touches of observation and description, which persons of loftier pretensions overlook and despise. I think I comprehend something of the characteristic part of Shakspeare; and in him indeed all is characteristic, even the nonsense and poetry. I believe it was the celebrated Sir Humphry Davy who used to say, that Shakspeare was rather a metaphysician than a poet. At any rate, it was not ill said. I wish that I had sooner known the dramatic writers contemporary with Shakspeare; for in looking them over about a year ago, I almost revived my old passion for reading, and my old delight in books, though they were very nearly new to me. The Periodical Essayists I read long ago. The Spectator I liked extremely: but the Tatler took my fancy most. I read the others soon after, the Rambler, the Adventurer, the World, the Connoisseur: I was not sorry to get to the end of them, and have no desire to go regularly through them again. I consider myself a thorough adept in Richardson. I like the longest of his novels best, and think no part of them tedious; nor should I ask to have any thing better to

do than to read them from beginning to end, to take them
up when I chose, and lay them down when I was tired,
in some old family mansion in the country, till every word
and syllable relating to the bright Clarissa, the divine
Clementina, the beautiful Pamela, " with every trick and
line of their sweet favour," were once more " graven in my
heart's table." [1]  I have a sneaking kindness for Mackenzie's Julia de Roubignè—for the deserted mansion, and
straggling gilliflowers on the mouldering garden-wall; and
still more for his Man of Feeling; not that it is better, nor
so good; but at the time I read it, I sometimes thought of
the heroine, Miss Walton, and of Miss —— together, and
" that ligament, fine as it was, was never broken! "—One
of the poets that I have always read with most pleasure,
and can wander about in for ever with a sort of voluptuous
indolence, is Spenser; and I like Chaucer even better.   The
only writer among the Italians I can pretend to any knowledge of, is Boccacio, and of him I cannot express half my
admiration.   His story of the Hawk I could read and think
of from day to day, just as I would look at a picture of
Titian's!—

I remember, as long ago as the year 1798, going to a
neighbouring town (Shrewsbury, where Farquhar has laid
the plot of his Recruiting Officer) and bringing home with
me, " at one proud swoop," a copy of Milton's Paradise
Lost, and another of Burke's Reflections on the French
Revolution—both which I have still; and I still recollect,

----

[1] During the peace of Amiens, a young English officer, of the
name of Lovelace, was presented at Buonaparte's levee.   Instead of
the usual question, " Where have you served, Sir? " the First Consul
immediately addressed him, " I perceive your name, Sir, is the same
as that of the hero of Richardson's Romance! "   Here was a Consul.
The young man's uncle, who was called Lovelace, told me this
anecdote while we were stopping together at Calais.   I had also been
thinking that his was the same name as that of the hero of Richardson's Romance.   This is one of my reasons for liking Buonaparte.

when I see the covers, the pleasure with which I dipped into
them as I returned with my double prize. I was set up
for one while. That time is past "with all its giddy raptures:" but I am still anxious to preserve its memory,
"embalmed with odours."—With respect to the first of
these works, I would be permitted to remark here in passing, that it is a sufficient answer to the German criticism
which has since been started against the character of Satan
(*viz.* that it is not one of disgusting deformity, or pure,
defecated malice) to say that Milton has there drawn, not
the abstract principle of evil, not a devil incarnate, but a
fallen angel. This is the Scriptural account, and the poet
has followed it. We may safely retain such passages as
that well-known one—

> ——His form had not yet lost
> All her original brightness; nor appear'd
> Less than archangel ruin'd; and the excess
> Of glory obscur'd—

for the theory, which is opposed to them, " falls flat upon
the grunsel edge, and shames its worshippers." Let us
hear no more then of this monkish cant, and bigotted outcry
for the restoration of the horns and tail of the devil!—
Again, as to the other work, Burke's Reflections, I took
a particular pride and pleasure in it, and read it to myself
and others for months afterwards. I had reason for my
prejudice in favour of this author. To understand an
adversary is some praise: to admire him is more. I thought
I did both: I knew I did one. From the first time I ever
cast my eyes on anything of Burke's (which was an extract from his Letter to a Noble Lord in a three-times a
week paper, The St. James's Chronicle, in 1796), I said to
myself, " This is true eloquence: this is a man pouring out
his mind on paper." All other style seemed to me pedantic

and impertinent. Dr. Johnson's was walking on stilts; and
even Junius's (who was at that time a favourite with me)
with all his terseness, shrunk up into little antithetic points
and well-trimmed sentences. But Burke's style was forked
and playful as the lightning, crested like the serpent. He
delivered plain things on a plain ground; but when he rose,
there was no end of his flights and circumgyrations—and
in this very Letter, " he, like an eagle in a dove-cot, fluttered *his* Volscians," (the Duke of Bedford and the Earl
of Lauderdale*) " in Corioli." I did not care for his doctrines. I was then, and am still, proof against their con-
tagion; but I admired the author, and was considered as
not a very staunch partisan of the opposite side, though I
thought myself that an abstract proposition was one thing—
a masterly transition, a brilliant metaphor, another. I conceived, too, that he might be wrong in his main argument,
and yet deliver fifty truths in arriving at a false conclusion.
I remember Coleridge assuring me, as a poetical and political set-off to my sceptical admiration, that Wordsworth
had written an Essay on Marriage, which, for manly
thought and nervous expression, he deemed incomparably
superior. As I had not, at that time, seen any specimens
of Mr. Wordsworth's prose style, I could not express my
doubts on the subject. If there are greater prose-writers
than Burke, they either lie out of my course of study, or
are beyond my sphere of comprehension. I am too old to
be a convert to a new mythology of genius. The niches
are occupied, the tables are full. If such is still my admiration of this man's misapplied powers, what must it have
been at a time when I myself was in vain trying, year after
year, to write a single Essay, nay, a single page or sentence; when I regarded the wonders of his pen with the
longing eyes of one who was dumb and a changeling; and

* He is there called " Citizen Lauderdale." Is this the present earl?

when, to be able to convey the slightest conception of my meaning to others in words, was the height of an almost hopeless ambition! But I never measured others' excellences by my own defects: though a sense of my own incapacity, and of the steep, impassable ascent from me to them, made me regard them with greater awe and fondness. I have thus run through most of my early studies and favourite authors, some of whom I have since criticised more at large. Whether those observations will survive me, I neither know nor do I much care: but to the works themselves, "worthy of all acceptation," and to the feelings they have always excited in me since I could distinguish a meaning in language, nothing shall ever prevent me from looking back with gratitude and triumph. To have lived in the cultivation of an intimacy with such works, and to have familiarly relished such names, is not to have lived quite in vain.

There are other authors whom I have never read, and yet whom I have frequently had a great desire to read, from some circumstance relating to them. Among these is Lord Clarendon's History of the Grand Rebellion, after which I have a hankering, from hearing it spoken of by good judges—from my interest in the events, and knowledge of the characters from other sources, and from having seen fine portraits of most of them. I like to read a well-penned character, and Clarendon is said to have been a master in this way. I should like to read Froissart's Chronicles, Hollinshed and Stowe, and Fuller's Worthies. I intend, whenever I can, to read Beaumont and Fletcher all through. There are fifty-two of their plays, and I have only read a dozen or fourteen of them. A Wife for a Month, and Thierry and Theodoret, are, I am told, delicious, and I can believe it. I should like to read the speeches in Thucydides, and Guicciardini's History of

Florence, and Don Quixote in the original. I have often thought of reading the Loves of Persiles and Sigismunda, and the Galatea of the same author. But I somehow reserve them like "another Yarrow." I should also like to read the last new novel (if I could be sure it was so) of the author of Waverley:—no one would be more glad than I to find it the best!—

# NOTES

[The annotations have not necessarily been introduced at the first occurrence of any name, and no cross-references have been supplied in the notes to names which occur in the text more than once. Such information as the notes supply can be found with the help of the index.—References, where no other indication is given, will be understood to be to the work under discussion. The Shakespeare references are to the one-volume Globe edition.]

## THE AGE OF ELIZABETH

This lecture forms the introduction to the series on the "Literature of the Age of Elizabeth." Hazlitt might have derived hints for it from Schlegel, who speaks of the zeal for the study of the ancients, the extensive communication with other lands, the interest in the literature of Italy and Spain, the progress in experimental philosophy represented by Bacon, and contrasts the achievements of that age, in a vein which must have captured Hazlitt's sympathy, with "the pretensions of modern enlightenment, as it is called, which looks with such contempt on all preceding ages." The Elizabethans, he goes on to say, "possessed a fullness of healthy vigour, which showed itself always with boldness, and sometimes also with petulance. The spirit of chivalry was not yet wholly extinct, and a queen, who was far more jealous in exacting homage to her sex than to her throne, and who, with her determination, wisdom, and magnanimity, was in fact, well qualified to inspire the minds of her subjects with an ardent enthusiasm, inflamed that spirit to the noblest love of glory and renown. The feudal independence also still survived in some measure; the nobility vied with each other in the splendour of dress and number of retinue, and every great lord had a sort of small court of his own. The distinction of ranks was as yet strongly marked: a state of things ardently to be desired by the dramatic poet." "Lectures on Dramatic Literature," ed. Bohn, p. 349.

P. 1. *Raleigh,* Sir Walter (1552-1618), the celebrated courtier, explorer, and man of letters.

*Drake,* Sir Francis (1545-1595), the famous sailor, hero of the Armada.

*Coke,* Sir Edward (1552-1634), the great jurist, whose "Institutes," better known as Coke upon Littleton, became a famous legal text-book.

*Hooker,* Richard (1553-1600), theologian, author of the "Laws of Ecclesiastical Polity" (1593), a defense of the Anglican Church against the Puritans and notable also as a masterpiece of English prose.

P. 2. *mere oblivion.* "As You Like It," ii, 7, 165.

*poor, poor dumb names* [mouths]. "Julius Cæsar," iii, 2, 229.

*Marston,* John (1575-1634). In the third lecture on the "Age of Elizabeth," Hazlitt calls him "a writer of great merit, who rose to tragedy from the ground of comedy, and whose *forte* was not sympathy, either with the stronger or softer emotions, but an impatient scorn and bitter indignation against the vices and follies of men, which vented itself either in comic irony or in lofty invective. He was properly a satirist. He was not a favourite with his contemporaries, nor they with him." Works, V, 224. His chief tragedy is "Antonio and Mellida."

*Middleton,* Thomas (1570?-1627), and *Rowley,* William (1585?-1642?). In the second lecture on the "Age of Elizabeth," Hazlitt associates these two names. "Rowley appears to have excelled in describing a certain amiable quietness of disposition and disinterested tone of morality, carried almost to a paradoxical excess, as in his Fair Quarrel, and in the comedy of A Woman Never Vexed, which is written, in many parts, with a pleasing simplicity and *naïveté* equal to the novelty of the conception. Middleton's style was not marked by any peculiar quality of his own, but was made up, in equal proportions, of the faults and excellences common to his contemporaries. . . . He is lamentably deficient in the plot and denouement of the story. It is like the rough draft of a tragedy with a number of fine things thrown in, and the best made use of first; but it tends to no fixed goal, and the interest decreases, instead of increasing, as we read on, for want of previous arrangement and an eye to the whole. . . . The author's power is *in* the subject, not *over* it; or he is in possession of excellent materials which he husbands very ill." Works, V, 214-5. For characters of other dramatists see notes to p. 326.

*How lov'd.* Pope's "Elegy to the Memory of an Unfortunate
Lady."

P. 3. *draw the curtain of time.* Cf. "we will draw the curtain
and show you the picture." "Twelfth Night," i, 5, 251.

*within reasonable bounds.* At this point Hazlitt digresses to re-
prove the age for its affectation of superiority over other ages and
the passage, not being relevant, has been omitted.

*less than smallest dwarfs.* "Paradise Lost," I, 779.

*desiring this man's art.* Shakespeare's Sonnets, XXIX.

*in shape and gesture.* "Paradise Lost," I, 590.

*Mr. Wordsworth says.* See Sonnet entitled "London, 1802."

P. 4. *drew after him.* "Paradise Lost," II, 692.

*Otway,* Thomas (1652-1685), author of "Venice Preserved," the
most popular post-Shakespearian tragedy of the English stage. Hazlitt notes in this play a "power of rivetting breathless attention, and
stirring the deepest yearnings of affection. . . . The awful suspense of the situations, the conflict of duties and passions, the intimate bonds that unite the characters together, and that are violently
rent asunder like the parting of soul and body, the solemn march
of the tragical events to the fatal catastrophe that winds up and
closes over all, give to this production of Otway's Muse a charm
and power that bind it like a spell on the public mind, and have made
it a proud and inseparable adjunct of the English stage." Works, V,
354-5.

*Jonson's learned sock.* Milton's "L'Allegro."

P. 6. *The translation of the Bible.* The first important 16th century translation of the Bible is William Tyndale's version of the
New Testament (1525) and of the Pentateuch (1530). The complete
translations are those of Miles Coverdale (1535), the Great Bible
(1539), the Geneva or Breeches Bible (1557), the Bishop's Bible
(1568), and the Rheims-Douay Bible—the New Testament (1582)
and the Old Testament (1609-1610). Finally came the Authorized
Version in 1611.

P. 8. *penetrable stuff.* "Hamlet," iii, 4, 36.

*his washing,* etc. St. John, xiii.

*above all art,* etc. Cf. Pope's "Epistle to the Earl of Oxford":
"Above all Pain, all Passion, and all Pride."

*My peace.* St. John, xiv, 27.

*they should love.* Ibid., xv, 12.

*Woman, behold.* Ibid., xix, 26.

*his treatment of the woman.* Ibid., viii, 1-12.

*the woman who poured precious ointment.* St. Matthew, xxvi, 6-13; St. Mark, xiv, 3-9.

*his discourse with the disciples.* St. Luke, xxiv, 13-31.

*his Sermon on the Mount.* St. Matthew, v-vii.

*parable of the Good Samaritan and of the Prodigal Son.* St. Luke, x, 25-37; xv, 11-32.

P. 9. *Who is our neighbour.* Ibid., x, 29.

*to the Jews,* etc. I Corinthians, i, 23.

P. 10. *Soft as sinews.* "Hamlet," iii, 3, 71.

*The best of men.* Dekker, "The Honest Whore," Part I, v, 2, sub fin.

P. 11. *Tasso by Fairfax.* Torquato Tasso (1544-1595), an Italian poet whose great epic, the "Gerusalemme Liberata," was finished in 1574. The English translation by Edward Fairfax was published in 1600 as "Godfrey of Bulloigne, or the Recoverie of Jerusalem."

*Ariosto by Harrington.* Lodovico Ariosto (1474-1533), whose romantic epic, "Orlando Furioso," was first published in 1516, and translated by Sir John Harrington in 1591.

*Homer and Hesiod by Chapman.* George Chapman (1559?-1634), poet and dramatist, published a complete translation of the "Iliad" in 1611, of the "Odyssey" in 1614, of Homer's "Battle of Frogs and Mice" in 1624, and of "The Georgicks of Hesiod" in 1618.

*Virgil.* A complete English translation of the "Æneid" was made by Gavin Douglas, a Scottish poet (1474?-1522), and first printed in London in 1553. There was a translation of the second and fourth books into blank verse by the Earl of Surrey, published in 1557, but the one most in use was by Thomas Phaer (1510?-1560), which appeared incompletely in 1558 and 1562 and was completed by Thomas Twyne in 1583.

*Ovid.* There were a number of translators of Ovid during this period, chief of whom was Arthur Golding, whose version of the "Metamorphoses" appeared in 1565 and 1567. "The Heroides" were translated by George Turberville in 1567.

*Sir Thomas North's translation of Plutarch.* The chief work of Plutarch, a Greek writer of the first century, is the "Parallel Lives," which was translated into French by Jacques Amyot in 1559. Sir Thomas North's translation of Amyot's version in 1579 was the most popular and influential of all Elizabethan translations.

P. 12. *Boccaccio,* Giovanni (1313-1375), Italian poet and novelist. Among the English his best known work is the "Decameron," a collection of a hundred prose tales. Versions of some of these stories appeared in various Elizabethan collections, such as the "Tragical Tales" translated by George Turberville in 1587. The first complete translation was published in 1620 and reprinted in the Tudor Translations in 1909.

*Petrarch* (1304-1374), Italian humanist and poet, whose sonnets were widely imitated by French and Italian poets during the Renaissance.

*Dante* (1265-1321). The author of the "Divine Comedy" was not very well known to Elizabethan readers. There was no English translation of his poem attempted till that of Rogers in 1782, and no version worthy of the name was produced till H. F. Cary's in 1814.

*Aretine.* The name of Pietro Aretino (1492-1556), an Italian satirist who called himself "the scourge of princes," was well known in England, but there was no translation of his works.

*Machiavel.* Nicolo Machiavelli (1468-1527), a Florentine statesman, whose name had an odious association because of the supposedly diabolical policy of government set forth in his "Prince." But this work was not translated till 1640. His "Art of War" had been rendered into English in 1560 and his "Florentine History" in 1595.

*Castiglione,* Baldassare (1478-1529). "Il Cortegiano," setting forth the idea of a gentleman, was translated as "The Courtier" by Thomas Hoby in 1561 and was very influential in English life.

*Ronsard,* Pierre de (1524-1585), the chief French lyric poet of the sixteenth century, whose sonnets had considerable vogue in England.

*Du Bartas,* Guillaume de Saluste (1544-1590), author of "La Semaine, ou la Création du Monde" (1578), "La Seconde Semaine" (1584), translated as the "Divine Weeks and Works" (1592 ff.) by Joshua Sylvester.

P. 13. *Fortunate fields.* "Paradise Lost," III, 568.

*Prospero's Enchanted Island.* Eden's "History of Travayle," 1577, is now given as the probable source of Setebos, etc.

*Right well I wote.* "Faërie Queene," II, Introduction, 1-3.

P. 14. *Lear is founded.* Shakespeare's actual sources were probably Geoffrey of Monmouth's "History of the Kings of Britain" (c. 1130) and Holinshed's "Chronicle."

*Othello on an Italian novel,* from the "Hecatommithi" of Giraldi Cinthio (1565).

*Hamlet on a Danish, Macbeth on a Scottish tradition.* The story of Hamlet is first found in Saxo Grammaticus, a Danish chronicler of the tenth century. Shakespeare probably drew it from the "His-

toires Tragiques" of Belleforest. "Macbeth" was based on Holinshed's "Chronicle of Scottish History."

P. 15. *those bodiless creations.* "Hamlet," iii, 4, 138.

*Your face.* "Macbeth," i, 5, 63.

*Tyrrell and Forrest,* persons hired by Richard III to murder the
young princes in the Tower. See "Richard III," iv, 2-3.

*thick and slab.* "Macbeth," iv, 1, 32.

*snatched a* [wild and] *fearful joy.* Gray's "Ode on a Distant
Prospect of Eton College."

P. 16. *Fletcher the poet.* John Fletcher the dramatist died of the
plague in 1625.

*The course of true love.* "Midsummer Night's Dream," i, 1, 34.

*The age of chivalry was not then quite gone.* Cf. Burke: "Reflections on the French Revolution" (ed. Bohn, II, 348): "But the
age of chivalry is gone. That of sophisters, economists, and cal-
culators, has succeeded; and the glory of Europe is extinguished
forever."

*fell a martyr.* Sir Philip Sidney (1554-1586), poet, soldier, and
statesman, received his mortal wound in the thigh at the battle of
Zutphen because, in emulation of Sir William Pelham, he threw off
his greaves before entering the fight.

*the gentle Surrey.* Henry Howard, Earl of Surrey (1518?-1547),
was distinguished as an innovator in English poetry as well as for his
knightly prowess.

*who prized black eyes.* "Sessions of the Poets," verse 20.

*Like strength reposing.* "'Tis might half slumb'ring on its own
right arm." Keats's "Sleep and Poetry," 237.

P. 17. *they heard the tumult,* "I behold the tumult and am still."
Cowper's "Task," IV, 99.

*descriptions of hunting and other athletic games.* See "Midsummer Night's Dream," iv, 1, 107 ff., and "Two Noble Kinsmen," iii.

*An ingenious and agreeable writer.* Nathan Drake (1766-1836),
author of "Shakespeare and his Times" (1817). In describing the
life of the country squire Drake remarks: "The luxury of eating
and of good cooking were well understood in the days of Elizabeth,
and the table of the country-squire frequently groaned beneath the
burden of its dishes; at Christmas and at Easter especially, the hall
became the scene of great festivity." Chap. V. (ed. 1838, p. 37).

*Return from Parnassus.* Hazlitt gives an account of this play in
the "Literature of the Age of Elizabeth," Lecture V.

P. 18. *it snowed.* "Canterbury Tales," Prologue, 345.

*as Mr. Lamb observes,* in a note to Marston's "What You Will"
in the "Specimens of Dramatic Literature" (ed. Lucas, I, 44):
" The blank uniformity to which all professional distinctions in ap-
parel have been long hastening, is one instance of the decay of
Symbols among us, which, whether it has contributed or not to make
us a more intellectual, has certainly made us a less imaginative
people." Cf. Schlegel's remark in the first note.

*in act.* "Othello," i, 1, 62.

*description of a mad-house.* "Honest Whore," Part 1, v, 2.

*A Mad World, My Masters,* the title of a comedy by Middleton.

P. 19. *Music and painting are not our forte.* Cf. Hazlitt's review
of the "Life of Reynolds" (X, 186-87): "Were our ancestors insensible to the charms of nature, to the music of thought, to deeds of
virtue or heroic enterprise? No. But they saw them in their mind's
eye: they felt them at their heart's core, and there only. They did
not translate their perceptions into the language of sense: they did
not embody them in visible images, but in breathing words. They
were more taken up with what an object suggested to combine with
the infinite stores of fancy or trains of feeling, than with the single
object itself; more intent upon the moral inference, the tendency and
the result, than the appearance of things, however imposing or expressive, at any given moment of time. . . . We should say that
the eye in warmer climates drinks in greater pleasure from external
sights, is more open and porous to them, as the ear is to sounds;
that the sense of immediate delight is fixed deeper in the beauty
of the object; that the greater life and animation of character gives
a greater spirit and intensity of expression to the face, making
finer subjects for history and portrait; and that the circumstances
in which a people are placed in a genial atmosphere, are more favourable to the study of nature and of the human form."

*like birdlime.* "Othello," ii, 1, 126.

P. 20. *Materiam superabat opus.* Ovid's "Metamorphoses," II, 5.

*Pan is a God.* Lyly's "Midas," iv, 1.


## SPENSER

This is the latter half of the lecture on Chaucer and Spenser from
the "English Poets."

P. 21. *Spenser flourished,* etc. Edmund Spenser (1552?-1599),
served as secretary to Sir Henry Sidney in Ireland in 1577, and went

again in 1580 as secretary to Lord Grey of Wilton, the Queen's new deputy to Ireland. He was driven out by a revolt of the Irish in 1598. "A View of the State of Ireland, written dialogue-wise between Eudoxus and Irenæus . . . in 1596" was first printed in 1633.

*description of the bog of Allan.* "Faërie Queene," II, ix, 16.

*Treatment he received from Burleigh.* Hazlitt refers to this treatment specifically in the essay "On Respectable People" (XI, 435) : " Spenser, kept waiting for the hundred pounds which Burleigh grudged him ' for a song,' might feel the mortification of his situation ; but the statesman never felt any diminution of his sovereign's favour in consequence of it." The facts, as they are recorded in the "Dictionary of National Biography," are as follows : " The queen gave proof of her appreciation by bestowing a pension on the poet. According to an anecdote, partly reported by Manningham, the diarist (Diary, p. 43), and told at length by Fuller, Lord Burghley, in his capacity of treasurer, protested against the largeness of the sum which the queen suggested, and was directed by her to give the poet what was reasonable. He received the formal grant of £50 a year in February 1590-1." Cf. Spenser's lines in "Mother Hubbard's Tale," 895 ff.

*Though much later than Chaucer.* The rest of this paragraph and most of the points elaborated in this lecture appeared in Hazlitt's review of Sismondi's "Literature of the South" in 1815 (X, 73 ff.).

*Spenser's poetry is all fairyland.* In a lecture delivered in February, 1818, three years after Hazlitt's remarks had appeared in the Edinburgh Review, Coleridge spoke as follows : "You will take especial note of the marvellous independence and true imaginative absence of all particular space or time in the Faery Queene. It is in the domains neither of history or geography ; it is ignorant of all artificial boundary, all material obstacles ; it is truly in the land of Faery, that is, of mental space. The poet has placed you in a dream, a charmed sleep, and you neither wish, nor have the power, to inquire where you are, or how you got there." Works, IV, 250.

P. 22. *clap on high.* "Faërie Queene," III, xii, 23.

*In green vine leaves.* I, iv, 22.

*Upon the top.* I, vii, 32.

P. 23. *In reading the Faërie Queene,* etc. See III, ix, 10; I, vii; II, vi, 5; III, xii.

*and mask.* "L'Allegro."

*And more to lull.* I, i, 41.

*honey-heavy dew of slumber.* "Julius Cæsar," ii, 1, 230.

*Eftsoons they heard.* II, xii, 70.

P. 25. *House of Pride.* I, iv, 4.

*Cave of Mammon.* II, vii, 28.

*Cave of Despair.* I, ix, 33.

*the account of Memory.* II, ix, 54.

*description of Belphœbe.* II, iii, 21.

*story of Florimel.* III, vii, 12.

*Gardens of Adonis.* III, vi, 29.

*Bower of Bliss.* II, xii, 42.

*Mask of Cupid.* III, xii.

*Colin Clout's Vision.* VI, x, 10-27.

P. 26. *Poussin,* Nicolas (1594-1665), French painter. See Hazlitt's delightful essay in "Table Talk" "On a Landscape by Nicholas Poussin."

*And eke.* III, ix, 20.

*the cold icicles.* III, viii, 35.

*That was Arion.* IV, xi, 23-24.

*Procession of the Passions.* I, iv, 16 ff.

P. 28. *Yet not more sweet.* Southey's "Carmen Nuptiale: Lay of the Laureate." In the "Character of Milton's Eve" in the "Round Table," Hazlitt remarks that Spenser "has an eye to the consequences, and steeps everything in pleasure, often not of the purest kind."

P. 30. *Rubens,* Peter Paul (1577-1640), Flemish painter. See the paper on "The Pictures at Oxford and Blenheim" (Works, IX, 71): "Rubens was the only artist that could have embodied some of our countryman Spenser's splendid and voluptuous allegories. If a painter among ourselves were to attempt a Spenser Gallery, (perhaps the finest subject for the pencil in the world after Heathen mythology and Scripture history), he ought to go and study the principles of his design at Blenheim."

*the account of Satyrane.* I, vi, 24.

*by the help.* III, x, 47.

*the change of Malbecco.* III, x, 56-60.

P. 31, n. *That all with one consent.* "Troilus and Cressida," iii, 3, 176.

P. 32. *High over hills.* III, x, 55.

*Pope who used to ask.* Pope is also quoted in Spence's "Anecdotes" (Section viii, 1743-4) as saying that "there is something in Spenser that pleases one as strongly in one's old age, as it did in one's youth. I read the 'Faërie Queene,' when I was about twelve, with infinite delight, and I think it gave me as much, when I read it over about a year or two ago." Waller-Glover.

*the account of Talus.* V, i, 12.

*episode of Pastorella.* VI, ix, 12.

P. 33. *in many a winding bout.* "L'Allegro."

## SHAKSPEARE

This selection is from the "Lectures on the English Poets." At the beginning of his lecture on Shakespeare and Milton, Hazlitt maintains that the arts reach their perfection in the early periods and are not continually progressive like the sciences—an idea which he frequently comes back to in his writings, notably in the "Round Table" paper, "Why the Arts are not Progressive."

P. 34. *the fault,* etc. Cf. "Julius Cæsar," i, 2, 140.

*Shakspeare as they would be.* Hazlitt may have had in mind Dr. Johnson's comment in his preface to Shakespeare's works: "the event which he represents will not happen, but if it were possible, its effect would probably be such as he had assigned; he has not only shewn human nature as it acts in real exigencies, but as it would be found in trials to which it cannot be exposed." (Nichol Smith: "Eighteenth Century Essays on Shakespeare," p. 117.)

P. 35. *its generic quality.* Coleridge applied the epithet "myriad-minded" to Shakespeare. See also Schlegel's "Lectures on the Drama," ed. Bohn, p. 363: "Never perhaps was there so comprehensive a talent for characterization as Shakespeare. It not only grasps the diversity of rank, age, and sex, down to the lispings of infancy; not only do the king and the beggar, the hero and the pickpocket, the sage and the idiot, speak and act with equal truthfulness . . . his human characters have not only such depth and individuality that they do not admit of being classed under common names, and are inexhaustible even in conception; no, this Prometheus not merely forms men, he opens the gates of the magical world of spirits, calls up the midnight ghost, exhibits before us the witches with their unhallowed rites, peoples the air with sportive fairies and sylphs; and these beings, though existing only in the imagination, nevertheless possess such truth and consistency, that even with such misshapen abortions as Caliban, he extorts the assenting conviction, that were there such beings they would so conduct themselves. In a word, as he carries a bold and pregnant fancy into the kingdom of nature, on the other hand, he carries nature into the region of fancy, which lies beyond the confines of reality. We are lost in astonishment at the close intimacy he brings us into with the extraordinary, the wonderful, and the unheard-of."

*a mind reflecting ages past.* "These words occur in the first lines of a laudatory poem on Shakespeare printed in the second folio (1632). The poem is signed ' J. M. S.' and was attributed by Coleridge to ' John Milton, Student.' See his ' Lectures on Shakespeare ' (ed. T. Ashe), pp. 129-130." Waller-Glover, IV, 411.

P. 36. *All corners,* etc. " Cymbeline," iii, 4, 39.

*nodded to him.* " Midsummer Night's Dream," iii, 1, 177.

*his so potent art.* " Tempest," v, 1, 50.

*When he conceived of a character,* etc. Cf. Maurice Morgann, " On the Character of Falstaff ": " But it was not enough for Shakespeare to. have formed his characters with the most perfect truth and coherence; it was further necessary that he should possess a wonderful facility of compressing, as it were, his own spirit into these images, and of giving alternate animation to the forms. This was not to be done *from without;* he must have *felt* every varied situation, and have spoken thro' the organ he had formed. Such an intuitive comprehension of things and such a facility must unite to produce a Shakespeare." (Nichol Smith : " Eighteenth Century Essays on Shakespeare," p. 247, n.)

*subject to the same skyey influences.* Cf. " Measure for Measure," iii, 1, 9: " servile to all the skyey influences."

*his frequent haunts.* Cf. " Comus," 314: " my daily walks and ancient neighborhood."

P. 37. *coheres semblably together.* Cf. 2 " Henry IV," v, 1, 72: " to see the semblable coherence."

*It has been ingeniously remarked,* by Coleridge, " Seven Lectures on Shakespeare and Milton," p. 116: " The power of poetry is, by a single word perhaps, to instil that energy into the mind, which compels the imagination to produce the picture. . . . Here, by introducing a single happy epithet, ' crying,' a complete picture is presented to the mind, and in the production of such pictures the power of genius consists."

*me and thy crying self.* " Tempest," i, 2, 132.

*What! man.* " Macbeth," iv, 3, 208.

*Rosencrans.* The early editions consistently misspell this name Rosencraus.

*Man delights not me.* " Hamlet," ii, 2, 321.

*a combination and a form.* "Hamlet," iii, 4, 60.

P. 39. *There is a willow,* etc.  See "Hamlet," iv, 7, 167:

"There is a willow grows aslant a brook
That shows his hoar leaves in the glassy stream."

*Now this is an instance,* etc.  Hazlitt elsewhere ascribes this observation to Lamb.  See p. 83, n.

*He's speaking now.* "Antony and Cleopatra," i, 5, 24.

*It is my birthday.* Ibid., iii, 13, 185.

P. 41. *nigh sphered in heaven.* Collins's "Ode on the Poetical Character."

*to make society.* "Macbeth," iii, 1, 42.

P. 42. *with a little act.* "Othello," iii, 3, 328.

P. 43. *while rage.* "Troilus and Cressida," i, 3, 52.

*in their untroubled elements,* etc.  Cf. Wordsworth's "Excursion," VI, 763-766:

"That glorious star
In its untroubled element will shine
As now it shines, when we are laid in earth
And safe from all our sorrows."

*Satan's address to the sun.* "Paradise Lost," IV, 31.

*Oh that I were.* "Richard II," iv, 1, 260.

P. 44. *His form.* "Paradise Lost," I, 591-594.

P. 45. *With what measure.* Mark, iv, 24; Luke, vi, 38.

*It glances.* "Midsummer Night's Dream," v, 1, 13.

*puts a girdle.* Ibid., ii, 1, 175.

*I ask.* "Troilus and Cressida," i, 3, 227.

*No man.* Ibid., iii, 3, 15.

P. 46. *Rouse yourself.* Ibid., iii, 3, 222.

*In Shakspeare, any other word,* etc.  In the essay "On Application to Study," in the "Plain Speaker," Hazlitt gives further illustrations of this point.

P. 47. *Light thickens.* "Macbeth," iii, 2, 50.

*the business of the state.* "Othello," iv, 2, 166.

*Of ditties highly penned.* 1 "Henry IV," iii, 1, 209.

*And so.* "Two Gentlemen of Verona," ii, 7, 31.

*The universality of his genius,* etc.  Cf. "On Gusto," "Round Table": "The infinite quality of dramatic invention in Shakspeare takes from his gusto.  The power he delights to show is not intense, but discursive.  He never insists on anything as much as he might, except a quibble."

P. 48. *He wrote for the great vulgar,* etc.  The same remark had been made by both Pope and Johnson. See Nichol Smith's "Eighteenth Century Essays on Shakespeare," pp. 49 and 141.

*the great vulgar and the small.* Cowley's "Translation of Horace's Ode III, i."

*his delights.* "Antony and Cleopatra," v, 2, 88.

P. 49. *His tragedies are better than his comedies.* Hazlitt is here deliberately opposing the view of Dr. Johnson expressed in the latter's preface to Shakespeare: "In tragedy he often writes with great appearance of toil and study, what is written at last with little felicity; but in his comick scenes, he seems to produce without labour, what no labour can improve. In tragedy he is always struggling after some occasion to be comick, but in comedy he seems to repose, or to luxuriate, as in a mode of thinking congenial to his nature. In his tragick scenes there is always something wanting, but his comedy often surpasses expectation or desire." (Nichol Smith's "Eighteenth Century Essays on Shakespeare," p. 121.) In the second lecture of the "English Comic Writers," Hazlitt recurs to this opinion of Johnson's with the following comment: "For my own part, I so far consider this preference given to the comic genius of the poet as erroneous and unfounded, that I should say that he is the only tragic poet in the world in the highest sense, as being on a par with, and the same as Nature, in her greatest heights and depths of action and suffering. There is but one who durst walk within that mighty circle, treading the utmost bound of nature and passion, showing us the dread abyss of woe in all its ghastly shapes and colours, and laying open all the faculties of the human soul to act, to think, and suffer, in direst extremities; whereas I think, on the other hand, that in comedy, though his talents there too were as wonderful as they were delightful, yet that there were some before him, others on a level with him, and many close behind him. . . . There is not only nothing so good (in my judgment) as Hamlet, or Lear, or Othello, or Macbeth, but there is nothing like Hamlet, or Lear, or Othello, or Macbeth. There is nothing, I believe, in the majestic Corneille, equal to the stern pride of Coriolanus, or which gives such an idea of the crumbling in pieces of the Roman grandeur, 'like an unsubstantial pageant faded,' as the Antony and Cleopatra. But to match the best serious comedies, such as Molière's Misanthrope and his Tartuffe, we must go to Shakspeare's tragic characters, the Timon of Athens or honest Iago, where we shall more than succeed. He put his strength into his tragedies and played with comedy. He was greatest in what was greatest; and his *forte* was not trifling, according to the opinion here combated, even though he might do that as well as any one else, unless he could do it better than anybody else." See also p. 99.

## CHARACTERS OF SHAKSPEARE'S PLAYS

### CYMBELINE

P. 51. *Dr. Johnson is of opinion.* "It may be observed that in many of his plays the latter part is evidently neglected. When he found himself near the end of his work, and in view of his reward, he shortened the labour to snatch the profit. He therefore remits his efforts where he should most vigorously exert them, and his catastrophe is improbably produced or imperfectly represented." (Nichol Smith: "Eighteenth Century Essays on Shakespeare," p. 123.)

*It is the peculiar excellence,* etc. Cf. Coleridge's Works, IV, 75-76: "In Shakespeare all the elements of womanhood are holy, and there is the sweet, yet dignified feeling of all that *continuates* society, a sense of ancestry and of sex, with a purity unassailable by sophistry, because it rests not in the analytic process, but in that sane equipoise of the faculties, during which the feelings are representative of all past experience,—not of the individual only, but of all those by whom she has been educated, and their predecessors even up to the first mother that lived. Shakespeare saw that the want of prominence which Pope notices for sarcasm, was the blessed beauty of the woman's character, and knew that it arose not from any deficiency, but from the exquisite harmony of all the parts of the moral being constituting one living total of head and heart. He has drawn it indeed in all its distinctive energies of faith, patience, constancy, fortitude,—shown in all of them as following the heart, which gives its results by a nice tact and happy intuition, without the intervention of the discursive faculty, sees all things in and by the light of the affections, and errs, if it ever err, in the exaggerations of love alone."

P. 52. *Cibber, in speaking.* See "Apology for the Life of Mr. Colley Cibber" (1740), I, iv.

*My lord.* i, 6, 112.

P. 53. *What cheer.* iii, 4, 41. The six quotations following are in the same scene.

P. 54. *My dear lord.* iii, 6, 14.
*And when with wild wood-leaves.* iv, 2, 389.
P. 55. *With fairest flowers.* iv, 2, 218.
*Cytherea, how bravely.* ii, 2, 14.
*Me of my lawful pleasure.* ii, 5, 9.
P. 56. *whose love-suit.* iii, 4, 136.
*the ancient critic.* Aristophanes of Byzantium, who lived in the third century before the Christian era.
*the principle of analogy.* This point is enforced by Hazlitt in connection with " Lear," " The Tempest," " Midsummer Night's Dream," and " As You Like It." Coleridge had previously remarked, " A unity of feeling and character pervades every drama of Shakespeare " (Works IV, 61), and Schlegel had written in the same manner concerning " Romeo and Juliet " · " The sweetest and the bitterest love and hatred, festive rejoicings and dark forebodings, tender embraces and sepulchral horrors, the fulness of life and self-annihilation, are here all brought close to each other ; and yet these contrasts are so blended into a unity of impression, that the echo which the whole leaves behind in the mind resembles a single but endless sigh." (ed. Bohn, p. 401).
P. 57. *Out of your proof.* iii, 3, 27.
P. 58. *The game's afoot.* " The game is up," iii, 3, 107.
*Under the shade.* " As You Like It," ii, 7, 111.
P. 59. *See, boys.* " Stoop, boys," iii, 3, 2.
*Nay, Cadwell.* iv, 2, 255.
*Stick to your journal course.* iv, 2, 10.
*Your highness.* i, 5, 23.

## MACBETH

P. 60. *The poet's eye.* " Midsummer Night's Dream," v, 1, 12.
*your only tragedy-maker.* An adaptation of " your only jig-maker," " Hamlet," iii, 2, 132.
*the air smells wooingly, the temple-haunting martlet.* i, 6, 4-6.
*blasted heath.* i, 3, 77.
*air-drawn dagger.* iii, 4, 62.
*the gracious Duncan.* iii, 1, 66.
P. 61. *blood-boultered Banquo.* iv, 1, 123.
*What are these.* i, 3, 39.
*bends up.* i, 7, 80.

P. 62. *The deed.* Cf. ii, 2, 11: "The attempt and not the deed confounds us."

*preter*[super]*natural solicitings.* i, 3, 130.

*Bring forth.* i, 7, 73.

P. 63. *Screw his courage.* i, 7, 60.

*lost so poorly.* Cf. ii, 2, 71: "Be not lost so poorly in your thoughts."

*a little water.* ii, 2, 68.

*the sides of his intent.* i, 7, 26.

*for their future days and nights.* Cf. i, 5, 70: "To all our days and nights to come." The next five quotations are from the same scene.

P. 64. *Mrs. Siddons.* Sarah Siddons (1775-1831), "The Tragic Muse," the most celebrated actress in the history of the English stage. Hazlitt wrote this passage for the Examiner (June 16, 1816) immediately after seeing a performance of the part by Mrs. Siddons. See Works, VIII, 312-373.

P. 65. *There is no art.* i, 4, 11.

*How goes the night.* ii, 1, 1.

P. 66. *Light thickens.* iii, 2, 50.

*Now spurs.* iii, 3, 6.

P. 67. *So fair and foul a day.* i, 3, 38.

*such welcome and unwelcome news together.* Cf. iv, 3, 138: "such welcome and unwelcome things at once."

*Men's lives are.* Cf. iv, 3, 171:

"and good men's lives
Expire before the flowers in their caps,
Dying or ere they sicken."

*Look like the innocent flower.* i, 5, 66.

*to him and all,* "to all and him." iii, 4, 91.

*Avaunt and quit my sight.* iii, 4, 93.

*himself again.* Cf. iii, 4, 107: "being gone, I am a man again."

*he may sleep.* iv, 1, 86.

*Then be thou jocund.* iii, 2, 40.

*Had he not resembled.* ii, 2, 13.

*should be women.* i, 3, 45.

*in deeper consequence.* i, 3, 126.

*Why stands.* iv, 1, 125.

P. 68. *He is as distinct a being,* etc. Cf. Pope (Nichol Smith's "Eighteenth Century Essays," p. 48): "Every single character in Shakespeare is as much an individual as those in life itself; it is impossible to find any two alike; and such as from their relation or affinity appear most to be twins, will upon comparison be found remarkably distinct." Beattie also had commented on "that wonderfully penetrating and plastic faculty, which is capable of representing every species of character, not as our ordinary poets do, by a high shoulder, a wry mouth, or gigantic stature, but by hitting off, with a delicate hand, the distinguishing feature, and that in such a manner as makes it easily known from all others whatsoever, however similar to a superficial eye." (Quoted in Drake's "Memorials of Shakespeare," 1828, p. 255.) Richard Cumberland had developed a parallel between Macbeth and Richard III in the Observer, Nos. 55-58, but it is to the suggestion of Thomas Whateley that Hazlitt is chiefly indebted. Both Richard III and Macbeth, says Whateley, "are soldiers, both usurpers; both attain the throne by the same means, by treason and murder; and both lose it too in the same manner, in battle against the person claiming it as lawful heir. Perfidy, violence, and tyranny are common to both; and these only, their obvious qualities, would have been attributed indiscriminately to both by an ordinary dramatic writer. But Shakespeare, in conformity to the truth of history as far as it led him, and by improving upon the fables which have been blended with it, has ascribed opposite principles and motives to the same designs and actions, and various effects to the operation of the same events upon different tempers. Richard and Macbeth, as represented by him, agree in nothing but their fortunes." (See the Variorum edition of "Richard III," p. 549.) Hazlitt makes similar discriminations between the characters of Iago and Richard III, between Henry VI and Richard II, and between Ariel and Puck.

*the milk of human kindness.* i, 5, 18.

*himself alone.* Cf. 3 "Henry VI," v, 6, 83: "I am myself alone."

P. 69. *For Banquo's issue.* iii, 1, 65.

*Duncan is in his grave.* iii, 2, 22.

*direness is rendered familiar.* v, 5, 14.

*troubled with thick coming fancies.* v, 3, 38.

P. 70. *subject to all.* "Measure for Measure," iii, 1, 9.

*My way of life.* v, 3, 22.

P. 71. *Lillo,* George (1693-1739), author of several "bourgeois" tragedies of which the best known is "George Barnwell" (1731).

*Specimens of Early English Dramatic Poets* by Charles Lamb, 1808. (Works, ed. Lucas, IV, 144.)

## IAGO

P. 73. *What a full fortune* and *Here is her father's house.* i, 1, 66-74.

P. 74. *I cannot believe.* ii, 1, 254.

*And yet how nature.* iii, 3, 227.

*milk of human kindness.* "Macbeth," i, 5, 18.

*relish of salvation.* "Hamlet," iii, 3, 92.

*Oh, you are well tuned.* ii, 1, 202.

P. 75. *My noble lord.* iii, 3, 92.

*O grace.* iii, 3, 373.

P. 76. *How is it.* iv, 1, 60.

*Zanga,* in the "Revenge" (1721), a tragedy by Edward Young (1683-1765).

## HAMLET

P. 76. *This goodly frame* and *Man delighted not.* ii, 2, 310-321.

P. 77. *too much i' th' sun.* i, 2, 67.

*the pangs.* iii, 1, 72.

P. 78. *There is no attempt to force an interest.* Professor Saintsbury ("History of Criticism," III, 258) calls this utterance an apex of Shakespearian criticism. Hazlitt makes a similar comment in the character of "Troilus and Cressida": "He has no prejudice for or against his characters: he saw both sides of a question; at once an actor and a spectator in the scene." Dr. Johnson had observed this attitude in Shakespeare, but he had seen in it a violation of the demands of poetic justice: "he carries his persons indifferently through right and wrong, and at the close dismisses them without further care, and leaves their examples to operate by chance. This fault the barbarity of his age cannot extenuate; for it is always a writer's duty to make the world better, and justice is a virtue independent on time or place." (Nichol Smith's "Eighteenth Century Essays on Shakespeare," p. 123.)

*outward pageant.* Cf. i, 2, 86: "the trappings and the suits of woe."

*we have that within.* i, 2, 85.

P. 79. *He kneels.* Cf. iii, 3, 73: "Now might I do it pat, now he is praying."

P. 80. *How all occasions.* iv, 4, 32.

P. 81. *that noble and liberal casuist.* Doubtless suggested by

Lamb's description of the old English dramatists as "those noble and liberal casuists." (Works, ed. Lucas, I, 46.)

*The Whole Duty of Man,* a popular treatise of morals (1659).

*Academy of Compliments,* or the Whole Duty of Courtship, being the nearest or most exact way of wooing a Maid or Widow, by the way of Dialogue or Complimental Expressions (1655, 1669).

*The neglect of punctilious exactness,* etc. The entire passage follows pretty closely the interpretation of Lamb: "Among the distinguishing features of that wonderful character, one of the most interesting (yet painful) is that soreness of mind which makes him treat the intrusions of Polonius with harshness, and that asperity which he puts on in his interviews with Ophelia. These tokens of an unhinged mind (if they be not mixed in the latter case with a profound artifice of love, to alienate Ophelia by affected discourtesies, so to prepare her mind for the breaking off of that loving intercourse, which can no longer find a place amidst business so serious as that which he has to do) are parts of his character, which to reconcile with our admiration of Hamlet, the most patient consideration of his situation is no more than necessary; they are what we *forgive afterwards,* and explain by the whole of his character, but *at the time* they are harsh and unpleasant. . . . [His behavior toward Ophelia] is not alienation, it is a distraction purely, and so it always makes itself to be felt by that object: it is not anger, but grief assuming the appearance of anger,—love awkwardly counterfeiting hate, as sweet countenances when they try to frown." "On the Tragedies of Shakespeare." (Works, ed. Lucas, I, 103-104.)

*He may be said to be amenable,* etc. Cf. Coleridge (Works, IV, 145): "His thoughts, and the images of his fancy, are far more vivid than his actual perceptions, and his very perceptions, instantly passing through the *medium* of his contemplations, acquire, as they pass, a form and a colour not naturally their own. Hence we see a great, an almost enormous, intellectual activity, and a proportionate aversion to real action, consequent upon it, with all its symptoms and accompanying qualities."

P. 82. *his father's spirit.* i, 2, 255.

*I loved Ophelia.* v, 1, 292.

*Sweets to the sweet.* v, 1, 266.

P. 83. *There is a willow.* See p. 39.

*our author's plays acted.* See pp. 70, 87.

P. 84. *Kemble,* John Philip (1757-1823), younger brother to Mrs. Siddons and noted as the leader of the stately school in tragedy.

Hazlitt often contrasted his manner with that of Kean: "We wish we had never seen Mr. Kean. He has destroyed the Kemble religion; and it is the religion in which we were brought up." Works, VIII, 345.

*a wave o' th' sea.* "Winter's Tale," iv, 4, 141.

*Kean,* Edmund (1787-1833), the great English tragic actor whom Hazlitt was instrumental in discovering for the London public. Shylock and Othello were his most successful rôles. For accounts of his various performances, see "A View of the English Stage" (Works, VIII). Most of the points in this essay are reproduced from the notice of Kean's Hamlet (VIII, 185-189).

## ROMEO AND JULIET

This extract is the opening paragraph of the sketch.

P. 84. *a great critic,* A. W. Schlegel. The passage alluded to by Hazlitt appears in Coleridge's Works (IV, 60-61) in what is little more than a free translation: "Read 'Romeo and Juliet';—all is youth and spring;—youth with its follies, its virtues, its precipitancies;—spring with its odors, its flowers, and its transiency; it is one and the same feeling that commences, goes through, and ends the play. The old men, the Capulets and the Montagues, are not common old men; they have an eagerness, a heartiness, a vehemence, the effect of spring; with Romeo, his change of passion, his sudden marriage, and his rash death, are all the effects of youth;—whilst in Juliet love has all that is tender and melancholy in the nightingale, all that is voluptuous in the rose, with whatever is sweet in the freshness of the spring; but it ends with a long deep sigh like the last breeze of the Italian evening."

P. 85. *fancies wan.* Cf. "Lycidas," "cowslips wan."

## MIDSUMMER NIGHT'S DREAM

These extracts are the second and last paragraphs of the essay.

P. 85. *Lord, what fools.* iii, 2, 115.

P. 86. *human mortals.* ii, 1, 101.

*gorgons and hydras,* "Paradise Lost," II, 628.

*a celebrated person,* Sir Humphry Davy; see p. 342. Cf.

Coleridge (Works, IV, 66) : "Shakespeare was not only a great poet, but a great philosopher."

P. 87. *Poetry and the stage.* Cf. Lamb, "On the Tragedies of Shakespeare" (ed. Lucas, I, 110) : "Spirits and fairies cannot be represented, they cannot even be painted,—they can only be believed. But the elaborate and anxious provision of scenery, which the luxury of the age demands, in these cases works a quite contrary effect to what is intended. That which in comedy, or plays of familiar life, adds so much to the life of the imitation, in plays which appeal to the higher faculties, positively destroys the illusion which it is introduced to aid."

## HENRY IV

Hazlitt's interpretation of Falstaff is worth comparing with that of Maurice Morgann in "An Essay on the Dramatic Character of Sir John Falstaff," although Hazlitt does not allude to Morgann's essay and is supposed to have had no knowledge of it. "To me then it appears that the leading quality in Falstaff's character, and that from which all the rest take their colour, is a high degree of wit and humour, accompanied with great natural vigour and alacrity of mind. . . . He seems, by nature, to have had a mind free of malice or any evil principle; but he never took the trouble of acquiring any *good* one. He found himself esteemed and beloved with all his faults; nay *for* his faults, which were all connected with humour, and for the most part grew out of it. As he had, possibly, no vices but such as he thought might be openly confessed, so he appeared more dissolute thro' ostentation. To the character of wit and humour, to which all his other qualities seem to have conformed themselves, he appears to have added a very necessary support, *that* of the profession of a *Soldier.* . . . Laughter and approbation attend his greatest excesses; and being governed visibly by no settled bad principle or ill design, fun and humour account for and cover all. By degrees, however, and thro' indulgence, he acquires bad habits, becomes an humourist, grows enormously corpulent, and falls into the infirmities of age; yet never quits, all the time, one single levity or vice of youth, or loses any of that cheerfulness of mind which had enabled him to pass thro' this course with ease to himself and delight to others; and thus, at last, mixing youth and age, enterprize and corpulency, wit and folly, poverty and expence, title and buffoonery, innocence as to purpose, and wickedness as to practice; neither incurring hatred by bad principle, or contempt by cowardice, yet involved in circumstances productive of imputation in both; a butt and a wit, a humourist and a man of humour, a touchstone and a laughing stock, a jester and a jest, has Sir *John Falstaff*, taken at that period of life in which we see him, become the most perfect comic character that perhaps ever was exhibited." (Nichol Smith's "Eighteenth Century Essays on Shakespeare," 226-7.)

P. 88. *we behold.* Cf. Colossians, ii, 9; "in him dwelleth all the fulness of the Godhead bodily."

*lards the lean earth.* 1 "Henry IV," ii, 2, 116.

*into thin air.* "Tempest," iv, 1, 150.

*three fingers deep.* Cf. 1 "Henry IV," iv, 2, 80: "three fingers on the ribs."

P. 89. *it snows.* Chaucer's Prologue to the "Canterbury Tales," 345.

*ascends me.* 2 "Henry IV," iv, 3, 105.

*a tun of man.* 1 "Henry IV," ii, 4, 493.

P. 91. *open, palpable.* Cf. 1 "Henry IV," ii, 4, 248: "These lies are like their father that begets them; gross as a mountain, open, palpable."

*By the lord.* Ibid., i, 2, 44.

*But Hal.* Ibid., i, 2, 91.

P. 92. *who grew.* Cf. ii, 4, 243: "eleven buckram men grown out of two."

*Harry, I do not.* ii, 4, 439.

P. 94. *What is the gross sum.* 2 "Henry IV," ii, 1, 91.

P. 95. *Would I were with him.* "Henry V," ii, 3, 6.

*turning his vices.* Cf. 2 "Henry IV," i, 2, 277: "I will turn diseases to commodity."

*their legs.* Ibid., ii, 4, 265.

*a man made after supper.* Ibid., iii, 2, 332.

*Would, Cousin Silence.* Ibid., iii, 2, 225.

*I did not think.* Ibid., v, 3, 40.

*in some authority.* Ibid., v, 3, 117.

*You have here.* Ibid., v, 3, 6.

## TWELFTH NIGHT

P. 96. *It aims at the ludicrous.* Cf. Hazlitt's remark in the Characters on " Much Ado About Nothing ": " Perhaps that middle point of comedy was never more nicely hit in which the ludicrous blends with the tender, and our follies, turning round against themselves in support of our affections, retain nothing but their humanity."

P. 97. *William Congreve* (1670-1729), *William Wycherley* (1640-1716), *Sir John Vanbrugh* (1664-1726), the chief masters of Restoration Comedy.

P. 98. *high fantastical.* i, 1, 15.

*Wherefore are these things hid.* i, 3, 133.

*rouse the night-owl.* ii, 3, 60.

*Dost thou think.* ii, 3, 123.

P. 99. *We cannot agree with Dr. Johnson.* See p. 49 and n.

*What's her history.* ii, 4, 12.

*Oh it came o'er.* i, 1, 5.

P. 100. *They give a very echo.* ii, 4, 21.

*Blame not this haste.* iv, 3, 22.

The essay concludes with the quotation of one of the songs and Malvolio's reading of the letter.

## MILTON

P. 101. *Blind Thamyris.* " Paradise Lost," III, 35.

P. 102. *with darkness.* VII, 27.

*piling up every stone.* XI, 324.

*For after I had from my first years.* " The Reason of Church Government," Book II, Introduction.

P. 103. *The noble heart.* " Faërie Queene," I, v, 1.

P. 104. *makes Ossa like a wart.* " Hamlet," v, 1, 306.

*Him followed Rimmon.* " Paradise Lost," I, 467.

*As when a vulture.* III, 431.

P. 105. *the pilot.* I, 204.

*It has been indeed objected to Milton.* Cf. Coleridge (Works, ed. Shedd, IV, 304) : " Milton is not a picturesque, but a musical, poet "; also Coleridge's " Table Talk," August 7, 1832 : " It is very remarkable that in no part of his writings does Milton take any notice of the great painters of Italy, nor, indeed, of painting as an art; while every other page breathes his love and taste for music. . . . Adam bending over the sleeping Eve, in Paradise Lost, and Dalilah approaching Samson, in the Agonistes, are the only two proper pictures I remember in Milton."

*Like a steam.* "Comus," 556.

P. 106. *He soon saw.* "Paradise Lost," III, 621.

P. 107. *With Atlantean shoulders.* II, 306.

*Lay floating.* I, 296.

*Dr. Johnson condemns the Paradise Lost.* See the conclusion of his "Life of Milton."

P. 108. *His hand was known.* "Paradise Lost," I, 732.

*But chief the spacious hall.* I, 762.

P. 109. *Round he surveys.* III, 555.

*Such as the meeting soul.* "L'Allegro."

*the hidden soul.* Ibid.

P. 110. *as Pope justly observes.* "First Epistle of the Second Book of Horace," 102.

P. 111. *As when Heaven's fire.* "Paradise Lost," I, 612.

*All is not lost.* I, 206.

*that intellectual being.* II, 147.

*being swallowed up.* II, 149.

P. 112. *Fallen cherub.* I, 157.

*rising aloft.* I, 225.

*the mystic German critics.* Cf. p. 344.

P. 113. *Is this the region.* "Paradise Lost," I, 242.

P. 114. *Salmasius.* At the request of Charles II, Claude de Saumaise (Claudius Salmasius), professor at Leyden, had written a vindication of Charles I, "Defensio pro Carolo I" (1649), to which Milton replied with the "Defensio pro Populo Anglicano" (1651). The controversy between the two is noted for the virulency of the personal invective.

*with hideous ruin.* "Paradise Lost," I, 46.

*retreated in a silent valley.* II, 547.

*a noted political writer.* Dr. Stoddart, editor of the Times and brother-in-law of Hazlitt, whom the critic bitterly hated, and Napoleon are here referred to. Cf. "Political Essays," III, 158-159.

P. 115. *Longinus preferred the Iliad.* "Whereas in the *Iliad,* which was written when his genius was in its prime, the whole structure of the poem is founded on action and struggle, in the *Odyssey* he generally prefers the narrative style, which is proper to old age. Hence Homer in his *Odyssey* may be compared to the setting sun: he is still as great as ever, but he has lost his fervent

heat. The strain is now pitched in a lower key than in the ' Tale
of Troy Divine': we begin to miss that high and equable sublimity
which never flags or sinks, that continuous current of moving incidents, those rapid transitions, that force of eloquence, that opulence
of imagery which is ever true to Nature. Like the sea when it
retires upon itself and leaves its shores waste and bare, henceforth
the tide of sublimity begins to ebb, and draws us away into the dim
region of myth and legend. In saying this I am not forgetting the
fine storm-pieces in the *Odyssey*, the story of the Cyclops, and other
striking passages. It is Homer grown old I am discussing, but
still it is Homer." On the Sublime, IX, trans. Havell.

*no kind of traffic.* Cf. "Tempest," ii, 1, 148.

*The generations were prepared.* Wordsworth's "Excursion," VI,
554.

*the unapparent deep.* "Paradise Lost," VII, 103.

P. 116. *know to know no more.* Cowper's "Truth," 327.

*They toiled not.* Matthew, vi, 28.

*In them the burthen.* Wordsworth's "Lines Composed above
Tintern Abbey."

*such as angels weep.* "Paradise Lost," I, 620.

P. 117. *In either hand.* XII, 637.

POPE

This selection begins with the second paragraph of the fourth
lecture on the "English Poets."

P. 118. *The question whether Pope was a poet.* Hazlitt had written a paper in answer to this question in the Edinburgh Magazine
for February, 1818 (Works, XII, 430-432), from which the following
paragraphs down to "Such at least is the best account" are copied.
The question had been previously answered by Dr. Johnson with
the same common sense as by Hazlitt: "It is surely superfluous to
answer the question that has once been asked, Whether Pope was a
poet? otherwise than by asking in return, If Pope be not a poet,
where is poetry to be found? To circumscribe poetry by a definition will only shew the narrowness of the definer, though a definition which shall exclude Pope will not easily be made." ("Life of
Pope," ed. B. Hill, III, 251). In their edition of Pope (II, 140),
Elwin and Courthope express the opinion that the doubt which both
Johnson and Hazlitt felt called upon to refute "was never main-

tained by a single person of reputation." Yet there is something very close to such a doubt implied in the utterances of Coleridge: " If we consider great exquisiteness of language and sweetness of metre alone, it is impossible to deny to Pope the character of a delightful writer; but whether he was a poet, must depend upon our definition of the word. . . . This, I must say, that poetry, as distinguished from other modes of composition, does not rest in metre, and that it is not poetry, if it make no appeal to our passions or our imagination." (Works, ed. Shedd, IV, 56.) Pope's verse was made the occasion of a long-winded controversy as to the relative value of the natural and artificial in poetry, lasting from 1819 to 1825, with William Bowles and Lord Byron as the principal combatants. Hazlitt contributed an article to the London Magazine for June, 1821, " Pope, Lord Byron and Mr. Bowles " (Works, XII, 486-508), in which he pointed out the fallacies in Byron's position and censured the clerical priggishness of Bowles in treating of Pope's life. The chief points in the discussion are best summed up in Prothero's edition of Byron's " Letters and Journals," Vol. V, Appendix III.

*If indeed by a great poet we mean.* Cf. Introduction, p. 1.

P. 120. *the pale reflex.* " Romeo and Juliet," iii, 5, 20.

P. 121. *Martha Blount* (1690-1762), the object of Pope's sentimental attachment throughout his life.

*In Fortune's ray.* " Troilus and Cressida," i, 3, 47.

*the gnarled oak . . . the soft myrtle.* " Faërie Qu.," II, ii, 116-117.

*calm contemplation.* Thomson's " Autumn," 1275.

P. 122. *More subtle web.* " Faërie Queene," II, xii, 77.

P. 123. *from her fair head.* " Rape of the Lock," III, 154.

*Now meet thy fate.* Ibid., V, 87-96.

P. 124. *Lutrin.* The " Lutrin " was a mock-heroic poem (1674-1683) of the French poet and critic, Nicolas Boileau Despreaux (1636-1711), the literary dictator of the age of Louis XIV.

*'Tis with our judgments.* " Essay on Criticism," I, 9.

*Still green with bays.* Ibid., I, 181.

P. 125. *the writer's despair.* Cf. Ibid., II, 278:

" No longer now that Golden Age appears,
When Patriarch-wits survived a thousand years:
Now length of fame (our second life) is lost,
And bare threescore is all ev'n that can boast:
Our sons their fathers' failing language see,
And such as Chaucer is shall Dryden be."

*with theirs should sail,* "attendant sail." " Essay on Man," IV, 383-6.

P. 126. *There died.* " Eloisa to Abelard," 40.

P. 127. *If ever chance.* Ibid., 347.

*Bolingbroke.* Henry St. John, Viscount Bolingbroke (1678-1751). " The Essay plainly appears the fabric of a poet: what Bolingbroke supplied could be only the first principles; the order, illustration, and embellishments must be all Pope's." Pope's Works, ed. Elwin and Courthope, II, 264.

P. 128. *he spins,* " draweth out." " Love's Labour's Lost," v, 1, 18.

*the very words.* Cf. " Macbeth," i, 3, 88: " the selfsame tune and words."

*Now night descending.* " Dunciad," I, 89.

*Virtue may choose.* " Epilogue to the Satires," Dialogue I, 137.

P. 129. *character of Chartres.* " Moral Essays, Epistle III."

*his compliments.* See p. 322.

*Where Murray.* " Imitations of Horace, Epistle VI," 52. William Murray (1705-1793), Chief Justice of England, created Lord Mansfield in 1776.

*Why rail.* " Epilogue to Satires," Dialogue II, 138.

*Despise low joys.* " Epistle to Mr. Murray," 60.

P. 130. *character of Addison.* " Epistle to Dr. Arbuthnot," 193-214.

*Buckingham.* George Villiers, second duke of Buckingham (1628-1687), statesman, wit, and poet.

*Alas! how changed.* " Moral Essays," III, 305.

*Arbuthnot,* John (1667-1735), physician and man of letters, whom Thackeray introduced in attendance at the death-bed of Francis Esmond. " He had a very notable share in the immortal History of John Bull, and the inimitable and praiseworthy Memoirs of Martinus Scriblerus. . . . Arbuthnot's style is distinguished from that of his contemporaries, even by a greater degree of terseness and conciseness. He leaves out every superfluous word; is sparing of connecting particles, and introductory phrases; uses always the simplest forms of construction; and is more a master of the idiomatic peculiarities and internal resources of the language than almost any other writer." " English Poets," Lecture VI.

*Charles Jervas* (1675-1739) gave Pope lessons in painting. He is also known as a translator of " Don Quixote."

*Why did I write.* " Epistle to Arbuthnot," 125.

P. 131. *Oh, lasting as those colours.* "Epistle to Mr. Jervas," 63.
*who have eyes.* Psalms, cxv, 5; cxxxv, 16, etc.
*It will never do.* Hazlitt was fond of mimicking this phrase with which Jeffrey so unfortunately opened his well-known review of Wordsworth's "Excursion."
*I lisp'd in numbers.* "Epistle to Arbuthnot," 128.
*Et quum conabar scribere.* Cf. Ovid's "Tristia," IV, x, 26: "Et, quod tentabam dicere, versus erat."

## PERIODICAL ESSAYISTS

The fifth lecture on the "Comic Writers."
P. 133. *the proper study.* Pope's "Essay on Man," II, 2.
*comes home.* Bacon's dedication of the Essays.
*Quicquid agunt homines.* "Whatever things men do form the mixed substance of our book." Juvenal's "Satires," I, 85. With occasional exceptions, this appears as the motto of the first 78 number of the Tatler.
*holds the mirror.* "Hamlet," iii, 2, 24.
*the act and practic.* Cf. "Henry V," i, 1, 51: "So that the art and practic part of life Must be the mistress to this theoric."
P. 134. *the web of our life.* "All's Well That Ends Well," iv, 3, 83.
*Quid sit pulchrum.* "It tells us what is fair, what foul, what is useful, what not, more amply and better than Chrysippus and Crantor." Horace's "Epistles," I, ii, 3-4.
*Montaigne,* Michel (1533-1592). "Essays," Books I and II, 1580; Book III, 1588.
P. 135. *not one of the angles.* Sterne's "Tristram Shandy," Bk. III, Ch. 12.
P. 136. *pour out.* "Imitation of Horace, Satire I," 51.
P. 136, n. *more wise Charron.* See Pope's "Moral Essays," I, 87. Pierre Charron (1541-1603), a friend of Montaigne, author of "De la Sagesse" (1601).
P. 137. *Pereant isti.* Ælius Donatus: St. Jerome's *Commentary on the Eucharist,* ch. 1. Mr. Carr's translation of the sentence is "Confound the fellows who have said our good things before us." (Camelot Hazlitt.)
P. 138. *Charles Cotton's* (1630-1687) translation of Montaigne was published in 1685. It was dedicated to George Savile, Marquis

of Halifax (1633-1695), who spoke of the essays as "the book in the world I am best entertained with."

*Cowley,* Abraham (1618-1667). "Several Discourses by way of Essays in Prose and Verse" appeared in the edition of his works in 1668.

*Sir William Temple* (1628-1699). His essays, entitled "Miscellanea," were published in 1680 and 1692.

*Lord Shaftesbury* (1671-1713), author of "Characteristics" (1711).

P. 139. *the perfect spy.* "Macbeth," iii, 1, 130.

*The Tatler* ran from April 12, 1709, to June 2, 1711. This paragraph and the larger portion of the next are substantially reproduced from the paper "On the Tatler" in the "Round Table."

*Isaac Bickerstaff.* Under the disguise of this name Swift had perpetrated an amusing hoax on an almanac-maker of the name of Partridge, and in launching his new periodical Steele availed himself of the notoriety of Bickerstaff's name and feigned his identity with that personage.

P. 140. *the disastrous stroke.* Cf. "Othello," i, 3, 157: "some distressful stroke that my youth suffered."

*the recollection of one of his mistresses.* Tatler, No. 107.

*the club at the Trumpet.* 132.

*the cavalcade.* 86.

*the upholsterer.* 155, 160, 178.

*If he walks out,* etc. '238.

P. 141. *Charles Lillie,* perfumer, at the corner of Beaufort Buildings in the Strand, was agent for the sale of the Tatler and Spectator and is several times mentioned in those periodicals.

*Betterton,* Thomas (1635?-1710), *Anne Oldfield* (1683-1730), *Will* [Richard] *Estcourt* (1668-1712), were popular actors of the day.

*Tom Durfey* (1653-1723) was a dramatist and song writer.

*Duke of Marlborough* (1650-1722), and *Marshal Turenne* (1611-1675).

*The Spectator* ran from March 1, 1711, to December 6, 1712, with an additional series from June 18 to December 20, 1714.

*the first sprightly runnings.* Dryden's "Aurengzebe," iv, 1.

P. 142. *Addison,* Joseph (1672-1719).

*the whiteness of her hand.* Cf. Spectator, No. 113. "She certainly has the finest hand of any woman in the world."

*the havoc he makes.* Spectator, 116, by Budgell.

*his speech from the bench* and *his unwillingness.* 122.

*his gentle reproof.* 130.

*his doubts.* 117.

P. 143. *his account of the family pictures.* 109, by Steele.

*his choice of a chaplain.* 106.

*his falling asleep at church* and *his reproof of John Williams,* i.e., John Matthews. 112.

*I once thought I knew.* Cf. " On ·the Conversation of Authors," where A—— (William Ayrton) is introduced as " the Will Honeycomb of our set."

*The Court of Honour.* Addison created the court in Tatler, 250. Its proceedings are recorded by himself and Steele in Nos. 253, 256, 259, 262, 265.

*Personification of Musical Instruments.* Tatler, 153, 157.

*the picture of the family.* Tatler, 95, of unknown authorship.

P. 144. *the account of the two sisters.* 151.

*the married lady.* 104.

*the lover and his mistress.* 94.

*the bridegroom.* 82.

*Mr. Eustace and his wife.* 172.

*the fine dream.* 117.

*Mandeville,* Bernard (d. 1733), author of the satirical " Fable of the Bees."

*reflections on cheerfulness.* Spectator, 381, 387, 393.

*those in Westminster Abbey.* 26.

*Royal Exchange.* 69.

P. 145. *the best criticism.* 226.

*Mr. Fuseli,* Henry (1741-1825), painter and art critic.

*an original copy.* Probably the octavo edition of 1711.

*The Guardian* ran from March 12, 1713, to October 1, 1713.

*The Rambler* ran from March 20, 1749-50, to March 14, 1752.

*Dr. Johnson,* Samuel (1709-1784).

P. 146. *give us pause.* " Hamlet," iii, 1, 68.

P. 147. *All his periods,* etc. See the " Character of Burke " and the preface to " The Characters of Shakespeare's Plays."

P. 148. *the elephant.* " Paradise Lost," IV, 345.

*If he were to write.* Boswell's " Johnson," ed. Birkbeck Hill, II, 231.

P. 149. *Rasselas,* an Oriental tale, published in 1759.

*abused Milton and patronized Lauder.* See Boswell's " Johnson," I, 228-231.

P. 150. *Boswell,* James (1740-1795), made his literary reputation by his "Life of Johnson."

*the king of good fellows.* Burns's "Auld Rab Morris."

*inventory of all he said.* Cf. Ben Jonson's "Alchemist," iii, 2: "And ta'en an inventory of what they are."

*Goldsmith asked.* Boswell's "Johnson," II, 260.

*If that fellow Burke.* II, 450.

*What, is it you.* I, 250.

P. 151. *with some unidead girls.* I, 251.

*Now, I think.* II, 362.

*his quitting the society.* I, 201.

*his dining with Wilkes.* III, 64.

*his sitting with the young ladies.* II, 120.

*his carrying the unfortunate victim.* IV, 321.

*an act which realises the parable.* Talfourd, who heard this lecture, reports that on Hazlitt's allusion to this incident "a titter arose from some who were struck by the picture as ludicrous, and a murmur from others who deemed the allusion unfit for ears polite: he paused for an instant, and then added, in his sturdiest and most impressive manner—'an act which realizes the parable of the Good Samaritan'—at which his moral, and his delicate hearers shrank, rebuked, into deep silence.

*where they.* Gray's "Elegy."

P. 152. *The Adventurer* ran from November 7, 1752, to March 9, 1754. John Hawkesworth (1715-1773) was its chief contributor.

*The World* ran from January 4, 1753, to December 30, 1756.

*The Connoisseur* ran from January 31, 1754, to September 30, 1756.

*one good idea.* The paper referred to is No. 176 of The World, by Edward Moore, the dramatist.

*Citizen of the World,* in two volumes, 1762.

*go about to cozen.* Cf. "Merchant of Venice," ii, 9, 37: "To cozen fortune and be honorable Without the stamp of merit."

*Persian Letters.* "Letters from a Persian in England to his Friend at Ispahan" (1735), by Lord Lyttleton.

P. 153. *The bonzes.* "Citizen of the World," Letter X.

*Edinburgh. We are positive.* Ibid., Letter V.

*Beau Tibbs.* Letters XXIX, LIV, LV, LXXXI.

*Lounger* ran from February 5, 1785, to January 6, 1786, *The Mirror* from January 23, 1779, to May 27, 1780. The chief contributor to both was Henry Mackenzie (1745-1831), author of the celebrated sentimental novels: "The Man of Feeling" (1771), "The Man of the World" (1773), "Julia de Roubigné" (1777). *the story of La Roche.* Mirror, 42, 43, 44. *the story of Le Fevre.* "Tristram Shandy," Bk. VI, ch. 6. P. 154. *author of Rosamond Gray.* Charles Lamb.


## THE ENGLISH NOVELISTS

From the sixth lecture on the "Comic Writers." Most of the matter had appeared in the Edinburgh Review for February, 1815, as a review of Madame D'Arblay's "Wanderer." (See Works, X, 25-44.) In "A Farewell to Essay-Writing" (Works, XII, 327) Hazlitt harks back to his days with Charles and Mary Lamb: "I will not compare our hashed mutton with Amelia's; but it put us in mind of it, and led to a discussion, sharply seasoned and well sustained, till midnight, the result of which appeared some years after in the Edinburgh Review."

P. 155. *Be mine to read.* To Richard West, April, 1742.

*Marivaux,* Pierre (1688-1763), and *Crebillon,* Claude Prosper (1707-1777), French novelists.

*something more divine.* Cf. p. 254.

P. 156. *Fielding . . . says.* "Joseph Andrews," Bk. III, ch. 1.

*description somewhere given.* "Reflections on the French Revolution," ed. Bohn, II, 351-352.

P. 157. *Echard.* John Eachard (1636-1697), author of "The Grounds and Occasions of the Contempt of the Clergy and Religion Enquired into." (1670.)

*worthy of all acceptation.* 1 Timothy, i, 15.

*the lecture.* "Joseph Andrews," Bk. IV, ch. 3.

*Blackstone,* Sir William (1723-1780), author of "Commentaries on the Laws of England" (1765-69).

*De Lolme,* John Louis (1740?-1807), author of "The Constitution of England" (1771).

*Cervantes,* Miguel (1547-1616), Spanish novelist whose most famous work is "Don Quixote."

*Le Sage,* Alain René (1668-1747), French novelist, author of "Gil Blas."

*Fielding,* Henry (1707-1754). His most important novels are "Joseph Andrews" (1742), "Tom Jones" (1749), "Amelia" (1751), "Jonathan Wild" (1743).

*Smollett,* Tobias (1721-1771), wrote "Roderick Random" (1748), "Peregrine Pickle" (1751), "Ferdinand Count Fathom" (1753), "Launcelot Greaves" (1762), "Humphrey Clinker" (1771).

*Richardson,* Samuel (1689-1761), wrote "Pamela" (1740), "Clarissa Harlowe" (1747-48), "Sir Richard Grandison" (1753).

*Sterne,* Laurence (1713-1768), wrote "Tristram Shandy" (1759-67), "A Sentimental Journey Through France and Italy" (1768).

P. 158. *in these several writers.* A few paragraphs are here omitted treating of "Don Quixote," "Lazarillo de Tormes" (1553), "Guzman d'Alfarache" by Mateo Aleman (1599), and "Gil Blas."

*They are thoroughly English.* In the review of Walpole's Letters (Works, X, 168), Hazlitt says: "There is nothing of a tea inspiration in any of his [Fielding's] novels. They are assuredly the finest thing of the kind in the language; and we are Englishmen enough to consider them the best in any language. They are indubitably the most English of all the works of Englishmen."

*Hogarth,* William (1697-1764), painter and engraver of moral and satirical subjects. His two most famous series of paintings are "The Rake's Progress" and "Marriage à la Mode." Lamb in his "Essay on the Genius and Character of Hogarth" observes: "Other pictures we look at,—his prints we read." Hazlitt, sharing this view, includes an account of Hogarth in the seventh lecture of the "Comic Writers," which opens as follows: "If the quantity of amusement, or of matter for more serious reflection which their works have afforded, is that by which we are to judge of precedence among the intellectual benefactors of mankind, there are, perhaps, few persons who can put in a stronger claim to our gratitude than Hogarth. It is not hazarding too much to assert, that he was one of the greatest comic geniuses that ever lived."

P. 159. *the gratitude of the elder Blifil.* Bk. I, ch. 13.

*the Latin dialogues,* etc. Bk. II, chs. 3-4.

P. 160. *honesty of Black George.* Bk. VI, ch. 13.

*I was never so handsome.* Bk. XVII, ch. 4.

*the adventure with the highwayman.* Bk. VII, ch. 9.

*Sophia and her muff.* Bk. V, ch. 4.

*coquetry of her cousin.* Bk. XVI, ch. 9.

*the modest overtures.* Bk. XV, ch. 11.

*the story of Tom Jones.* Cf. Coleridge's "Table Talk," July 5, 1834: "I think the Œdipus Tyrannus, the Alchemist, and Tom Jones, the three most perfect plots ever planned."

account of Miss Matthews and Ensign Hibbert [Hebbers]. Bk. I, chs. 7-9.

P. 161. *the story of the miniature picture.* Bk. XI, ch. 6.

*the hashed mutton.* Bk. X, ch. 6.

*the masquerade.* Bk. X, ch. 2.

*the interview.* Bk. X, chs. 2, 8.

P. 162. *His declaring.* Bk. III, ch. 3.

*his consoling himself.* Bk. III, ch. 2.

*the night-adventures.* Bk. IV, ch. 14.

*that with the huntsman.* Bk. III, ch. 6.

*Wilson's account.* Bk. III, ch. 3.

P. 163. *Roderick Random's carroty locks.* ch. 13.

*Strap's ignorance.* ch. 14.

*intus et in cute.* Persius' "Satires," III, 30.

P. 164. *scene on ship-board.* ch. 24.

*profligate French friar.* chs. 42-43.

P. 165. *the Count's address.* ch. 27.

*the robber-scene.* chs. 20-21.

*the Parisian swindler.* ch. 24.

*the seduction.* ch. 34.

P. 166. *the long description.* The allusions to Miss Byron's dress in Vol. VII, Letter III, can scarcely be called a long description.

P. 167. *Dr. Johnson seems to have preferred.* Cf. Boswell's " Johnson," ed. Hill, II, 174 : " Sir, there is more knowledge of the heart in one letter of Richardson's, than in all Tom Jones."

P. 168. *reproaches to her "lumpish heart."* " Pamela," ed. Dobson and Phelps, I, 268.

*its lightness.* I, 276.

*the joy.* II, 7-25.

*the artifice of the stuff-gown.* I, 51.

*the meeting with Lady Davers.* II, 145 ff.

*the trial-scene with her husband.* IV, 122 ff.

P. 169. *her long dying-scene.* " Clarissa Harlowe," ed. Dobson and Phelps, Vol. VIII, Letter 29.

*the closing of the coffin-lid.* VIII, Letter 50.

*the heart-breaking reflections.* VI, Letter 29.

*Books are a real world.* Wordsworth's " Personal Talk."

*Lovelace's reception and description of Hickman.* VI, Letter 86.

*the scene at the glove-shop.* VII, Letter 70.

*Belton, so pert.* I, Letter 31.

*his systematically preferring.* Cf. " Why the Heroes of Ro-

mances are Insipid " (Works, XII, 62) : " There is not a single thing
that Sir Charles Grandison does or says all through the book from
liking to any person or object but himself, and with a view to answer to a certain standard of perfection for which he pragmatically
sets up. He is always thinking of himself, and trying to show that
he is the wisest, happiest, and most virtuous person in the whole
world. He is (or would be thought) a code of Christian ethics;
a compilation and abstract of all gentlemanly accomplishments.
There is nothing, I conceive, that excites so little sympathy as this
inordinate egotism; or so much disgust as this everlasting self-
complacency. Yet this self-admiration, brought forward on every
occasion as the incentive to every action and reflected from all
around him, is the burden and pivot of the story."

P. 170. *a dull fellow.* Boswell's " Johnson," ed. Birkbeck Hill, II,
222.
  *the tale of Maria.* Bk. IX, ch. 24.
  *the apostrophe to the recording angel.* Bk. VI, ch. 8.
  *the story of Le Fevre.* Bk. VI, ch. 6.
The rest of the lecture treats of Fanny Burney, Anne Radcliffe,
Elizabeth Inchbald, William Godwin, and Sir Walter Scott.


## CHARACTER OF MR. BURKE

First published in the " Eloquence of the British Senate " and republished in " Political Essays."
  P. 172. *The following speech.* Hazlitt refers to the speech On
the Economic Reform (February 11, 1780). See Burke's Works,
ed. Bohn, II, 55-126.
  P. 174. *the elephant to make them sport.* " Paradise Lost,".IV,
345.
  *native and endued.* " Hamlet," iv, 7, 180.
  *Lord Chatham.* William Pitt, Earl of Chatham (1708-1778), the
great English statesman.
  P. 176. *a new creation.* Goldsmith's " Traveler," 296.
  P. 178. *All the great changes.* Cf. Morley's " Life of Burke,"
ch. 8: " All really profound speculation about society comes in time
to touch the heart of every other object of speculation, not by
directly contributing new truths or directly corroborating old ones,
but by setting men to consider the consequences to life of different
opinions on these abstract subjects, and their relations to the great

paramount interests of society, however those interests may happen at the time to be conceived. Burke's book marks a turning-point in literary history, because it was the signal for that reaction over the whole field of thought, into which the Revolution drove many of the finest minds of the next generation, by showing the supposed consequences of pure individualistic rationalism."

P. 179. *Alas! Leviathan.* Cowper's "Task," II, 322.

*the corner stone.* Psalms, cxvii, 22.

*to the Jews.* 1 Corinthians, i, 23.

P. 183. *the consequences of his writings.* In this view Hazlitt has the full support of Lord Morley.

P. 184. *How charming.* Milton's " Comus," 476.

*He was one of the severest writers we have.* The description of Burke's style which follows should be compared with that given on pp. 344-5 and with the splendid passage in the " Plain Speaker " essay "On the Prose Style of Poets," beginning: " It has always appeared to me that the most perfect prose-style, the most powerful, the most dazzling, the most daring, that which went the nearest to the verge of poetry, and yet never fell over, was Burke's. It has the solidity, and sparkling effect of the diamond; all other *fine writing* is like French paste or Bristol-stones in the comparison. Burke's style is airy, flighty, adventurous, but it never loses sight of the subject; nay, is always in contact with, and derives its increased or varying impulse from it. It may be said to pass yawning gulfs ' on the unsteadfast footing of a spear: ' still it has an actual resting-place and tangible support under it—it is not suspended on nothing. It differs from poetry, as I conceive, like the chamois from the eagle: it climbs to an almost equal height, touches upon a cloud, overlooks a precipice, is picturesque, sublime—but all the while, instead of soaring through the air, it stands upon a rocky cliff, clambers up by abrupt and intricate ways, and browzes on the roughest bark, or crops the tender flower."

P. 186. *the set or formal style.* See pp. 147-8.

P. 187. *Thoughts on the Cause of the Present Discontents* (1770), a criticism of the ministerial policy of the English government under George III.

*Reflections on the Revolution in France* (1790), a severe arraignment of the principles which inspired the revolution and a prophetic warning of its consequences.

*Letter to the Duke of Bedford.* A Letter from the Right Hon. Edmund Burke, to a Noble Lord, on the attacks made upon him and his pension, in the House of Lords, by the Duke of Bedford and the Earl of Lauderdale, early in the present session of Parliament. (1796.)

*Regicide Peace.* Three Letters addressed to a Member of the Present Parliament, on the proposals for peace with the regicide Directory of France. (1796.)

P. 188. *Fox,* Charles James (1749-1806), the famous Whig statesman who was frequently the opponent of Burke and of the younger Pitt.

P. 189. *Dr. Johnson observed,* in his "Life of Pope" (ed. Birkbeck Hill, III, 230): "In their similes the greatest writers have sometimes failed: the ship-race, compared with the chariot-race, is neither illustrated nor aggrandised; land and water make all the difference: when Apollo running after Daphne is likened to a greyhound chasing a hare, there is nothing gained; the ideas of pursuit and flight are too plain to be made plainer, and a god and the daughter of a god are not represented much to their advantage by a hare and a dog."

*a person.* Conjecturally Joseph Fawcett. In the essay "On Criticism" ("Table Talk") Hazlitt says: "The person of the most refined and least contracted taste I ever knew was the late Joseph Fawcett, the friend of my youth. He was almost the first literary acquaintance I ever made, and I think the most candid and unsophisticated. He had a masterly perception of all styles and of every kind and degree of excellence, sublime or beautiful, from Milton's Paradise Lost to Shenstone's Pastoral Ballad, from Butler's Analogy down to Humphrey Clinker."

P. 189, n. *the comparison of the British Constitution.* "Letter to a Noble Lord," Works, ed. Bohn, V, 137.


## MR. WORDSWORTH

From "The Spirit of the Age." Characterizations of Wordsworth also occur in the lecture "On the Living Poets" and in the Essay "On Genius and Common Sense" in "Table Talk."

P. 191. *lowliness is young ambition's ladder.* "Julius Cæsar," ii, 1, 22.

*no figures.* Cf. "Julius Cæsar," ii, 1, 231: "Thou hast no figures nor no fantasies Which busy care draws in the brains of men."

*skyey influences.* "Measure for Measure," iii, 1, 9.

P. 192. *nihil humani.* Terence: "Heautontimoroumenos," i, 1, 25.
*the cloud-capt towers.* "Tempest," iv, 1, 151.
P. 193. *the judge's robe.* Cf. "Measure for Measure," ii, 2, 59:
"No ceremony that to great ones 'longs,
    Not the king's crown, nor the deputed sword,
    The marshal's truncheon, nor the judge's robe."
*Pindar and Alcæus.* Greek lyric poets.
*a sense of joy.* Wordsworth's "To My Sister."
P. 194. *Beneath the hills.* Cf. Wordsworth's "Excursion," VI,
531:
    "Amid the groves, under the shadowy hills
        The generations are prepared . . ."
P. 195. *To him the meanest flower.* "Ode on the Intimations of
Immortality."
P. 196. *Grasmere* was the residence of Wordsworth between 1799
and 1813.
*Cole-Orton* was the residence of Wordsworth's friend, Sir George
Beaumont, to whom he dedicated the 1815 edition of his poems:
"Some of the best pieces were composed under the shade of your
own groves, upon the classic ground of Cole-Orton."
P. 197. *Calm contemplation.* Cf. "Laodamia": "Calm pleasures
there abide, majestic pains."
*Fall blunted* "from each indurated heart." Goldsmith's
"Traveler," 232.
*and fit audience.* Wordsworth quotes this line from "Paradise
Lost," VII, 31, in "The Recluse," 776:
    "'Fit audience let me find though few!'
        So prayed, more gaining than he asked, the Bard—
        In holiest mood."
P. 198. *The Excursion.* Hazlitt wrote a review of this poem for
the *Examiner* which not only aroused Wordsworth's resentment
but led to one of his disagreements with Lamb. The review appears
in the "Round Table."
*toujours perdrix,* "always partridges," alluding to a story of a
French king, who, on being reproved by his confessor for faithless-
ness to his wife, punished the offender by causing him to be fed on
nothing but his favorite dish, which was partridge. See Notes and
Queries, Series IV, Vol. III, p. 336.
*In his person.* In 1803, while on a visit to the Lake Country,
Hazlitt had painted a portrait of Wordsworth. "He has painted
Wordsworth," writes Southey, "but so dismally, though Words-

worth's face is his idea of physiognomical perfection, that one of his friends, on seeing it, exclaimed, ' At the gallows—deeply affected by his deserved fate—yet determined to die like a man; ' and if you saw the picture, you would admire the criticism." " Life and Correspondence," II, 238.

*His manner of reading.* See p. 295.

*a man of no mark.* 1 "Henry IV," iii, 2, 45.

P. 199. *He finds fault with Dryden's description.* Hazlitt adopted this criticism in his lecture " On Pope and Dryden."

P. 200. *Titian* (c. 1477-1576), the great Venetian painter.

*Chaucer.* Wordsworth's modernizations of Chaucer are " The Prioress's Tale," " The Cuckoo and the Nightingale," and a part of " Troilus and Cressida."

*a tragedy.* "The Borderers" was written in 1795-96 but not published till 1842. The quotation which follows is from Act iii, 1, 405, and should read:

> "Action is transitory—a step, a blow,
> The motion of a muscle—this way or that—
> 'Tis done, and in the after-vacancy
> We wonder at ourselves like men betrayed:
> Suffering is permanent, obscure and dark,
> And shares the nature of infinity."

Wordsworth quoted these lines after the dedication to " The White Doe of Rylstone" and later added a note: " This and the five lines that follow were either read or recited by me more than thirty years since, to the late Mr. Hazlitt, who quoted some expressions in them (imperfectly remembered) in a work of his published several years ago."

P. 201. *Let observation.* Cf. De Quincey's " Rhetoric " (Works, ed. Masson, X, 128) : " We recollect a little biographic sketch of Dr. Johnson, published immediately after his death, in which, among other instances of desperate tautology, the author quotes the well-known lines from the Doctor's imitation of Juvenal—' Let observation,' etc., and contends with some reason that this is saying in effect,—' *Let observation with extensive observation observe mankind extensively.*' " Coleridge somewhere makes the same remark.

*Drawcansir.* A character in " The Rehearsal" by the Duke of Buckingham.

> " Let petty kings the names of Parties know :
> Where'er I am, I slay both friend and foe." v, 1.

*Walton's Angler.* In the fifth lecture of the " English Poets "

Hazlitt writes: "Perhaps the best pastoral in the language is that prose-poem, Walton's Complete Angler. That well-known work has a beauty and romantic interest equal to its simplicity, and arising out of it. In the description of a fishing-tackle, you perceive the piety and humanity of the author's mind. It is to be doubted whether Sannazarius's Piscatory Eclogues are equal to the scenes described by Walton on the banks of the river Lea. He gives the feeling of the open air: we walk with him along the dusty roadside, or repose on the banks of a river under a shady tree; and in watching for the finny prey, imbibe what he beautifully calls 'the patience and simplicity of poor honest fishermen.' We accompany them to their inn at night, and partake of their simple, but delicious fare; while Maud, the pretty milkmaid, at her mother's desire, sings the classical ditties of the poet Marlow; 'Come live with me, and be my love.'"

*Paley,* William (1743-1805), a noted theologian. Cf. "On the Clerical Character" in "Political Essays" (Works, III, 276) : "This same shuffling divine is the same Dr. Paley, who afterwards employed the whole of his life, and his moderate second-hand abilities, in tampering with religion, morality, and politics,—in trimming between his convenience and his conscience,—in crawling between heaven and earth, and trying to cajole both. His celebrated and popular work on Moral Philosophy, is celebrated and popular for no other reason, than that it is a somewhat ingenious and amusing apology for existing abuses of any description, by which any thing is to be got. It is a very elaborate and consolatory elucidation of the text, *that men should not quarrel with their bread and butter.* It is not an attempt to show what is right, but to palliate and find out plausible excuses for what is wrong. It is a work without the least value, except as a convenient commonplace book or *vade mecum,* for tyro politicians and young divines, to smooth their progress in the Church or the State. This work is a text-book in the University: its morality is the acknowledged morality of the House of Commons." See also Coleridge's opinion of Paley on p. 288.

*Bewick,* Thomas (1753-1828), a well-known wood-engraver.

*Waterloo,* Antoine (1609?-1676?), a French engraver, painter, and etcher.

*Rembrandt,* Harmans van Rijn (1606-1669), Dutch painter, whose mastery of light and shade was the object of Hazlitt's special admiration.

P. 202. *He hates conchology,* etc. See the lecture "On the Living

Poets": "He hates all science and all art; he hates chemistry, he
hates conchology; he hates Voltaire; he hates Sir Isaac Newton; he
hates wisdom; he hates wit; he hates metaphysics, which he says are
unintelligible, and yet he would be thought to understand them; he
hates prose; he hates all poetry but his own; he hates the dialogues in
Shakespeare; he hates music, dancing, and painting; he hates
Rubens, he hates Rembrandt; he hates Raphael, he hates Titian;
he hates Vandyke; he hates the antique; he hates the Apollo Bel-
videre; he hates the Venus of Medicis."

*Where one for sense.* Butler's "Hudibras," II, 29.

P. 203. *take the good.* Plautus's "Rudens," iv, 7.

## MR. COLERIDGE

### From the "Spirit of the Age."

P. 205. *and thank.* Cf. "Comus," 176: "In wanton dance they
praise the bounteous Pan."

*a mind reflecting.* See p. 35 and n.

*dark rearward.* Cf. "Tempest," i, 2, 50: "In the dark backward
and abysm of time."

P. 206. *That which was.* "Antony and Cleopatra," iv, 14, 9.

*quick, forgetive.* 2 "Henry IV," iv, 3, 107.

*what in him is weak.* Cf. "Paradise Lost," I, 22: "What in me
is dark Illumine, what is low raise and support."

P. 207. *and by the force.* Cf. "Macbeth," iii, 5, 28: "As by the
strength of their illusion Shall draw him on to his confusion."

*rich strond.* "Faërie Queene," III, iv, 18, 29, 34.

*goes sounding.* "Hazlitt seems to have had a hazy recollection
of two passages in Chaucer's *Prologue.* In his essay on 'My First
Acquaintance with Poets,' he says, 'the scholar in Chaucer is described as going "sounding on his way,"' and in his *Lectures on
the English Poets* he says, 'the merchant, as described in Chaucer,
went on his way "sounding always the increase of his winning."'
The scholar is not described as 'sounding on his way,' but Chaucer
says of him, 'Souninge in moral vertu was his speche,' while the
merchant, though 'souninge alway th' encrees of his winning,' is not
described as going on his way. Wordsworth has a line ('Excursion,' Book III), 'Went sounding on a dim and perilous way,' but
it seems clear that Hazlitt thought he was quoting Chaucer." Waller-
Glover, IV, 412.

P. 208. *his own nothings.* "Coriolanus," ii, 2, 81.

*letting contemplation.* Cf. Dyer's "Grongar Hill," 26: "till contemplation have its fill."

*Sailing with supreme dominion.* Gray's "Progress of Poesy."

*He lisped.* Pope's " Prologue to the Satires," 128.

*Ode on Chatterton.* " Monody on the Death of Chatterton," written by Coleridge in 1790, at the age of eighteen.

P. 209. *gained several prizes.* "At Cambridge Coleridge won the Browne Gold Medal for a Greek Ode in 1792." Waller-Glover.

*At Christ's Hospital,* a London school which Leigh Hunt and Lamb attended about the same time as Coleridge. The former has left a record of its life in his " Autobiography," and Lamb has written of it, with special reference to Coleridge, in his " Recollections of Christ's Hospital" and "Christ's Hospital Five-and-Thirty Years Ago."

*Struggling in vain.* " Excursion," VI, 557.

P. 210. *Hartley,* David (1705-1757), author of "Observations on Man" (1749), and identified chiefly with the theory of association. Cf. Coleridge's "Religious Musings," 368: "and he of mortal kind Wisest, he first who marked the ideal tribes Up the fine fibres through the sentient brain."

*Dr. Priestley,* Joseph (1733-1804), scientist and philosopher of the materialistic school, author of "The Doctrine of Philosophical Necessity Illustrated" (1777). "See! Priestley there, patriot, and saint, and sage." "Religious Musings," 371.

*Bishop Berkeley's fairy-world.* George Berkeley (1685-1753), idealistic philosopher. Cf. p. 287.

*Malebranche,* Nicholas (1638-1715), author of "De la Recherche de la Vérité" (1674).

*Cudworth,* Ralph (1617-1688), author of "The True Intellectual System of the Universe" (1678).

*Lord Brook's hieroglyphical theories.* Fulke Greville, Lord Brooke (1554-1628), friend and biographer of Sir Philip Sidney.

*Bishop Butler's Sermons.* Joseph Butler (1692-1752), author of "Fifteen Sermons Preached at the Rolls Chapel" (1726), and "The Analogy of Religion, Natural and Revealed, to the Constitution and Course of Nature" (1736).

*Duchess of Newcastle.* Margaret Cavendish (1624?-1674), published about a dozen folio volumes of philosophical fancies, poems, and plays. In " Mackery End in Hertfordshire " Lamb refers to her as "the thrice noble, chaste, and virtuous, but again somewhat fantastical and original-brained, generous Margaret Newcastle."

*Clarke,* Samuel (1675-1729), English theologian of latitudinarian principles.

*South,* Robert (1634-1716), controversial writer and preacher.

*Tillotson,* John (1630-1694), a popular theological writer of rationalistic tendency.

*Leibnitz's Pre-established Harmony.* Gottfried Wilhelm Leibnitz (1646-1716), a German philosopher, represented the world as consisting of an infinite number of independent substances or monads related to each other in such a way (by the pre-established harmony) as to form one universe. Cf. Coleridge's "Destiny of Nations," 38 ff.:

> "Others boldlier think
> That as one body seems the aggregate
> Of atoms numberless, each organized;
> So by a strange and dim similitude
> Infinite myriads of self-conscious minds
> Are an all-conscious spirit, which informs
> With absolute ubiquity of thought
> (His own eternal self-affirming act!)
> All his involved Monads, that yet seem
> With various province and apt agency
> Each to pursue its own self-centering end."

P. 210, n. *And so by many.* "Two Gentlemen of Verona," ii, 7, 30.

P. 211. *hortus siccus* [dry garden] *of Dissent.* Burke's "Reflections on the French Revolution," Works, ed. Bohn, II, 287.

*John Huss* (1373?-1415), Bohemian reformer and martyr.

*Jerome of Prague,* a follower of Huss who was burnt for heresy in 1416.

*Socinus.* Fausto Paulo Sozzini (1539-1604), an Italian theologian who sought to simplify the doctrine of the Trinity.

*John Zisca* (1370?-1424), a leader of the extreme Hussite party.

*Neal's History.* Daniel Neal (1648-1743) published his "History of the Puritans" 1732-38.

*Calamy,* Edmund (1671-1732) published an "Account of the Ministers, Lecturers, Masters and Fellows of Colleges, and Schoolmasters who were Ejected or Silenced after the Restoration of 1660" (1702 and 1713).

*Spinoza,* Baruch (1632-1677), a Dutch philosopher of Jewish parentage, the chief representative of Pantheism, "the doctrine of one infinite substance, of which all finite existences are modes or limitations."

*When he saw.* Cf. Coleridge's "Remorse," iv, 2, 100:
"When we saw nought but beauty; when we heard
The voice of that Almighty One who loved us
In every gale that breathed, and wave that murmur'd!"

*Proclus* (410-485) and *Plotinus* (204-270), philosophers of the Neo-Platonic school. In "Biographia Literaria" (chap. 9) Coleridge refers to his "early study of Plato and of Plotinus, with the commentaries and the 'Theologia Platonica' of the illustrious Florentine; of Proclus, and Gemistius Pletho."

*Duns Scotus* (1265 or 1275-1308) and *Thomas Aquinas* (1227-1274), two great theologians of the Catholic Church.

*Jacob Behmen* or Böhme (1575-1624), a German religious mystic who exerted considerable influence on English religious thought in the eighteenth century. In the "Biographia Literaria" (chap. 9) Coleridge writes: "A meek and shy quietist, his intellectual powers were never stimulated into feverous energy by crowds of proselytes, or by the ambition of proselyting. Jacob Behmen was an enthusiast in the strictest sense, as not merely distinguished, but as contradistinguished from a fanatic. . . . The writings of these Mystics acted in no slight degree to prevent my mind from being imprisoned within the outline of any single dogmatic system."

*Swedenborg,* Emanuel (1688-1772), the Swedish scientist and mystic from whom have sprung some of the modern theosophical cults.

*Religious Musings,* published in his "Poems on Various Subjects" (1796).

*the glad prose of Jeremy Taylor.* Cf. "Literature of the Age of Elizabeth," Lecture VII: "In his writings, the frail stalk of human life reclines on the bosom of eternity. His Holy Living and Dying is a divine pastoral. He writes to the faithful followers of Christ, as the shepherd pipes to his flock. He introduces touching and heartfelt appeals to familiar life; condescends to men of low estate; and his pious page blushes with modesty and beauty. His style is prismatic. It unfolds the colours of the rainbow; it floats like the bubble through the air; it is like innumerable dew-drops that glitter on the face of morning, and tremble as they glitter. He does not dig his way underground, but slides upon ice, borne on the winged car of fancy. The dancing light he throws upon objects is like an Aurora Borealis, playing betwixt heaven and earth. . . . In a word, his writings are more like fine poetry than any other prose whatever; they are a choral song in praise of virtue, and a hymn to the Spirit of the Universe."

*Bowles,* William Lisle (1762-1850), published "Fourteen Sonnets" in 1789, and a second edition containing twenty-one in the same year. In the first chapter of the "Biographia Literaria," Coleridge credits the sonnets of Bowles with saving him from a premature absorption in metaphysics and theology and with introducing him to the excellences of the new school of poetry. In his enthusiasm he went about making proselytes for Bowles and "as my school finances did not permit me to purchase copies, I made, within less than a year and a half, more than forty transcriptions, as the best presents I could offer to those, who had in any way won my regard. And with almost equal delight did I receive the three or four following publications of the same author." Coleridge also addressed a "Sonnet to Bowles," opening

"My heart hath thanked thee, Bowles! for those soft strains,
   That on the still air floating tremblingly,
   Wak'd in me Fancy, Love, and Sympathy!"

P. 212. *John Bull.* Croker's John Bull was a scurrilous newspaper edited by Theodore Hook, the first number of which appeared December 17, 1820.

*Mr. Croker,* John Wilson (1780-1857), politician and man of letters, one of Hazlitt's pet aversions, and the same who comes in for such a severe chastisement in Macaulay's review of his edition of Boswell's "Johnson."

*Junius,* the mysterious author of a famous series of political letters which appeared in the London Public Advertiser from January 21, 1769, to January 21, 1772, collected as the "Letters of Junius" in 1772. The name of Sir Philip Francis is the one most persistently associated with the composition of these letters.

*Godwin,* William (1756-1836), leader of the philosophical radicals in England and a believer in the perfectibility of man, wrote "An Enquiry concerning Political Justice" (1793), "Caleb Williams" (1794), and other novels and miscellaneous works. Godwin was the husband of Mary Wolstonecraft, and the father-in-law of Shelley. Hazlitt wrote a sketch of him in the "Spirit of the Age" and reviewed his last novel, "Cloudesley," in the Edinburgh Review. Coleridge has a Sonnet to William Godwin:

"Nor will I not thy holy guidance bless,
   And hymn thee, Godwin! with an ardent lay;

For that thy voice, in Passion's stormy day
When wild I roam'd the bleak Heath of Distress,
Bade the bright form of Justice meet my way—
And told me that her name was Happiness."

*Sorrows of Werter,* a sentimental novel of Goethe's, the work by which he was most generally known to English readers in Hazlitt's day.

*laugh'd with Rabelais.* Cf. Pope's "Dunciad," I, 22: "Or laugh and shake in Rab'lais easy chair."

*spoke with rapture of Raphael.* Coleridge had visited Italy in 1806 on his return from a stay in Malta, and had devoted his time there to a study of Italian art. See p. 298 n.

*Giotto* (d. 1337), *Ghirlandaio,* whose real name was Domenico Bigardi (1449-1494), and *Massaccio* (1402-1429) were early Florentine painters.

*wandered into Germany.* Coleridge's visit to Germany and his introduction to the leading German philosophers dates back to 1798-99.

*Kantean philosophy.* Immanuel Kant (1724-1804) was the leader of modern philosophy. "The writings of the illustrious sage of Königsberg, the founder of the Critical Philosophy, more than any other work, at once invigorated and disciplined my understanding. The originality, the depth, and the compression of the thoughts; the novelty and subtlety, yet solidity and importance of the distinctions; the adamantine chain of the logic; and I will venture to add—(paradox as it will appear to those who have taken their notion of Immanuel Kant from Reviewers and Frenchmen)—the clearness and evidence, of the Critique of Pure Reason; and Critique of the Judgment; of the Metaphysical Elements of Natural Philosophy; and of his Religion within the bounds of Pure Reason, took possession of me as with a giant's hand. After fifteen years' familiarity with them, I still read these and all his other productions with undiminished delight and increasing admiration." "Biographia Literaria," chap. IX.

*Fichte,* J. Gottlieb (1762-1814). "Fichte's *Wissenschaftslehre,* or Lore of Ultimate Science, was to add the key-stone of the arch" of Kant's system. Ibid.

*Schelling,* Friedrich Wilhelm Joseph (1775-1829). "In Schelling's *Natur-Philosophie,* and the *System des Transcendentalen Idealismus,* I first found a genial coincidence with much that I had toiled out for myself, and a powerful assistance in what I had yet to do. . . . Many of the most striking resemblances, indeed all the main and fundamental ideas, were born and matured in my mind before I had ever seen a single page of the German Philosopher; and I might indeed affirm with truth, before the most important works of Schelling had been written, or at least made public. Nor is this coincidence at all to be wondered at. We had studied in the same school; been disciplined by the same preparatory philosophy, namely, the writings of Kant; we had both equal obligations to the polar logic and dynamic philosophy of Giordano Bruno; and Schelling has lately, and, as of recent acquisition, avowed that same affectionate reverence for the labors of Behmen, and other mystics, which I had formed at a much earlier period." Ibid.

*Lessing,* Gotthold Ephraim (1729-1781), German dramatist and critic.

*sang for joy.* Coleridge had in 1789 composed some stanzas " On the Destruction of the Bastille," but these were not published till 1834.

*would have floated his bark.* Coleridge and Southey with some other friends had in 1794 formed a plan for an ideal colony, the Pantisocracy, on the banks of the Susquehanna.

*In Philharmonia's.* Cf. Coleridge's " Monody on the Death of Chatterton," 140: " O'er peaceful Freedom's undivided dale."

P. 213. *Frailty.* Cf. " Hamlet," i, 2, 146: " thy name is woman."

*writing paragraphs.* Coleridge was connected with the staff of the Courier as a sort of assistant-editor for five months in 1811. His contributions during this period appeared as the " Essays on His Own Times " in 1850.

*poet-laureate* and *stamp-distributor* are references respectively to Southey and Wordsworth.

*bourne from whence.* " Hamlet," iii, 1, 79.

*tantalized by useless resources.* Compare this with Coleridge's own lines of bitter self-reproach addressed " To a Gentleman":
" Sense of past youth, and manhood come in vain,
And genius given, and knowledge won in vain."

P. 214. *one splendid passage.* The lines beginning " Alas! they had been friends in youth " (408-426). The same passage had been singled out for praise by Hazlitt in his lecture " On the Living Poets " and in the review of " Christabel " which had appeared in the Examiner of June 2, 1816. The authorship of this review has been disputed but should on internal evidence, despite its failure in appreciation, be ascribed to Hazlitt. See Works, XI, 580-582.

*Translation of Schiller's Wallenstein,* made by Coleridge in 1799-1800.

*Remorse.* This tragedy was played at the Drury Lane Theatre with considerable popular success in 1813. It was a recast of an early play entitled "Osorio," composed in 1797.

P. 215. *The Friend;* a literary, moral, and political weekly paper, excluding personal and party politics and the events of the day (1809-1810), was reissued in one volume in 1812, and with additions and alterations (rather a rifacimento than a new edition) in 1818.

The sketch in the Spirit of the Age concludes with a contrast between Coleridge and William Godwin.

## MR. SOUTHEY

This selection forms the conclusion of a sketch of Southey in the "Spirit of the Age." It illustrates, even more strikingly than the "Character of Burke," Hazlitt's power of dissociating his judgments from his prejudices, inasmuch as there had been exchanges of rancorous personalities between the two men.

P. 216. *Like the high leaves.* Southey's "The Holly Tree."

*of any poet.* In an essay in the "Plain Speaker" "On the Prose Style of Poets," Hazlitt elaborates his theory that poets turned out inferior prose. "I have but an indifferent opinion of the prose-style of poets: not that it is not sometimes good, nay, excellent; but it is never the better, and generally the worse from the habit of writing verse."

*full of wise saws.* "As You Like It," ii, 7, 156.

P. 217. *historian and prose-translator.* Southey wrote the "History of Brazil," the "History of the Peninsular War," the "Book of the Church," and lives of Wesley, Cowper, and Nelson. He translated from the Spanish the romances of "Amadis of Gaul," "Palmerin of England," and "The Cid."

P. 219. *Pindaric or Shandean,* i.e., whimsical. Pindaric should of course be understood as a reference to Peter Pindar, the name under which John Wolcot (1738-1819) wrote his coarse and whimsical satires. Hazlitt mentions him at the end of his lectures "On the Comic Writers": "The bard in whom the nation and the king delighted, is old and blind, but still merry and wise:—remembering how he has made the world laugh in his time, and not repenting of the mirth he has given; with an involuntary smile lighted up at the mad pranks of his Muse, and the lucky hits of his pen." Shandean is derived from Sterne's novel, "Tristram Shandy."

*And follows so.* "Henry V," iv, 1, 293.

*his political inconsistency.* This is the subject of Hazlitt's attacks on Southey. See "Political Essays" (Works, III, 109-120, 192-232).

## ELIA

The last essay in the "Spirit of the Age" is entitled "Elia and Geoffrey Crayon." An edition published at Paris by Galignani in 1825 omits the account of Washington Irving, and this text, as it is in all respects unexceptionable, has been here adopted for the sake of coherence. In a letter to Bernard Barton, February 10, 1825, Lamb refers to Hazlitt's sketch: "He has laid too many colours on my likeness, but I have had so much injustice done me in my own name, that I make a rule of accepting as much over-measure to 'Elia' as Gentlemen think proper to bestow."

P. 221. *shuffle off.* "Hamlet," iii, 1, 67.

*The self-applauding bird.* Cowper's "Truth," 58.

P. 222. *New-born gauds* and *give to dust.* "Troilus and Cressida," iii, 3, 176-79.

*do not in broad rumor lie;* and the two following quotations are free renderings of "Lycidas," 78-82.

*Mr. Lamb rather affects.* Hazlitt had Lamb in his eye when he described the *Occult School* in the essay "On Criticism" ("Table Talk"): "There is another race of critics who might be designated as the *Occult School—verè adępti.* They discern no beauties but what are concealed from superficial eyes, and overlook all that are obvious to the vulgar part of mankind. Their art is the transmutation of styles. By happy alchemy of mind they convert dross into gold— and gold into tinsel. They see farther into a millstone than most others. If an author is utterly unreadable, they can read him for ever: his intricacies are their delight, his mysteries are their study. They prefer Sir Thomas Brown to the Rambler by Dr. Johnson, and Burton's Anatomy of Melancholy to all the writers of the Georgian Age. They judge of works of genius as misers do of hid treasure—it is of no value unless they have it all to themselves. They will no more share a book than a mistress with a friend. If they suspected their favourite volumes of delighting any eyes but their own, they would immediately discard them from the list. Theirs are superannuated beauties that every one else has left off intriguing with, bed-ridden hags, a 'stud of night-mares.' This is not envy or affectation, but a natural proneness to singularity, a love of what is odd and out of the way. They must come at their pleasures with difficulty, and support admiration by an uneasy sense of ridicule and opposition. They despise those qualities in a work which are cheap and obvious. They like a monopoly of taste, and are shocked at the prostitution of intellect implied in popular productions. In like manner, they would chuse a friend or recommend a mistress for gross defects; and tolerate the sweetness of an actress's voice only for the ugliness of her face. Pure pleasures are in their judgment cloying and insipid—

'An ounce of sour is worth a pound of sweet!'

Nothing goes down with them but what is *caviare* to the multitude. They are eaters of olives and readers of black-letter. Yet they smack of genius, and would be worth any money, were it only for the rarity of the thing!"

P. 223. *fine fretwork.* "Essays of Elia," "The South-Sea House."

*the chimes at midnight.* 2 "Henry IV," iii, 2, 228.

P. 224. *cheese and pippins.* Ibid., v, 3.

*inns and courts of law.* "The Old Benchers of the Inner Temple," in "Essays of Elia."

*a certain writer.* Hazlitt himself. It is known to everybody that the friendship of Lamb for Hazlitt suffered certain strains, and various attempts have been made to guess at the provocations. Mutual recriminations in regard to literary borrowings have been thought to be responsible for more than one breach. So Mr. Bertram Dobell, in his "Sidelights on Lamb," 212-14, imagines that the mystery is solved in a letter of Hazlitt's to the editor of the London Magazine (April 12, 1820) charging Lamb with appropriating his ideas: "Do you keep the Past and Future? You see Lamb argues the same view of the subject. That 'young master' will anticipate all my discoveries if I don't mind." The similarity of idea between Hazlitt's "Past and Future" and Lamb's "New Year's Eve," and the appearance in Lamb's essay of the phrase "young masters" makes it clear enough what Hazlitt is referring to, but that either man should have taken the matter very seriously is hard to believe. It is easier to look upon Hazlitt's expression as banter of the same kind that Lamb allowed himself in connection with the essay on "Guy Faux" alluded to in the present sketch. This subject had been proposed by Lamb, as we are informed in "Of Persons One Would Wish to Have Seen," and had been written up by Hazlitt in the Examiner in 1821 (Works, XI, 317-334). Two years later Lamb contributed a paper on the same subject to the London Magazine, founded partly on an essay in the Reflector (1811), entitled "On the Probable Effects of the Gunpowder Treason." The essay in the London Magazine (Lamb's Works, ed. Lucas, I, 236 ff.) opens with a facetious thrust at Hazlitt: "A very ingenious and subtle writer, whom there is good reason for suspecting to be an ex-Jesuit, not unknown at Douay some five-and-twenty years since (he will not obtrude himself at M—th again in a hurry), about a twelvemonth back, set himself to prove the character of the Powder Plot conspirators to have been that of heroic self-devotedness and true Christian martyrdom. Under the mask of Protestant candour, he actually gained admission for his treatise into a London weekly paper, not particularly distinguished for its zeal towards either religion. But, admitting Catholic principles, his arguments are shrewd and incontrovertible. [Then follows a quotation from Hazlitt setting forth the Catholic standpoint.] It is impossible, upon Catholic principles, not to admit the force of this reasoning; we can only not help smiling (with the writer) at the simplicity of the gulled editor, swallowing the dregs of Loyola for the very quintessence of sublimated reason in England at the commencement of the nineteenth century. We will just, as a contrast, show what we Protestants (who are a party concerned) thought upon the same subject, at a period rather nearer to the heroic project in question." This is the kind of resentment we would expect Lamb to show at the appropriation of his ideas. That there were not wanting grounds for real grievance against Hazlitt may be gathered from a letter to Wordsworth, September 23, 1816 (Lamb's Works, ed. Lucas, VI, 491): "There was a cut at me a few months back by the same hand. . . . It was a pretty compendium of observation, which the author has collected in my disparagement, from some hundred of social evenings which we had spent together,—however in spite of all, there is something tough in my attachment to H—— which these violent strainings cannot quite dislocate or sever asunder. I get no conversation in London that is absolutely worth attending to but his." To one of his quarrels with Lamb Hazlitt owes the finest compliment he ever received, and happily it marks the termination of all differences between them. It occurs in the well-known "Letter of Elia to Robert Southey" which Lamb published in the London Magazine when Southey reproached him with his friendship for Hazlitt (Works, I, 233): "I stood well with him for fifteen years (the proudest of my life), and have ever spoke my full mind of him to some, to whom his panegyric must naturally be least tasteful. I never in thought swerved from him, I never betrayed him, I never slackened in my admiration for him, I was the same to him (neither better nor worse) though he could not see it, as in the days when he thought fit to trust me. At this instant, he may be preparing for me some compliment, above my deserts, as he has sprinkled many such among his admirable books, for which I rest his debtor; or, for any thing I know, or can guess to the contrary, he may be about to read a lecture on my weaknesses. He is welcome to them (as he was to my humble hearth), if they can divert a spleen, or ventilate a fit of sullenness. I wish he would not quarrel with the world at the rate he does; but the reconciliation must be effected by himself, and I despair of living to see that day. But, protesting against much that he has written, and some things he chooses to do; judging him by his conversation which I enjoyed so long, and relished so deeply; or by his books, in those places where no clouding passion intervenes—I should belie my own conscience, if I said less, than that I think W. H. to be, in his natural and healthy state, one of the wisest and finest spirits breathing. So far from being ashamed of that intimacy, which was betwixt us, it is my boast that I was able for so many years to have preserved it entire; and I think I shall go to my grave without finding, or expecting to find, such another companion."

*Burton's Anatomy of Melancholy* was published in 1621. Its quaint prose was often imitated by Lamb and had a direct effect on his style.

*Sir Thomas Browne* (1605-1682), physician and essayist, author of "Religio Medici" (1642), "Pseudodoxia Epidemica" (1646), and "Hydriotaphia or Urn Burial" (1658).

*Fuller's Worthies.* The "History of the Worthies of England" (1662) is the best known work of Thomas Fuller (1608-1661), an English divine and writer on church history.

*does not make him despise Pope.* See p. 322.

*Parnell,* Thomas (1679-1717). In the sixth lecture on the "English Poets" Hazlitt says: "Parnell, though a good-natured, easy man, and a friend to poets and the Muses, was himself little more than an occasional versifier."

*Gay,* John (1685-1732), is best known by his "Beggar's Opera" (1728) and "Fables" (1727 and 1738). Hazlitt writes of Gay in the sixth lecture on the "English Poets" and has a paper on "The Beggar's Opera" in the "Round Table."

*His taste in French and German.* Cf. "On Old English Writers and Speakers" in the "Plain Speaker": "Mr. Lamb has lately taken it into his head to read St. Evremont, and works of that stamp. I neither praise nor blame him for it. He observed, that St. Evremont was a writer half-way between Montaigne and Voltaire, with a spice of the wit of the one and the sense of the other. I said I was always of the opinion that there had been a great many clever people in the world, both in France and England, but I had been sometimes rebuked for it. Lamb took this as a slight reproach; for he had been a little exclusive and national in his tastes."

P. 225. *His admiration of Hogarth.* See note to p. 158.

*Leonardo da Vinci* (1452-1519), Italian painter, sculptor, architect.

*fine Titian head.* Hazlitt painted a portrait of Lamb in the costume of a Venetian senator. This portrait now hangs in the National Gallery.

P. 226. *to have coined.* Cf. "Julius Cæsar," iv, 3, 72: "I had rather coin my heart, And drop my blood for drachmas."

*Mr. Waithman,* Robert (1764-1833), was Lord Mayor in 1823.

*Rosamond Gray,* a tale, was published in 1798 and "John Woodvill," a tragedy, in 1802. The lines in the footnote are from the second act of "John Woodvill."


## SIR WALTER SCOTT

This selection forms the latter half of the sketch of Scott in the "Spirit of the Age." The following dialogue between Northcote and Hazlitt, "Conversations of Northcote," XVI, represents Hazlitt's feelings for Scott: "N. 'You don't know him, do you? He'd be a pattern to you. Oh! he has a very fine manner. You would learn to rub off some of your asperities. But you admire him, I believe.' H. 'Yes; on this side of idolatry and Toryism.' N. 'That is your prejudice.' H. 'Nay, it rather shows my liberality, if I am a devoted enthusiast notwithstanding. There are two things I admire

in Sir Walter, his capacity and his simplicity; which indeed I am apt
to think are much the same.'"

P. 227. *more lively.* Cf. "Coriolanus," iv, 5, 237: "it's spritely,
waking, audible, and full of vent."

*their habits.* "Hamlet," iii, 4, 135.

P. 228. *Baron of Bradwardine* and the others mentioned in this
sentence appear in "Waverley."

*Paul Veronese* (1528-1588), a painter of the Venetian school.

*Balfour of Burley* and the others in this sentence appear in
"Old Mortality." The quotation is from chapter 38.

*Meg Merilees* to *Dominie Sampson,* in "Guy Mannering."

P. 229. *her head to the east.* Cf. "Guy Mannering," chap. 15:
"Na, na! not that way, the feet to the east."

*Rob Roy* to *Die Vernon,* in "Rob Roy."

*thick coming.* Cf. "Macbeth," v, 3, 38: "thick-coming fancies."

*Earl of Glenallan,* in "The Antiquary."

*Black Dwarf* to *Grace Armstrong,* in the "Black Dwarf."

*Children of the Mist,* in "Legend of Montrose."

*Amy* (Robsart) and *Varney,* in "Kenilworth."

*George of Douglas,* in "The Abbot."

P. 229, n. *the finest scene.* "Guy Mannering," chap. 51.

P. 231. *a consummation.* "Hamlet," iii, 1, 63.

*by referring to the authentic history.* At this point Hazlitt reproduces in a footnote one of Scott's historical quotations in "Ivanhoe."

*flints and dungs.* See "Ivanhoe," chap. 43.

P. 232. *calls backing.* 1 "Henry IV," ii, 4, 165.

*Mr. MacAdam,* John Loudon (1756-1836).

*Sixty years since.* The sub-title of "Waverley" was "'Tis Sixty
Years Since."

*Wickliff,* John (c. 1320-1384), an important English forerunner
of the Protestant Reformation, the first translator of the Bible
into English.

*Luther,* Martin (1483-1546), led the first successful revolt against
the authority of the Catholic Church.

*Hampden,* John (c. 1595-1643), an English patriot who by his
refusal to pay ship-money precipitated the rebellion against Charles
I which ended in the beheading of that monarch.

*Sidney,* Algernon (1622-1683), an English patriot who fought on
the side of Parliament against Charles I, and who, in the reign of
Charles II, was tried for treason by Jeffreys, the hanging judge, and

condemned to execution without proof. Sidney is the author of "Discourses Concerning Government" in which he vindicates the right of resistance to the misrule of kings.

*Somers,* John (1651-1716), took an important part in bringing about the bloodless Revolution which drove James II from England in 1688.

P. 233. *Red Reiver, in* "The Black Dwarf."

*Claverhouse,* in "Old Mortality."

*Tristan the Hermit* and *Petit André,* in "Quentin Durward."

*but himself.* Though Scott composed many of his own mottoes, he never quoted his own previous verse but pretended to be using an Old Play or an Old Poem.

P. 234. *born for the universe.* Goldsmith's "Retaliation," 31.

*winked and shut.* Marston's "Antonio's Revenge," Prologue.

P. 235. *Who would not grieve.* Cf. Pope's "Prologue to the Satires," 213:

"Who but must laugh, if such a man there be?
Who would not weep if Atticus were he?"


# LORD BYRON

From the "Spirit of the Age." Discussions of Byron's poetry are also to be found in the review of "Childe Harold's Pilgrimage" (Works, XI, 420-426) and in "Pope, Lord Byron and Mr. Bowles" (XI, 486-508).

P. 236. *As if a man.* "Coriolanus," v, 3, 36.

*cloud-capt.* "Tempest," iv, 1, 152.

P. 237. *prouder than.* Cf. Shakespeare's "Troilus and Cressida," i, 3, 380: "His crest that prouder than blue Iris bends."

*silly sooth.* "Twelfth Night," ii, 4, 47.

P. 239. *denotes a foregone conclusion.* "Othello," iii, 3, 428.

P. 240. *in cell monastic.* Cf. "As You Like It," iii, 2, 441: "To live in a nook merely monastic."

P. 241. *thoughts that breathe.* Gray's "Progress of Poesy," 110.

P. 242. *Lord Byron does not exhibit a new view of nature.* In the paper on "Pope, Lord Byron and Mr. Bowles," Hazlitt's tone is more generous: "His Lordship likes the poetry, the imaginative part of art, and so do we. . . . He likes the *sombre* part of it, the thoughtful, the decayed, the ideal, the spectral shadow of human greatness, the departed spirit of human power. He sympathizes

not with art as a display of ingenuity, as the triumph of vanity or
luxury, as it is connected with the idiot, superficial, petty self-
complacency of the individual and the moment (these are to him
not 'luscious as locusts, but bitter as coloquintida'); but he sympathizes with the triumphs of Time and Fate over the proudest
works of man—with the crumbling monuments of human glory—
with the dim vestiges and countless generations of men—with that
which claims alliance with the grave, or kindred with the elements
of nature." Works, XI, 496.

*poor men's cottages.* "Merchant of Venice," i, 2, 14.

*reasons high.* "Paradise Lost," II, 558.

P. 243. *Till Contemplation.* Dyer's "Grongar Hill," 26.

*this bank.* "Macbeth," i, 7, 6.

P. 244. *The Liberal*: Verse and Prose from the South, a quarterly published in Italy by Leigh Hunt and Byron, 1822-23, to
which Hazlitt also contributed. In the second of its four numbers
appeared Byron's "Heaven and Earth: A Mystery."

*the deluge,* in "Heaven and Earth."

*his aversion.* See "Don Juan," III, stanza 94:

> "A drowsy frowzy poem, called the Excursion,
> Writ in a manner which is my aversion."

*born in a garret.* In the "English Bards and Scotch Reviewers,"
Byron, speaking of Jeffrey, refers to "the sixteenth story, where
himself was born."

*Letter to the Editor.* The Letter to William Roberts, editor of
the British Review, appeared in the first number of the Liberal.

*Long's,* a restaurant in Bond Street.

P. 245. *the controversy about Pope.* See note to p. 118.

*Scrub,* in Farquhar's "Beaux' Stratagem."

*very.tolerable.* "Much Ado About Nothing," iii, 3, 37.

P. 246. *a chartered libertine.* "Henry V," i, 1, 48.

P. 247. *Like proud seas.* "Two Noble Kinsmen," ii, 2, 23.

*Did the latter ever acknowledge the obligation?* Scott wrote
to Byron's publisher, John Murray, December 17, 1821: "I accept
with feelings of great obligation, the flattering proposal of Lord
Byron to prefix my name to the very grand and tremendous
drama of 'Cain.' I may be partial to it, and you will allow I have
cause; but I do not think that his Muse has ever taken so lofty a
flight amid her former soarings."

*Farthest from them.* "Paradise Lost," I, 247.

P. 248. *the first Vision of Judgment,* the one composed by

Southey on the occasion of the death of George III, celebrating that monarch's entry into heaven and provoking a spirited travesty from Byron.

*None but itself.* This line is quoted by Burke in the "Letters on a Regicide Peace," from a play written or adapted by Lewis Theobald, "The Double Falsehood" (1727). Waller-Glover.

*the tenth transmitter.* Richard Savage's "The Bastard."

P. 250. *Nothing can cover.* Beaumont and Fletcher's "The False One," ii, 1.

## ON POETRY IN GENERAL

This is the first of the "Lectures on the English Poets."

P. 251. *spreads its sweet leaves.* "Romeo and Juliet," i, 1, 158.

P. 252. *the stuff.* "Tempest," iv, 1, 156.

*mere oblivion.* "As You Like It," ii, 7, 166.

*man's life.* "King Lear," ii, 4, 270.

P. 253. *There is warrant.* "Richard III," i, 4, 112.

*such seething brains.* "Midsummer Night's Dream," v, 1, 4.

*Angelica and Medoro.* Characters in "Orlando Furioso."

P. 254. *which ecstacy is very cunning in.* "Hamlet," iii, 4, 138.

*Poetry, according to Lord Bacon.* Cf. Bacon's "Advancement of Learning," Book II: "Because *true Historie* representeth Actions and Euents more ordinarie and lesse interchanged, therefore *Poesie* endueth them with more Rarenesse and more vnexpected and alternatiue Variations: So as it appeareth that *Poesie* serueth and conferreth to Magnanimitie, Moralitie, and to delectation. And therefore it was euer thought to haue some participation of diuinesse, because it doth raise and erect the Minde, by submitting the shewes of things to the desires of the Mind, whereas reason doth buckle and bowe the Mind unto the Nature of things."

P. 255. *Our eyes are made the fools.* "Macbeth," ii, 1, 44.

*That if it would.* "Midsummer Night's Dream," v, 1, 19.

*The flame o' th' taper.* "Cymbeline," ii, 2, 19.

P. 256. *for they are old.* Cf. "Lear," ii, 4, 194.

*Nothing but his unkind daughters.* Cf. "King Lear," iii, 4, 72:

"Nothing could have subdued nature
    To such a lowness but his unkind daughters."

P. 257. *The little dogs.* Ibid., iii, 6, 65.

*So I am.* Ibid., iv, 7, 70.

*O now, for ever.* "Othello," iii, 3, 347.

*Never, Iago.* Ibid., iii, 3, 453.

P. 258. *But there.* Ibid., iv, 2, 57.

*To be discarded thence!* The first edition at this point adds: "This is like that fine stroke of pathos in 'Paradise Lost,' where Milton makes Adam say to Eve,

'Should God create another Eve, and I
Another·rib afford, yet loss of thee
Would never from my heart!'"

*Impassioned poetry is an emanation of the moral and intellectual part of our nature.* Cf. "On People of Sense" in "Plain Speaker": "Poetry acts by sympathy with nature, that is, with the natural impulses, customs, and imaginations of men, and is, on that account, always popular, delightful, and at the same time instructive. It is nature moralizing and *idealizing* for us; inasmuch as, by shewing us things as they are, it implicitly teaches us what they ought to be; and the grosser feelings, by passing through the strainers of this imaginary, wide-extended experience, acquire an involuntary tendency to higher objects. Shakspeare was, in this sense, not only one of the greatest poets, but one of the greatest moralists that we have. Those who read him are the happier, better, and wiser for it."

*Moore,* Edward (1712-1757), author of "The Gamester" (1753),

P. 259. *As Mr. Burke observes,* in "A Philosophical Enquiry into the Origin of Our Ideas of the Sublime and Beautiful," Part I, Section 15: "Choose a day on which to represent the most sublime and affecting tragedy we have; appoint the most favourite actors; spare no cost upon the scenes and decorations; unite the greatest efforts of poetry, painting, and music; and when you have collected your audience, just at the moment when their minds are erect with expectation, let it be reported that a state criminal of high rank is on the point of being executed in the adjoining square; in a moment the emptiness of the theatre would demonstrate the comparative weakness of the imitative arts, and proclaim the triumph of the real sympathy."

*Masterless passion.* Cf. "Merchant of Venice," iv, 1, 51: "For affection, Mistress of passion, sways it to the mood," etc.

P. 260. *satisfaction to the thought.* "Othello," iii, 3, 97.

*Now night descending.* See p. 128.

*Throw him.* Collins's "Ode to Fear."

*Ingratitude.* Cf. "King Lear," i, 4, 281 : "More hideous, when thou show'st thee in a child."

P. 261. *both at the first.* "Hamlet," iii, 2, 23.

P. 262. *And visions.* Hazlitt uses this quotation in his paper on "Wordsworth's Excursion" in the "Round Table" with the change of *poetic* to *prophetic.* "This couplet occurs in a letter from Gray to Walpole ('Letters,' ed. Tovey I, 7-8). The lines are apparently a translation by Gray of Virgil, 'Æneid,' VI, 282-84." Waller-Glover, XII, 504.

P. 263. *Doctor Chalmers's Discourses.* Thomas Chalmers (1780-1847), a celebrated divine and preacher of Scotland, published in 1817 "A Series of Discourses on the Christian Revelation, Viewed in Connection with Modern Astronomy."

*bandit fierce.* Milton's "Comus," 426.

*our fell of hair.* "Macbeth," v, 5, 11.

*Macbeth . . . for the sake of the music.* Some copies of the first edition misprint *Macheath,* the name of the leading character in Gay's "Beggar's Opera." In writing "On Commonplace Critics," in the "Round Table," Hazlitt represents the commonplace critic as questioning whether any one of Shakespeare's plays, "if brought out now for the first time, would succeed. He thinks that 'Macbeth' would be the most likely, from the music which has been introduced into it." The reference is to the music written for D'Avenant's version of the play, produced in 1672. According to Waller-Glover (I, 436), "this music, traditionally assigned to Matthew Locke, is now attributed to Purcell"; but Furness, in the Variorum edition of "Macbeth," accepts the conclusion of Chappell in Grove's "Dictionary of Music," "that Purcell could not have been the composer of a work which appeared when he was in his fourteenth year," especially as "the only reason that can be assigned why modern musicians should have doubted Locke's authorship is that a manuscript of it exists in the handwriting of Henry Purcell."

P. 264. *Between the acting.* "Julius Cæsar," ii, 1, 63.

P. 265. *Thoughts that voluntary move.* "Paradise Lost," III, 37.

*the words of Mercury.* Cf. "Love's Labour's Lost," v, 2, 940: "The words of Mercury are harsh after the songs of Apollo."

*So from the ground.* "Faërie Queene," I, vi, 13.

P. 266. *the secret* [hidden] *soul.* Milton's "L'Allegro."

P. 267. *the golden cadences.* "Love's Labour's Lost," iv, 2, 126.

*Sailing with supreme dominion.* Gray's "Progress of Poesy."

*sounding always.* See p. 207 and n.

*except poets.* Cf. "On the Prose Style of Poets" in the "Plain Speaker": "What is a little extraordinary, there is a want of *rhythmus* and cadence in what they write without the help of metrical rules. Like persons who have been accustomed to sing to music, they are at a loss in the absence of the habitual accompaniment and guide to their judgment. Their style halts, totters, is loose, disjointed, and without expressive pauses or rapid movements. The measured cadence and regular *sing-song* of rhyme or blank verse have destroyed, as it were, their natural ear for the mere characteristic harmony which ought to subsist between the sound and the sense. I should almost guess the Author of Waverley to be a writer of ambling verses from the desultory vacillation and want of firmness in the march of his style. There is neither *momentum* nor elasticity in it; I mean as to the *score,* or effect upon the ear. He has improved since in his other works: to be sure, he has had practice enough. Poets either get into this incoherent, undetermined, shuffling style, made up of 'unpleasing flats and sharps,' of unaccountable starts and pauses, of doubtful odds and ends, flirted about like straws in a gust of wind; or, to avoid it and steady themselves, mount into a sustained and measured prose (like the translation of Ossian's Poems, or some parts of Shaftesbury's Characteristics) which is more odious still, and as bad as being at sea in a calm." Hazlitt's views on this question are peculiar, though his examples are well chosen. The more common opinion is that voiced by Coleridge in his remarks "On Style": "It is, indeed, worthy of remark that all our great poets have been good prose writers, as Chaucer, Spenser, Milton; and this probably arose from their just sense of metre. For a true poet will never confound verse and prose; whereas it is almost characteristic of indifferent prose writers that they should be constantly slipping into scraps of metre." Works, IV, 342.

P. 268. *Addison's Campaign* (1705), written in honor of Marlborough's victory at Blenheim, was described as "that gazette in rhyme" by Joseph Warton (1722-1800) in his "Essay on the Writings and Genius of Pope," I, 29.

*Chaucer.* Cf. A. W. Pollard's "Chaucer," p. 35: "To Boccaccio's 'Teseide' and 'Filostrato,' he was indebted for something more than the groundwork of two of his most important poems; and he was also acquainted with three of his works in Latin prose. If, as is somewhat hardily maintained, he also knew the *Decamerone,* and took from it, in however improved a fashion, the idea of his Canterbury Pilgrimage and the plots of any or all of the four tales (besides that of Grisilde) to which resemblances have been traced in his own work, his obligations to Boccaccio become immense. Yet he never mentions his name, and it has been contended that he was himself unaware of the authorship of the poems and treatises to which he was so greatly indebted."

*Dryden.* His translations from Boccaccio are "Sigismonda and Guiscardo," "Theodore and Honoria," "Cymon and Iphigenia."

P. 269. *married to immortal verse.* "L'Allegro."

*John Bunyan* (1628-1688), author of "Pilgrim's Progress" (1678).

*Daniel Defoe* (c. 1659-1731), journalist and novelist. His masterpiece, "Robinson Crusoe," appeared in 1719.

*dipped in dews.* Cf. T. Heywood's "Ben Jonson, though his learned pen Was dipt in Castaly, is still but Ben."

*Philoctetes.* The story of the Greek hero who, on the voyage to the siege of Troy, was abandoned on an uninhabited island, is the subject of a play by Sophocles.

*As I walked about.* "Robinson Crusoe," Part I, p. 125 (ed. G. A. Aitken).

P. 270. *give an echo.* "Twelfth Night," ii, 4, 21.

P. 271. *Our poesy.* "Timon of Athens," i, 1, 21.

P. 272. *all plumed.* Cf. 1 "Henry IV," iv, 1, 98:

> "All plumed like estridges that with the wind
> Baited like eagles having lately bathed;
> Glittering in golden coats, like images;
> As full of spirits as the month of May,
> And gorgeous as the sun at midsummer;
> Wanton as youthful goats, wild as young bulls."

*If we fly.* Psalms, cxxxix, 9.

P. 275. *Pope Anastatius.* "Inferno," xi, 8.

*Count Ugolino.* Ibid., xxxiii.

*Ossian.* James Macpherson (1736-1796) published between 1760 and 1765 what he alleged to be a translation of the ancient Gaelic hero-bard, Oisin or Ossian. The poems fed the romantic appetite of the generation and were translated into practically every European language. In Germany especially the influence of "Ossian" wrought powerfully through the enthusiasm it aroused in the young Goethe and in Schiller. In England, the poems, immediately upon their appearance, gave rise to a long controversy as to their authenticity, Dr. Johnson being among the first to attack the belief in their antiquity. The truth seems to be that, though there really is a legendary hero answering to Ossian, no such poems as Macpherson attributed to him were ever transmitted. The whole work is to all intents the original creation of Macpherson himself. The supposed Gaelic originals, which were published by the Highland Society of London in 1807, have been proved by philologists to be spurious, to be nothing in fact but translations into bad Gaelic from Macpherson's good English. This conclusion is further supported by the mass of borrowings from the Bible and the classics which have been found in "Ossian." See J. C. Smart: "James Macpherson, An Episode in Literature" (1905).

P. 276. *lamentation of Selma.* Lament of Colma in "Songs of Selma," Ossian, ed. William Sharp, p. 410.

*Roll on.* Cf. ibid., p. 417: "ye bring no joy on your course!

## MY FIRST ACQUAINTANCE WITH POETS

[The identification of quotations has been omitted for this essay in order to allow students an opportunity to try it for themselves.]

The third and fourth paragraphs of this essay had appeared in a letter of Hazlitt's to the Examiner (Works, III, 152). The entire essay was first published in the third number of the Liberal (see note to p. 244).

P. 277. *W—m,* Wem.

P. 281. *Murillo* (1617-1682) and *Velasquez* (1599-1660) are the two greatest Spanish painters.

*nothing—like what he has done.* In the essay "On Depth and Superficiality" ("Plain Speaker"), Hazlitt characterizes Coleridge as "a great but useless thinker."

P. 282. *Adam Smith* (1723-1790), founder of the science of political economy, author of "The Wealth of Nations" (1776).

*huge folios.* In the essay "On Pedantry" ("Round Table") Hazlitt writes: "In the library of the family where we were brought up, stood the *Fratres Poloni;* and we can never forget or describe the feeling with which not only their appearance, but the names of the authors on the outside inspired us. Pripscovius, we remember, was one of the easiest to pronounce. The gravity of the contents seemed in proportion to the weight of the volumes; the importance of the subjects increased with our ignorance of them."

P. 283, n. Hazlitt's father was the author of "Discourses for the Use of Families on the Advantages of a Free Enquiry and on the Study of the Scriptures" (1790) and of "Sermons for the Use of Families" in two volumes (1808).

P. 284. *Mary Wolstonecraft* (1759-1797), author of the "Vindication of the Rights of Woman" (1792).

*Mackintosh,* Sir James (1765-1832), wrote "Vindiciæ Gallicæ, a Defence of the French Revolution and its English Admirers against the Accusations of the Right Hon. Edmund Burke." Hazlitt writes of Mackintosh in the "Spirit of the Age" as "one of the ablest and most accomplished men of the age, both as a writer, a speaker, and a converser," and comparing him with Coleridge, he remarks, "They have nearly an equal range of reading and of topics of conversation; but in the mind of the one we see nothing but *fixtures,* in the other every thing is fluid."

*Tom Wedgwood* (1771-1805) was an associate of some of the literary men of his day.

P. 285. *Holcroft,* Thomas (1745-1809), actor, dramatist, novelist, a member of Godwin's group of radicals. His chief writings are "The Road to Ruin" (1792), "Anna St. Ives" (1792), and "Hugh Trevor" (1794-97). Holcroft's "Memoirs," written by himself, were edited and completed by Hazlitt and published in 1816 (Works, II).

P. 286. *Hume,* David (1711-1776), historian and sceptic philosopher, described by Hazlitt as "one of the subtlest and most metaphysical of all metaphysicians." His chief writings are "A Treatise on Human Nature, being an Attempt to Introduce the Experimental Method of Reasoning into Moral Subjects" (1739-40), "Philosophical Essays" (1748), "Four Dissertations" (1757).

P. 287. *Essay on Vision.* Hazlitt calls this "the greatest by far of all his works and the most complete example of elaborate analytical reasoning and particular induction joined together that perhaps ever existed." (Works, XI, 108).

*Tom Paine* (1737-1809), an influential revolutionary writer, author of "Common Sense" (1776), a pamphlet advocating American independence, "Rights of Man" (1791), a reply to Burke's "Reflections on the French Revolution," and "The Age of Reason" (1795). He also took an active part in both the American and French revolutions.

*prefer the unknown to the known.* Cf. the first essay "On the Conversation of Authors": "Coleridge withholds his tribute of applause from every person, in whom any mortal but himself can descry the least glimpse of understanding. He would be thought to look farther into a millstone than any body else. He would have others see with his eyes, and take their opinions from him on trust, in spite of their senses. The more obscure and defective the indications of merit, the greater his sagacity and candour in being the first to point them out. He looks upon what he nicknames *a man of genius,* but as the breath of his nostrils, and the clay in the potter's hands. If any such inert, unconscious mass, under the fostering care of the modern Prometheus, is kindled into life,—begins to see, speak, and move, so as to attract the notice of other people,—our jealous patroniser of latent worth in that case throws aside, scorns, and hates his own handy-work; and deserts his intellectual offspring from the moment they can go alone and shift for themselves."

*a discovery on the same subject.* Hazlitt's first publication, " On the Principles of Human Action."

P. 288. *I sat down to the task,* etc. Cf. " On Application to Study " (" Plain Speaker ") : " If what I write at present is worth nothing, at least it costs me nothing. But it cost me a great deal twenty years ago. I have added little to my stock since then, and taken little from it. I 'unfold the book and volume of the brain,' and transcribe the characters I see there as mechanically as any one might copy the letters in a sampler. I do not say they came there mechanically—I transfer them to the paper mechanically." See also p. 345.

P. 289. *which . . . he has somewhere told himself.* " Biographia Literaria," ch. 10.

*that other Vision of Judgment.* Byron's.

*Bridge-Street Junto.* " The Constitutional Association or, as it was called by its opponents, 'The Bridge Street Gang,' founded in 1821 'to support the laws for suppressing seditious publications, and for defending the country from the fatal influence of disloyalty and sedition.' The Association was an ill-conducted party organisation and created so much opposition by its imprudent prosecutions that it very soon disappeared. See an article in the Edinburgh Review for June, 1822." Waller-Glover, VI, 487.

P. 290. *at Tewkesbury.* In the essay " On Going a Journey," Hazlitt refers to this episode as occurring at Bridgewater : " I remember sitting up half the night to read Paul and Virginia, which I picked up at an inn in Bridgewater, after being drenched in the rain all day; and at the same place I got through two volumes of Madame D'Arblay's Camilla."

*Paul and Virginia* (1788), a sentimental novel by Bernardin St. Pierre (1737-1814).

P. 291. *Camilla* (1796), a novel by Fanny Burney (1752-1840).

*a friend of the poet's.* "This is a mistake. Wordsworth paid £23 a year for Alfoxden. The agreement is given in Mrs. Henry Sandford's 'Thomas Poole and His Friends,' I, 225." Waller-Glover.

P. 292. *In the outset of life.* Alongside of this paragraph should be read the essay "On the Feeling of Immortality in Youth," Works, XII, 150.

P. 294. *Chantrey,* Sir Francis (1781-1842). His bust of Wordsworth is now at Cole-Orton.

*Haydon,* Benjamin Robert (1786-1846), a celebrated English painter who was intimate with many literary men. In the picture referred to Haydon also introduced a portrait of Hazlitt.

*Monk Lewis.* Matthew Gregory Lewis (1775-1818) wrote among other things a sensational novel, "The Monk" (1795), which gained him his nickname. "The Castle Spectre" was originally produced at the Drury Lane Theatre in 1797.

P. 295. *Tom Poole* (1765-1837), friend and patron of Coleridge.

P. 296. *Sir Walter Scott's,* etc. Probably a reference to' the banquet given to George IV by the Magistrates of Edinburgh and attended by Scott, August 24, 1822.

*Blackwood,* William (1776-1834), the Edinburgh publisher.

*Gaspar Poussin* (1613-1675). His real name was Dughet, but he changed it out of respect to his brother-in-law, Nicholas Poussin.

*Domenichino* or Domenico Zampieri (1581-1641), a painter of Bologna.

P. 297. *Death of Abel* (1758), an idyllic-pastoral poem by Solomon Gessner (1730-1788), a German poet of the Swiss school who enjoyed a wide popularity in the eighteenth century.

P. 298. *since the days of Henry II.* As Henry II lived in the twelfth century, and as neither Coleridge nor Wordsworth ever refer to the language of Henry II as their standard, the statement in the text may probably be considered as a blunder of Hazlitt's.

*He spoke with contempt of Gray and with intolerance of Pope.* Cf. "Biographia Literaria," ch. 2: "I felt almost as if I had been newly couched, when, by Mr. Wordsworth's conversation, I had

been induced to re-examine with impartial strictness Gray's celebrated Elegy. I had long before detected the defects in The
Bard; but the Elegy I had considered as proof against all fair
attacks; and to this day I can not read either without delight, and a
portion of enthusiasm. At all events whatever pleasure I may have
lost by the clearer perception of the faults in certain passages, has
been more than repaid to me by the additional delight with which
I read the remainder." In his "Table Talk," October 23, 1833,
Coleridge says again: "I think there is something very majestic in
Gray's Installation Ode; but as to the Bard and the rest of his
lyrics, I must say I think them frigid and artificial." Of Pope
and his followers he writes ("Biographia Literaria," ch. I): "I
was not blind to the merits of this school, yet, as from inexperience
of the world, and consequent want of sympathy with the general
subjects of these poems, they gave me little pleasure, I doubtless
undervalued the kind, and with the presumption of youth withheld
from its masters the legitimate name of poets. I saw that the
excellence of this kind consisted in just and acute observations on
men and manners in an artificial state of society, as its matter and
substance, and in the logic of wit, conveyed in smooth and strong
epigrammatic couplets, as its form; that even when the subject was
addressed to the fancy, or the intellect, as in the Rape of the
Lock, or the Essay on Man; nay, when it was a consecutive
narration, as in that astonishing product of matchless talent and
ingenuity, Pope's Translation of the Iliad; still a point was looked
for at the end of each second line, and the whole was, as it were, a
*sorites,* or, if I may exchange a logical for a grammatical metaphor,
a conjunction disjunctive, of epigrams. Meantime, the matter and
diction seemed to me characterized not so much by poetic thoughts,
as by thoughts translated into the language of poetry."

*he thought little of Junius as a writer.* Cf. Coleridge's "Table
Talk," July 3, 1833: "The style of Junius is a sort of metre, the law
of which is a balance of thesis and antithesis. When he gets out of
his aphorismic metre into a sentence of five or six lines long, nothing can exceed the slovenliness of the English."

*dislike for Dr. Johnson.* Cf. "Table Talk," July 4, 1833: "Dr.
Johnson's fame now rests principally upon Boswell. It is impossible not to be amused with such a book. But his *bow-wow* manner
must have had a good deal to do with the effect produced. . . .
As to Burke's testimony to Johnson's powers, you must remember
that Burke was a great courtier; and after all. Burke said and

wrote more than once that he thought Johnson greater in talking than in writing, and greater in Boswell than in real life."

*opinion of Burke.* Cf. " Table Talk," April 8, 1833: " Burke was indeed a great man. No one ever read history so philosophically as he seems to have done. . . . He would have been more influential if he had less surpassed his contemporaries, as Fox and Pitt, men of much inferior minds, in all respects."

*He liked Richardson, but not Fielding.* On this subject Coleridge evidently changed his mind. Cf. " Table Talk," July 5, 1834: " What a master of composition Fielding was! Upon my word, I think the Œdipus Tyrannus, the Alchemist, and Tom Jones the three most perfect plots ever planned. And how charming, how wholesome, Fielding always is! To take him up after Richardson is like emerging from a sickroom heated by stoves into an open lawn on a breezy day in May."

*Caleb Williams,* the chief novel of William Godwin.

P. 298, n. *He had no idea of pictures.* See p. 212.

*Buffamalco.* Cristofani Buonamico (1262-1351), also known as Buffalmacco, a painter of Florence.

P. 300. *Elliston,* Robert William (1774-1813), actor and later manager of the Drury Lane Theatre.

*still continues.* See p. 224 and n.


## ON THE CONVERSATION OF AUTHORS

This is the title of Essays III and IV of the " Plain Speaker." Our selection begins with the last paragraph of the first, which forms a fitting introduction to the account of one of Lamb's celebrated Wednesday evenings. Lamb tells us that his sister was accustomed to read this essay with unmixed delight.

P. 301. *When Greek meets Greek.* Nathaniel Lee's " Alexander the Great," iv, 2.

*C——.* Coleridge.

P. 302. *small-coal man.* Thomas Britton (1654?-1714), a dealer in small coal, who on the floor of his hut above the coal-shop held weekly concerts of vocal and instrumental music, at which the greatest performers of the day, even Handel, were to be heard.

*And, in our flowing cups.* Cf. " Henry V," iv, 3, 51:

"then shall our names
Familiar in his mouth as household words . . .
Be in their flowing cups freely remember'd."

P. 303. *the cartoons.* See Hazlitt's account of Raphael's cartoons in "The Pictures at Hampton Court" (Works, IX, 43).

*Donne,* John (1573-1631), poet and divine. Hazlitt in the "Lectures on the English Poets" confesses that he knows nothing of him save "some beautiful verses to his wife, dissuading her from accompanying him on his travels abroad (see p. 318), and some quaint riddles in verse, which the Sphinx could not unravel." V, 83.

P. 304. *Ned P——.* Edward Phillips. Lamb speaks of him as "that poor card-playing Phillips, that has felt himself for so many years the outcast of Fortune." (Works, ed. Lucas, VII, 972.)

*Captain ——.* Rear-Admiral James Burney (1750-1821), brother of Fanny Burney the novelist, author of a "Chronological History of the Voyages and Discoveries in the South Sea or Pacific Ocean" in five volumes (1803-1817). "The captain was himself a character, a fine, noble creature—gentle, with a rough exterior, as became the associate of Captain Cook in his voyages round the world, and the literary historian of all these acts of circumnavigation." Crabb-Robinson's Diary, 1810.

*Jem White.* James White (1775-1820), of whom Lamb has left us a sketch in the essay "On the Praise of Chimney-Sweepers": "He carried away half the fun of the world when he died." He wrote, it is supposed with some cooperation from Lamb, the "Original Letters, etc., of Sir John Falstaff and his Friends" (1796), which were described by Lamb as "without exception the best imitations I ever saw." (Works, ed. Lucas, VI, 2.) A review of this book by Lamb, consisting chiefly of specimens, appeared in the Examiner in 1819 (Works, ed. Lucas, I, 191 ff.).

*turning like the latter end.* This phrase occurs in one of the extracts in Lamb's review of Falstaff's Letters just mentioned (p. 194).

*A——.* William Aryton (1777-1858), a musical critic and director of the King's Theatre in the Haymarket. In the letter of Elia to Robert Southey (Lamb's Works, I, 230) he is spoken of as "the last and steadiest left me of that little knot of whist-players, that used to assemble weekly, for so many years, at the Queen's Gate."

*Mrs. R——.* Mrs. Reynolds, who had been Lamb's schoolmistress.

*M. B.* Martin Charles Burney, son of Admiral Burney. "Martin Burney is as odd as ever. . . . He came down here, and insisted on reading Virgil's 'Eneid' all through with me (which he did,) because a Counsel must know Latin. Another time he read out all the Gospel of St. John, because Biblical quotations are very emphatic in a Court of Justice. A third time, he would carve a fowl, which he did very ill-favoredly, because 'we did not know how indispensable it was for a Barrister to do all those sort of things well. Those little things were of more consequence than we supposed.' So he goes on, harassing about the way to prosperity, and losing it. With a long head, but somewhat wrong one— harum-scarum. Why does not his guardian angel look to him? He deserves one—: may be, he has tired him out." Lamb's Works, VII, 855.

*Author of the Road to Ruin.* Thomas Holcroft.

P. 305. *Critique of Pure Reason,* by Kant.

*Biographia Literaria.* Coleridge's account of his literary life, published in 1817.

*Those days are over!* The event here referred to may be Waterloo. Mr. Lucas thinks that Hazlitt's share in Lamb's gatherings "ceased after an unfortunate discussion of Fanny Burney's Wanderer, which Hazlitt condemned in terms that her brother, the Admiral, could not forgive." (Lamb's Works, I, 482.) It is likely that Mr. Lucas has been led astray by the statement in Crabb-Robinson's Diary to the effect that Hazlitt used to attend Captain Burney's whist-parties "till he affronted the Captain by severe criticisms on the works of his sister," presumably by his article in the Edinburgh Review in 1814. Hazlitt commemorates Lamb's evenings in the "Pleasure of Hating" ("Plain Speaker"): "What is become of 'that set of whist players,' celebrated by Elia in his notable *Epistle to Robert Southey, Esq. . . .* 'that for so many years called Admiral Burney friend?' They are scattered, like last year's snow. Some of them are dead—or gone to live at a distance—or pass one another in the street like strangers; or if they stop to speak, do it as coolly and try to *cut* one another as soon as possible. Some of us have grown rich—others poor. Some have got places under Government—others a *niche* in the Quarterly Review. Some of us have dearly earned a name in the world; whilst others remain in their original privacy. We despise the one, and envy and are glad to mortify the other."

*Like angels' visits.* Cf. Blair's "The Grave," 582: "Like those of angels, short and far between." Hazlitt was fond of pointing out this source for Campbell's famous line "Like angels' visits few and far between," and of insisting that the alteration spoiled the sense. Therel y he is said to have incurred Campbell's bitter hostility.

P. 306. *Mr. Douce,* Francis (1757-1834), Shakespearian scholar and keeper of the manuscripts in the British Museum.

*L. H——.* Leigh Hunt. There is a sketch of him in the "Spirit of the Age."

*aliquando sufflaminandus erat.* "He sometimes had to be checked." This is a quotation from Seneca which Ben Jonson in "Timber" (ed. Schelling, p. 23) had applied to Shakespeare.

P. 307. *The Indicator.* Leigh Hunt's most successful series of essays, which began their run in 1819.

*Mr. Northcote,* James (1746-1831), the painter of whose talk Hazlitt has left an entertaining record in the "Conversations of James Northcote" (1830), a book which inspired Crabb-Robinson to say, " I do not believe that Boswell gives so much good talk in an equal quantity of his life of Johnson."

P. 308. *Sir Joshua's.* Sir Joshua Reynolds (1723-1792), the famous English painter.

P. 309. *Horne Tooke* (1736-1812), politician and author of a celebrated philological volume, "The Diversions of Purley" (1786, 1805). His portrait is included in the "Spirit of the Age": "He was without a rival (almost) in private conversation, an expert public speaker, a keen politician, a first-rate grammarian, and the finest gentleman (to say the least) of his own party. He had no imagination (or he would not have scorned it!)—no delicacy of taste, no rooted prejudices or strong attachments: his intellect was like a bow of polished steel, from which he shot sharp-pointed poisoned arrows at his friends in private, at his enemies in public."

*hear a sound so fine.* J. S. Knowles's "Virginius," v, 2.

P. 310. *silenced a learned professor.* Cf. "Spirit of the Age" " He used to plague Fuseli by asking him after the origin of the Teutonic dialects, and Dr. Parr, by wishing to know the meaning of the common copulative, *Is.*"

*Curran,* John Philpot (1750-1817), member of Parliament from Ireland, orator and wit.

P. 311. *Mrs. Inchbald,* Elizabeth (1753-1821), a well-known actress, dramatist, and novelist. In literature she is associated with the group of William Godwin, and her best-known works are " A Simple Story" and " Nature and Art."

*from noon to dewy eve.* "Paradise Lost," I, 743.

*Mrs. M——.* Mrs. Montagu, wife of Basil Montagu. In the

"Pleasure of Hating" ("Plain Speaker") there is another allusion to Mrs. Montagu "whose dark raven locks made a picturesque background to our discourse."

*H—t's.* Leigh Hunt's.

*N—'s.* Northcote's.

*H—yd—n's.* Haydon's.

*Doctor Tronchin.* Theodore Tronchin, a physician of Geneva, figures in Rousseau's "Confessions."

*P. 312. Sir Fopling Flutter,* a character in George Etherege's comedy, "The Man of Mode."

*For wit is like a rest.* "Master Francis Beaumont's Letter to Ben Jonson." For *players* read *gamesters.*

*came down into the country.* Charles and Mary Lamb with a few of their friends paid a visit to Hazlitt at Winterslow in 1810.

*Like the most capricious poet.* "As You Like It," iii, 3, 8.

*walked gowned.* Lamb's "Sonnet Written at Cambridge, August 15, 1819."

*P. 313. the person I mean.* George Dyer (1755-1841), an amiable hack-writer and a friend of Lamb. He figures prominently in two of the Essays of Elia, "Oxford in the Vacation" and "Amicus Redivivus," and in many of Lamb's letters. "To G. D. a poem is a poem. His own as good as any bodie's, and god bless him, any bodie's as good as his own, for I do not think he has the most distant guess of the possibility of one poem being better than another. The Gods by denying him the very faculty itself of discrimination have effectually cut off every seed of envy in his bosom." Letter to Wordsworth (Lamb's Works, ed. Lucas, VI, 519).

## OF PERSONS ONE WOULD WISH TO HAVE SEEN

This, like the preceding essay, is a record of one of Lamb's Wednesday evenings. It was originally published in the New Monthly Magazine for January, 1826, from which the present text is reproduced. It was republished by Hazlitt's son in "Literary Remains" (1836) and "Winterslow" (1850).

*P. 315. Come like shadows.* "Macbeth," iv, 1, 111.

*B——.* Lamb. The name is supplied in "Literary Remains."

*defence of Guy Faux.* See p. 224 and n.

*Never so sure.* Pope's "Moral Essays," II, 51.

*A*——. William Ayrton.

P. 316. *in his habit.* "Hamlet," iii, 4, 135.

P. 317. *And call up him.* "Il Penseroso," 109.

*wished that mankind.* Browne's "Religio Medici," Part II, section 9.

*Prologues spoken.* See Prologue to Fulke Greville's tragedy of "Alaham."

P. 318. *old edition.* Mr. W. C. Hazlitt suggests that it is the edition of 1609 of which Lamb owned a copy. "Memoirs of Hazlitt," I, 276.

*Here lies.* "An Epithalamion on the Lady Elizabeth and Count Palatine." Muses' Library, I, 86.

*By our first strange.* "Elegy on his Mistress," I, 139.

P. 320. *lisped in numbers.* Pope's "Prologue to Satires," 128.

*His meeting with Petrarch.* Chaucer was in Italy in 1372-3, but his meeting with Petrarch is only a matter of conjecture. He probably did not meet Boccaccio, the author of the "Decameron."

*Ugolino.* See p. 275.

*portrait of Ariosto.* Hazlitt probably refers to the Portrait of a Poet in the National Gallery, now ascribed to Palma.

P. 321. *the mighty dead.* Thomson's "Winter," 432.

*creature of the element.* Cf. "Comus," 299:
> "Of some gay creatures of the element,
> That in the colors of the rainbow live,
> And play i' the plighted clouds."

*That was Arion.* "Faërie Queene," IV, ix, 23.

*For Captain C., M. C., Miss D*——, "Literary Remains" supplies Admiral Burney, Martin Burney, Miss Reynolds.

*with lack-luster eye.* "As You Like It," ii, 7, 21.

P. 322. *his compliments.* See p. 129.

P. 323. *But why then publish.* "Prologue to Satires," 135.

*Gay's verses.* "Mr. Pope's Welcome from Greece" (ed. Muses' Library, I, 207).

P. 324. *E*——. In "Literary Remains" the name supplied is Erasmus Phillips, probably a mistake for Edward Phillips.

*nigh-sphered in heaven.* Collins's "Ode on the Poetical Character," 66.

*Garrick,* David (1717-1779), the celebrated actor.

*J. F*——. According to "Literary Remains," Barron Field (1786-1846), Lamb's friend and correspondent.

*Handel,* George Frederick (1685-1759), the musical composer, German by birth but naturalized in England.

P. 325. *Wildair,* in Farquhar's comedy "Sir Harry Wildair."

*Abel Drugger,* in Ben Jonson's "Alchemist," was one of Garrick's famous parts.

P. 326. *author of Mustapha.* Fulke Greville.

*Kit Marlowe* (1564-1593), the most brilliant writer of tragedy before Shakespeare. He wrote "Tamburlaine the Great," "The Tragical History of Dr. Faustus," "The Jew of Malta," and "Edward the Second." In the "Age of Elizabeth" Hazlitt says of him, "There is a lust of power in his writings, a hunger and thirst after unrighteousness, a glow of the imagination, unhallowed by any thing but its own energies."

*Webster,* John, wrote during the first quarter of the seventeenth century. His chief plays are "The White Devil" and the "Duchess of Malfy." *Dekker,* Thomas (c. 1570-1641). "The Shoemaker's Holiday," "The Honest Whore," and "Old Fortunatus" are his best plays. In the third lecture of the "Age of Elizabeth" Hazlitt thus compares Webster and Dekker: "Webster would, I think, be a greater dramatic genius than Deckar, if he had the same originality; and perhaps is so, even without it. His White Devil and Duchess of Malfy, upon the whole perhaps, come the nearest to Shakspeare of anything we have upon record; the only drawback to them, the only shade of imputation that can be thrown upon them, 'by which they lose some colour,' is, that they are too like Shakspeare, and often direct imitations of him, both in general conception and individual expression. . . . Deckar has, I think, more truth of character, more instinctive depth of sentiment, more of the unconscious simplicity of nature; but he does not, out of his own stores, clothe his subject with the same richness of imagination, or the same glowing colours of language. Deckar excels in giving expression to certain habitual, deeply-rooted feelings, which remain pretty much the same in all circumstances, the simple uncompounded elements of nature and passion:—Webster gives more scope to their various combinations and changeable aspects, brings them into dramatic play by contrast and comparison, flings them into a state of fusion by a kindled fancy, makes them describe a wider arc of oscillation from the impulse of unbridled passion, and carries both terror and pity to a more painful and sometimes unwarrantable excess. Deckar is content with the historic picture of suffering; Webster goes on to suggest horrible imaginings. The pathos of the one tells home and for itself; the other adorns his sentiments with some image of tender or awful beauty. In a word, Deckar is more like Chaucer or Boccaccio; as Webster's mind appears to have been cast more in the mould of Shakespeare's, as well naturally as from studious emulation."

*Heywood*, Thomas (d. c. 1650), a prolific dramatist who excelled in the homely vein. His best-known play is "The Woman Killed with Kindness."

*Beaumont*, Francis (1584-1616), and *Fletcher*, John (1579-1625), composed their dramas in collaboration. In the "Age of Elizabeth" Hazlitt calls them lyric and descriptive poets of the first order, but as regards drama "the first writers who in some measure departed from the genuine tragic style of the age of Shakspeare. They thought less of their subject, and more of themselves, than some others. They had a great and unquestioned command over the stores both of fancy and passion; but they availed themselves too often of commonplace extravagances and theatrical trick. . . . The example of preceding or contemporary writers had given them facility; the frequency of dramatic exhibition had advanced the popular taste; and this facility of production, and the necessity for appealing to popular applause, tended to vitiate their own taste, and to make them willing to pamper that of the public for novelty and extraordinary effect. There wants something of the sincerity and modesty of the older writers. They do not wait nature's time, or work out her materials patiently and faithfully, but try to anticipate her, and so far defeat themselves. They would have a catastrophe in every scene; so that you have none at last: they would raise admiration to its height in every line; so that the impression of the whole is comparatively loose and desultory. They pitch the characters at first in too high a key, and exhaust themselves by the eagerness and impatience of their efforts. We find all the prodigality of youth, the confidence inspired by success, an enthusiasm bordering on extravagance, richness running riot, beauty dissolving in its own sweetness. They are like heirs just come to their estates, like lovers in the honeymoon. In the economy of nature's gifts, they 'misuse the bounteous Pan, and thank the Gods amiss.' Their productions shoot up in haste, but bear the marks of precocity and premature decay. Or they are two goodly trees, the stateliest of the forest, crowned with blossoms, and with the verdure springing at their feet; but they do not strike their roots far enough into the ground, and the fruit can hardly ripen for the flowers!"

*Jonson,* Ben (1573-1637), was the originator of the "comedy of humors." Hazlitt, in discussing him at length in the second lecture on the "Comic Writers," confesses a disrelish for his style. "He was a great man in himself, but one cannot readily sympathise with him. His works, as the characteristic productions of an individual mind, or as records of the manners of a particular age, cannot be valued too highly; but they have little charm for the mere general reader. Schlegel observes, that whereas Shakspeare gives the springs of human nature, which are always the same, or sufficiently so to be interesting and intelligible; Jonson chiefly gives the *humours* of men, as connected with certain arbitrary and conventional modes of dress, action, and expression, which are intelligible only while they last, and not very interesting at any time. Shakspeare's characters are men; Ben Jonson's are more like machines, governed by mere routine, or by the convenience of the poet, whose property they are. . . . His portraits are caricatures by dint of their very likeness, being extravagant tautologies of themselves; as his plots are improbable by an excess of consistency; for he goes thoroughstitch with whatever he takes in hand, makes one contrivance answer all purposes, and every obstacle give way to a predetermined theory. . . . Old Ben was of a scholastic turn and had dealt a little in the occult sciences and controversial divinity. He was a man of strong crabbed sense, retentive memory, acute observation, great fidelity of description and keeping in character, a power of working out an idea so as to make it painfully true and oppressive, and with great honesty and manliness of feeling, as well as directness of understanding: but with all this, he wanted, to my thinking, that genial spirit of enjoyment and finer fancy, which constitute the essence of poetry and wit. . . . There was nothing spontaneous, no impulse or ease about his genius: it was all forced, up-hill work, making a toil of pleasure. And hence his overweening admiration of his own works, from the effort they had cost him, and the apprehension that they were not proportionably admired by others, who knew nothing of the pangs and throes of his Muse in child-bearing." Works, VIII, 39-41. Of Ben Jonson's tragedies Hazlitt held a higher opinion than of his comedies. "The richer the soil in which he labours, the less dross and rubbish we have. . . . His tenaciousness of what is grand and lofty, is more praiseworthy than his delight in what is low and disagreeable. His pedantry accords better with didactic pomp than with illiterate and vulgar gabble; his learning engrafted on romantic tradition or classical history, looks like genius. . . . His tragedy of the Fall of Sejanus, in particular, is an admirable piece of ancient mosaic. . . . The depth of knowledge and gravity of expression sustain one another throughout: the poet has worked out the historian's outline, so that the vices and passions, the ambition and servility of public men, in the heated and poisonous atmosphere of a luxurious and despotic court, were never described in fuller or more glowing colours." Works, V, 262-3.

*a vast species alone.* Cowley's " The Praise of Pindar."

*G——.* Godwin, according to " Literary Remains."

*Drummond of Hawthornden.* William Drummond (1585-1649), the poet who recorded his conversation with Ben Jonson on the occasion of a visit paid to him by the latter in 1618. " He has not done himself or Jonson any credit by his account of their conversation," says Hazlitt in the " Lectures on the Age of Elizabeth." Works, V, 299.

*Eugene Aram* was hanged in 1759 for a murder he had committed several years earlier.

*Admirable Crichton.* James Crichton (1560?-1582), a Scotchman of noble birth who, in a brief life, gained the reputation of universal genius and concerning whose powers many legends arose.

P. 327. *H——.* Hunt, according to " Literary Remains."

*Hobbes,* Thomas (1588-1679), the English philosopher. His chief work is " Leviathan, or the Matter, Form, and Power of a Commonwealth, Ecclesiastical and Civil" (1651). Hazlitt vindicated the superiority of Hobbes as a thinker at a time when his fame was overshadowed by other reputations. He calls him the founder of the modern material philosophy and maintains that "the true reason of the fate which this author's writings met with was that his views of things were too original and comprehensive to be immediately understood, without passing through the hands of several successive generations of commentators and interpreters. Ignorance of another's meaning is a sufficient cause of fear, and fear produces hatred." Works, XI, 25-48.

*Jonathan Edwards* (1703-1758). In writing " On the Tendency of Sects " in the " Round Table," Hazlitt had alluded to Edwards as an Englishman and had spoken of his work on the Will as "written with as much power of logic, and more in the true spirit of philosophy, than any other metaphysical work in the language."

P. 327, n. *Lord Bacon,* Francis (1561-1626), statesman, scientist, and man of letters. His chief works are the " Essays " (1597), the " Advancement of Learning" (1604), " Novum Organum" (1620), "History of Henry VII " (1622).

P. 328. *Dugald Stewart* (1753-1828), Scotch philosopher.

*Duchess of Bolton.* Lavinia Fenton (1708-1760), the original Polly in Gay's " Beggar's Opera," married the Duke of Bolton in 1751.

P. 329. *Raphael,* Sanzio (1483-1520), the greatest of all the Italian painters.

*Lucretia Borgia with calm golden locks.* This sounds like a striking anticipation of Landor's fine line, " Calm hair meandering in pellucid gold " in his poem " On Lucretia Borgia's Hair." Or had Hazlitt seen the poem before it was published?

*Michael Angelo* (1475-1564), poet, painter, architect, and sculptor, the most famous of the great Italian artists.

*Correggio* (1494-1534), *Giorgione* (1477-1510), *Guido* (1575-1642), *Cimabue* (1240-1302), *Vandyke* (1599-1641). The other painters are mentioned elsewhere in this volume.

*whose names on earth.* In his review of Sismondi's "Literature of the South" (Works, X, 62) Hazlitt cites among the proofs of Dante's poetic power " his description of the poets and great men of antiquity, whom he represents ' serene and smiling,' though in the shades of death, ' because on earth their names in fame's eternal records shine for aye.' " As these lines have not been located in Dante, they have been ascribed to the lying memory of Lamb, from whose lips Hazlitt learned them.

P. 330. *Mrs. Hutchinson,* Lucy (b. 1620), whose life of her Puritan husband, Colonel Hutchinson, had appeared in 1806, presumably shortly before the conversation recorded in this essay.

*one in the room.* Mary Lamb, the sister of the essayist.

*Ninon de Lenclos* (1615-1705), for a long time the leader of fashion in Paris and the patroness of poets.

*Voltaire* (1694-1778), the sceptical philosopher of the Enlightenment; *Rabelais* (1490-1553), the greatest French humorist, author of " Gargantua and Pantagruel"; *Molière* (1622-1673), the master of French comedy; *Racine* (1639-1699), the master of French classic tragedy; *La Fontaine* (1621-1695), author of the "Fables"; *La Rochefoucauld* (1613-1680), celebrated for his book of cynical "Maxims," which Hazlitt imitated in his "Characteristics"; *St. Evremont* (1610-1703), a critic.

P. 331. *Your most exquisite reason.* Cf. " Twelfth Night," ii, 3, 155.

*Oh, ever right.* " Coriolanus," ii, 1, 208.

*H——.* This speech is attributed to Lamb in " Literary Remains," but wrongly so according to Waller and Glover " because, in the first place, the speech seems more characteristic of Hunt than of Lamb, and, secondly, because the volume of the New Monthly in which the essay appeared contains a list of errata in which two corrections (one of them relating to initials) are made in the essay and yet this ' H——' is left uncorrected."

## ON READING OLD BOOKS

This essay was first published in the London Magazine for February, 1821, and republished in the " Plain Speaker."

P. 333. *I hate to read new books.* It would take too long to recall all the passages in which Hazlitt voices his sentimental attachment to the writers with whom he first became acquainted. " The greatest pleasure in life," he says in one essay, " is that of reading when we are young," and at the conclusion of his lectures on the " Age of Elizabeth " he remarks : " Were I to live much longer than I have any chance of doing, the books which I ˙read when I was young, I can never forget." Patmore's statement concerning Hazlitt's later reading may be exaggerated, but it is interesting in this connection : " I do not believe Hazlitt ever read the half of any work that he reviewed—not even the Scotch novels, of which he read more than of any other modern productions, and has written better perhaps, than any other of their critics. I am certain that of many works that he has reviewed, and of many writers whose general pretensions he has estimated better than anybody else has done, he never read one tithe." " My Friends and Acquaintances," III, 122.

*Tales of my Landlord.* Scott's.

*Lady Morgan* (1783?-1859), a writer of Irish stories, of which the best-known is " The Wild Irish Girl " (1806). She is also the author of certain miscellaneous productions, among which is a " Life of Salvator Rosa " reviewed by Hazlitt for the Edinburgh Review, July, 1824. Works, X, 276-310.

*Anastatius,* an Eastern romance by Thomas Hope (1770-1831).

*Delphine* (1802), a novel by Madame De Staël (1766-1817), the celebrated French bluestocking.

*in their newest gloss.* "Macbeth," i, 7, 34.

*Andrew Millar* (1707-1768), the publisher of Thomson's and Fielding's works.

*Thurloe's State Papers.* "A Collection of State Papers" (1742) by John Thurloe (1616-1668), Secretary of State under Cromwell.

*Sir Godfrey Kneller* (1648-1723), a portrait painter of German birth whose work and reputation belong to England.

P. 335. *for thoughts.* Cf. "Hamlet," iv, 5, 175: "There's rosemary, that's for remembrance; pray, love, remember: and there is pansies, that's for thoughts."

*Fortunatus's Wishing Cap,* in Dekker's play of "Old Fortunatus."

*Bruscambille.* "Tristram Shandy," Bk. III, ch. 35.

*the masquerade.* "Tom Jones," Bk. XIII, ch. 7.

*the disputes.* Bk. III, ch. 3.

*the escape of Molly.* Bk. IV, ch. 8.

*Sophia and her muff.* Bk. V, ch. 4.

*her aunt's lecture.* Bk. VII, ch. 3.

*the puppets dallying.* "Hamlet," iii, 2, 257.

P. 336. *ignorance was bliss.* Gray's "Ode on a Distant Prospect of Eton."

*Ballantyne press.* The printing firm of John and James Ballantyne in Edinburgh with which Scott was associated, and in whose financial ruin he was so disastrously involved.

*Minerva Press.* The sponsor of popular romances.

P. 337. *Mrs. Radcliffe,* Anne (1764-1823), a very popular writer of novels in which romance, sentiment, and terror are combined in cunning proportions. Her chief novels are "The Romance of the Forest" (1791), "The Mysteries of Udolpho" (1794) and "The Italian" (1797). Hazlitt writes of her in the lecture "On the English Novelists."

*sweet in the mouth.* Revelation, x, 9.

*gay creatures.* "Comus," 299.

*Tom Jones discovers Square.* Bk. V, ch. 5.

*where Parson Adams.* "Joseph Andrews," Bk. IV, ch. 14.

P. 338. *Chubb's Tracts.* Thomas Chubb (1679-1747), a tallow-chandler who devoted his leisure hours to the deistic controversy. His "Tracts and Posthumous Works" were published in six volumes in 1754.

*fate, free-will.* "Paradise Lost," II, 560.

*Would I had never seen.* Marlowe's "Dr. Faustus," Scene 19.

P. 339. *New Eloise.* "Julie, ou La Nouvelle Héloise" (1760), a novel by the great French sentimentalist, Jean Jacques Rousseau (1712-1778), who was the most powerful personal force in the revolutionary movement of the eighteenth century and whose writings have left a deep impression on the political and educational systems of the nineteenth. His other important works are "The Social Contract" and "Émile" (1762) and the "Confessions" (1782). Hazlitt has a "Character of Rousseau" in the "Round Table" (see p. xliv, n.).

*scattered like stray-gifts.* Wordsworth's "Stray Pleasures."

*Sir Fopling Flutter,* in Sir George Etherege's comedy "The Man of Mode" (1676).

P. 339, n. *a friend.* Charles Lamb.

P. 340. *leurre de dupe,* a decoy. The expression occurs in the fourth book of Rousseau's "Confessions."

*a load to sink a navy.* "Henry VIII," iii, 2, 383.

*Marcian Colonna is a dainty book.* Lamb's "Sonnet to the Author of Poems Published under the Name of Barry Cornwall."

P. 341. *Keats.* Hazlitt shared the popular conception of Keats as an effeminate poet. He concludes the essay "On Effeminacy of Character" in "Table Talk" with a reference to Keats: "I cannot help thinking that the fault of Mr. Keats's poems was a deficiency in masculine energy of style. He had beauty, tenderness, delicacy, in an uncommon degree, but there was a want of strength and substance. His Endymion is a very delightful description of the illusions of a youthful imagination, given up to airy dreams—we have flowers, clouds, rainbows, moonlight, all sweet sounds and smells, and Oreads and Dryads flitting by—but there is nothing tangible in it, nothing marked or palpable—we have none of the hardy spirit or rigid forms of antiquity. He painted his own thoughts and character; and did not transport himself into the fabulous and heroic ages. There is a want of action, of character, and so far, of imagination, but there is exquisite fancy. All is soft and fleshy, without bone or muscle. We see in him the youth, without the manhood of poetry. His genius breathed 'vernal delight and joy.'—'Like Maia's son he stood and shook his plumes,' with fragrance filled. His mind was redolent of spring. He had not the fierceness of summer, nor the richness of autumn, and winter he seemed not to have known, till he felt the icy hand of death!" Again in the introduction to the "Select British Poets" (Works, V, 378), he says that Keats "gave the greatest promise of genius of any poet of his day. He displayed extreme tenderness, beauty, originality, and delicacy of fancy; all he wanted was manly strength and fortitude to reject the temptations of singularity in sentiment and expression. Some of his shorter and later pieces are, however, as free from faults as they are full of beauties."

*Come like shadows.* "Macbeth," iv, 1, 111.

*Tiger-moth's wings* and *Blushes with blood.* Keats's "Eve of St. Agnes."

*Words, words.* "Hamlet," ii, 2, 194.

*the great preacher.* Edward Irving.

*as the hart.* Psalms, xlii, 1.

*Giving my stock* [sum]. "As You Like It," ii, 1, 48.

P. 342. *Valentine, Tattle and Prue,* characters in Congreve's "Love for Love" (1695).

*know my cue.* Cf. "Othello," i, 2, 83.

*Intus et in cute.* See p. 163.

*Sir Humphry Davy* (1778-1829), the celebrated chemist.

P. 343. *with every trick and line* [line and trick]. "All's Well That Ends Well," i, 1, 107.

*the divine Clementina,* in Richardson's "Sir Charles Grandison."

*that ligament.* Sterne's "Tristram Shandy," Bk. VI, ch. 10.

*story of the hawk.* "Decameron," Fifth Day, ninth story.

*at one proud* [fell] *swoop.* "Macbeth," iv, 3, 219.

P. 344. *with all its giddy* [dizzy] *raptures.* Wordsworth's "Tintern Abbey," 85.

*embalmed with odours.* "Paradise Lost," II, 843.

*the German criticism.* See p. 112.

*His form.* "Paradise Lost," I, 591.

*Falls flat.* Ibid., I, 460.

P. 345. *For Dr. Johnson's and Junius's style.* See pp. 147-9, 186, 190.

*he, like an eagle.* "Coriolanus," v, 6, 115.

*An Essay on Marriage.* "No such essay by Wordsworth is at present known to exist. It would seem either that 'Marriage' is a misprint for some other word, or that Hazlitt was mistaken in the subject of the essay referred to by Coleridge. Hazlitt is probably recalling a conversation with Coleridge in Shropshire at the beginning of 1798 (cf. 'My First Acquaintance with Poets'), at which time *A Letter to the Bishop of Llandaff* (1793) was the only notable prose work which Wordsworth had published." Waller-Glover.

P. 345, 11. *Is this the present earl?* "James Maitland, eighth Earl of Lauderdale (1759-1839), succeeded his father in August, 1789." Waller-Glover.

P. 346. *worthy of all acceptation.* 1 Timothy, i, 15.

*Clarendon.* Edward Hyde, Earl of Clarendon (1609-1674), English statesman and author of the "History of the Rebellion" (1704-1707).

*Froissart,* Jean (1338-1410), the chronicler of the Hundred Years' War.

*Holinshed,* Ralph (d. 1580?), author of "Chronicles of England, Scotlande, and Irelande" (1578).

*Stowe,* John (1525?-1605), author of "Englysh Chronicles" (1561).

*Thucydides* (460?B.C.-399?), the historian of the Peloponnesian War.

*Guicciardini,* Francesco (1483-1540), Italian statesman and author of a "History of Italy from 1494 to 1532."

P. 347. *The Loves of Persiles and Sigismunda,* the last work of Cervantes (translated into English in 1619) and *Galatea,* his first work (1585).

*another Yarrow.* Cf. Wordsworth's "Yarrow Revisited."

# INDEX

# INDEX

5'